ADVANCES IN PRESENCING

ADVANCES IN PRESENCING

Volume 2

Edited by
Olen Gunnlaugson, Ph.D.
William Brendel, Ed.D.

TRIFOSS BUSINESS PRESS

Dedicated to the emergence of presencing as a viable field of research and practice

About the Editors

Olen Gunnlaugson, Ph.D. is an Associate Professor in Leadership and Organizational Development at Université Laval (Canada) where he teaches MBA courses in leadership, management skills and group communications to managers, leaders and executives. With a research background in Leadership Development, Group Communication and Leadership Coaching, he received his Ph.D. at the University of British Columbia and did his Post-Doctorate at Simon Fraser University, Vancouver.

To date, his work has been published in 13 books as well as 35 articles and chapters in leading academic journals and books. He has presented and keynoted at numerous international conferences, received five faculty level awards for teaching from universities in Canada and the USA and taught several thousand emerging leaders and executives at leading schools in Canada, USA, Austria, Sweden and South Korea. Over the past several years, he has been researching and developing Dynamic Presencing, with a book released early 2020. Dynamic Presencing is a five journey method for developing our existing presencing practice into an orienting way of being and leading.

William Brendel, Ph.D. is an Assistant Professor of Organization Development and Change at Penn State University and is the CEO of the Transformative Learning Institute. William has over 20 years of experience as an organization development consultant, researcher, author and trainer. His publications on mindful leadership and organizational change span academic journals and popular press. His consultation and workshops have led to measurable transformations in organizational culture and performance across the U.S., China, India and Africa. William has previously held academic positions at Texas A&M, Temple University, and the University of St Thomas, where he has taught graduate courses in Organization Development, Leadership Development, Change Management, Talent Management, Group Dynamics, and Transformative Learning. William received his Doctorate in Adult Learning and Leadership, and Master's degree in Organizational Psychology at Columbia University in New York.

Table of Contents

CHAPTER 1

Reflections on Advances in Presencing - Volume II

Olen Gunnlaugson and William Brendel

It is with great pleasure that we introduce the book series: Advances in Presencing. Over the past fifteen years Otto Scharmer and colleagues work with Theory U has played a vitalizing role in bringing together an international community of practice comprised of progressively minded organizations, communities and leaders who are committed to stewarding a more promising future for humanity. Since the last scholar-practitioner book on Theory U was released in 2013, there has been a growing collective interest in deepening and broadening the conversation with Theory U.

This three volume Series invites contributing voices from the Presencing Institute, independent researchers, scholar practitioners, consultants and many others into the conversation. Where the last research volume *Perspectives on Theory U: Insights from the Field* (Gunnlaugson et. al, 2013) focused more on the voices of academics and management scholar-practitioners, given how the Theory U community has grown over the past five years, we felt it was important to offer an updated practitioner focus on Theory U as a whole, with an interest in how this work, including the practice of presencing is being applied both individually and collectively.

As editors, we faced a number of thought-provoking challenges while developing this series. The first is that presencing
presents a paradox. While it values a form of knowing beyond
conventional thinking or downloading, in order to be considered
a full-fledged paradigm of knowledge creation there needs to be
some bracketing of its own conceptual real estate. In reading
through the chapters in this book one will quickly discover that
presencing as a practice, is in a phase of exploration, with no fi-
nite horizon or boundary informing its development. Intentional
or not, presencing concepts and practices include and subsume
neighboring practices and paradigms, most notably those of Buddhist, Existentialist and the consciousness-based wisdom
traditions.

For instance, Vipassana or insight meditation tradition, which
predates presencing by 2,600 years, is itself a methodology of letting go of the ego in order to let new insight into the nature of the
self present itself freshly each moment. Not surprisingly, presencing resembles separate, modern Buddhist applications such as
mindful leadership, which positions meditation as a secular inlet
for organizational influence and creativity. Similarly, Theory U,
for which presencing plays a central role, incorporates concepts
from design thinking such as the use of empathy and
rapid-prototyping.

Theory U practitioners also refer to presencing as a social
field, which is very similar to the Buddhist concept of codepen-
dent origination, and what existentialists like Heidegger refer to
as a field of care. Following from these observations, the question
then becomes going forward, what essential differences distinguish presencing from its counterpart orientations and practices?
What does presencing actualize and bring into being that these
similar approaches do not? Given its growing significance in personal change, shared learning and social transformation projects
across a wide cross section of fields, as academic practitioners
continue to explore and develop upon their own sense and application of presencing, how might presencing begin to emerge as a
field of research and praxis in the coming years and decades
ahead?

One of the current values of presencing is how the aforementioned and other perspectives and practices are being woven together and updated in our current global context, an effort that is echoed through each of the three volumes of this book series. This has the effect of bringing these respective approaches to life in an experimental fashion, aligned with a growing collective human effort for a hopeful future versus a profitable quarter or immediate sense of stress reduction. How does presencing accomplish this? For one, scholars and practitioners have been compelled to upcycle English verb tenses and adjectives in order to describe particular nuances of learning in new ways with particular points of emphasis.

Those who are new to the concept of presencing often report a sensitivity to this shift in "languaging", and the same will be true for those who read this series; each chapter pushes the limits and limiting nature of the English language. This is necessary to the extent that presencing introduces concepts that the English language fails to describe. For instance, in drawing from Scharmer's distinctions in Theory U, presencing practitioners often talk about the connection of the head, heart, and hands as a more holistic framework for moving from a space of understanding to a space of knowing. In contrast, Sanskrit does not treat these concepts as separate and distinct, but rather, through the term "Citta" refers to a single heart-mind integration.

At some point readers may find themselves asking, is presencing a process that makes all other learning paradigms and activities more creative and useful, or is it the other way around? To navigate these conceptual challenges, this book series includes a tapestry of applications from a variety of contexts across the globe, spanning multiple languages, and accomplishing a variety of aims. It also honors ancient wisdom traditions from which presencing borrows and benefits, while at the same time cultivating emerging lineages and practices such as Dynamic Presencing.

To accomplish these eclectic aims, this three volume book series incorporates insight from both presencing scholars and practitioners, ensuring a balance of critical and creative perspectives that have been peer-reviewed, offering current perspectives on how Theory U is being adapted across a broad range of organizations, companies and contexts that are united in the deeper impulse of learning to shape and build a life-affirming emerging future for all stakeholders. By weaving these and other perspectives into the larger conversation of Theory U, we are of the mindset that these and other updates will ensure that the Series reaches a wider scope of reading audience and catalyzes interest across both the Academic and Practitioner world. Finally, we are at point in history where these two cultures intersect and it is our interest to shine the light on this intersection in a way that inspires a myriad of applications in the world with real projects and research efforts that are not only informed by this framework and but also practitioners capable of co-facilitating and co-leading and embodying these initiatives.

A guiding intention of this Series since its inception has been to raise further awareness of the applicability of critical and creative applications of Theory U to our colleagues, students, ULAB hubs, international communities of practice and beyond, further conveying how this body of work is informing, enriching, and sustaining new developments across a wide variety of disciplines. In effect, this Series will give a current pulse on the current scholar practitioner voices and perspectives on Theory U and presencing through featured writings on the experiences, challenges, and promise of this emerging field. It is our estimation that this work as a whole has the real promise to open up a new space of possibility for engaging a more coherent and resonant future for all concerned, which we know is not only possible but essential for humanity to shift its current course of risks that threaten our shared future in the twenty first century.

Inspired by the Theory U projects of Otto Scharmer and colleagues of the Presencing Institute, Theory U and presencing are approaching a tipping point as a viable, comprehensive praxis for stewarding change and global transformation. To illustrate and support this development, *Advances in Presencing* includes perspectives and applications by academics, researchers, teachers, change makers, consultants, community activists and thought leaders.

Overview of Chapters

In chapter two, "Gestures of the Mind as an Invisible Force for Social Change: A Phenomenological Exploration of what it is to Listen", Dr. Ursula Versteegen and Jill Jakimetz suggest that only by understanding the inner practice component of Theory U, one may become able to unpack its full potential. Specifically, they explore listening as one essential tool for becoming aware of awareness, connecting to others, and putting oneself into a place from which meaningful action becomes possible. Taking a phenomenological perspective, they first describe how they came to recognize listening as a crucial component within the Theory U process. In part two, they discuss case examples and a listening exercise to reflect on the interplay of listening, intentionality, and the boundaries of self and other. Contending listening as a powerful tool to reveal more profound levels of knowledge within the social field, they conclude that the quality of listening has to be taken much more into account when striving for social change. Finally, suggestions for future research are briefly outlined.

In chapter 3, "Theory U: From potentials and co-becoming to bringing forth emergent innovation and shaping a thriving future: on what it means to "learn from the future as it emerges" Markus F. Peschl establishes that in order to bring forth such purposeful innovations and novelty, it is necessary to turn things on their head. Instead of learning from the past and extrapolating past knowledge into the future, we have to start from the future. In his chapter, Peschl develops an alternative approach to innovation that is driven by future potentials, developing an epistemological/ontological framework that provides a theoretical foundation both for Theory U and, as we refer to it, for Emergent Innovation. Bloch´s "not yet", Aristotle´s potentials (vs. actuality), S.Kauffman´s "adjacent possibles", Ingold´s "correspondence", as well as Scharmer´s "Source" and "Higher Purpose" play a central role in this approach. Peschl shows that innovation is not so much dependent on the (creative) activity of an agent/ innovator. Rather, he suggests to turn things on their head: if we want to shape an unfolding reality in an open-ended and purposeful manner, we have to acknowledge that we have to give up epistemic control and have to engage in an emergent process of co-becoming and co-creation with future potentials. We have to learn how to listen to, identify, and cultivate the emergent purpose/final cause and that it will "pull" us towards sustainable innovation. In the last part of this paper he discusses practical implications for organizations, skills and mindsets, Theory U, as well as for innovation strategies.

In Chapter 4 "Developing our Presencing Self through Four Levels of Leadership Presence" Olen Gunnlaugson introduces the first Dynamic Presencing Journey, Primary Presence, which involves a phenomenological excavation of our presencing nature through four lifeworlds: *Being Real; Being Witness; Being Essence and Being Source*. Each lifeworld introduces a particular presencing self-sense, mode of presence, and relationality as well as a distinct inscape from which to engage presencing from as a way of being. The focus of this initial journey is to uncover the inherent activation site of presence that exists within each of us and as it turns out, contains a particular ground that is indispensable to developing our overall presencing capacity. As each level of presence is uncovered, enacted and lived into, key transformative conditions come online, clarifying and opening a path into a ground of presence that supports and drives presencing as an overall movement as we learn to uncover and embody the inner dimensions of our presencing nature.

In Chapter 5, "The Importance of Presencing in Creativity" Gareth Loudon and Gina Deininger review some key findings from creativity research and present a new model for creativity where the ideas of presencing play an important role. The LCD model (Listen, Connect, Do) for creativity puts dynamic movement and a person's state of being at its core. They describe the key features of the model and reflect on the similarities and differences between these features and the core elements of Theory U and presencing. Next, they share their thoughts on practical steps organizations can take to enhance the creativity of their staff and how these steps map to the ideas highlighted in Theory U. Finally, they discuss how Theory U can be extended to incorporate some of the ideas from their LCD model and suggest that presencing could be at the heart of all Theory U activities, whether that is listening, observing, connecting, making, collaborating or reflecting.

In chapter 6, "Earthrise: On the interplay of States and Structures in Theory U" Karsten Skipper explores the distinction between State changes and Structural development, and how to further integrate these two dimensions in the application and understanding of Theory U. To this end, Skipper discusses how Terri O'Fallon's STAGES model may help unifying structural and phenomenological approaches. By identifying similarities between Scharmers' four field structures and the four phases of learning in STAGES, the chapter opens the possibility of distinguishing concrete (early level) from subtle (later level) expressions of the transformation processes described by Theory U. Through this distinction, the transition from ego-system awareness to eco-system awareness may be viewed as a subtle transformation that echoes earlier, concrete development. The chapter stresses the importance of grounding the emerging eco-system awareness through continuous efforts to express subtle insights in concrete structures and reinterpret concrete values in light of emerging subtle structures. It presents nonlinear ways to portray the relation between concrete and subtle structures, and points to the gestures used in Social Presencing Theater (SPT) as a model example of bridging developmental levels. It further shows how this capacity for vertical span and integration may be generalized through awareness of keywords, keys situations and key moments in history (keystones) that are significant across developmental levels.

In chapter 7, "From Social Technology to Technologies of the Self to Larger Scale Social Technology" Tom Karp makes a case for the need for 'global presencing' in action. In his chapter, he focuses on the development of Theory U in both time and space, as well as vertically and horizontally, encompassing systemic, group and individual levels. The linear model suggested by Theory U should be supplemented with the 'messiness' of change and learning. This involves acknowledging that factors at macro and meso levels affect insight, knowledge and cognition, as well as interaction and interpersonal learning. Identity, feelings, needs, power and processes are important. Individuals must change in order for systems to change, and actions, movement and change at an individual level come together to create the aggregate systemic change. Karp makes a case that leaders', change agents' and individuals' ability to be self-aware and regulate their inner forces that work both for and against action is the factor that enables them to be more receptive to new knowledge and to act in accordance with it. In Karp's view, this may enable Theory U to evolve from being a processual tool to a theory for full-scale systemic change.

In chapter 8, "Deep Listening at the Eye of the Needle: Music Improvisation & Co-creation In the Social Field of Presencing" Bobby Rickets explores Theory U and Presencing from the perspective of improvisational music performance, illustrating specific qualities of the music improvisor's mindset and way of being relevant to extending Presencing mastery. Emphasis is placed on a heightened capacity for listening, Deep Listening, which masterful, improvising musicians utilize to inform instantaneous, co-creative action resulting in artful outcomes. His chapter also discusses how musicians develop an ability to sustain and direct consciousness in the present, thereby allowing for a deepening of consciousness in that present moment. Additionally, he describes a potential additional dimension or dynamic of Deep Listening and Presencing, revealing itself as a collective capacity for discerning the profoundly new, one step beyond an immediate acknowledgment of the future as it emerges. A range of critical skillsets possessed by masterful music improvisors are described, which facilitate a heightened capacity for Deep Listening and Presencing, and are conceivably scalable to Presencing practitioners in non-musical contexts. In the interest of bringing Presencing to diverse fractals of society, the author proposes connecting models for achieving expertise, skill in perceiving meaning through various modes of listening and sensing, and a capacity for collaboration, as a scaffolding upon which to extend Presencing ability.

In chapter 9, "Arts-based Interventions as a Series of Methods to Access Presencing" Lotte Darsø and Cecilie Meltzer focus on the question: How can arts-based interventions prepare and support Presencing, and thereby learning from the future as it emerges? They propose that arts-based interventions can be a way to access deeper layers of tacit knowing and lead to new realizations and new solutions to our perceived problems. The theoretical framework includes research on thought processes, brainwaves, consciousness and applied quantum theory as well as research on arts-based interventions. Four empirical cases from the Nordic educational sector demonstrate how arts-based interventions can support accessing and transcending the deeper layers of the U-process: Sensing, Presencing and Crystallizing. These cases illustrate how selected arts-based methods, such as movement, drama, sculpting and painting, can be applied for accessing unconscious material and reveal hidden insights and energy sources that help learning, transformation and healing. Identifying with a chosen artefact, person, material or artwork may change our perspective and redirect our attention towards what is truly meaningful and inspirational. They conclude that arts-based interventions are well suited for preparing and supporting individuals and groups in the deepest phases of the U.

In chapter 10, "Presencing and Negative Capability: Identical Twins or Relatives?" Suneetha Saggurthi and Munish Thakur seek to explore the relationship between Presencing and Negative capability (NC), a phrase given by the poet John Keats. We discuss their common ontological and epistemological assumptions and point out the ways in which they differ. We posit that NC helps "presence" the moment of truth and beauty. The seeing, sensing, and presencing aspects are related to passive receptivity, sympathetic identification, and imagination, the three elements of NC, connecting with the social technology of open heart, open mind and open will. NC point out that it helps open the creative doors of perception and brings in the sensuous and sensing body. Moments of presencing come about with NC with its imagination as an essential aspect. The chapter ends with a discussion on how NC helps in presencing, especially in the context of meaning and leadership, with its "holiness of heart's affections and the truth of imagination."

In chapter 11, "Crossing the Threshold of Presencing Using Values and Narrative Coaching" Christine Cavanaugh Simmons, Marcy Strong, Victor Shewchuk provides leadership coaches with a means to access the state of presencing in a coaching setting. Through deep listening to the use of language in personal narratives, and interconnecting the language used to the values the leader holds, the authors have supported leaders to access the "Source," resulting in generative and agentic identity constituting moments. From their experiences and those of other coaches, the authors share the process of diving down the pathway of Theory U, noting the shifts in language and the levels of listening for the opening of the crack for presencing to emerge. This chapter concludes by exploring the unique role of the coach in this setting as well as the interior condition of the coach that is necessary to hold the space for the possibility of presencing.

In chapter 12, "Perspectives on Voices of Resistance with Experience-based Coaching" Katherine J. Train presents mechanisms and methods to bring a language and process to coaching that helps coaches skilfully manage these limiting voices by identify them and clearing them before they trigger absencing, The chapter aims to contribute to an understanding of interior constraints expressed through the voices that come about partly through inherent human characteristics and partly through biographical conditioning influences. She firstly proposes a mechanism to aid in the recognition and understanding of the appearance of the voices of resistance. She then follows with coaching methods drawing on Psychophonetics (Tagar, 2006), and a descriptive phenomenological (Merleau-Ponty, 2002) and enactive (Thompson, 2007) approach to disarm and transform inherent and conditioned influences. Methods are described in the context of the voices of resistance and intending toward their transformation to open mind, heart and will. The mechanisms and methods are illustrated with examples from leadership coaching case studies in organizational scenarios where open mind, heart and will are compromised by judgment, cynicism or fear.

In chapter 13, "Criticality and Creativity in Presencing" Hayo Reinders and Jay Hays introduce Critical Presencing, a merging of presencing and Critical Learnership. This fusion permits the greatest possible value from presence and presencing, criticality, and continuous and purposeful learning. In this context (and as a simplification), Critical Presencing is a mindful constructive process. An individual who is critically presencing would be aware of these springboards and their potential value, as well as how he or she is attending to and dealing with them. The more conscious thinkers are of these thoughts and when and how they come, the more productive they will be. Greater critical awareness, along with discipline in applying certain learning habits and skills, can lead to faster and more repeatable innovations and successful responses. A highlight of the chapter is a mini-case portraying a moment in the life of a busy executive faced with a seemingly insurmountable dilemma. The authors analyze the executive's thoughts and actions with respect to Critical Presencing, revealing concretely the principles, concepts, attitudes, and behaviors that define Critical Presencing and bear on outcomes likely more positive than other problem-solving, decision-making, and design processes might be.

Finally, in chapter 14, "Sensory Templates and Presencing" Klaus Springborg proposes that recent research in cognitive science can help us better understand and facilitate the learning-process described in Theory U. In particular, he focuses on the Theory of Sensory Templates, which identifies the neurological mechanism whereby humans ground abstract concepts in somatic states as the deepest assumptions upon which actions, thoughts, and emotions are based, i.e. as the place from which we act. The Theory of Sensory Templates can help facilitators working with Theory U translate theory into concrete, pragmatic methods, such as cultivating awareness of felt sense, describing felt sense using sensorimotor vocabulary, grounding key concepts, such as commitment, freedom, self, leadership, motivation, collaboration and competition in the somatic states felt at the bottom of the U, and other Somatic-Linguistic Practices. In short, Theory U tells us what to do. Theory of Sensory Templates tells us how to do it.

Closing Remarks

In closing, a guiding intention of this Series is to raise further awareness of the applicability of Theory U and presencing to our colleagues, students, ULAB hubs, international communities of practice and beyond, further conveying how this growing body of work is informing, enriching, and sustaining new developments across a wide variety of disciplines globally. In effect, by showcasing current voices and perspectives on Theory U and presencing, this Series also seeds the participation of future critical and appreciative streams of research on the different methods of presencing, their respective communities of practice and the value derived from such scholarly-practitioner undertakings. In this sense, Advances in Presencing offers important guidance and inspiration to colleagues currently involved in this work. By encouraging not only further elaboration and refinement of the Theory U framework and presencing approaches that are currently being explored and applied globally, this Series is also encouraging paradigmatic breakthroughs that may also provide new updates and prototypes to be followed and possibly further developed elsewhere. As a whole, Advances in Presencing affirms our convictions, and those of many of the invited authors, that this new, exciting, and extraordinarily important emerging field is one that has the promise to be of great service to humanity in the years and decades ahead.

CHAPTER 2

Gestures of the Mind as an Invisible Force for Social Change: A Phenomenological Exploration of what it is to Listen

Dr. Ursula Versteegen and Jill Jakimetz

> "Every object well contemplated creates an organ of perception in us" (Zajonc, 2009, p.182 f).

Connecting Inner Transformation to Social Innovation

We face an unprecedented challenge requiring social innovation of unknown complexity and authenticity. Disconnected from the lived experience of citizens, democracies in the US, Europe, and elsewhere fail to provide solutions on a governmental level. Institutions, such as hospitals or schools, face demands that cannot be satisfied with the approaches of the past centuries. Earth's web of life is the fundamental foundation of our societies. Extreme weather events and changing regional climates, along with mass extinction of species, profoundly destabilizes this foundation, desperately testing our capacities for peace, justice and cooperation.

To act differently than we have done before, we must think differently. We must be different. In 2007, after ten years of research and practice in the field of social change, Otto Scharmer (2007) published Theory U, "The Social Technology of Presencing", suggesting that in order to cope with systemic challenges, we needed to "learn from the future as it emerges" (2009, p.7). To propose "the future" as a new "source of learning" turned out to be the tip of an iceberg. The more we explore it, the more the future is revealed as a place of possibility and a place of engagement. Theory U is an expedition into the inner worlds of our social existence.

At its core, Theory U offers a new paradigm of how we relate to ourselves and the world and, consequently, opens a new perspective and set of skills to support this new way of being, thinking, and acting in the world. "Presencing blends the words 'presence' and 'sensing.' It means to sense, tune in, and act from one's highest future potential – the future that depends on us to bring it into being" (Scharmer, 2009, p. 8). Note that the person in the first half of the sentence, the one who is sensing and tuning in, is not the same as in the second part of the sentence, the one who is addressed by the potentiality that needs to come into being. What is action in Scharmer's Theory U and who is acting? If the experience of the past is not the only source for learning, what are we accessing when learning from the future? How is the nature of what we might learn from the future different from what we have been learning from the past? How can we access a knowing that we are not aware of?

For decades, management theories of change have tended to focus on the outer side of change, creating change through restructuring, re-engineering, or exchanging people. In 1990, Peter Senge (1990) started to turn the perspective from a third-person perspective inwards, logging into our own experience. Doing so, he started to bring the power of the invisible levels of intervention for change to consciousness, including systems thinking, mental models, team learning, dialogue, and personal mastery.

Echoing this development, another silent revolution in research started to arise, which aimed to support the exploration of inner worlds. Consciousness, the biology of cognition, and neurophenomenology (Depraz 2003; Petitmengin, 2009; Varela, 2000), as well as microphenomenology (Petitmengin-Peugeot, 1999; Petitmengin, 2006; Petitmengin, Van Beek, Bitbol, & Nissou, 2017), contemplative learning (Gunnlaugson, Sarath, Scott & Bai, 2014), such as meditation and compassion, and their impact on body, mind, and brain (Goleman & Davidson, 2017; Klimecki, Leiberg, Lamm, & Singer, 2012) increasingly became of interest.

With Theory U, a new line of theories of change has been entering the field of management and leadership theory, linking inner practice to social innovation. Based on Lewin's *Field Theory* (1997), Theory U seeks to unite action and awareness. However, it sometimes remains unclear how action and awareness fuel each other and create dynamics for change. For all Theory U's unique focus on the journey through the U, it sometimes feels that the radical importance of the sequential steps of inner experiences (suspending, seeing, redirecting, sensing, letting go, presencing, letting come, crystallizing, prototyping, embodying) may get muffled as we are planning to help realign a system. In working within the world of broad systems change, we can sometimes stay at the top of the U, even while moving through it. Without knowing more about how action and awareness work together, we may be missing opportunities for greater collective learning and organizational impact.

Ten years later, many of the core concepts and tools of Theory U have been broadly spread and used by thousands of practitioners in many different contexts, organizations, countries, and cultures. To our knowledge, little research has been done to understand the inner side – the lived experience – of the process of creating change from the perspective of U-practitioners. What seems to be true for contemplative practice in general, "what it is like to meditate – from moment to moment, at different stages of a practice – has barely been addressed in contemporary contemplative science" (Petitmengin, et al., 2017), seems to be the same for the practice of awareness-based social technologies. Nevertheless, we cannot make fruitful a source of knowledge that we are not aware of, let alone compare notes on how awareness-based social technologies do or do not help create innovation and change. For knowledge to become actionable, it has to be grounded in the awareness of the people who are creating changes. We need to develop a kind of vision that relates the invisible dynamic of our own inner experience as change makers to the visible effects evolving in the current moment of the social process we are just about to create. What skill is needed so that we can we catch up with ourselves real time? The cultivation of the seed of awareness and related changes in the quality of thinking in the person-in-change herself, it seems, is the fertile ground and point of departure for interesting and instructive phenomena to unfold themselves.

To take responsibility for the outcomes of their work, U-practitioners (and any person involved in social innovation) need to become more aware of the inner dimensions of their work. Bringing awareness to the activity of experiencing the human journey as such, rather than just addressing the content of that experience, is a crucial precursor to bringing awareness to the sources that give rise to the activity of experience. The practice of cultivating these forms of awareness within oneself must intentionally guide the course of any intervention. Theory U hypothesizes that changing levels of self-other-awareness based on functioning with an open mind, open heart, and open will, results in shifting relationships in the social field. In short, a social field shifts based on a change in consciousness of those who constitute the field (Scharmer, 2018). The capacity of a social field to co-enact a new social reality co-emerges with the capacity of its players to become aware of their own way of being in it.

It seems to us that the journey of becoming aware of deeper levels of knowing follows three co-evolving streams: First, accessing and reflecting one's own lived experience as a U-practitioner concerning a specific tool or practice in certain case contexts. Second, continuously deepening contemplative practice to increase capacity for awareness, loving-kindness, and compassion to bring to work. Third, researching experience, forming terms, and conceptualizing frames to capture and make accessible the most invisible yet active and effective drivers of our existence. Scharmer's *Matrix of Social Evolution: Embodying an Evolving Consciousness* (2017, 2018) is a first sketch trying to surface, bring together, name and trace the visible results of action with the yet-invisible impulses of inner activity. In this article, our focus of exploration will be the lived experience of listening residing at the cross-section of awareness and action.

Specifically, from an impact perspective, listening is a core practice underlying Theory U. As Scharmer (2018) pointed to: "Listening is probably the most underrated leadership skill" (p.25). Listening and speaking may not be everything. However, without the capacity to shift the quality of listening and speaking, Theory U can do nothing.

The purpose of this paper is to explore the workings of Theory U through the lens of listening and its impact on social field transformation from our perspective as practitioners. How is listening effectively creating change? We will focus on listening because of three reasons. First, it is a practice for which we have personal case examples. Second, we have used listening as a contemplative practice over time, and third, with the four types of listening and the four social fields provided by Scharmer (2009; 2018), we have some initial grammar and a framework to work with. We thus ask how listening functions as a discriminative and productive inner activity that, if consciously experienced and mastered, can be effective to link the invisible world of thought with the visible world of behaviors, thus making social innovation possible. Put differently, what is the inner experiential process of becoming aware of one's listening as an invisible and mostly unconscious intermediary activity that either connects or disconnects us to ourselves, to each other and the whole?

The chapter is organized into two parts. The first part reconstructs the broader social context from which the "need" for Theory U as a new theory of change has evolved from a phenomenological point of view. The framework of the four types of listening is reviewed. The second part will explore the experience of listening from a phenomenological point of view. Through case stories, we will examine how Theory U serves as a phenomenological approach that cues awareness of the lived experience of people and makes space for change-makers to immerse themselves into the reality of their interiors, thereby observing the workings of co-creation from within. We will put the cases in the context of Scharmer's framework of social system change (2018).

Part I: Theory U as Phenomenological Approach

The Crack: Unexpected Awareness (1st Person Perspective as a Theory U Practitioner– 1).

My, Ursula's, personal starting point into the riddle of listening and the nature of the challenges of our time was as a Ph.D. student in Psychology and early on in my professional career in the health policy department of a global health company. I was confronted with some incidents that made me recognize a stunning gap between the intentions that institutions held about what they were supposedly doing and my own experience about what I felt was happening.

For instance, I learned that meetings as a collaborative infrastructure were supposedly bringing people together to collaborate and tap into collective intelligence. My experience of them, however, was that in most meetings, a couple of people spoke forever, usually elderly, white, male leaders. The majority of people did not speak at all or very little. Nonetheless, when the rare moments happened that one of them would speak up, it sometimes felt like an opening into a new world. However, what was that opening and what made it different? At one point, we were organizing a big cultural transformation program, involving tens of thousands of people to create a more participatory employee-driven and entrepreneurial culture. However, our employee survey turned out to be an all multiple-choice survey with predetermined categories of what the consultant experts wanted to know, except for one open, so-called "qualitative" question. Here, employees could share their experience of the day-to-day lived reality of the company.

After we had analyzed the data, we ended up having one company, but two worlds. On the one hand, we had the quantitative data depicting an organization with infrastructures and processes that employees rated as more or less satisfactory. On the other hand, qualitative data sometimes revealed heartbreaking stories about how it felt to work for the company. Both sets of data were talking about the same company, with the same people as the "database." However, it seemed that the quantitative part of the survey had tapped into a completely different reality and knowledge base than the "qualitative" part.

My studies in psychology had been similarly ambivalent. I had hoped to understand more of what it meant to be human. I was interested to learn how it was possible that despite the many good intentions of human beings, we were still faced with a deeply complex and challenging world. Instead, I ended up learning a lot of analytical concepts about being human. It felt as if we had been studying aliens from another planet. I was told that what I experienced as highly relevant inside of myself could not be talked about in the "real" world of academia and later, corporate life. It was considered non-representative and subjective and thus in a way, irrelevant and non-existing. How could something I saw from within be so real and tangible and yet simultaneously be so irrelevant at the same time? Expressing subjective experience became the fast track to losing credibility at that time, so I shut up. The piles of so-called representative data became weighty testimonials of another world impossible to grapple with and from which I grew disconnected. As nobody else questioned the significance of that data, I quietly resigned myself from it. I grieved about the everyday world becoming a boring, if not harmful realm, as this deeper inner divide created a profound loss of something deep inside that I did not have words for. At some point, the pain numbed and I soldiered on.

Reconnecting Inner And Outer World (1st Person Perspective as a Theory U Practitioner– 2)

After three years into my career, in the early '90s, something equally surprising, but in a reverse sense, happened. I had been trying to meet Peter Senge, head of the Organizational Learning Center at MIT. He turned out not to be in. Instead, I was told to wait to meet the new teaching assistant in the department. I decided to stay. Surprised by myself, I wondered why I would be waiting for someone I did not know, for an unknown amount of time not knowing whether he would even want to talk to me? Where did that come from? At the same time, there was some faint sense of calling I realized inside of myself that I could not ignore either. Despite all the uncertainty on the who, when, if, and why level, on another level, there was something more real and promising in the unexpected turn of the situation. Some part of me knew I had to wait for however long it would take. I was not waiting for someone. I was holding onto to a possibility that needed to land.

Once the unknown teaching assistant arrived, he readily agreed to go for a cup of coffee. He then explained to me why he had come to the US. He wanted to bring a new dimension to the theory of organizational leadership and learning that he felt was lacking. The way he spoke touched me profoundly, and something inside of me cracked open. MIT, as today, was one of the most prestigious, highly respected, frontline, and academic places in the world of whole systems change, leadership, and organizational learning. He and I, sitting there, greenhorns who just finished their PhDs, thinking about the missing piece in the change approaches of some of the world's most famous experts in the field. It felt disturbing and inspiring at once.

The teaching assistant outlined three threads of reasoning for me. As he spoke, my world spun. I did not understand a word of the content of what he was saying, but I was confident of his meaning. How could I possibly know without understanding? Watching myself, I realized I was not even looking at him. My gaze was hanging somewhere between his hands and his coffee. The whole set appeared to be the backdrop of something else happening. Nothing was in focus. The entire scene seemed to be dimmed down weirdly despite the bright morning sun pooling around the Au Bon Pain in Harvard Square. Although he was sitting right next to me, his voice seemed distant. Technically, I heard the words, but I realized I was listening to something else. I was listening to the pauses during the search, the activity behind the words, the trying to push them out. At some point, my listening had taken the guy out of the picture. It was not about him. It was about a larger story that had taken a ride through him. I had a profound experience of a synchronicity. There seemed to be a space of resonance emerging above and beyond me that I was soaked into, connecting to a deep sense of longing, of being human, and of uncompromising certainty. I could feel being opened, turned, and connected to a larger stream. A reality that I seemingly knew, that I vaguely recognized but was not keenly aware of, began to stir. Here was proof confirming some deep layer of my experience and I was taking it all in. I had met Otto Scharmer.

A Recurring Crisis: The Mismatch Between Collective Awareness and Systems Reality

Years later, I came to understand that one of the observations Otto Scharmer had tried to share with me that morning at Harvard Square was that the reality of our systems, be it education, health care, business, or government, often do not match the experience of learners, patients, customers, employees, and citizens. In the Global Health Company, both groups saw different parts of a reality that they could not recognize as one. From one perspective, the leaders viewed the company from the perspective of their intentions and ideas. From the other, employees experienced it from the perspective of suffering the behavioral consequences from an institutional body that they felt was long outdated. From the mindset of their leaders, they had to be mobilized to engage. From their own experience, the institutional body kept them from realizing their aspiration. In their minds, they were effective *despite* and not *because* of the existing institutional body. They were self-organized along real needs growing vital connections and relationships into a social body of their own that felt young and alive.

The difference between third and first-person data mirrored the gap of awareness between thinking and acting in the collective social body. The leaders were aware of their intentions but not of the impact of their actions. The employees suffered from the impact of the consequences but were not aware of the intentions that had caused them. The organization was meant to move as a whole, but the limbs seemed to take a different course than the head. Together they created something nobody wanted.

Twenty years later, these patterns of social bodies and their outdated institutional forms, leading increasingly separate lives in a somewhat uncomfortable marriage, have sped up, deepened, and widened. Not only within organizations, but also across systems, societies, continents, and planet spheres, pain and suffering seem to have increased in all living beings, be them humans, animals, plants, or soil. We seem deeply estranged from our institutional creations that have become sclerotic reminders of past mental models. We are stuck in the dead bodies of our institutions, unable to see ourselves in light of the future forces that would lever us ahead. Scharmer and Kaeufer (2013) have summarized the outcomes of our limited capacity to synchronize awareness and action within ourselves, amongst each other, and on a broader, societal and planetary scale as the "three divides" (pp. 37-39), with this expressing the outer symptoms of profound inner disconnects:

> "Today, in most social systems, we collectively produce results that no one wants. These results show up in the form of environmental, social, and cultural destruction. The ecological divide (which disconnects self from nature), the social divide (which disconnects self from other), and the spiritual divide (which disconnects self from self) shape the larger context in every large system change today." (Scharmer, 2017)

Scharmer (2017) describes the structural challenge we face as a society as the "double split of the social field" (p.10), the combined effect of disconnect from each other and between collective awareness and action, both of which we are not (yet) present enough to experience them as they drive our behaviors: "Case in point: climate change. We collectively produce results that no one wants: severe climate destabilization. That is the body-mind split. Why, then, don't we wake up? Because at this point the second split kicks in: I am so remote from the people who are beginning to feel the worst impact of climate destabilization that in spite of their suffering, nothing motivates me to move from beginning awareness to action." (Scharmer 2016, p. 12).

Reconnecting Action to Awareness and Them To Us: An Evolutionary Grammar for the Social Field

From a phenomenological point of view, the challenge of Theory U practitioners is to design social processes that are effective with regards to "learn[ing] to understand what we see" (Zajonc, 2009, p.150), but taking into account at the same time "what we know is a reflection of who we are... who we are also determines how we act and the ethics we embody. In this way, being, knowing, and acting are invariably interconnected." (Zajonc, 2009, p.188). To close the three divides, we have to understand what we see, but our seeing itself is a reflection of our understanding who we are. Scharmer's *Matrix of Social Evolution* (2017, 2018), depicted in Table 1, shows the resulting interdependencies of "being, knowing, and acting" and how their specific configurations give birth to evolving consciousness.

Table 1 shows four different stages of attention (first column on the left) translating into four types of listening, speaking, organizing, and coordinating. Scharmer (2017) comments that "consciousness is the independent variable that can facilitate a change in the degree of separation between body and mind (or action and awareness). The development of social fields is the embodiment of a human consciousness that is evolving from ego to eco." Henceforth, we use the notion of the *social field* as the phenomenological version of social systems, meaning that social fields are social systems seen from within (Scharmer, 2017).

Each social field evolves through the contingencies among the triad of being, knowing, and action. Zajoncs' (2009) careful and extensive research points exactly to what we are dealing with. If we want to upgrade our capacities as human beings to the level of successfully dealing with the complexity of our time, the transformational approach chosen needs to match the fundamental nature of the challenge. Being, knowing, and acting are inseparable.

Ecological Divide: Self ≠ Nature		Social Divide: Self ≠ Other	Spiritual Divide: Self ≠ Self	
Attention	Micro: Listening	Meso: Conversing	Macro: Organizing	Mundo: Coordinating
1.0 Habitual	Downloading Habitual	Downloading Polite Phrases	Centralized Hierarchy	Centralized Commanding
2.0 Ego-System	Factual Open-Minded	Debate "I am my point of view" Speaking my view	Decentralized Divisions	Free Market Competing
3.0 Stakeholder	Empathic Open-Hearted	Dialogue "I have a point of view" Speaking from the whole inquiry	Networked Stakeholder Groups	Social Market Negotiating
4.0 Eco-System	Generative Open-Presence	Collective Creativity Presencing, flow speaking from what is moving through	Eco-System Co-Creating	Co-Creative Eco-System Awareness based collective action

Table 1. Being, knowing, and acting social evolution. Adapted with permission from Scharmer (2017 b, p.5)

However, what does it take for a transformation in consciousness to happen in a way that we can transform what we see and who we are as a seer simultaneously? *Mirroring* is one of the 19 points Scharmer (2017a) names as a condition for a social field to be able to metamorphose:

> "To change the operating levels of a social field, people need a mechanism that helps them *bend the beam of observation back onto the observing self.* When this happens for the individual (micro), we call it mindfulness. Mindfulness is the capacity to pay attention to your attention. When this happens in a group, we call it dialogue. Dialogue is not people talking to each other. Dialogue is the capacity of a system to see itself. What's missing in today's capitalism is a set of enabling or mirroring infrastructures that would help our systems to sense and see themselves and thereby remove the barriers preventing the next round of profound institutional innovation and systems change. " (Scharmer 2017).

Zajonc (2009), reflecting on what is needed to create new thinking, notes:

- "new experience must be joined with new thinking if new knowledge is to result.
- New insight requires new concepts as well as new percepts. We require a way of
- bringing experience and reason together, a way of perceiving meaning in the
- given, even when the given arises through deep meditation." (p.179)

Zajonc (2009) and Varela (2000) have pointed to new organs of perception tending to build as a consequence of their functional use, not as their prerequisite. Being exposed to new experiences stimulates the use of otherwise dormant capacities. The formation of new organs of perception will, in turn, improve the capacity to explore the experience entirely. As Varela (2000, as cited in Scharmer, 2009) has shown in his famous experiment with cats, cats learn seeing by being nudged into it. Born blind, the capacity to use their eyes will arise pending on the experience of hurting themselves on an unseen object. Cats that are carried around do not hit any walls and do not learn to see. Extending these dynamics to human development, this implies that we may be holding the potential of new organs of perception that we are unaware of. This potential will remain dormant as long as we are not exposed to the experience relevant to their awakening. Applying the dynamics to the future of human development, Zajonc (2009) suggests that we may have to develop seeing beyond the sensual world: "We need more than material mastery of the outer world; we require an inner knowledge and spiritual mastery as well" (p.155). If we stay blind for the inner knowing, we may hit the invisible walls within ourselves, between us, and between us and the planet.. Zajonc (2009) notes that "the organs we need for insight are fashioned by attention and immersion in the object of contemplation. With every repetition, the cycle of attention and formation is at work fashioning the organs required for contemplative knowing." (p. 183).

Relating this to the Matrix of Social Evolution (Table 1), this implies that transforming our capacity to listen from downloading to factual, empathic, and generative will create new circuits of functionalities forming new organs of perception that embody a higher quality of consciousness through an open mind, open heart, and open will.

Throughout the chapter, we will refer to the four types of listening, L1-4, as outlined in the 'micro' scale of Table 1. Each mode of listening is an activity associated with a social field structure of attention (1-4), as outlined in the first column of the same table. These structures of attention relate to the development of the three organs of perception, which are open mind (suspending judgment and observing), open heart (connecting through feelings), and open will (letting go and connecting to what is at the edge of becoming). The open mind helps to move from habitual (L1) to factual listening (L2). The open heart facilitates moving from listening to the other (L2) as an object to tuning into the subjective experience finding "Thou" (L3; Buber, 1997). Lastly, the open will allows to let go of ego and connect to what wants to come into being.

In conclusion, experiential awareness of each of these fields is essential if we are to mindfully maneuver among them while navigating towards knowledge and change creation. Listening is an activity that defines the absence-presence, self-other, and inner-outer divides and is therefore ideal for exploring the relationship between consciousness, the social field, and its results. If the central challenge to making the presencing level of the social field visible and tangible is the degree of its interiority, then the scientific study of one's own experience is well worth recruiting. In the next section, we will present phenomenology as a method of inquiry into an experience and present phenomenological studies in an attempt to add language to the grammar of the social field.

Part II: Tuning in: Making the Invisible Process of Social Reality Formation Visible, Speakable, and Tangible

To become knowledgeable about who we are, we need to become researchers in the science of studying our own experience. Knowledge, in this context, is "knowledge (...) constituted from two sides: in the act of cognition, each percept from the sense world is united to a concept of our minds" (Zajonc, 2009, p.147). Theory U practitioners seek to design social processes for multiple stakeholders to make new experiences to be joined with new thinking, aiming to create actionable insights and innovation. Zajonc (2009) describes the difficulty of this task, stating that once we turn from the study of outer to inner phenomena and begin developing the organs of perception described before (open mind, open heart, open will), new things begin to happen:

> "Its character becomes richer, our dreams change, and life itself seems to gain other dimensions. In order to discover authentic meaning in these experiences of inner life, our thinking must become free and mobile in ways that are quite unfamiliar to us. For this reason, it is extremely difficult to capture in thought and give expression in words to that which is within" (Zajonc, 2009, p.151).

Zajonc (2009) further argues that turning the within outward "requires the joining of intelligence to impression, and concept to percept" (p.151). For this reason, we view Scharmer's (2009) four types of listening as an excellent tool and prototype of giving *outwardness* (Zajonc, 2009) to impressions of the inward listening experience. Each percept from experience in the sense world is associated with a concept of mind. In other words, following the four types of listening, I can either listen to myself as the center of my world (Level 1), listen to discern my world vs. their world (2), listen from the within world of the other (3), or listen from the collectively-arising potentiality (4). These four types of listening are reflected in four different mindsets, namely, a "downloading" awareness (habit-driven; 1), a "factual", open mind awareness (ego-driven; 2), an "empathetic" stakeholder awareness (open heart-driven), or, finally, a "generative" open-presence awareness (eco-system-driven; 4). The social technologies of Theory U give language to a world of knowledge that we all share but are often not aware of. The "known" thus carries a potential for meaning once we become aware of it.

Becoming Aware of Awareness

What makes it so difficult to access deeper levels of human experience? Petitmengin and colleagues (2017) argue:

"a large part of our experience remains unnoticed or 'pre-reflective' in the language of phenomenology. This is because our attention is almost completely absorbed in the content, the 'what' of our activity, largely or entirely excluding the activity itself, the 'how'".

Aiming "to help subjects redirect their attention from the content of the experience towards the mode and dynamics of appearance of this content and to describe it precisely," (Petitmengin et al., 2017, p. 3), they have developed so-called "micro-phenomenological interviews."

At a deep level it seems, we are faced with both the remarkable capacity and the challenge to unconsciously imprint our-selves into sensual life in a way that makes us believe that the re-sulting affect is coming from the outside. We become victims of our inattentiveness. To track our own minds' activity, we have to learn to bracket or withhold the content level we take for a given: "I withhold my assent to the ontological status of the perceived: I 'bracket' its facticity." (Husserl, 1982). We suspend the assump-tion that what we see is there for real.

> "This redirection is like the gesture of phenomenological reduction as described by Edmund Husserl: withdrawing from our exclusive focusing on objects and broadening our attentional gaze (Bitbol, 2014) so as to reveal and de-scribe the underlying 'intentional life' of consciousness (Husserl, 2002), and, even deeper, the pre-intentional lay-er of the "self-affection" of life" (Henry, 2000)" (as cited in Petitmengin et al., 2017, p. 3)

Petitmengin and colleagues' (2017) micro-phenomenological work dramatically enhances the granularity of the picture of how we are co-creators of the reality we live in, helping us discern imagination from perception, ego from eco. What is it like, in concrete terms, to be listening generatively, to be presencing?

Observing Becoming Aware of Awareness in the Social Field (1st Person Perspective as a Theory U Practitioner– 3)

Otto Scharmer and I, Ursula, had been working with a group of physicians in central Germany (cf. Kaeufer, Scharmer, & Ver-steegen, 2003; Scharmer, 2009; Scharmer 2018) who wanted to set up a seamless 24/7 emergency call system for a rural area. Together, they had co-created a health care system that did not provide a single emergency call number that was always working for the whole population. Instead, various parallel infrastruc-tures operated as independent emergency systems with different emergency numbers, call centers, staff, and emergency helpers independent from each other. All of them were stretched thin in capacity, eventually ending up with situations that were both confusing and possibly dangerous.

A meeting was organized by the doctors who had initiated the change project. They had invited most of the stakeholders who needed each other to change the regional emergency system. 15-20 people were sitting in the room, including leaders from local insurance companies, physician associations, emergency call centers of various organizations, local politicians, and us, the action researchers and process consultants. Patients and citizens – the lived experience of the system from within - were missing. During the initial check-in round, each person spoke from the perspective and the organization they were representing. Everyone went on explaining their good intentions as they were trying to do the best for the patient as they saw it, but for reasons beyond their scope, their intentions were stymied by the system's workings. As they went on and on for about an hour, making their statements and putting forth their claims about their expectations for everyone else, I sensed that with each of them speaking, the mood got increasingly heavy, and we were drifting apart. The way we spoke out of our own perspective regenerated all the systemic fault lines we were talking about. The climate in the room dropped. We were pulled into different directions by a mysterious invisible force. The walls that separated us were almost palpable. We were stuck.

There was dead silence. Some of us were wondering how we would ever be able to raise ourselves out of our chairs again, let alone elevate the health care system to its next level. As the heaviness sank in, Otto Scharmer started talking. He talked into that dead space of isolated units of what supposedly was a health care system. He started describing what he saw in a very calm and slow way. He spoke about how everyone had been trying so hard to do the right thing and the frustration that despite all the hard work the outcome was not satisfying. However, it was not so much *what* he said, but *how* he spoke. It was like soothing a baby. He progressed through what he felt to be the predominant experience in the room. Although he did not move, it was more like a movement pervaded the room than words. First, there was a soft

40

breeze, a gentle stirring of the space between all of us, and as his stirring went around and touched deeper layers in each of us, the various fragmented health care islands one after the other started bursting like little soap bubbles and became part of a more substantial soup.

The longer he spoke, the more time slowed down, from time to time small nods and sighs started coming up, accompanied by a softening of body language. As everyone was letting go, that what had been sealing individual knowing peeled itself off like a decal, revealing the mess from a safe distance with a rising awareness and disbelief: Wow, this is *us* creating that mess?

While all of this was happening between all of us in the room, connections amongst us started to root and move into the foreground. The single institutional units started to pull away into the background like heavy furniture being pushed aside. The relational space became palpable, revealing a soft, warm, and wobbly substance extending itself and including everyone to become part of the new skin of the emerging collective social body that all of our senses started to attend to. Color and mood in the room had shifted. The whole scene felt like we had been actors going through a collective dream state of a yet emerging play that we were co-producing without being aware of it, with Otto Scharmer being the scene shifter. He was clearing out the stage setting of act one: "Experts doing Health Care Systems Change" to act two: "Human-beings-in-development caring about those in need of emergency help." It became evident that a real shift in health care might not be done by reassembling existing expert pieces. The shift needed to be a relational and intentional revolution about how to cooperate and to co-create towards an activation of the life forces of a caring love-impulse bringing forth the system, instead of changing the institutional surface of an already dead body.

Where is the entry point into a world of thought that matches our experience of ourselves and the world as one whole, breathing organism? If we are estranged from our own experience, we may neither know ourselves nor the other. In my unexpected awareness of something compelling me to wait at MIT, I had an embodied experience of understanding. I was aware of dissonance between my intellectual understanding of the moment, my behavior, and a felt understanding. From a second-person perspective, I could see in this meeting how Otto Scharmer was able to access, name, and reframe the experience we were having. He was stitch-by-stitch interweaving the precepts with the language and concepts that helped us to understand what was going on. I intuitively realized that there was a level of knowing in the room that I had not been aware of but that his speaking had revealed. He had listened to the painful experiences of human beings in the room who had tried to do something amazing for their fellow-humans, while I had been listening to arrogant experts and their little ego-silos trying to maximize their power on behalf of everyone else. Through Otto Scharmer's intervention, we all could start attending to the highest future potential that tried to come into being, but needed the force of love to come through.

Theory U is designed to develop a shared sense of the existence of this experiential dimension of "I-in-Now", which Scharmer describes in *The Blind Spot: Uncovering the Grammar of the Social Field* (2017) and what we refer to as "L4", generative listening, or "listening from the source." Drawing from the work of Petitmengin and colleagues (2017), whose research invites us to "reflect (...) on the basis of experience and on the basis of the experience of its description", this portion delves into the micro-phenomenological research on listening, confirming and enriching Scharmer's (2017) grammar of first-person experience of the social field.

Phenomena of Listening and Dimensions of Experience: Activating Organs of Perception Along the Double Split of the Social Field

What is listening? Do we listen with our ears? As must be taught to children – and relearned by most of us adults – we listen with our whole bodies. We are listening with our hands and feet by keeping them still, listening with our mouths by being silent, and listening with our brains by paying attention to the speaker (Truesdale, 1990). When listening to another, we do not just listen to the meaning of words, signed or spoken, but we also listen for meaning by observing a whole array of non-verbal signs (Burgoon, 2016), and by reading cultural contexts and group dynamics (Schein, 1993). We listen for the whole meaning, conveyed within and among all the parts (Bortoft, 2007, p.8).

Hearing offers an immense world of experiences from which to explore what it is like to listen. An example below, Petitmengin and Bitbol's (2009) micro-phenomenological study of listening to a sound, provides the kind of 'thick description' (Geertz, 1973) that reveals rich layers of sensing, cognition, and consciousness. We can listen with our ears, but this is only one of many starting points.

To hear with our ears, sound waves manifest themselves through our vibrating eardrum, ossicles, and cochlea, and transform to electricity at our nerves. The electrical brain transforms vibration into information through a "flexible and adaptable processing system" (Imhof, 1985). As brain imaging has shown and as many in the deaf community validate, one can listen visually (Vox, 2017) and tactilely (Shibata, 2001), as much as aurally. Indeed, "hearing is basically a specialized form of touch," says deaf percussionist Evelyn Glennie, who hears with her feet (Kassabian, 2013, p. xv). In this way, listening is a networked sense of touch. As Scharmer (2009) alludes to in the *Grammar of the Social Field* and as we saw in the palpable atmosphere in the example above, listening's haptic sensibility is one of the clearest wavelengths for attuning attention and social field.

Dimensions of Experience: Self-Other

Who are we as listeners? I listen, unaware, through my first-person perspective on the world. I listen to others from within this perspective, a second person listening out to another. I may use my senses of curiosity, empathy, and imagination, activating the open mind and open heart organs to come close to a first-person perspective of another. Using these senses and organs, I begin walking in their shoes, seeing what they see, feeling what they may feel. Through dialogue, through exchanging subtleties of intersubjective experiences, we confirm one another (Brown & Keller, 1979, p. 304, as cited in Floyd, 1984). I may listen, that is, apply a sense of curiosity, concern, or anxiety (Nancy, 2007, p. 5) from a third-person position, trying to understand the whole from outside the whole. I listen, aware that I am listening, to myself, watching what I think, sense, or feel.

> "To be listening is thus to enter into tension and to be on the lookout for a relation to self: not...a relationship to 'me'...or to the 'self' of the other, ... but to the relationship in self,...as it forms a 'self'...Consequently, listening is passing over to the register of presence to self, it being understood that the 'self' is precisely nothing substantial...but precisely the resonance of a return" (Nancy, 2007, p. 12).

In this way, the self is a reverberation. The self is knotted, enmeshed, and becoming-with (Haraway, 2008). "Listening in its entangled form is dialogical listening which stretches a radical openness towards interconnections and 'listening with'" (Heddon, 2017). A self who listens *with* (rather than listens *to*; L3+4 rather than L1+2) is the place from which we may leverage collective understanding and mobilize ourselves into meaningful, concerted action.

In Petitmengin and colleagues' (2009) phenomenological study of listening to a sound, they uncovered a generic structure relating one's attentional disposition to the experience of self-other. For example, when listening to a sound with the intention of discerning its source, there was a clear distinction between self and other, namely the self in the role of the listener, the other, the sound, and the imagined source of the sound. Listeners reached out from their ears, across space, to the source of the sound. However, when listeners shifted their attention to the characteristics of the sound – its pitch, timbre, and volume – there was a parallel shift in the relationship experienced between self and other. At this moment, space became denser, physical boundaries opened, and sound mixed with visual, tactile, and other kinesthetic sensations. When listeners then focused attention on the felt experience of sound, this shift was even more dramatic. In order to bring attention to felt sound – which can be described as the resonance of sound within themselves – listeners activated their entire bodies and prepared a 'receptive' inner stance. What they felt brought about the synchronization between interior and exterior space: "as though [the sound] got hold of me somewhere inside myself and forced me to follow, led me to follow..." (Petitmengin et al., 2017, p. 273).

Beyond synchronization, listeners experienced a complete shift in identity, ego to eco, with subject and object rendered meaningless: "The sound, it abolishes the limit between me and the outside...there is no more skin, or a skin which is much more permeable" (Petitmengin et al., 2017, p. 273). Another quote supports this impression: "There are [...] moments when truly I am no longer there...There is a coalescence at a given moment between what I am and the music" (p. 273). A nimble, relational, pluralistic self is demonstrated through these shifts in attention. By deploying a self who can experience the dissolution of the subject vs. object split, a hidden organ of perception is activated, allowing conscious access inside of the blind spot.

Emerging Common Gestures.

We can observe similar gestures in Petitmengin's study of the intuitive experience (Petitmengin-Peugeot 1999). Participants in the study examined an array of reflective and pre-reflective procedures for accessing intuition. In the example given at the beginning of this chapter, when deciding to stay to meet the unknown teaching assistant, intuitive certainty came as a surprise. The mode of its delivery was barely conscious, and my conscious response was to stay put and wonder why. Petitmengin-Peugeot's (1999) project was to come up with a model "of the structure of intuitive experience, which is made up of a succession of very precise interior gestures" (p. 60). This model contained four major gestures, which were "letting go", "connection", "listening" for signs of a coming intuition (what we would call generative listening, where attention is simultaneously "panoramic" and "discriminating"), and the arrival of "the intuition" itself, in three phases (p. 60).

Additionally, eight other gestures were, although not brought to conscious awareness in all participants, common enough to suggest a more nuanced generic structure of the experience and, therefore, may be fruitful clues to follow for fleshing out the grammar of the social field. These other gestures were "maintaining", "anchoring", "disconnecting", "getting out of the intuitive state and back to usual functioning", "protection", "distinguishing intuition from projection", "interpretation" of the intuition, and "translating the intuition into a communicable form, such as words, drawings, or scientific hypothesis" (p.60).

We highlight the volume and particularity of gestures involved in one type of experience. Petitmengin-Peugeot (1999) notes that these were the gestures that came via the explication interview through layers of consciousness into a reflective awareness allowing a clear, verbal description. There may be others that stayed within pre-reflective experience; there may be gestures that are particular to both the intuitive experience and a particular context involving the individual, environment, or intuition.

Each gesture can be broken down into common "experiential variables" and "descriptive traits" (p.60), some of which chime in with Scharmer's "seven dimensions of first-person experience of social fields" (2017) and 19 quality "points" of the social field (2017). The seven dimensions of first-person experience are akin to variables within "interiority", one of the points along the journey through the social field. These variables show quality changes as a person experiences moving from one social field to another. For example, what it is like to experience moving from "downloading" to listening with empathy. We present some of these terms below as sketch of associations (See Table 2). The loose and overlapping relationships point to both broader and more granular categories, and perhaps to other organizing frameworks entirely.

Petitmengin (1999, p.60)	**Scharmer (2017)**
"experimental variables" and "descriptive traits"	"Seven dimensions of first person experience" and "points" of the social field
Sensorial modalities	Materiality
Attentional modes, internal and external	Interiority
Mental activities	Field structures of attention, thinking
Non-voluntary gestures	Co-creativity
Perception of body and space	Time, space, boundaries, materiality, non-locality
Processes of connection	Source, self, other
Internal state	Wholeness

Table 2. Comparison of key terms used in Petitmengin (1999) and Scharmer (2017)

If we compare the two studies of Petitmengin (Petitmengin, 2009, p.277; Petitmengin-Peugeot, 1999) with Scharmer's (2017) first-person descriptions of experiencing a generative social field, balanced with the personal case above, we could come up with a rough approximation that we are talking about common aspects of basic human capacities and, for lack of better words, spiritual functioning in the material world. Time slows. Space widens, it expands from a point-source trajectory to distributed presence where attention is non-directional, unfocused, and receptive. The experience of otherness slides into an experience of connection and wholeness. The experience of self is de-centered, featuring a "panoramic awareness" (Scharmer, 2017), which both creates a sense of "unified self" and a "synchronization" with others (Petitmengin, 2009 p. 70). The materiality of the field is perceptible. It is "warming," "thickening" (Scharmer, 2017), densifying, becoming a beam of light, or like a fabric (Petitmengin, 2009;

Petitmengin-Peugeot, 1999). Scharmer's (2017) "source" dimension of collective awareness, seeing from "the surrounding sphere," may be akin to Petitmengin-Peugeot's (1999) description of the experience of being "completely mobilized" (p. 71). Scharmer (2017) describes the "thinking" dimension in terms of "emerging possibilities" "at the source of the social field," Petitmengin-Peugeot (1999) categorizes listening experience as moving from mapping cause-effect, to qualities and resonance, which are tracked through increasingly transmodal sensations. She documents a "feeling of coherence" (p. 70) within the experience of accessing intuition.

Theory U plots the journey to presencing and the experiential tools of Listening 1-4 along the gestures of epochè- suspension, redirection, letting go. Research of first-person experience of listening activity supports this alignment. Along this journey, evidence of a distributed self emerges: a self that is rooted in the individual and directly in touch with the collective. A self that resembles a vessel whose definition shifts but is always spacious within. We cannot think of ourselves as only single, prepackaged entities whose wills either stimulate or respond. We are also demonstrably anchored in interbeingness and we, our*selves,* emerge and evolve in concert with ever-changing social-ecological contexts (Scharmer, 2000; Zahavi, 2005). To be ourselves, we become with others (Haraway, 2008). Our own listening lets us experience this.

Two Sides Linking Awareness and Action: Observing and Doing.

As Zajonc (2009) states, "What we know is a reflection of who we are." (p. 188), we can comprehend Listening 1-4 as activities imprinted on the process of becoming aware of awareness. Listening changes our sense of the self and the world. We may direct our attention to L1, 2, 3, and 4, but the process of listening, *doing* the listening is what changes our perceptive lens. By listening through each level, we develop a capacity to perceive the otherwise imperceptible.

At pre-reflective levels, we may know that these fields exist, but only through effective listening, we can directly observe those fields and the transformation of their realities. To quote Zajonc (2009), "the organs we need for insight are fashioned by attention and immersion in the object of contemplation. With every repetition, the cycle of attention and formation is at work fashioning the organs required for contemplative knowing." (p. 183). Thus, awareness of and experiencing the different listening modes reveals an abundance of ways to engage with an abundance of being. Generative listening is the organ we use to perceive the energetic affluence of life. Listening allows us the conscious experience of exchanging breath with this life. It is this kind of heightened vitality that John Dewey posits as essential to growth and learning (Dewey, 2005):

> "Instead of signifying being shut up within one's own private feelings and sensations, [an aesthetic experience] signifies active and alert commerce with the world; at its height it signifies complete interpenetration of self and the world of objects and events" (p.18).

"Active and alert commerce with the world" echoes the way writer Nan Shepherd (as cited in Macfarlane, 2012), referring to her experience of herself, all the parts, and the whole of the "living mountain" of the Cairngorm as a "traffic of love", with traffic implying exchange and mutuality rather than congestion or blockage (Macfarlane, 2012, p. 193). The personal relationship between attention, generative listening, and the self is clear. However, what does listening do "out there"? If listening is simultaneously perception and action, which, like touch, orients and settles us into a position in the world, what is the outer result? What impression does our touch leave on others? Perhaps as traffic smooths pathways, commerce softens cash, mycorrhizae make and holds space, generative listening is a movement that massages the soils, a passage that ripples the waters, a holding that warms the whole.

Doing generative listening may be a "homeopathic medicine" (McKanan, 2019) for the social system. Once done, the experience of generative listening is a map of an otherwise invisible territory, the social field. Awareness of the experience is guiding knowledge for entering into the field and way-making-with the other inhabitants of this place. Our work as researchers and practitioners of an "applied metaphysics" is to ride the phenomenological lemniscate of experience and observation of experience: centered in source, going out deeply, attentively into direct experience, connecting with self and other; swooping back through center, bringing attention to the way inner and outer was experienced, increasing the granularity of our picture of the social field and the way our consciousness brings us agency within it.

Observing the self, "the I," we see that as an individual attunes their attention and awareness to the "frequency" of vibration, intuition, or presencing, we are no longer observing a strictly first-person perspective, but something more akin to an expanded first-person perspective, or perhaps an embodied third-person perspective, which is a transcendental subjective perspective, saying something like: "I see the whole from the outside, but I have not removed my thinking-acting self from the whole." Becoming aware of this perspective is one thing, reliably entering into it is another. Do we possess agency over our "distributed selves" (Debarba et al., 2017) in the collective simply by inhabiting this self? Is there another layer of awareness to become conscious of? How does an individual "generative self" produce a "generative outcome" as laid out in the grammar of the social field (Scharmer, 2015)?

Examining our lived experience is an intermediary to linking thinking and action. If we can describe the inner gestures of activating the organs of perception – open mind, open heart, open will – through listening, if we can share the description of what it is like to make these gestures and experience these organ functions, we can raise the question of what the next gestures are. This may be either at the microscale or at the larger scales we discuss below, which allow us to coordinate our functioning as organs of a larger social body.

Observing Listening as an Activity in the Social Field

As we have seen, listening is an expression of the degree to which we can master our attention. It is an internal activity that allows us to transcend the boundary of our "I (Ego)-organization." In that sense, it is important to note, that listening is not just a means to observe what is going on in the outside world, but also has an immediate presence in the sensual outside world. That is, our counterparts can sense whether or not and how we are listening. This immediate presence through non-physical action, such as listening, will change the experience of what one can say and hence, the experience of social reality.

I, Ursula, once had a pre-program interview with a top leader from a global consumer goods company. The phone conversation was meant to help him reflect his leadership to prepare for the program. However, he was so busy that we had to postpone the call twice. Once we spoke, he was still under so much pressure that he poured out like a waterfall all the reasons why he did not have time to talk at all. I did not get to ask a single of my pre-prepared questions for 45 minutes, the time the conversation was initially meant to take in total.

I sat there, overwhelmed by the massive volume of content that felt raining down onto me, under pressure myself not being able to achieve what I was meant to do, torn between either hanging up or yelling at him to stop. The second I noticed my own downloading and realized that what I had been hearing all along but did not listen to, was the suffering and pain of an overwhelmed human being, the exact moment my heart opened and connected to the place from where he was speaking, precisely in that very instance, he stopped. He dropped the sentence.

There was absolute silence. I was stunned. Then it was as if he turned around 180 degrees and for the first time addressed me as a real person: "Are you still listening?" I had a sensation of immediate tangible physical presence, though we were still 1000 miles apart. Boundaries ceased to be. Time stood still. I responded: "I only started now." I could almost hear an in-between space open that we both started tuning. That space was empty and beautiful. Each of us seemed to be putting words into it like into a shared bowl.

We spoke for a long time. This was one of the most formative experiences of listening presence in my career. This other layer of the reality of something waiting to be seen by us seems always to be there. The future is present. What makes it a future is that it takes time to let go of our mental distractions and open our will to step into it. Once we do, the world spins around.

The following points to some evidence we have found over and over with regards to the workings of the networked self, in this case in dyads of people practicing listening 1-4. My colleagues Beth Jandernoa and Glennifer Jillespie have developed a small exercise called "paired listening." After having been introduced to some small listening practices and the four types of listening, participants are invited to experiment with the "unwanted side effects of non-listening." In pairs, sitting opposite to each other, they move through three rounds of listening, with only the listener getting instructions about how to listen. It can be a handful or a ballroom full of pairs, but each pair always has its own dyadic space and is part of a larger social field at the same time. The speaker is asked to share an activity or story that she loves . The speakers do not know what the listeners are instructed to do. Depending on the instruction (i.e., whether the instruction is "open mind, open heart, open will", a subset of those, or, to the contrary, "closed mind, heart, will"), two fundamentally different types of social fields will arise. With the instruction of "open mind" and "open heart", the listeners generate a social field of compassion that makes the whole room buzz like a beehive. Why is this the case if the speakers do not know what the listeners have been instructed to do? The intended level of quality of listening remains invisible to them. They speak their minds into unknown territory. When debriefing the "open mind, open heart, open will" set of instructions, we have heard speakers repeatedly report patterns of experience such as that they had said more than they initially intended to. They surprised themselves and started discovering dimensions of the experience they have not been aware of. They got to say things they did not know that they knew. It helped them to reconnect to the deeper layers of themselves. They loved the listeners for their listening. The listeners noted that the growing enthusiasm of the speakers touched them and helped them to open their hearts even more. The more the invisible dance between listeners and speakers kept unfolding, the deeper became the wish of the listeners for the speakers to be happy. On the opposite end, when the listeners were instructed to close their organs of perception – mind, heart and will – and to listen "full of judgement" and "as if they did not genuinely believe what the speaker said", the collective buzz died down. Speakers report that after a moment of disbelief and confusion, they start turning inwards, checking whether there is something wrong about them. They try harder, starting to entertain the listeners, hoping to re-connect to them and on the way begin to lose themselves. After a few moments, the motivation of the speakers dies down, not much is coming to their minds any more.

The "paired listening" practice does not take more than 6-8 minutes. It teaches everyone in the room the difference between a social field of presencing and one of absencing. In a nutshell, the practice brings together cause and effect in time and space of an invisible, inner activity, with the visible results of social reality creation as the co-enacted drama put on stage. Everyone knows this from daily life but most often, most take it for granted. The realization that it is not a natural law unfolding but *us* who unwittingly create the double split of the social matrix is stunning. Here, we can see the phenomenon unfold in slow motion in front of our eyes. By closing down one's organs of perception, we cause the other to experience relational disconnect. By the other trying to re-connect to me being in offline mode, she or he disconnects from herself. Ideas that seemed to be flying in from nowhere, seizing the speakers to speak more and the listeners to listen even better, cease. That is the disconnect from the social field, a dying down of human relation and creativity. In order to deal with the confusion of their speaking partners, the listeners have to disconnect too. They turn inwards as well, shutting further down their sensing. The traffic of the buzz subsides. I am no longer part of the other's experience and she is no longer part of mine. We both go offline from the generative source that was fueling us, returning into the isolation of our physical bodies. The room is getting cold.

By contrast, the upwards movement with mind, heart, and will wide open, started a dissemination process causing something to travel within the dyads and across the room as a whole. A kind of social soil builds, nurturing and inspiring speakers and listeners, transcending the ego-boundaries of their speaking and listening, giving room to the non-physical presence of a larger sense of resonance. All this is the social field, the container, and the holding space of the collective activity of compassion. Our counterparts sense our listening. They tune in with their whole bodies into the opening of mind, heart and will, co-creating an inter-relational space and collectively shifting the forces of the social field. Further research is needed to understand how collective dialogic encounter shifts the forces of the social field towards either experiencing it as a body of generative resonance and creativity (presencing) or the opposite (absencing).

The experimental practice above consciously induced micro-changes in the quality of listening. Bringing together the experience of self, other and whole within the boundaries of time and space the practice suggest a threefold experience of Self. First, one experiences in real-time the effectiveness of listening as an activity modulated by three different inner micro-gestures of the mind. For instance, noticing confusion and enthusiasm triggered in the speaker as a direct consequence of either closing down or opening one's mind. Second, as the feedback loop between listening action and impact awareness is instantly closed, listeners often experience both types of results as if it was happening to themselves and not to a separate person. Third, from a peripheral perspective participants get a sense of temperature shifts in the surrounding larger holding body, either cooling down or warming up, as the space reflects back their listening beyond the dyads. By being able to experience the relatedness of causes and conditions of the incident, a new sense of self turns into a longing to help the speaker to feel well again.

Listening is an activity to cultivate a field, including one's own inwardly. Luckily, as the paired listening practice is a constructed space of seeing oneself through collapsing time and space, people have a chance to immediately apologize, laugh, hug, and heal right away. The container makes it possible for them to become aware of the consequences of their own behavior, hurting themselves as much as the other. Conducting this exercise in such a controlled setting thus allows direct experience of how quality of listening, as well as its consequences, can be guided by intention, without exposing our participants to a non-cushioned shock outside that echo chamber.

What this exercise tells us about the thinking-acting circuit in the evolution of the social system is that we are overdue to take the next evolutionary step, which is to put the development of compassion into focus. The enormous formative forces of our challenges are pushing hard for new types of social coordination mechanisms. Yet, the development of the "inner light," that cultivation of empathy and compassion produce to meet the outer light, seems to have a hard time keeping up. Though mindfulness is in everyone's mouth, mindfulness without compassion seems to leave the world cold.

As the "paired listening" exercise shows, it does not take more than a tiny shift in our inner field to change the world. The freedom for intentional action lies within. With our lack of intention, we create random social fields of disconnect that turn back to us with the bold package of intended consequences. Whereas non-intentionality creates disconnect, absence and isolation, intentionality gives form- scaffolding to possibilities. The quality of listening as a gesture of awareness can create social asphalt or a healthy soil for humanity.

Conclusion

One core aspect of listening is to be simultaneously perceiving and creating. It is a breathing process between deepening one's vertical connection of accessing deeper levels of experience and cognition, and at the same time, it means to expand and reach out beyond oneself into some sense of self. A key question in the work of transforming social fields from Ego-awareness-based systems to Eco-awareness-based systems is how local, personal states of quality attendance exactly give rise to the global, systemic properties of a social field. One movement that we have explored so far is to turn away from habitual thinking about content into one's own experience, and another one is to turning into experiencing together. How do we get there? What does the experience of the fourth level of cognition or being look like on the level of the collective? Is there something like a "collective contemplative knowing" (Gunnlaugson et al., 2014)? Answering these questions could be a fruitful field of research.

In this article, we have applied a phenomenological approach to get a better understanding of what transformation as an intuiting agent in the collective may be.

Concluding on a higher level, recall that the paired listening exercises have shown that listening can have a global effect on all people in a given environment. Thus, a promising question for future research asks how we can activate our own and others' listening in a way that contributes to the greater good of society. An implication related to this idea is that we can only transform as a whole but not as separated or fragmented pieces. As long as we cannot see ourselves as part of the problem, we cannot be part of the solution.

The moment the entire system sees itself, it shifts as inner light meets outer light and creates insight. As long as the experience is individualized in isolated bubbles, we cannot become relevant. Like each note in a piece of a composition cannot create and change anything by itself, it is only on the level of patterns of relationships that the voids become places for human beings to step in and intuit the new relationships. These relationships can and should reorganize over time, but let our transformations be agencies of love.

Acknowledgments:

With deep thanks to Rachel Schneider for inspiration and to Luca Versteegen for helpful comments, review and constant support throughout the entire work process for this article.

References

Beuys, J. (1990). Eine Innere Mongolei. Dschingis Khan, Schamanen, Akticen. Ölfarben, Wasserfarben und Bleistiftzeichnungen aus der Sammlung van der Grinten. In C.
Haenlein (Ed.). Hannover: Kestnergesellschaft.

Bitbol, M. (2014). *La conscience a-t-elle une origine?: Des neurosciences à la pleine conscience: une nouvelle approche de l'esprit.* Paris: Flammarion.

Bohm, D. (2004). Thought as a System. London Routledge.

Bohm, D. (2013). On dialogue. London: Routledge.

Bortoft, H. (1986). Goethes naturwissenschaftliche Methode. Verlag Freies Geistesleben.
Stuttgart.

Bortoft, H. (2007). The Wholeness of Nature: Goethes Way of Science. Edinburg: Floris Books.

Bortoft, H. (1999). Imagination Becomes an Organ of Perception. Conversation with Otto

Scharmer London, July 14, 1999, retrieved from https://www.presencing.org/assets/images/aboutus/theory-u/leadership-interview/doc_bortoft-1999.pdf March 17th, 2019.

Bortoft, H. (2014). Taking Appearance seriously: The Dynamic Way of Seeing in Goethe and

European Thought. Edinburgh. Edinburgh: Floris Books.

Brown, C.T., and P.W. Keller. (1979). Monologue to dialogue: An exploration of interpersonal communication, 2nd edition. Englewood Cliffs, NJ: Prentice-Hall.

Buber, M. (1958). I and thou. In R.G. Smith (Ed.). I and thou. New York: Scribners.

Buber, M. (1999). Das dialogische Prinzip: Ich und Du. Zwiesprache. Die Frage an den

Einzelnen. Elemente des Zwischenmenschlichen. Zur Geschichte des dialogischen Prinzips (14th ed.). Gütersloh: Gütersloher Verlagshaus.

Burgoon, J. K., Guerrero, L. K., & Floyd, K. (2016). *Nonverbal communication.* London: Routledge.

Ceraso, S. (2014). (Re) Educating the Senses: Multimodal Listening, Bodily Learning, and the Composition of Sonic Experiences. *College English*, 77, 102–123.

Cheetham, T. (2015). Imaginal Love. The Meanings of Imagination in Henry Corbin and James Hillman. Thompson: Spring Publications.

Coakley, C. G., Halone, K. K., & Wolvin, A. D. (1996). Perceptions of listening ability across the life-span: Implications for understanding listening competence. *International Journal of Listening*, *10*, 21–48.

Debarba, H. G., Bovet, S., Salomon, R., Blanke, O., Herbelin, B., & Boulic, R. (2017).

Characterizing first and third person viewpoints and their alternation for embodied interaction in virtual reality. *PloS one*, *12*. doi: doi. org/10.1371/journal.pone.0190109

Decety, J. E., & Ickes, W. E. (2009). The social neuroscience of empathy. MIT Press.

Deleuze, G., & Guattari, F. (1987). A thousand plateaus: Capitalism and schizophrenia.

Minneapolis: University of Minnesota Press.

Depraz, N., Varela, F. J., & Vermersch P. (2003). On Becoming Aware. A Pragmatics of Experiencing. Amsterdam: John Benjamins Publishing Co.

Depraz, N., Varela, F.J. & Vermersch P. (1999) "The Gesture of Awareness, An Account of Its Structural Dynamics,". In M. Velmans, (Ed). Investigating Phenomenological Consciousness. Amsterdam: Benjamin Publishers.

Dewey, J. (1934). Art as Experience. New York: Berkley Publishing Group, 2005.

Eidsheim, N.S. (2015). Sensing Sound: Singing and Listening as Vibrational Practice. Duke University Press.

Floyd, J.J. (1984). Dialogic listening. Paper presented at International Listening Association Convention, Scottsdale, AR.

Floyd, J. (2010). Listening: A Dialogic Perspective. In A. D. Wolvin, (Ed.). Listening and Human Communication in the 21st Century. Hoboken: Wiley-Blackwell.

Gagliano, M. (2015). In a green frame of mind: perspectives on the be-havioural ecology and cognitive nature of plants. *AoB PLANTS*, *7*, 1–8

Geertz, C. (1994). Thick description: Toward an interpretive theory of culture. *Readings in the Philosophy of Social Science*, 213-231.

Goethe, J.W. (1984/1790). Die Metamorphose der Pflanzen. Acta hu-maniora. Weinheim: LPZ Verlag.

Goleman, D, & Davidson, R.J., (2017). Altered Traits: Science reveals how meditation changes your mind, brain, and body. New York, NY: Avery.

Gunnlaugson, O., Sarath, E.W., Scott C. & Bai, H. (2014). Contemplative Learning and Inquiry across Disciplines. Albany: NY Press.

Hamilton, L., & Taylor, N. (2017). Listening for the Voices of Animals.

In: Ethnography after Humanism. London: Palgrave Macmillan.

Haraway, D. J. (2008). *When species meet*. Minneapolis: University of Minnesota Press.

Heddon, D. (2017). The cultivation of entangled listening: an ensemble of more-than-human participants. In: Harpin, A. and Nicholson, H. (eds.) *Performance and Participation: Practices, Audiences, Politics*, pp. 19-40. Basingstoke: Palgrave.

Henry, M. (2000). Incarnation. Une philosophie de la chair. Paris: Editions du Seuil.

Hurlburt, R. T. (2009). Iteratively apprehending pristine experience. *Journal of Consciousness Studies, 16*, 156-188.

Husserl, E. (1982). Ideas pertaining to a pure phenomenology and to a phenomenological philosophy: First book, General introduction to a pure phenomenology. Boston: Kluwer Academic Publishers.

Husserl, E. (2002). *Phantasia, conscience d'image, souvenir: de la phénoménologie des présentifications intuitives: textes posthumes (1898-1925)*. Grenoble: Editions Jérôme Millon.

Hendricks, M. (2009). Experiencing Level An instance of developing a variable from a first person process so it can be reliably measured and taught." In C. Petitmengin (Ed.). Ten Years of Viewing from Within: The Legacy of Francisco Varela. Exeter: Imprint Academic

Imhof, M (1985). The Cognitive Psychology of Listening.

Johannesen, R.L. (2002). Ethics in human communication (5th ed.). Prospect Heights, IL Waveland Press.

Jung, S. , Petzenhauser, C., & Tuckermann, H. (2001). Im Dialog mit Patienten. Anatomie einer Transformation im Gesundheitswesen. (2nd ed.). Heidelberg: Carl-Auer-Systeme Verlag.

Kaeufer, K., Scharmer O. & Versteegen U. (2003). Breathing Life into a Dying System.

Recreating Healthcare from Within. In: Reflections. The SoL Journal on Knowledge, Learning and Change. *5*, 1–12.

Kassabian, A. (2013). Ubiquitous Listening: Affect, Attention, and Distributed Subjectivity. University of California Press.

Klimecki, O. M., Leiberg, S., Lamm, C., & Singer, T. (2012). Functional neural plasticity and associated changes in positive affect after com-passion training. *Cerebral Cortex, 23*, 1552-1561.

Kurt, H. (2017). Die Neue Muse. Versuch über die Zukunftsfähigkeit. Klein Jasedow: thinkOya.

Latour, B. (2018). Down to Earth: Politics in the New Climate Regime. Cambridge, UK: Polity Press, 2018

Lewin, K. (1997). Resolving social conflicts and field theory in social science. Washington, DC: American Psychological Association. doi: http://dx.doi.org/10.1037/10269-000

Macfarlane, R. (2012). The Old Ways: A Journey On Foot. London: Penguin Books

Maurel, M. (2009). The Explication Interview: Examles and Applications. In C. Petitmengin (Ed.). Ten Years of Viewing from Within: The Legacy of Francisco Varela. Exeter: Imprint Academic.

Merleau-Ponty, M. (1945). The Phenomenology of Perception. London: Routledge.

Nagel, T. (2012). Mind and Cosmos: Why the Materialist Neo-Darwinian Conception of Nature is Almost Certainly False. Oxford University Press.

Nancy, J.L. (2008). Listen. A history of our ears. Fordam University Press.

Nhat Hanh, T. (2013). Walking the Noble Path. The Five Mindfulness Trainings. Berkeley: Parallax Press.

Petitmengin, C. (2006). Describing one's subjective experience in the second person: An interview method for the science of consciousness. *Phenomenology and the Cognitive Sciences*. 5:229-269 p 236). DOI 10.1007/s11097-006-9022-2.

Petitmengin, C. (2009). The validity of first-person descriptions as authenticity and coherence. *Journal of Consciousness Studies, 16,* 252-284.

Petitmengin-Peugeot, C. (1999). The Intuitive Experience. In F.J. Varela & J. Shear, (Eds.). The View From Within. First person approaches to the study of consciousness. London, Imprint Academic.

Petitmengin, C., & Bitbol, M. (2009). Listening from within. *Journal of Consciousness Studies, 16*, 363–404.

Petitmengin, C., Bitbol, M., Nissou, J.-M., Pachoud, B., Curallucci, H., Cermolacce, M., & Vion-Dury, J.(2009) Listening from Within. In C. Petitmengin (Ed.). Ten Years of Viewing from Within. The Legacy of Francisco Varela. Charlottesville: Imprint Academic Philosophy Documentation Center.

Petitmengin, C., Van Beek, M., Bitbol, M., & Nissou, J. M. (2017). What is it Like to Meditate?: Methods and Issues for a Micro-phenomenological Description of Meditative Experience. *Journal of Consciousness Studies, 24*, 170-198.

Rogers, C. R. (1995a). *On becoming a person: A therapist's view of psychotherapy*. Boston, MA: Houghton Mifflin Harcourt.

Rogers, C. R. (1995b). *A way of being*. Boston, MA: Houghton Mifflin Harcourt.

Sacks, S. (2011). Social Sculpture and New Organs of Perception: New practices and new pedagogy for a humane and ecologically viable future. 80-97. In: Lerm Hayes, C. & Walters, V. (Eds.). *Beuysian Legacies in Ireland and Beyond. Art, Culture and Politics.* München: LIT Verlag.

Rosch, E., & Scharmer, C. O. (1999). Primary knowing: When perception happens from the whole field. Interview with Elanor Rosch. (Personal Communication, October 15th, 2005)

Scharmer, C.O. (2000). The Three Gestures of Becoming Aware: Interview with Francisco Varela Paris, France January 2000. Online. www.presencing.com/dol/varela. Retrieved November 20, 2017).

Scharmer, C.O. (2007). Theory U. Leading from the Future as it Emerges. Cambridge: SoL (The Society for Organizational Learning).

Scharmer, C. O. (2009). Theory U. Leading from the Future as it Emerges. San Francisco: Berrett-Koehler Publishers, Inc.

Scharmer, C.O. (2011). Durch den Tod und aus der Zukunft. *Das Goetheanum*, 7, 1-3

Scharmer, C. O., & Kaeufer, K. (2013). Leading from the Emerging Future. From Ego-System To Eco-System Economies. San Francisco: Berrett-Koehler Publishers, Inc. Scharmer, C.O. (2017a) The Blind Spot: Uncovering the Grammar of the Social Field.

Huffington Post Blog, retrieved from https://www.huffingtonpost.com/otto-scharmer/uncovering-the-grammar-of-the-social-field_b_7524910.html on March 17th, 2019. Scharmer, C.O. (2018). The Essentials of Theory U. Core Principles and Applications. Oakland, CA: Berrett-Koehler Publishers, Inc.

Scharmer, C.O. (2017b) The Blind Spot: Investigating the Landscape of the Social Field. Unpublished draft version of Scharmer, C.O. (2017a).

Schein, E. H. (1993). On dialogue, culture, and organizational learning. *Organizational Dynamics*, 22, 40–51.

Schein, E.H. (1995). Kurt Lewin´s change theory in the field and in the classroom: Notes toward a model of managed learning. *Systems Practice*, 9, 27–27. doi:10.1007/BF02173417

Scheler, M. (2017). The nature of sympathy. London: Routledge.

Senge, P., Scharmer, C. O., Jaworski, J., & Flowers, B. S. (2004). Presence. Human. Human Purpose and the Field of the Future. Cambridge: SoL (The Society for Organizational Learning).

Sermijn, J., Devlieger P., & Loots G. (2008). The Narrative Construction of the Self: Selfhood as a Rhizomatic Story. *Qualitative Inquiry, 14*,

632–650.

Shepherd, N. (2011). The Living Mountain. Re-issue edition. Edinburgh: Canongate Books.

Shibata, D. K., Kwok, E., Zhong, J., Shrier, D., & Numaguchi, Y. (2001). Functional MR imaging of vision in the deaf. *Academic Radiology, 8*, 598-604.

Simard, S. (2016). How Trees Talk to Each Other. Video File. https://www.ted.com/talks/suzanne_simard_how_trees_talk_to_each_other, retrieved on December 31, 2017.

Singer, T., & Bolz, M. (2013). *Compassion: Bridging practice and science.* Max Planck Institute for Human Cognitive and Brain Sciences.

Steiner, R. (2008). Goethes Theory of Knowledge. An Outline of the Epistemology of his Worldview. Great Barrington, MA: Steiner Books.

Stolorow, R.D. (2013). Intersubjective-Systems Theory: A Phenomenological-Contextualist Psychoanalytic Perspective. In: Psychoanalytic Dialogue, *23*, 383–389. London: Routledge.

Süddeutsche Zeitung (1980). Zeige deine Wunde (Beuys Installation). January 27th-28th, 1980.

Truesdale, S. P. (1990). Whole-body listening: Developing active auditory skills. *Language, Speech, and Hearing Services in Schools, 21*, 183–184.

Varela, F. (2000). Three Gestures of Becoming Aware. Conversation with Francisco Varela, January 12th, 2000, retrieved from www.presencing.com on March 17th, 2019.

Varela, F. J. (1996). Neurophenomenology: A methodological remedy for the hard problem. *Journal of Consciousness Studies, 3*, 330–349.

Velmans, M. (2000). Investigating Phenomenal Consciousness. New Methodologies and Maps. Amsterdam: John Benjamins Publishing Co.

Vermersch, P. (2009). Describing the practice of introspection. *Journal of Consciousness Studies, 16*, 20–57.

Voegelin, S. (2014). Sonic Possible Worlds. Hearing the Continuum of Sound. New York: Bloomsbury Publishing.

Vox. (2007). Visualizing rhythms and rhymes through American Sign Language. Retrieved from https://www.youtube.com/watch?v=EuD-2iNVMS_4 on December 31, 2017.

Weber, A. (2016). The Biology of Wonder. Aliveness, Feeling, and the Metamorphosis of Science. Gabriola Island, Canda: New Society Publishers.

Zajonc, A. (2009). Meditation as contemplative inquiry: When knowing becomes love. Great Barrington, MA: Lindisfarne Books.

Zumdick, R. (2013). Death Keeps Me Awake: Joseph Beuys and Rudolf Steiner. Bamberg: AADR – Spurbuchverlag.

CHAPTER 3

Theory U: From potentials and co-becoming to bringing forth emergent innovation and shaping a thriving future
On what it means to "learn from the future as it emerges"

Markus F. Peschl

"Every human being is not one but two. One is the person who we have become through the journey of the past. The other one is the dormant being of the future we could become through our forward journey. Who we become will depend on the choices we make and the actions we take now. That being of the future is our highest or best future possibility... The essence of presencing is to get these two selves, these two beings, to talk and listen to each other, to resonate, both individually and collectively." (Scharmer 2007, p 401)

Introduction—context and challenges

How can we bring about new and thriving futures facing complex (global) challenges in a rapidly changing, unpredictable, and uncertain world? This is one of the most pressing questions of today's knowledge economy and society in which innovation and (disruptive) change have become one of the key drivers for social, economic, educational, cultural, as well as technological dynamics. The more the focus is on creating novelty, in particular on creating novelty that brings forth *sustainable change* and *thriving innovations*, the more we are tempted to search for recipes or mechanisms that generate new knowledge by applying or following rules or well-proven methods/procedures.

Taking a closer look reveals however that such an approach is doomed to failure. For reasons of formal logic, rules or algorithms cannot generate radically new knowledge, as, by definition, they rely on past knowledge and only make explicit what is already implicitly given in these rules/algorithms. Innovation can*not* be "made" or predicted by adapting or extrapolating past experiences, knowledge, innovations, or technologies into the future. And even if we apply highly creative methods or "out-of-the-box" thinking, that is no guarantee that the resulting "creative" solutions or so-called radical innovations will be sustainable or will lead to a thriving future (compare the innovation paradox; Peschl & Fundneider (2017)). We refer to such an alternative form of innovation as *future-driven/-oriented innovation* (as opposed to innovation that is primarily driven by the (extrapolation of the) past; cf. Peschl et al. 2015).

The claim of this paper is that—in order to bring forth sustainable and purposeful innovations and novelty—it is necessary to turn things on their head: instead of learning from the past (e.g., Kolb 1984, Scharmer and Kaeufer 2010) and extrapolating past knowledge/experiences into the future, we have to start from the future. In this context Scharmer's *Theory U* (Scharmer 2007/2016) plays an important role as one of its main claims is to understand change and innovation as *"Learning from the future as it emerges."* (Scharmer 2007, p 52)

Although Scharmer's Theory U had a huge impact in a wide variety of domains (organizational, political, personal, social, coaching, etc.) over the last decade(s), there has been little further research on its theoretical foundations with respect to philosophical and epistemological issues. By questioning classical mechanistic and Newtonian approaches of innovation and prediction, this paper focuses on the question of what is exactly meant by *"Learning from the future as it emerges"* in the context of future-driven innovation and proposes an alternative framework providing a theoretical foundation for this question.

This paper is organized as follows: For the first step we will take a closer look at the situation which we find ourselves in when we try to innovate in a future-oriented manner. We will see that we are at the interface between past, present, and future, and that we are always confronted with an open-ended unfolding future that is "not yet" (Bloch 1975, 1986). The challenge is to come up with innovation artifacts that are "not yet", that want to emerge. In this context Aristotle's concepts of form and matter and how matter receives its form (i.e., the production of an artifact) turn out to be central. As an illustration and metaphor, we will develop what we refer to as "Innovation Zipper" depicting this situation of entering the space of an unknown future.

In the second step we will introduce the concept of adjacent possibles as a theoretical foundation and staring point for identifying and exploring future potentials. It turns out that they are compatible with what Aristotle (1991a) refers to as potentiality and actuality. We will relate these concepts to Scharmer's "learning from the future as it emerges" which can be reformulated as bringing potentials into actuality. One of the main requirements and challenges for achieving this is to give up epistemological control: i.e., will have to leave behind a hylomorphic approach to innovation and discover the importance of emergent purpose or final cause in such processes. In the final sections we will discuss the implications for such an approach to future-oriented innovation.

The becoming and unfolding of reality as being in a state of "not yet"

Before entering into the emerging future, let's have a closer look at the situation we are confronted with whenever we are innovating or initiating change processes. In fact, this is the situation, in which we find ourselves in every moment of our being. "Like the world, human life is a venture, a series of risks, that is radically open to an indefinite future without a certain conclusion." (Kellner 1976, p 22) Following E.Bloch´s (1975) idea of the world being an "experiment" ("Experimentum mundi"), one can see that the world in general, our being as humans as well as organizations are in a constant process of becoming and unfolding over time. They are in an unfinished and incomplete state and process of "*not yet*". We do not know (exactly) where this unfolding is leading to; due to this open-endedness we have just a rough idea about its (current) determination or finality at best (as it might change over time as well). As a consequence, future states of reality are categorically open (Poli 2006, p 77) meaning that the process of unfolding brings to light novel qualities, phenomena, categories, behavioral patterns, new determinations (in the sense of Aristotle´s (1991, 1991a) causa formalis/finalis) etc. that have been present only in a hidden and/or latent manner; they have "not yet" been perceivable or realized. They are potentials waiting to be developed or triggered either by internal activities, maturation processes, by external triggers, or environmental events.

At the interface between past, present, and future: ontological considerations on the role of matter, form, and potentials

On the "Not yet"

What is this "not yet" about? How is it related to and what is the role of potentials or "latents" (e.g. Poli 2011) in this context? What do we mean by talking about a human, an organization, or reality unfolding or becoming? How are these issues related to innovation, profound change, presencing (Scharmer 2007), and shaping the future? In order to find an answer to these questions we suggest to take a look at E.Bloch´s philosophical considerations in the first step. Although being rooted in a political and Marxist tradition, his concepts reveal a lot about our approach and understanding of innovation and future-orientedness as it is suggested by Scharmer´s Theory U (2007/2016). One of Bloch´s (1975, 1986) starting points is his observation that the past illuminates the present and that this may lead us into a (better) future. As is shown by Kellner and O´Hara (1976) in their discussion on Bloch, the present is characterized by *latency* and *tendency*. These concepts can be described as "the unrealized potentialities that are latent in the present, and the signs and foreshadowings that indicate the tendency of the direction and movement of the present into the future." (Kellner and O´Hara 1976, p 16) In other words, our actual present world, our human existence, or an organization is in a permanent state of potentiality, of needs, and desires. It is waiting to unfold into something that is "not yet here"; the present state is the unrealized potential and it is our task to bring what-is-not-yet-realized (or the not-yet-come-into-being ["noch-nicht-Gewordenes"]) into the world by changing or transforming both the world and ourselves in accordance with what could be, with what could lead into a thriving future.

From that perspective, any existing reality (meaning the world, an object, a phenomenon, our human existence, or an organization) is *always more than it is in the current moment*, it surpasses itself and—in a way—is *"ahead of itself"* by being driven by its potentials, by what is yet to come, by the "not yet", and by its surrounding influences. "Being ahead of itself" can be seen in a temporal sense as well as in the sense of final and/or formal cause. Such a dynamic is the very foundation for any process of bringing forth novelty, change, or innovation. In the context of humans and living as well as social systems in general, it is rooted in the process of life itself and its intrinsic dynamics and drive to thrive and grow and to bring to live what is "not yet".

How can we characterize this "not yet", how does it come into being? First of all, is important to note that novelty, innovation, or change always realizes itself in *material artifacts*, which we refer to as *innovation artifacts* (see later sections for details). In general, an artifact is an object that has been intentionally made or produced for a specific purpose (Risto 2011). In other words, there has to be one or more "authors" or agents (cognitive systems) who are responsible for having brought forth this artifact. Conceptually speaking, Aristotle (1991, 1991a) suggests that an artifact or an object is constituted as a *unity or compound of form and matter*. Form (formal cause/causa formalis) gives matter (material cause/causa materialis) its determination, its "meaning", its purpose, its intelligibility, its *"what* it is". As will be discussed (and challenged) later every (innovation) artifact, but also all natural objects, have a material basis that has or receives a specific form. In the case of artifacts, this form has its roots in a cognitive system´s knowledge: simply speaking, knowledge (form) or a "(new) idea" in a cognitive system's mind is transformed into action/behavior itself shaping matter (i.e., artifacts, environmental structures) according to this knowledge or idea. In other words, form "in-forms" and is engraved into matter and this unity of form and matter constitutes an object or (innovation) artifact. It is, for instance, the artist and his/her idea or knowledge (i.e., formal cause) bringing form to bronze (matter/material cause) and, by this artistic activity (efficient cause), shapes a statue (concrete object).

This perspective is referred to as the *hylomorphic* framework/approach and has been discussed (as well as put into question) widely in various fields (e.g., Ainsworth 2016; Ingold 2013). The basic idea is that a specific piece of matter (an object) qua matter has a potentiality to be (in-) formed, to receive a specific shape or form, functionality, meaning, etc. through the intentional activity of an agent (e.g., a designer, artist, entrepreneur, or innovator). The resulting artifact *embodies* the original idea or knowledge of its creator(s).There is, however, a challenging question hidden in the hylomorphic approach that is especially interesting in the context of (future-oriented) innovation, organizational design, and Theory U: If matter is in a state of potentiality, it may receive a whole range of different forms, determinations, meanings, etc. Which strategies do we have to employ so that the resulting artifact leads to interaction patterns that are truly beneficial for its user(s) and supports his/her purposeful thriving? What has been described as "form in-forms matter" above can be seen as a process of *"actualizing"* matter, bringing it from a state of (more of less pure) potentiality into a (more or less) determined state of being a specific object (see below for a more detailed discussion on potentiality and actuality) with a specific functionality and meaning. In most cases, this will be realized as a process of *transforming* existing (less/differently determined) objects into new objects, e.g., by reshaping, combining, connecting, etc. them. In other words, matter receives a (new) form, it is trans-formed into something different/novel, something that we refer to as (innovation) *artifact*.

For the context of innovation processes this implies that we are responsible for bringing (novel) form and final cause/purpose to matter by realizing its future potentials (i.e., realizing its "not yet"). Hence, the *becoming of reality* can be understood as a process of disclosing its potentials in a process of (self- and/or external) actualization: i.e., bringing the "not yet (known/realized)" into an actually existing state. In this context Bloch´s (1986, e.g. chapter 17) concepts of "Front" and "Novum" are important: *Front* is the foremost segment of time, where what is next is determined. In the following section we will see that this is an important state, as it opens up the space of possible successor states. *"Novum* is the real possibility of the not-yet-known, not-yet-wrought-into-being, with the accent of the good novum (the realm of freedom), when the trend toward it has been activated." (Kellner and O´Hara 1976, p 32) This also implies that matter can*not* be transformed in a completely arbitrary manner. The more or less loosely coupled existing compound of matter and form (to be changed/transformed) always imposes some *constraints* and *resistance* on its transformability. Whenever one is doing art or science, this is a well known experience: one is confronted with exactly this resistance emanating from reality, for instance, in the process of falsification in scientific experiments (e.g., Popper 1959) or failing to shape a lump of clay according to one's ideas and plans. As we will see, this is an important insight for any innovation and change process as, in most cases, they are highly constrained by internal and external factors.

Although being rather abstract, one can see that there is a deep connection between these theoretical considerations above and Scharmer´s (2007/2016) Theory U/Presencing framework (see below for further details). They provide a sound philosophical/ontological foundation for the processes and dynamics taking place in the course of Presencing; the latter is exactly about identifying future potentials that "want to emerge", that want to break forth, and that (hopefully) shape future states of the environment in a beneficial and thriving manner as they have been intrinsically present in the "not yet". Understanding this approach as being grounded in an Aristotelian (1991a, 981b28) sense of metaphysics, we are dealing here with looking at things from the rather abstract perspective of wisdom, first causes, and principles. However, as we will see below, these concepts have crucial implications and applications in almost every (practical) domain ranging from humans, over the realm of natural objects and phenomena, artifacts, social systems, organizations, to future-oriented innovation processes (Peschl and Fundneider 2017, 2017a). In the final section we will discuss some of these implications in more detail.

Zipper metaphor: (Shaping the) "Becoming of reality"

In order to illustrate the situation we are in whenever we are producing, making (in the sense of Ingold 2013), or designing something, or creating an innovation (having been described above) in a more comprehensible way, I suggest to make use of the metaphor of a zipper[1] (see Figure 1). From a system´s science perspective (e.g., Kauffman 1993, 2000; Senge 1990; Weinberg 2011), the current state of reality and of a cognitive system is the result of its respective and joint history of transformations and interactions between the environment and a cognitive system at any moment in time. These interactions manifest themselves as transformations or reshaping of matter and as giving or changing the form (and sometimes meaning and/or final cause) of the material objects at hand (see discussion in the section above). Actually, the present point in time is the very moment where things are "put together", transformed, re-shaped, combined, etc. by the behavioral activities and interactions of a cognitive system with the environmental dynamics and the internal dynamics of the object.

As a result of these processes, a (novel) artifact emerges in the course of time. Metaphorically speaking, in the moment, when the two parts of the zipper are conjoined a new artifact is created or emerges. As we will see below, we refer to this artifact as a (new) Actual (e.g., Kauffman 2014). Over time they form a specific "path" or they leave a "trace" of interaction and transformation patterns which we refer to as the "past" or history of interactions (compare also the concept of path dependency; e.g., Stack and Gartland 2003). An artifact represents such a (historical) trace that results from behavioral interactions between a cognitive system and its environment (see the "zipped path" in Figure 1).

Assuming a different perspective that takes into account the development over time, this metaphor describes the process of reality *unfolding* over time. What we are looking at is the process of *becoming* as it has been discussed in various contexts (e.g., in organizational theory, systems science, or in the theory of artifacts; e.g., Clegg et al. 2005; Cooper 2006; Ingold 2013, 2014; Kauffman 2014; Tsoukas and Chia 2002). In the following sections, we will discuss what "becoming" means and how we can study and shape it in diverse contexts.

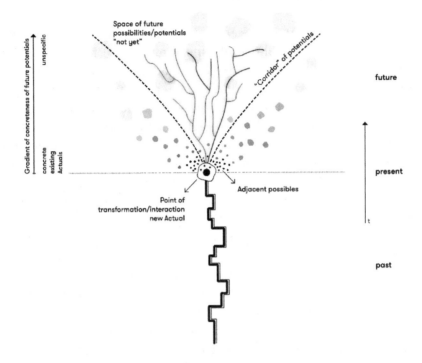

Figure 1: "Innovation-Zipper" metaphor: Moving from the past via Actuals and adjacent possibles to future potentials/Possibles. Becoming and shaping of reality and artifacts in a process of future-driven innovation.

What can we learn from the "zipper metaphor" from an innovation and Theory U perspective?

1. The present point in time and state/situation is the point of getting in contact with *potentiality* and the interface between the past and the future (see discussion above and below).

2. The present state is (partly) the result of the past: I.e., the present state is the product of an interaction- and transformation-history from the past. The "zipper-path" has emerged with each interaction/transformation decision and activity at each point in time. As a consequence, for

creating (sensible) novelty and future-driven innovation it is critical to take the history of the Actual into consideration. Otherwise, any created future state becomes completely arbitrary.

3. The Future is neither completely deterministic nor completely open (at least for the mid-range future). For Theory U this implies that it is one of the challenges to identify a good balance on the polarity between openness and a deterministic perspective. In a way, it is paradoxically: with respect to a current state, future potentials are partly determined by the current state (itself being partly the result of its history) and at the same time they have capacity to develop in an open-ended manner (ideally towards its "(highest) Self/highest possible future") (Scharmer 2007, p 41f, 401f).

4. Actually being in a certain state/situation in the present implies that there is only a limited space of future possibilities and possible development paths into the future ("potentials"). At each point in time we have only a limited number of possible decisions/activities of how we might interact with the environment and/or how we might transform it. In other words, the space of potentials opens up a kind of "corridor" that is constrained by boundaries. For Theory U this implies that the future state will not only lie within the boundaries of the corridor, but, above that, has to relate to the "(highest) Self/highest possible future" (e.g., Scharmer 2007, p 41f, 401f); hence, it is necessary to identify a path leading to such a desired thriving future state. We are going to discuss this rather crucial issue in the section(s) to come.

5. Gradient of concreteness from the present to the future: The further potentials lie in the future, the more fuzzy and unspecific they become. Potentials lying in the near future are more concrete. The situation at the present point in time comprises concrete (material) realized elements ("Actuals") that may be used by the creator/cognitive system(s) as building blocks for shaping the next instantiation of the artifact in an (creative) act of

transformation. As will be shown in the next section, the totality of next possible instantiations forms the space of "adjacent possibles" (Kauffman 2000, 2014).

6. In most cases—for economical reasons—not all future possibilities will necessarily be explored and become expressed.

7. Open question: if we have some understanding of the space of future possibilities, which path should we choose at a specific point in time, how, and why?

The final points direct our attention toward an important issue that is highly relevant both for Theory U and our initial question of how to bring about innovations that are future-driven, that serve a (higher) purpose, and that are sustainable, as well as contribute to shaping a thriving future. In the subsequent sections we will develop these ideas as well as this zipper metaphor further with respect to these questions.

Becoming: From adjacent possibles to Actuals

As an illustration of the above situation (being inspired by Kauffman 2000) think about the situation of a child (or innovator) building a complex object from Lego bricks: By starting with one brick you attach another brick to it and, step by step, you end up with a more or less complex object having a specific shape, meaning, purpose, and functionality. This object is the result of subsequent steps of transformations. In this context it is important to introduce the notion of the *adjacent possible*: "The adjacent possible is just that set of unique novel objects, not yet constructed, that can be constructed from the current set of Lego objects in a single construction step. Of course, within the limited world of Lego we can think of the technologically adjacent possible from any actual. A Lego economy might flow persistently from simple primitive objects into the adjacent possible, building up evermore complex objects." (Kauffman 2000, p 224)

Returning to our zipper metaphor above, the adjacent possible describes the situation we are in when we are transforming an existing artifact/Actual by, for instance, combining or extending it with other existing objects into a new Actual. As a result, these newly created Actuals might offer a new use, purpose, or meaning. If we are interested in future-oriented innovation aiming at bringing forth profound novelty (and not just incremental adaptations or extensions of existing systems or objects), the processes having been described above cannot be executed in a purely mechanistic manner. In other words, we have to *question the classical mechanistic worldview* (as well as the state of consciousness and the mindset standing behind this view); in most cases, such a classical approach is based on Newton's laws expressing what *actually is* happening in the world (and not what *potentially could* happen; see also Kauffman 2000, 2014; Felin et al. 2014; Koppl et al. 2014; Longo and Montevil 2013). One of these laws' premises is that the dynamics or becoming of the material world can be expressed by entailing laws in a more or less deterministic and mechanistic manner (e.g., by calculating predictions from a formula or rule system in a deductive manner). Such a worldview reduces reality to Aristotle's efficient (and material) cause.

However, in his Metaphysics (V 2) and Physics (II 3) Aristotle (1991, 1991a) (and in large parts of philosophy) develops the idea that, if we want to understand and explain reality in a *comprehensive* manner, we have to take into account and search for four causes: material, efficient, formal, and final cause. In the efficient (and material) cause perspective (in most cases assumed by the natural sciences) the world is (a) reduced to its material aspects and (b) is described by entailing laws or rules (e.g., in the form of differential equations). This results in a mechanistic understanding of the world, because applying these laws (for instance in predictions) only covers and makes explicit what *actually is* (and *will be*) and what is already implicitly given in the structure of the laws or rules. As an implication, we can neither expect a lot of novelty or creativity arising from them; nor can we hope for insights about potentials or what *could be possible*. However, this limitatioin is contradictory to our experience of a world that is characterized by a high level of richness, creativity, uncertainty, and unpredictability.

As a consequence, for understanding and designing/shaping

a world that is heavily driven by socio-technological dynamics, knowledge economics, and innovation we do not only have to take into consideration materially based cause-effect relation-ships/laws, but also the domains of *meaning, purpose/use,* and *goals* (i.e., formal and final cause). Being open to the emergence of novelty, of new functions, or of new purposes and meaning im-plies that we have to surpass the realm of a mechanistic and de-terministic perspective on systems and on their unfolding and becoming. We have to introduce a shift from Actuals/actuality to Possibles/possibility. The question we are facing in the context of future-oriented innovation as well as in Scharmer's (2007) Theo-ry U is: How do entirely novel Actuals with new meaning, pur-poses, or uses arise (that cannot only be derived from the mecha-nistic laws of physics)?

Following Kauffman (2000, 2014) let's take a look at living systems and their evolution in the biosphere in order to achieve a better understanding of the challenges in the context of fu-ture-oriented innovation. Evolutionary dynamics unceasingly brings forth (sometimes radical) novelty; it is not predictable and not describable by entailing laws (Longo et al. 2012). Kauffman (2014) introduces the differentiation between *Actuals* and *Possi-bles*: Actuals "define the existing and not merely potential or pos-sible (p 3)... Actuals and Probables obey the law of the excluded middle, Possibles do not... I have proposed a new dualism, *Res potentia*, ontologically real possibles (that do not obey the law of the excluded middle) and *Res extensa*, ontologically real Actuals (that do obey the law of the excluded middle) (p 6)" Kauffman 2014, p 3 & 6)[2] The fascinating thing about Possibles is that they can be both ontologically real, they may physically materialize, and at the same time their functionality or purposefulness resists prediction, they are *"unprestatable"* (Kauffman 2000, 2014; Longo et al. 2012).

In other words, final cause and/or formal cause can*not* be pre-dicted (Kauffman uses the term *unprestatability* in this context); they emerge as a result of the interaction between the new Actual and its environment in the moment of transformation. Addition-ally, we have to be aware that—in most cases—the complexity increases, as the environment itself changes with the emergence of the new Actual and, therefore, the space of possible interactions (implying new functionalities, uses, and purposes) changes and increases as well. Hence, we can conclude the following: yes, we can predict all possible material configurations with high accuracy by making use of entailing laws (Aristotle's efficient and material cause), for example, from Newtonian physics or by computing all possible combinations of, for instance, Lego bricks. However, it is *not* possible to prestate/predict (all) its purposes, uses, or meanings (i.e., final and formal cause). For finding answers to these questions we have to go beyond classical deductive rules and laws and develop an alternative framework. As we will see, such a framework is rooted in Aristotle's potentials, in Bloch's "not yet", and in the concept of Possibles having been developed above. Furthermore, we will show that they are the theoretical foundation for what is happening in Scharmer's (2007) presencing.

The original question we are addressing in this paper is how to bring forth an innovation (artifact) having a reasonable and sustainable purpose and use in an emergent process of co-becoming and co-creation (with a creative agent)? Although Kauffman (2014) argues from an evolutionary perspective, we can derive several interesting learnings from this account for the context of innovation and Theory U:

1. The current state of an innovation artifact (= Actual) plus its surrounding objects (= the "zipping situation") are constraining the next step of transformation.
2. However, this transformation does not happen in a mechanistic manner; rather, the "zipping situation" acts as an *enabler* for *adjacent possible opportunities* that can not be fully predicted in their functionality or purpose.
3. New Actuals (embodying unpredictable and new purposes and functionalities) arise from this process in a radically *emergent* manner.
4. They act as a new starting point for the next step in the transformation process. New Actuals *enable* (but do *not* entail) new (adjacent) possibles.
5. In a sense, this process is recursive/self-referential as it

shapes and produces its own future environment in which the subsequent steps of this process will happen.

6. However, these recursive dynamics do not necessarily imply a limitation concerning the scope of opportunities, but rather an opening up to new spaces of possibles and opportunities that are appearing in the process of transformation. Actuals create new adjacent possibles enabling the emergence of new Actuals which in turn enable new adjacent possibles...

Enabling and Creating New Niches

Pushing this idea of creating one's own environment that functions recursively as a new point of departure for the next step of the subsequent transformation creation processes one step further leads us to two related concepts. They are important both in the domain of evolution and (future-oriented) innovation: the phenomenon of *preadaptation* and the creation of an *(empty) niche* (e.g., Felin et al. 2014; Kauffman 1993, 2014; Longo and Montevil 2013). Each newly created Actual constitutes a set of boundary conditions functioning as *enabling constraints* by establishing a space of potentials/adjacent possibles in which new Actuals may emerge. In evolutionary terms this new Actual embodies an (yet) *empty niche*. It is empty, because its potential use (or purpose) is not (yet) known, does not yet serve a particular purpose/use, and might become essential at a later point in time.

This novel use might emerge in a later step of transformation when both the environment and/or the artifact and the user are "ready" (in the sense of "considering it useful") to make mutual use of these newly created structures. In other words, the (empty) niche gets filled with a useful, sensible, purposeful, and/or thriving interaction pattern (e.g., between a user and the newly emerged innovation artifact). In Darwinian terms, such an empty niche can be understood as a *preadaptation*; an adaptation that does not yet have any (or a different) use in the present moment. It opens up a space of (yet unknown) opportunities that might become useful at a later point in time. However, at the present point in time we do not have (a good or) any understanding of the possible future use(s) that might eventually emerge in subsequent transformation steps. This is an intrinsically *creative* process that does not follow a specific plan or goal from the outset. It is unprestatable; metaphorically speaking, we do not know the next possible use of a screwdriver. The (next) use, purpose, or meaning *emerges* in this process of creating niches providing a new enabling environment that gives rise to and creates yet new niches… that, at some later point, makes these pre-adaptations useful (without selection processes explicitly or "intentionally creating" them). We propose to apply these concepts to the domain of co-creation processes and future-oriented innovation as well as using them as a theoretical foundation for Theory U. This process of pre-adaptive niche creation is one of the theoretical foundations for the approach of Emergent Innovation (Peschl and Fundneider 2015, 2017a).

Challenging the "ideology" of planning and controlling in classic management, such a perspective gives rise to the alternative *paradigm of enabling*. As an implication (see, for instance, Peschl and Fundneider 2017a) we will have to question and rethink these classic approaches of management by acknowledging radical uncertainty and unpredictability especially in our time that is characterized by high levels of complexity, uncertainty, unpredictability, exponential dynamics, digital technologies, and networks. We will show that the concepts having been discussed above in combination with the approach of Theory U offer a powerful theoretical foundation and framework for such an alternative understanding of future-oriented management and innovation. This is in line with Kauffman's (2014) perspective that we "do not yet recognize the potentially enormous power of this often unstatable emerging adjacent possibles, the very opportunities evolution creates… for itself, the very opportunities the evolving economy, governmental structures, laws, regulations and enabled behaviors, strategies, that create yet new adjacent possible opportunities into which we become. If so, and for human life if we cannot know what we enable, how do we do so wisely? How in human life do we garden the partially unprestatable and unintended adjacent possibles into which we become,

81

flowering or metastasizing?" (Kauffman 2014, p 7) As we will see in the following section, the Presencing (Scharmer 2007) approach might point into an interesting direction for providing a possible answer to this question.

Innovation by learning from the future and cultivating emerging potentials

In order to innovate in a future-oriented manner, we have to shift our perspective from the past and present to the future. This kind of innovation has to go beyond problem solving, out-of-the-box-thinking, trial-and-error learning, as well as learning and extrapolating solutions from the past to the future (Peschl, Fundneider, and Kulick 2015). Rather, we have to address the core issue of this paper, namely, *how should we innovate and design for a thriving and prosperous future?* How can we realize *innovation* that is understood as "Emergent Innovation" (Peschl and Fundneider 2013, 2017) within this ontological/epistemological framework? More specifically, we have to deal with the following guiding questions: How do we develop new Actuals and adjacent possibles in the flow of the becoming of reality? How do we identify potentials in a new niche and what are its possible new not yet known (sensible) uses, purposes, and/or meanings? How do we create and/or identify them in a meaningful and sustainable manner?

From such a perspective, the future allows for, offers, and affords (Gibson 1986; Chemero 2003; Peschl and Fundneider 2017) opportunities for specific (novel) behavioral actions (possibly leading to new innovation artifacts). We are confronted with what we refer to as one of the innovation paradoxes that concerns the polarity between (radical) novelty vs. connectedness, intelligibility and transferability to existing structures ("Anschlussfähigkeit"): on the one hand innovative behavior or artifacts should be novel or even radically new. On the other hand, there is the requirement that the level of novelty is not so "far out" that nobody can understand it or cope with it any more. This paradox concerns the ability of a cognitive system (or market) to "understand", cognitively accept, and fit into existing mental frameworks/models what this completely novel artifact is about or how it could be useful (for instance, for a possibly not yet known use or purpose). Finding an optimal balance between these two poles seems to be the key challenge for every radical and future-oriented form of innovation.

Looking more closely at this paradox and at classic approaches to innovation, such as stage gate processes or creativity techniques (Cooper 1990; Baregheh, Rowley, and Sambrook 2009; Tidd and Bessant 2009), reveals that the key issues can be summarized as follows: (i) It is primarily our thinking and creative acts that generate ideas in our mind. (ii) These ideas are the result of a process of extrapolation from our past experiences into the future (compare the predictive mind hypothesis from cognitive science; e.g., Clark, 2013, 2016; Hohwy, 2013). (iii) From an epistemological perspective, reality only plays a minor role in this process of generating novelty, as it is our mind that wants to shape reality according to its own ideas (hylomorphic approach) rather than being shaped by reality. (iv) The Future plays almost no role in these classic approaches. Hence, following such classic approaches to innovation and creating novelty we are in a mode of trying to take *control* over our environment rather than entering into a mode of *cooperation, co-becoming* (Roth et al. 2016), or *correspondence* (Ingold 2013) between our cognition and our (future) environment (compare also Peschl 2019). How can such an alternative approach to innovation be realized? That is the point where Scharmer's (2007/2016) Theory U/Presencing comes in.

Tapping unfolding reality

The underlying question we are confronted with here is *what is the source of the future purpose or final cause?* Where does a possible sensible use come from? Is it primarily our mind, our thinking, our creativity, ideas, or concepts according to which we try to shape our environment and/or innovation artifacts? Or is it the environment, the space of adjacent possibles, the (future) potentials that shape our minds and, by that, guide our transformation activities resulting in new Actuals, innovation artifacts, new behavioral interaction patterns, etc.? We will see that it is not an either-or question. What can be said from the onset, however, is that the important role of reality and its future potentials as well as giving up control are at the center of our considerations.

One of Scharmer's (2007) main claims is that we have to acknowledge that the environment plays a major role in innovation processes (and not only the creative mind of the innovator). This implies that we have to give up the idea of having a clearly defined goal or purpose for the innovation in mind before starting to interact with the environment (compare the discussion on (Aristotle's) hylomorphic approach to innovation, design, or making; Ingold 2013; Ainsworth 2016; Peschl 2019). Furthermore, if this goal or purpose might emerge (Mitleton-Kelly 2007) and co-become in the process of engaging with and "corresponding" to the environment (Ingold 2013, Roth et al. 2016), we are facing the question of how to identify this purpose and what are "adequate" goals worth pursuing so that a successful and thriving innovation might emerge. In other words, the challenge is to develop strategies avoiding that the resulting novelty or innovation is *not completely arbitrary* (as it is the case in most "out-of-the-box-thinking" driven creative processes) and fulfills a deeper purpose that is coherent with emergent (future) environmental potentials/adjacent possibles and dynamics (compare innovation paradox above).

In the field of innovation this is one of the key issues, if the aspiration of the planned innovation activities goes beyond incremental innovation, adaptation, or optimization (Ettlie, Bridges, and O´Keefe 1984; Baregheh, Rowley, and Sambrook 2009). Understanding innovation as radical, disruptive, profound, future-driven and/or emergent (Hopp et al. 2018; Peschl and Fundneider 2013, 2017) leads to these questions concerning the source of the deeper purpose and meaning. The perspective having been developed in the sections above can give us a pointer how this challenge could be addressed in an alternative manner. Combining it with Scharmer's (2007/2016) Presencing approach both sheds a new light on these issues and gives some theoretical foundation to Theory U.

One key challenge in such a future-driven form of innovation is the issue on how much *control* we are exerting on the becoming of reality. In this context "control" refers to the fact that our mind and cognition functions like a prediction machine; as is shown by the predictive mind/coding approach in cognitive science (e.g., Clark 2013, 2016; Hohwy 2013) there is empirical/neuroscientific evidence that the main function of our cognition consists in projecting experiences from the past and verifying them in the reality. This implies that our perception and cognition are heavily determined by our already existing knowledge and that we almost can *not* "see" what we do not expect and what does not fit into our patterns of knowledge. What we are facing here is what I want to refer to *"epistemological or cognitive control"*; it is the biggest obstacle for opening up to an unfolding, uncertain, and unknown future, and, hence, for bringing forth novelty. Epistemological control defines and constrains the space of possibilities, the space of what may emerge in the realm of adjacent possibles.

On the other hand, giving up control implies opening up our mind for unexpected Possibles, for exploring a future and a succession of spaces of adjacent possibles that is open-ended, for a world that is *novel* and that wants to *emerge* beyond our projections, expectations, and our predetermined frames of reference. "Not restricting what you will consider to what you know already opens you up to experiencing the vast unknown; and in that you are likely to encounter what is to you the new… Being out of control… can be seen as offering more options than we could, ourselves, imagine. Thus, it is a way of increasing our creativity because we have access to (for instance) ideas which would otherwise not have come to our minds." (Glanville 2007, p 1189 & 1195) Only if we let go from our past experiences we will be able to "see" potentials that are going beyond our projections from the past (both individually and organizationally). This process of letting go and reframing is also at the center of Scharmer's (2007) first phases of his Theory U approach. It is the prerequisite that we may enter openly into the yet unknown space of novelty, the space of "not yet" and of adjacent possibles potentially leading us into new purposes and uses.

Giving up (epistemological) control does not only imply that we try to perceive reality with an open or beginner's mind and with "fresh eyes" (Scharmer 2007, p 39 & 244), but also that we learn to see the *future of reality as an emergent and unfolding phenomenon carrying in itself a dynamics of bringing things into actuality*. I.e., the goal or the purpose is not clear from the outset, but (co-) emerges in a process of cooperation and co-becoming with the environment. What do we mean, when we understand the purpose or the final cause (for instance, of an innovation) as being an emergent phenomenon developing in a process of co-becoming? Concepts from Aristotelian philosophy, from system's science and second order cybernetics, as well as from Scharmer's Theory U can shed some light on this question.

As we will discuss later, Ingold (2013 [p 115], 2014), Roth et al. (2016), or Peschl (2019) show that producing an innovation artifact can be compared to a kind of ongoing dialogue between the creator and his/her material. Both systems are interacting, engaging actively, and mutually changing and transforming themselves in a recursive manner; they co-become (see zipper metaphor above). This is not only a process of interaction, but a form of *correspondence*. Both creator and material "find to each other" by *mutually shaping each other* according to the (yet unknown) purpose that wants to emerge. The final (innovation) artifact is not known in advance but reveals its form and purpose in a process of correspondence and co-becoming.

On the role of adjacent possibles and potentials in an understanding of innovation as learning from the future as it emerges

"...the cause lies in the future... Closed circular causality, thus, bridges the gap between effective and final cause, between motive and purpose...no longer does one have to concern oneself with the starting conditions—as they are automatically provided by the end conditions. To be sure, this is the case, but the matter is anything but simple: only certain values of those conditions provide a solution for the processes within the circle; the problem has become an "Eigen-value" problem. (H.v.Foerster 2003, p 230)

In this section we are going to expand on the concept of adjacent possibles and potentials and what role they play in the context of Theory U. We will show that potentials are about "*what is not yet here*", or, in Scharmer´s (2007) terms, what still has to be born, what wants to emerge. We will develop further our theoretical framework that will act as a foundation for the process of Theory U, in particular, for the phase of Presencing. We will establish a link between the concept of Presencing on the one hand and sensing, identifying, and cultivating potentials as well as the concept of "adjacent possibles" on the other hand. Based on this framework, we will relate these insights to the principles of Presencing (e.g., Scharmer 2007, p 183ff) and develop a more profound understanding of what it means to "learn from the future as it emerges".

Learning from the future as it emerges

At the center of Scharmer's Theory U we can find his concept of a future-based understanding of learning (and innovation). It is opposed to a concept of learning from the past (Scharmer 2007, p 467; Kolb 1984) and finds its expression in, what Scharmer refers to as the discipline of *presencing* or in his idea of "*learning from the future as it emerges*". (Scharmer 2007, p 52) Let's take a closer look at what Scharmer says about this concept and on which principles it is based.

Presencing happens at the interface between the past and the future: as we have seen in the zipper metaphor (see Figure 1) a system (be it a person, as social system, or an artifact) is always the result of its history, a result of its process of becoming. At the present point in time a new space opens up, the space of adjacent possibles or potentials, "the *dormant* self, *the one that is waiting within us to be born*, to be brought into existence, to come into reality through our journey ahead. Presencing is the process of connecting these two selves. To connect our current with our authentic self. To move toward our real self from the future." (Scharmer

2007, p 189) Abstracting from our classic understanding of "self", one can see that this process is about bringing into existence what is already dormant or latent in a system and what is driven by and directed towards a thriving future.

Scharmer explains the neologism of presencing as blend of "sensing" and "presence". By being in a state of mindfulness (see, for instance, Rigg 2018) and of being completely in the present and not only perceiving what is there ("Actuals"), but what could be, we may move into a process of sensing from the future. By doing so, we connect to what Scharmer (mysteriously) refers to as "the Source", a source that lies in a thriving future and that attracts us and that "wants" to come into being, a potential that strives for coming into actuality; "...perception begins to happen from a future possibility that depends on us to come into reality. In that state we step into our real being, who we really are, our authentic self. Presencing is a movement where we approach our self *from the emerging future*." (Scharmer 2007, p 163) Furthermore, he states that "Presencing happens when our perception begins to connect to the source of our emerging future." (Scharmer 2007, p165). How could we possibly understand this ("mysterious and anecdotal") notion of (higher) "Self", purpose, and "Source" and its relation to presencing?

Although being rather on an operational side, Scharmer develops several principles on which the approach of presencing is based. Let's take a brief look at the most important ones:

1. *Presence and awareness*: In order to enter into the process of presencing one has to be in a state of high awareness and presence; being open to and aware of what is (in the outside and inside world) is key for identifying and understanding emerging potentials.

2. *Sensing and knowing from the inside*: normally, we perceive phenomena from the outside, we consider their shape, qualities that can be detected by our sensory systems, functions, behaviors, etc. For tapping future potentials it is necessary to switch perspective and deeply immerse into the world and try to achieve an understanding from the inside (out) (Scharmer 2007, p165f; Bortoft 1996;

Peschl and Fundneider 2013,).

3. *Primary knowing and wisdom*: Closely related to the previous point is what Scharmer quoting Varela, Thompson, and Rosch (1991) refers to as primary knowing: a perspective of wisdom is suggested in which it is essential to have a profound understanding of the phenomenon/world on the level of its being, of what it is in its *core* or *essence* (compare also Peschl and Fundneider 2013, 2015). As we will see, only if we know the very core of a phenomenon we will be able to "see" its future potentials that have not been tapped yet and might lead to fundamental and thriving innovations. This is achieved by assuming a perspective of wisdom.

4. *Blurring the border between mind and the world*: This point is related to the requirement of deep immersion and of reducing (epistemological) control. It is about discovering the deep interrelatedness and embeddedness between mind/cognition and world. The environment is part of our mind and vice versa.

5. *Correspondence and surrendering*: Although Scharmer (2007) does not explicitly refer to this concept[3,] it is a consequence of the previous point. As we have seen already, it is about the process of co-becoming between cognitive system/creator and his/her material, shaping and being shaped in an unfolding reality. It is a form of surrendering or, as Ingold (2014) refers to it, undergoing to the world and its unfolding (see our discussion below).

6. *Letting go and the eye of the needle*: If one wants to encounter the unknown and an emergent future it is essential to let go; however we consider this to be more than "everything that is not essential must go" (Scharmer 2007; p 184) Rather, it concerns actively lowering our epistemological control and projections, leaving behind our past experiences, judgments, and plans, and get free for what wants to emerge. Normally, this is not going to happen automatically or spontaneously; it takes an active effort and, in many cases, also courage. It implies that we have to leave our comfort zone and certainties and move into a space of

the unknown and uncertainty. It is like passing through the eye of a needle, a kind of "rebirth" of our mind. In the beginning, this might lead to an unpleasant emotional state of fear, uncertainty, or instability and one (or an organization) has to learn to bear it and to deal with such emotions.

7. *Empty space and silence*: The activity of letting go leads us to entering an empty space both in our mind and in our environment. It is this emptiness and stillness that gives novelty some space to emerge and enables us to listen to novelty in the form of highly fragile and subtle potentials that want to emerge in the field.

8. *The power of place, body, and Enabling Spaces*: For such a sophisticated and fragile embodied process involving cognition, emotions, and the body to be successful it is necessary to provide an adequate environment which we refer to as Enabling Spaces (Peschl and Fundneider 2012, 2014) or, as Scharmer (2007, p 187) calls them, a holding space of deep listening. It is a space that facilitates getting in resonance with oneself and coming into contact with an emerging future.

What we can learn from Aristotle: Reconsidering potentials and Actuals

Future-driven innovation always implies having to acknowledge that we are dealing with an unfolding, incomplete, and open-ended reality. As has been shown in our discussion about Bloch (1975, 1986) and adjacent possibles, reality is always in a state of "not-yet", it is always more than what we can perceive in the current moment. *Innovation* understood in this sense, similarly as presencing, is an *emergent process trying to bring to life what is "not yet"*. This is what Foerster (2003, p 230) means when stating that the "cause lies in the future"; as we will see in this section, this idea is closely related to Aristotle's final cause. It leads us to understanding that the *future (at least partly) drives the present* and that we have to shift our focus from *efficient cause to final cause* if we want to innovate in a future-oriented manner. If future states (at least partly) determine present states and how they might develop and unfold and if we want to understand the processes involved more profoundly, we will have to take a closer look at the concepts of potentiality/potentials and actuality/Actuals. As we have seen above, Bloch's (1976, 1986) "not-yet" and Kauffman's (2008, 2014) notion of Actuals and (adjacent) Possibles were a first approach to these issues. However, we suggest to go back as far as to Aristotle's (1991a) Metaphysics in order to dig deeper and achieve a more profound understanding of what is at stake if we take seriously the importance of the future's influence in the context of innovation and Theory U.

As we have seen above any object or phenomenon is always a composition of matter and form. I.e., material cause represents its material basis or substance and form is the way how this material substratum is put together. Together they form a unity with a specific meaning, functionality, and purpose. In this context it is important to introduce Aristotle's distinction between *potential(-ity)* (Latin: potentia) and *actuality* (Latin: actus). The Ancient Greek term for *potentiality* is dunamis (δύναμις) and refers to potential, capacity, (cap-)ability, or possibility. Aristotle (1991a) distinguishes between two forms of dunamis: (i) in its first sense dunamis means that a thing has (in itself) the capacity and the power to produce a change, it can be the source of change into something else or into itself qua other (1046a12). For instance, the dispersed Lego bricks have the implicit capacity to be assembled into a meaningful and functional object. This can be achieved by an external force, action, transformation, or movement ("κίνησῐς/kinesis") in the Aristotelian sense.

(ii) The second meaning of dunamis is not so much related to movement (or being moved/transformed), but rather to *actuality* (energeia [ενέργεια] and entelechia/entelechy [ἐντελέχεια]) (Aristotle 1991a, 1048a25). Without going into the details of this sophisticated discussion by Aristotle and his interpreters (e.g., Cohen 2016) this means: rather than putting an emphasis on change, actuality focuses on the capacity of an entity to be in a different and more *complete* or "*perfect*" state. It refers to an object's tendency to reach its complete state, its actuality. In this sense, reality (and any cognitive system, object, artifact, entity, social system, organization, etc.) is conceived as being an unfolding process that has in itself a latent directedness towards the realization of its (highest) potentials leading to its (emergent) actuality, telos, purpose, and entelechia. This tendency towards an emergent telos is closely related to the entity's potentiality and *final cause*. Aristotle (1991a, 1048b1–3) makes an analogy comparing the relationship between actuality and potentiality to someone who is awake vs. someone who is asleep or a lump of matter vs. a finished sculpture or piece of art.

As an illustration, Cohen (2016) introduces the example of a piece of wood that can be shaped into a table or into a bowl. Hence, the piece of wood has at least two potentialities: it can become potentially a table or a bowl. The more complete state of wood, its actuality, is a table or a bowl. The piece of wood has in it the potentiality to become a table or bowl. This is exactly the situation we are in when we are innovating or in the process of presencing: we are confronted with more or less (un-/pre-)formed matter and have to find ways for bringing or transforming this potentiality into a more complete state of (sustainable or thriving) actuality (i.e., the innovation artifact). Here we are facing a shift towards a new form (formal cause) and purpose (final cause).

In this context it is important to understand that this shift implies a *priority of actuality over potentiality* (in analogy to the priority of form over matter). Actuality has priority through final (and formal) cause: "Things that come to be moved toward an end (telos)—the boy becomes a man... Form or actuality is the end toward which natural processes are directed. Actuality is therefore a cause in more than one sense of a thing's realizing its potential... one and the same thing may be the final, formal, and efficient cause of another." (Cohen 2016, p 13f) That is the (metaphysical) reason, why we suggested that *future-oriented innovation should primarily focus on final cause and purpose*.

The zipper metaphor reconsidered

As an implication we suggest to revise the zipper metaphor and add a third dimension: from the perspective of our discussion about potentials and actuals as well as from Theory U it has become clear that it is no longer sufficient to look at innovation processes only as more or less undirected transformation and/or combination of (adjacent) possibles into new actuals. Rather, the dimension of final cause, "perfection" or, as Scharmer (2007) puts it, of "higher purpose"/highest future possibility has to be considered as well (see Figure 2).

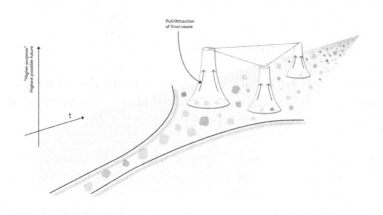

Figure 2: The zipper metaphor 2.0 — adding the aspect of "highest possible future" and purpose as a third dimension gives a direction to the transformation process. The final cause exerts a pull to this process and is co-responsible for bringing forth a thriving future.

Introducing the domains of meaning, (higher) purpose, and goals in this revised version of the zipper metaphor implies that we are going beyond the almost exclusively material or mechanistic realm of cause-effect relationships. The space of adjacent possibles receives a semantic change and (future-)purpose dimension. By identifying the core of the object of innovation and its potentials we are entering not only a perspective of wisdom (e.g., by radically changing the standpoint and knowing it "from within" (Scharmer 2007)), but, by doing so, we touch upon a future aspect: we are getting in touch with the highest future possibility and by making sense out of and relating such future possibilities the whole process receives an orientation; it is pulled by final cause and attracted by a potentially thriving future. It is not only the creator´s (or the innovation team´s) mind(s) that are responsible for bringing forth novelty and creativity; rather, it is a process of co-becoming and co-creation between the environmental structures and (future) dynamics and the involved extended cognitive processes leading to a new stable interaction pattern. New niches might emerge with formerly unknown uses and novel possibilities of interaction patterns serving potentially profound (future) human needs.

Discussion and implications

In this section we are going to bring together the concepts having been developed and discussed above. Let us recap what are the overall goals of this paper:

i.   Figuring out what happens when we move from the domain of the known to an unknown and uncertain future (see Figure 1 and 2);

ii. Understanding more thoroughly what Theory U implies by the concept of "learning from the future";

iii. Developing a sound theoretical framework into which Scharmer's Theory U approach, and more specifically, the process of presencing can be embedded and

iv. what are the implications and learnings from this framework for our understanding of Theory U and how they can be applied in future-oriented innovation processes.

In the previous sections we have developed a good understanding of what are potentials and adjacent possibles and how they might be used in order to cultivate and evolve the "not yet" and how it might be brought to life. In the following sections we are going to take a closer look at some of the implications for Theory U and what such a perspective that is deeply rooted in potentials means for innovation processes that are driven by the future.

Potentials/potentiality and Actuals/actuality in Theory U

In the context of Scharmer's (2007) Theory U the relationship between potentiality and actuality plays a central role although Scharmer only implicitly refers to these concepts, for instance, when he states: "Connecting with the highest future possibility and/or with the highest (future) Self." (Scharmer 2007, Table 20.1, p 366); or: "Presencing, the blending of sensing and presence, means to connect with the Source of the highest future possibility and to bring it into the now." (Scharmer 2007, p 163); or: "As a consequence, the essence of this view of the human being is to create through connecting to one's highest future possibility, one's authentic Self." (Scharmer 2007, p 444) It is also closely related to Scharmer's (2001) concept of self-transcending knowledge.

What is common in these statements is the idea of bringing or transforming potentiality into actuality. As an illustration, Scharmer (2007, p 402) uses the metaphor of a seed that needs continuous cultivation, nurturing, and attention in order to grow, and finally evolve its highest potential (i.e., bringing forth fruits). This metaphor also shows that such a process is open-ended, directed towards the future, driven by final cause or purpose (bearing fruits and perhaps leading to reproduction), and that the seed has to die in order to develop its full potential and finally can bring its full actuality to life. Furthermore, such a seed needs a nurturing environment to make these processes happen (cf. Enabling Spaces; Peschl and Fundneider 2012, 2014).

Thus, Theory U suggests a move from the known to the unknown (future opportunities, potentials, "not yet") and back to the known (see Figure 3); however this movement must not be seen as a process of adaptation or reaction to (known) problems and challenges. Rather, it is about (pro-)actively co-creating/ co-evolving new environments, problem spaces and niches, and shape the future in a sustainable and thriving manner. It is about connecting the past to the future (Scharmer 2007, p 401) and about tuning into, listening to, and getting in resonance with future potentials and developing them in a process of mutual correspondence (cf. Ingold 2013; Peschl 2019).

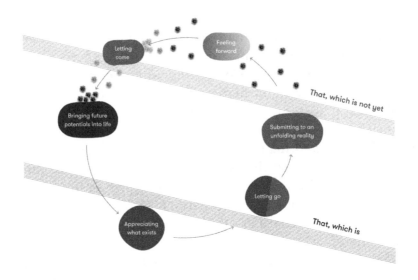

Figure 3: Innovation and Theory U as a process moving from the known (i.e., what is, Actuals) to the unknown ("not yet", potentials) and back to the known (new Actual or new artifact) in a circular manner (this figure has been co-developed with Carina Rohrbach).

Innovation as undergoing, submitting, and corresponding to reality

One of the most important implications of the approach having been discussed here as well as of Theory U/Presencing is a radical shift in mindsets and skills: it is about the *role of the environ-*

ment in future-driven innovation and knowledge creation processes. While classic approaches are based on the (implicit) assumption of a creative mind "dominating" over reality, we suggest to *reverse* this relationship. I.e., the hylomorphic perspective is replaced by a relationship of *co-becoming* and *correspondence* (see also Peschl 2019). This issue is closely related to our discussion of giving up epistemological control and developing an attitude/virtue of humbleness.

As Ingold (2014) suggests, creativity and creation of new knowledge do not (only) happen inside the creator's mind/brain, "but in their attending upon a world in formation. In this kind of creativity, undergone rather than done, imagination is not so much the capacity to come up with new ideas as the aspirational impulse of a life that is not just lived but led. But where it leads is not yet given. In opening to the unknown—in exposure—imagination leads not by mastery but by submission. Thus the creativity of undergoing, of action without agency, is that of life itself." (Ingold 2014, p 124) In a way this calls for an agent to *"think and act with the material"* (rather than thinking only with his/her mind/brain). However, "thinking with the environment" is not meant primarily in the sense of offloading cognitive effort, cognitive load, or tasks to the environment (such as when using a computer for doing complex computations or storing huge amounts of data; compare the extended approach to cognition; Clark 2008; Clark and Chalmers 1998; Menary 2010).

Rather, it is about anticipating (not in the narrow sense of predicting) possible future states of the world by intimately engaging with the world. In his work on craftsmanship Sennett (2008) stresses the role both of the material and the hand. By developing what he refers to as "material consciousness" (Sennett 2008, 199ff) he shows the importance of being curious about one's material and of knowing it deeply. In our terminology this can be translated into having a profound knowledge about potentialities and adjacent possibles by knowing them "from within." In this context "thinking with the hand" does not only mean to "think about" the world, but to enter into a (n existential) process of co-becoming and corresponding with the world (Ingold 2013; Roth et al. 2016; Peschl 2019), or to submit to the world. In being so close to the material, we can be both with and "one step ahead of the material" (Sennett 2008, p 175). We are not imposing our ideas on the material, but we are "feeling-forward" (Ingold 2014, p 136f; see also Figure 3) together with the material. Both the material and the creator/agent co-become and enter into an emerging unity going in the direction of a yet unknown creation.

"This is a matter not of predetermining the final forms of things and all the steps needed to get there, but of opening up a path and improvising a passage. To foresee, in this sense, is to see into the future, not to project a future state of affairs in the present; it is to look where you are going, not to fix an end point. Such foresight is about prophecy, not prediction." (Ingold 2013, p 69)

What Ingold calls foreseeing is closely related to the processes happening in the context of one possible interpretation of presencing, namely, in the sense of "*pre-sensing*". As we have seen, such a perspective on creating novelty and innovation emphasizes the role of the environment. Instead of a creative mind, reality itself is the primary source of novelty by providing a space of adjacent possibles/potentials. The temporal sequence/causality is reversed: it is not the creative idea leading to a transformation of the environment, but the potentials in the environment leading the dynamics of the mind and inviting it into a close cooperation, co-creation, and co-development of its potentials with the environment. As a consequence, we have to *undergo* reality. This means that we have to "move upstream, to a fount of incipience where ideas have yet to crystallize out from the flow of action... imagination is another word for the aspiration of not-yet-being. As such, it leads from the front rather than directing from behind. But *where* it leads is not yet plotted out before the act begins." (Ingold 2014, p 135) What Ingold describes here is in accordance with our discussion about the importance and priority of emergent final cause (over efficient cause) and bringing potentiality into actuality. "Leading from the front" implies that the emergent final cause/purpose attracts, "pulls", or leads the dynamics of the transformation/innovation processes rather than "being directed from behind" by the efficient cause of the mind trying to shape or manipulate reality according to its own ideas. The creative mind is engaged with the material and follows its form-generating potentials by entering in a joint process of growing and co-becoming. This is what we refer to as (innovation by) *correspondence* (see also Ingold 2013, Roth et al. 2016; Peschl 2019).

One final important point that follows from this approach: it might seem that the cognitive agent is put into a rather passive role in such an understanding of innovation and knowledge creation processes. This is misleading, however, as the innovator has to be not only highly engaged in deeply knowing his/her material (from within), but he/she has to *actively listen* to and interact with the material and its potentials. Hence, undergoing is not passive, it is "active undergoing, in which submission leads, [it] is a kind of *action without agency...* you do not initiate it; rather, it *behooves* to you... It has no point of origin; it cannot be traced to an intention... It is rather part of a never-ending process of attention and response... Just as the 'already' is always behind us,... so the 'not yet' will always escape ahead of us, beyond the horizon of our expectations." (Ingold 2014, p 137f) Hence, what we are dealing here with is a kind of "active passivity" in the sense of actively giving up (epistemological) control and switching to a mode of attentively molding the environment and at the same time being molded by it, of leading and being led at the same time.

The importance of a mindset of leisure

As we have seen in our discussion about the process of presencing, a special enabling environment is necessary for entering into such a state of submitting and being receptive to future potentials. One key ingredient for such a process is a state of mind that can be characterized best as *re-creation* (cf. also Scharmer 2007) or *leisure* (the German word is "Muße"). Pieper (1989) describes leisure as a "form of that stillness that is the necessary preparation for accepting reality" and "it means, that the soul's power, as real, of responding to the real—a co-respondence, eternally established in nature—has not yet descended into words.

Leisure is the disposition of receptive understanding, of contemplative beholding, and immersion—in the real." (Pieper 1998, p 50) Hence, leisure is a form of "active stillness" and a mindset of listening in which one opens up and immerses into reality (see also Beatty and Torbert 2003). It is a process of re-creating a current state or phenomenon by responding and corresponding to the potentials/adjacent possibles that want to emerge. This acceptance of reality (as a result of giving up epistemological control) is a precondition for novelty to be able to arise.

In listening to what wants emerge, one has to (learn to) accept that we are dealing with potentials. I.e., we are confronted with the domain of the yet unknown that is—per definitionem—not fully graspable. In this context, the mindset of leisure is necessary, as we have to rely on intuition, deep immersion and knowledge, on knowing from within (empathic knowledge) as well as on the humbleness and trust that the "right" potentials will be brought to life. This kind of "understanding" is qualitative (rather than "facts" or quantitative knowledge) and fragmentary and we have to engage in processes of deep sense making. As a consequence, we have to reduce our control as "leisure is not the attitude of the one who intervenes but of the one who opens himself; not of someone who seizes but of one who lets go, who lets himself go, and ,go under." (Pieper 1998, p 51) Only such an attitude will lead to an open mind and re-creation of our thinking and innovation processes.

Implications for education, organizational capacities, and personal development

Necessity of acquiring new sets of skills and mindsets

If one is intending to apply such processes for innovation and knowledge creation, we will have to acquire and cultivate future-oriented (epistemic) skills, practices, and mindsets that go beyond classic (innovation) management and leadership skills as they are taught in most MBA programs (mostly focusing on analytical skills, control, planning, etc.). Only then we will be able to enter into a process of co-creating a thriving future by learning from it as it emerges (compare also Miller 2015, 2018):

- *Openness and mindset of enabling (in leadership)*: While classic management has a strong focus on planning and control our approach to innovation suggests to establish a culture and mindset of openness (e.g., by providing strategic timeouts or routines in which employees get some "free time" to engage in observation or deep listening exercises, etc.). From a management perspective this means that management has to be understood rather in these sense of providing an enabling infrastructure: "Enabling Spaces" (Peschl and Fundneider 2012, 2014) or holding spaces (Scharmer 2007, p 187).
- *Receptivity and humbleness to be "im-pressed" and changed by an environmental dynamics that does not follow one's expectations*: As an implication of openness both attitudes and skills have to be developed that leave behind the mindset of (epistemic) control: i.e., they enable to embrace the unexpected and to be ready to not only reflect, but also to question and change deeply rooted hypotheses, premises, and mindsets (both on an individual and organizational level (compare also Grisold and Peschl´s (2017a) discussion on "Organizational Predictive Mind").
- *Being able to wait/patience*: Emergent processes cannot be "made" or completely controlled. One has to provide enabling (organizational, personal) infrastructures and develop an attitude and culture of patience and humbleness in the sense of being open to wait what "wants" to emerge.
- *Engaging with and immersing into one's environment, unknown opportunities and the space of adjacent possibles*
- *Being able to listen to what wants to emerge and the capacity to identify and to develop a sense for potentials*: We have to learn not to think in or search for solutions in the first place, but in appreciating an uncertain and unpredictable environment that is about potentials and untapped opportunities rather than a given problem- and solution-space. Both the problem- and solution-space are permanently chang-

ing (if they exist at all) and dynamically developing; the challenge is to wait for, listen to, and identify these future/emergent potentials leading to thriving innovations.

- *Capacity to acquire deep knowledge and understanding and knowing from within*: Instead of looking and observing from the outside only, one should try to penetrate deeper into the core or essence of the object to be changed (e.g., Scharmer 2007; Bortroft 1996). It is not only about classic perception or observation, learning or knowledge acquisition processes, or about reflecting premises and identifying knowledge frameworks, but about actively interacting with the (organizational) environment: one changes the perspective of an external observer only to an internal perspective of actively being part of and involved/engaged in the processes of intervention and enacting. It is a kind of "thinking with the environment", which does not only result in knowing the (organizational) system and its ecosystem from the inside (out), its core, but also in getting an understanding of its future potentials that are emerging in this process.

- *Being prepared to be "pulled" and attracted by purpose/final cause emerging from potentials*: We do not only have to learn to observe, deeply understand from within, and to listen to potentials, but also to understand that the purpose or the final cause itself is emerging. As an implication, it is not primarily the creative agent who is responsible for bringing about novelty or novel uses/purposes by him-/herself, but the unfolding and enabled environmental dynamics exerts a kind of "pull" towards an emerging purpose. The challenge of the agent/innovator is to create an enabling environment for such a process (see zipper metaphor 2.0 above; Figure 2) and to be open for sensing and bringing this emergent purpose from a state of potentiality into actuality.

- *Love for details and "weak signals"*: In most cases, future potentials are not "obvious", they are not visible or directly accessible to our senses. Rather, they are hidden and latent (Poli 2006, 2011), they are fragile and need to be brought to the fore as they are not "shouting out loudly". That is why it is important to learn to listen closely to details and to things that are not explicit, that are silent and in the domain of the "not yet".

It is important to keep in mind that this applies both to the individual and organizational domain.

Future-driven innovation requires personal change

Any process of future-driven innovation is based on personal involvement. However, as we have seen in the co-becoming/correspondence approach above, it is not sufficient to just apply a technique and/or preconceived concept to the environment and to react to what does not work in the process of realizing one's idea or concept. Rather, it has become evident that the innovator (and his/her idea or concept) has to fully engage and co-develop with his/her material or artifact in a process of co-becoming. From a learning perspective, this means that one has to change *first* on a personal and existential level (deeply reflecting and reframing attitudes, mindsets, skills, etc.) and only then will be capable of engaging with the material/environment in such an intimate manner as has been sketched above.

The innovator becomes his/her work/artifact

This implies that in such a perspective, we cannot make a clear distinction between the creator and the designed object any longer. The innovator cannot separate him-/herself from the object as he/she is involved and engaged in an existential and personal (and not only cognitive) process of *co-becoming*, of personal change, of being *exposed* to, as well as being *together* and growing with the material. Instead of mastery of the material it is a process of *undergoing* (leading to mastery) (compare Ingold 2014). As a consequence of the previous point we do not only have to acknowledge that the border between the agent and his/her environment/material gets blurred, but that—in a way—the agent becomes what he or she creates (and vice versa). In other words, the process of understanding innovation in such a way is *transformative* on both sides and both have to undergo a process of mutual profound change. Hence, future-oriented innovation as has been developed in this paper always implies a personal transformation as a necessary prerequisite; contrary to most classical approaches to innovation and creativity the creative agent has to change his/her patterns of perception, thinking, as well as of behaviors and even hast to go through a more existential transformation.

Conclusion

Coming back to our initial question of how it is possible to come up with innovations that are not only "creative" and (radically) novel, but that are sustainable and may lead to a thriving future, we have seen that the approach being suggested by Theory U/presencing is a promising strategy. We have shown that the concept of (future) potentials as well as understanding, exploring, and developing the space of adjacent possibles is key for such an approach. As we have seen in the zipper metaphor it is crucial to understand innovation not primarily as a "creative activity", but as an endeavor of being open to, identifying, and being attracted by future potentials as is suggested by Theory U. Only, if we understand this space of adjacent possibles as the domain of an emergent and unfolding future we will be able to "learn from the future as it emerges" and develop thriving innovations by combining to submit to this domain with the (highest) Self/highest possible future (e.g., Scharmer 2007, p 41f, 401f).

Furthermore, it has become clear that an innovation strategy that is based on the concept of being driven by the future implies that we have to turn most of our assumptions about "innovation management" on their head; most importantly, it is not primarily about "management", but about *enabling*; we have to give up (epistemological) control and enter into a mode and mindset of co-becoming and correspondence with our world. By doing so we come to understand the object of innovation "from within" and may identify its future potentials that have not been tapped yet. The challenge is to "listen to" or "feel forward" what wants to emerge from these potentials, what wants to be activated and break forth in the untapped potentials of the core of the object of innovation, and make sense of and cultivate opportunities and what wants to be brought to life and actuality.

The resulting purpose or possible value/use (of the innovation artifact) can neither be planned nor is it given in advance, but emerges and unfolds in the process of co-becoming as final cause. As a consequence, we may arrive at an innovation that resolves one of the major challenges and paradoxa in innovation: for being a thriving and sustainable future-driven innovation, it does not suffice to be just novel, creative, or radical/disruptive (Christensen, Raynor, and McDonald 2015), but it has to fulfill somehow in a deeper purpose, it has to be connected to a—perhaps, in some cases not yet known—deep human need. Or, as Hekkert, Snelders, and van Wieringen (2003) put it in the context of industrial design and aesthetics, such an innovation has to be "most advanced, yet acceptable".

Following the approach and mindset having been outlined in this paper, this results in what we are referring to as emergent innovation (Peschl and Fundneider 2013, 2017): on the one hand, it has its roots in the (potentials of the) core of an existing Actual (be it a product, service, business model, organizational purpose, etc.). Hence, it is compatible with existing mindsets, assumptions, conceptual frameworks, or mental models (of potential uses and users, markets, user needs, or organizational capabilities). On the other hand, it may be completely and radically novel (and not only in the sense of just "out-of-the-box" or "creative"), as it is driven by unknown future potentials that have emerged from the core in this process. As we have seen, this might lead to completely new needs and niches that have been unknown at the outset and that open up the opportunity for a new and thriving future.

Another important implication is that in order to arrive at such future-driven innovations which follow the Theory U based approach, it is necessary that the involved persons (or organization) has to undergo a profound personal/existential transformation as well. In other words, such a process cannot be executed like an abstract and mechanical activity, but the involved stakeholders go through a transformation of their mindsets, attitudes, as well as skill sets (see section above). We cannot expect to shape the future in a thriving manner without being shaped by her in return.

References

Ainsworth, T. (2016). Form vs. Matter. In E. N. Zalta (ed.), The Stanford Encyclopedia of Philosophy (Spring 2016). Metaphysics Research Lab, Stanford University.
https://plato.stanford.edu/archives/spr2016/entries/form-matter/

Aristotle (1991). Physics (fourth ed.). In J. Barnes and Aristotle (Eds.), The complete works of Aristotle. The revised Oxford Translation (Vol 1) Princeton, N.J.: Princeton University Press.

Aristotle (1991a). Metaphysics. In J. Barnes and Aristotle (Eds.), The complete works of Aristotle. The revised Oxford Translation (Vol 2) Princeton, N.J.: Princeton University Press.

Beatty, J. E., & Torbert, W. R. (2003). The False Duality of Work and Leisure. Journal of Management Inquiry, 12(3), 239–252. https://doi.org/10.1177/1056492603256340

Bloch, E. (1975). Experimentum Mundi. Frage, Kategorien des Herausbringens, Praxis. Frankfurt/M.: Suhrkamp Verlag.

Bloch, E. (1986). The principle of hope (3 Volumes). Cambridge, MA: MIT Press.

Bortoft, H. (1996). The wholeness of nature. Goethe´s way of science. Edinburgh: Floris Books.

Brown, T. (2008). Design Thinking. Harvard Business Review 86(6), 84–93.

Brown, T. (2009). Change by design. How design thinking transforms organizations and inspires innovation. New York, NY: Harper Collins.

Chemero, A. (2003). An outline of a theory of affordances. Ecological Psychology 15(2), 181–195.

Chia, R. and I.W. King (1998). The organizational structuring of novelty. Organization 5(4), 461-478.

Christensen, C.M., M. Raynor, and R. McDonald (2015). What is disruptive innovation?. Harvard Business Review 2015(12), 44–53.

Clark, A. (2008). Supersizing the mind. Embodiment, action, and cognitive extension. Oxford, New York: Oxford University Press.

Clark, A. (2013). Whatever next? Predictive brains, situated agents, and the future of cognitive science. Behavioral and Brain Sciences 36(3), 1–73.

Clark, A. (2016). Surfing uncertainty. Prediction, action, and the embodied mind. Oxford, New York: Oxford University Press.

Clark, A. and D. Chalmers (1998). The extended mind. Analysis 58(1), 7–19.

Clegg, S. R., Kornberger, M., & Rhodes, C. (2005). Learning/Becoming/ Organizing. *Organization*, 12(2), 147–167.

Cohen, S.M. (2016). Aristotle's Metaphysics. In E.N. Zalta (Ed.), The Stanford encyclopedia of philosophy Stanford; https://plato.stanford.edu: Metaphysics Research Lab, Stanford University.

Cooper, R.G. (1990). Stage-gate systems: a new tool for managing new products. Business Horizons 33(3), 44–54.

Cooper, R. (2006). Making present. Autopoiesis as human production. *Organization*, 13(1), 59–81.

Dodgson, M. and D. Gann (2010). Innovation. A very short introduction. Oxford: Oxford University Press.

Ettlie, J.E., W.P. Bridges, and R.D. O´Keefe (1984). Organisational strategic and structural differences for radical vs. incremental innovation. Management Science 30(6), 682–695.

Felin, T., S. Kauffman, R. Koppl, and G. Longo (2014). Economic opportunity and evolution: beyond landscapes and bounded rationality. Strategic Entrepreneurship Journal 8(4), 269–282.

Foerster, H.v. (Ed.) (2003). Understanding understanding. Essays on cybernetics and cognition. New York: Springer-Verlag.

Gibson, J.J. (1986). The ecological approach to visual perception (new ed.). New York: Psychology Press. Taylor and Francis Group.

Goldspink, C. and R. Kay (2003). Organizations as self-organizing and sustaining systems. A complex and autopoietic systems perspective. International Journal of General Systems 32(5), 459–474.

Grisold, T. and M.F. Peschl (2017). Why a systems thinking perspective on cognition matters for innovation and knowledge creation. A framework towards leaving behind our projections from the past for creating new futures. Systems Research and Behavioral Science 34(3), 335–353.

Grisold, T and M.F. Peschl (2017a). Change from the inside out. Towards a culture of unlearning by overcoming Organizational Predictive

Mind. In N. Tomaschek and D. Unterdorfer (Eds.), Veränderung. Der Wandel als Konstante unserer Zeit, pp. 45–63. Münster, New York: Waxmann.

Hekkert, P., D. Snelders, and P.C.W. van Wieringen (2003). Most advanced, yet acceptable. Typicality and novelty as joint predictors of aesthetic preference in industrial design. British Journal of Psychology 94(1), 111–124.

Hohwy, J. (2013). The Predictive Mind. Oxford: Oxford University Press.

Hopp, C., D. Antons, J. Kaminski, and T.O. Salge (2018). What 40 years of research reveals about the difference between disruptive and radical innovation. Harvard Business Review 2018(4).

Ingold, T. (2013). *Making. Anthropology, archaeology, art and architecture.* Abingdon, Oxon; New York, NY: Routledge.

Ingold, T. (2014). The creativity of undergoing. *Pragmatics & Cognition*, 22(1), 124–139.

Kauffman, S.A. (1993). The origins of order: Self-organisation and selection in evolution. Oxford: Oxford University Press.

Kauffman, S.A. (2000). Investigations. New York: Oxford University Press.

Kauffman, S.A. (2008). Reinventing the sacred. A new view of science, reason, and religion. New York: Basic Books.

Kauffman, S. A. (2014). Prolegomenon to patterns in evolution. *BioSystems*, 123(2014), 3–8.

Kauffman, S.A. (2016). Humanity in a creative universe. New York: Oxford University Press.

Kay, R. (2001). Are organizations autopoietic? A call for new debate. Systems Research and Behavioral Science 18, 461–477.

Kelley, T. (2004). The art of innovation. Lessons in creativity from IDEO, America's leading design firm. London: Profile Books.

Kellner, D. and H. O´Hara (1976). Utopia and Marxism in Ernst Bloch. New German Critique Autumn 1976(9), 11–34.

Kolb, D. A. (1984). *Experiential learning: experience as the source of learning and development.* Englewood Cliffs, NJ: Prentice Hall.

Koppl, R., S. Kauffman, T. Felin, and G. Longo (2014). Economics for a creative world. Journal of Institutional Economics 2014, 1–31.

Krippendorff, K. (1989). On the essential contexts of artifacts or on the proposition that "Design is making sense (of things)". Design Issues 5(2), 9–39.

Longo, G., M. Montevil, and S. Kauffman (2012). No entailing laws, but enablement in the evolution of the biosphere. In (Ed.), Proceedings of the Fourteenth International Conference on Genetic and Evolutionary Computation, pp. 1379–1392. Philadelphia, PA.

Longo, G. and M. Montevil (2013). Extended criticality, phase spaces and enablement in biology. Chaos, Solitons & Fractals 55, 64–79.

Maturana, H.R. (1970). Biology of cognition. In H.R. Maturana and F.J. Varela (Eds.), Autopoiesis and cognition: the realization of the living, pp. 2–60. Dordrecht, Boston: Reidel Pub.

Maturana, H.R. and F.J. Varela (Eds.) (1980). Autopoiesis and cognition: the realization of the living. Dordrecht, Boston: Reidel Pub.

Menary, R. (Ed.) (2010). The extended mind. Cambridge, MA: MIT Press.

Miller, R. (2015). Making Experimentalist Leadership practical. The theory and practice of futures literacy. Victoria: Centre for Strategic Education Seminar Series Paper. (24).

Miller, R. (Ed.) (2018). Transforming the future. Anticipation in the 21st century. Oxon, New York: Routledge.

Mitleton-Kelly, E. (2003). Ten principles of complexity and enabling infrastructures. In E. Mitleton-Kelly (Ed.), Complex systems and evolutionary perspectives on organisations: the application of complexity theory to organisations, pp. 23–50. Oxford: Elsevier.

Mitleton-Kelly, E. (2007). The emergence of final cause. In M. Aaltonen (Ed.), The third lens. Multi-ontology sense-making and strategic decision-making, pp. 111–124. Adlershot: Ashgate Publishing.

Paulus, B.P. et al. (2002). Social and cognitive influences in group brainstorming. Predicting production gains and losses. European Review of Social Psychology 12(1), 299–325.

Paulus, B.P., M. Dzindolet, and N.W. Kohn (2012). Collaborative creativity. Group creativity and team innovation. In M. Mumford (Ed.), Handbook of organizational creativity, pp. 327–357. San Diego, CA: Academic Press.

Peschl, M.F. (2006). Learning and teaching as socio-epistemological engineering. Enabling spaces of profound cogntive change, innovation, and knowledge ceation. In A. Mettinger, P.

Oberhuemer, and C. Zwieauer (Eds.), eLearning an der Universtät Wien. Forschung - Entwicklung - Einführung, pp. 112–135. Münster: Waxmann.

Peschl, M.F. (2019). Design and innovation as co-creating and co-becoming with the future. Design Management Journal 14(1), 4–14.

Peschl, M.F. and T. Fundneider (2012). Spaces enabling game-changing and sustaining innovations: Why space matters for knowledge creation and innovation. Journal of Organisational Transformation and Social Change (OTSC) 9(1), 41–61.

Peschl, M.F. and T. Fundneider (2013). Theory-U and Emergent Innovation. Presencing as a method of bringing forth profoundly new knowledge and realities. In O. Gunnlaugson, C. Baron, and M. Cayer (Eds.), Perspectives on Theory U: Insights from the field, pp. 207–233. Hershey, PA: Business Science Reference/IGI Global.

Peschl, M.F. and T. Fundneider (2014). Designing and enabling interfaces for collaborative knowledge creation and innovation. From managing to enabling innovation as socio-epistemological technology. Computers and Human Behavior 37, 346–359.

Peschl, M.F., T. Fundneider, and A. Kulick (2015). On the limitations of classical approaches to innovation. From predicting the future to enabling "thinking from the future as it emerges". In Austrian Council for Research and Technology Development (Ed.), Designing the Future: Economic, Societal and Political Dimensions of Innovation, pp. 454–475. Wien: Echomedia.

Peschl, M. F., & Fundneider, T. (2016). Design as anticipation and innovation. In D. R. Society (Ed.), *Proceedings of DRS 2016, Design Research Society 50th Anniversary Conference* (pp. 1–14). Brighton, UK: DRS.

Peschl, M., & Fundneider, F. (2017). Future-oriented innovation. How affordances and potentials can teach us how to learn from the future as it emerges. In W. Hofkirchner & M. Burgin (Eds.), *The future information society. Social and technological problems* (pp. 223–240). Singapore: World Scientific Publishing.

Peschl, M.F. and T. Fundneider (2017a). Uncertainty and opportunity as drivers for re-thinking management: Future-oriented organizations by going beyond a mechanistic culture in organizations. In W. Küpers, S. Sonnenburg, and M. Zierold (Eds.), ReThinking Management: Perspectives and impacts of cultural turns and beyond, pp. 79–96. Wiesbaden: Springer.

Poli, R. (2006). The ontology of what is not there. In J. Malinowski and A. Pietruszczak (Eds.), Essays in Logic and Ontology (Poznan Studies in the Philosophy of the Sciences and the Humanities, vol. 91), pp. 73–80. Amsterdam/New York: Rodopi.

Poli, R. (2010). An introduction to the ontology of anticipation. Futures 42(7), 769–776.

Poli, R. (2010a). The many aspects of anticipation. Foresight 12(3), 7–17.

Poli, R. (2011). Ontological categories, latents and the irrational. In J. Cumpa and E. Tegtmeier (Eds.), Ontological categories, pp. 153–163. Heusenstamm: Ontos Verlag.

Popper, K.R. (1959). The logic of scientific discovery. London: Hutchinson.

Rigg, C. (2018). Somatic learning. Bringing the body into critical reflection. Management Learning 49(2), 150–167.

Risto, H. (2011). Artifact. In E.N. Zalta (Ed.), The Stanford encyclopedia of philosophy Stanford; https://plato.stanford.edu: Metaphysics Research Lab, Stanford University.

Roth, W.M., D. Socha, and J. Tenenberg (2016). Becoming-design in corresponding: re/theorising the co- in codesigning. CoDesign 12(1).

Sarasvathy, S. D., Dew, N., Velamuri, S. R., & Venkataraman, S. (2003). Three Views of Entrepreneurial Opportunity. In Z. D. Acs & D. B. Audretsch (Eds.), *Handbook of entrepreneurship research* (pp. 141–160). Dordrecht, NL: Kluwer Academic Publishers.

Scharmer, C.O. (2001). Self-transcending knowledge. Sensing and organizing around emerging opportunities. Journal of Knowledge Management 5(2), 137–150.

Scharmer, C. O. (2007). *Theory U. Leading from the future as it emerges. The social technology of presencing*. Cambridge, MA: Society for Organizational Learning.

Scharmer, C.O. (2016). Theory U. Leading from the future as it emerges. The social technology of presencing (second ed.). San Francisco, CA: Berrett-Koehler Publishers.

Scharmer, C. O., & Kaeufer, K. (2010). In front of the blank canvas. Sensing emerging futures. *Journal of Business Strategy*, 31(4), 21–29.

Sennett, R. (2008). The craftsman. New Haven and London: Yale University Press.

Simonton, D.K. (2011). Creativity and discovery as blind variation. Campbell's (1960) BVSR model after the half-century mark. Review of General Psychology 15(2), 158–174.

Stack, M. and M.P. Gartland (2003). Path creation, path dependency, and alternative theories of the firm. Journal of Economic Issues 37(2), 487–494.

Tidd, J. (2006). A review of innovation models. London: Imperial College. (Discussion Paper 1).

Tidd, J and J. Bessant (2009). Managing innovation. Integrating technological, market and organizational change (fourth ed.). Chichester: John Wiley & Sons.

Tsoukas, H., & Chia, R. (2002). On organizational becoming: Rethinking organizational change. *Organization Science*, 13(5), 567–582.

Varela, F.J., E. Thompson, and E. Rosch (1991). The embodied mind: cognitive science and human experience. Cambridge, MA: MIT Press.

CHAPTER 4

Developing our Presencing Self through Four Levels of Leadership Presence

Olen Gunnlaugson, Ph.D.

Background & Introduction

This chapter introduces my current research in Dynamic Presencing,[4] which is focused on establishing presencing as a core leadership ability that is accessible in any situation, whether in a coaching conversation, high performance team or in solitude. Presencing initially developed through Otto Scharmer and colleagues' *Theory U* (Jaworski, 2012; Scharmer, 2007, 2000a, 2000b; Scharmer & Kaufer, 2013), drawing upon important insights gathered from interviews with 150 thought leaders worldwide as part of MIT Sloan School of Management's *Global Dialogue Project,* as well as various consulting initiatives associated with the *Society for Organizational Learning.* More recent perspectives have been applied from the field of management in the book *Perspectives on Theory U: Insights From the Field* (Gunnlaugson et al., 2013) as well as the international U. Lab MOOC (Massive Open Online Course), which started in the spring of 2015, where over 100,000 registered participants to date from over 185 countries have worked with applying Theory U to various societal, organizational and leadership challenges.

Before I introduce Dynamic Presencing, I will give some brief context on presencing. Let's start with Scharmer's (2007) initial description of the presencing process: When moving into the state of presencing, perception begins to happen from a future possibility that depends on us to come into reality. In that state we step into our real being, who we really are, our authentic self. Presencing is a movement where we approach our self *from the emerging future.* (p.163)

Scharmer defines presencing as the "blending of the words "presence" and "sensing." It means to sense, to tune in, and to act from one's highest future potential" (p.8). The main injunction for accessing presencing is to "go to the place of individual and collective stillness, open up to the deeper Source of knowing and connect to the future that wants to emerge through you" (p.18). Senge et al.'s (2004) initial account of presencing in the book *Presence*, Scharmer's subsequent work with *Theory U* (2013; 2007; 2000a; 2000b) and Jaworski's more recent book *Source* (2012) have all made important inroads into identifying the presencing process as being fundamentally about a way of leading from our emerging self and future.

Dynamic Presencing builds from this body of work in supporting an overall creative restoration and re-embodiment of our presencing nature in service of learning how to engage a more sustained presencing mode of experience. In this way, Dynamic Presencing is focused on developing our core presencing capacities to more effectively unearth, shape and discern the emerging future in a sustained and effortless manner. Mastering the methods of Dynamic Presencing opens a path into the heart of a generative perception of reality that is grounded in a way of being and relating to our experience that are united interiorly, in turn making presencing actionable in day to day life. Senge's insight "collectively becoming aware of our inner places from which we operate in real time—may well be the single most important leverage point for shifting the social field in this century and beyond" (Scharmer, 2007, p.10) brings important clarity to a current leadership challenge. Dynamic Presencing builds upon

Senge's insight by supporting us in building capacities to access this inner region of presencing more effectively.

To make this aim realizable, Dynamic Presencing introduces an updated process-method and language that begins where Scharmer and colleagues left off at the bottom of the U. Introducing five new transformative journeys, Dynamic Presencing is designed to help *Theory U* practitioners build capacity to access and effectively work from inside this blind spot of our time, which to date has not been well understood (Jaworski, 2012), as a way of leading. Each journey works through a process of reweaving presencing through our different experiential faculties, bringing forth an overall approach that supports the evolution of a more advanced presencing that functions more seamlessly as an embodied generative capacity at the level of our overall perception and action. As practitioners learn how to integrate these inner dimensions of their experience in day to day work and life, this work catalyzes significant shifts, re-grounding and a re-orientation of presencing from the inside-out. Through an immersion in each of the five journeys, Dynamic Presencing clarifies a means for directly accessing and leading from the underlying regions of our immediate experience.

For the purposes of this chapter, I will focus on the first Dynamic Presencing Journey, Primary Presence, which involves an excavation of four lifeworlds, each of which encompasses a distinct layer or dimension of our presencing nature: *Being Real; Being Witness; Being Essence and Being Source.* Each lifeworld introduces a particular synergistic self-sense, mode of presence and relationality as well as a distinct inscape from which to engage presencing from as a way of being. I refer to each of these micro cultures of being as *lifeworlds*, a term borrowed from phenomenology (i.e. Husserl) that represents the immersive sensory world of experience that each of us lives in that is distinct from say the more objective measurable world we experience as outside ourselves. Though we engage with a variety of lifeworlds on a daily basis, in Primary Presence, the focus of this initial journey is to uncover the inherent activation site of presence that exists within each of us and as it turns out, contains a particular ground that is indispensable to developing our overall ontological presencing capacity. As each level of presence is uncovered, enacted and lived into, key transformative conditions come online, clarifying and opening a path into a ground of presence that supports and drives presencing as an overall movement. I will now turn to introducing the core movement of Primary Presence (Figure 1.0), which consists of a descent into the four lifeworlds that support us in uncovering and embodying the inner dimensions of our presencing nature.

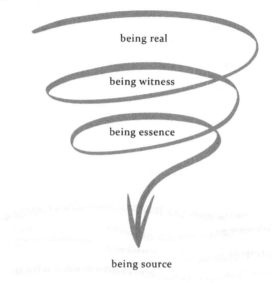

Figure 1.0. The Core Movement of Primary Presence

Being Real

The first lifeworld, being real, provides an initial reference point to begin letting go of whatever is obstructing us from a more transparent and grounded contact with our experience and underlying humanity. The initial focus here is to get in touch with ourselves in a more centered and undefended way. Contact with this initial lifeworld makes it possible to begin from a place that is trustable and aligned with our actual phenomenological ground, which brings us back into contact with our senses and existential sense of presence. Making contact with being real helps us connect with our immediate experience as its arising, making it possible to connect with a quality of seeing and presence that is uncontrived and unassuming.

Inside the real, the initial work involves connecting through to the places where our immediate experience is arising and discovering whatever lies in wait there. This encounter with the first layer of who we are invites a discernment process, a willingness to look, see and more importantly feel into where the actual ground of our presence lies at its source. The process of coming home into the real is guided by a listening and sensing into this quality of being inside our actual individual nature, again letting go of our socially and culturally mediated senses of self. By relaxing into this first ground level of presence, we come into contact with *what-is* through an unconditional support, interest and trust in whatever is arising. Encountering the real invites a more transparent meeting with ourselves directly.

Moving into being real is an invitation to let go of the burden of holding certain social masks, personas or images of ourselves that are keeping us at some remove from the immediacy of living from a more transparent contact with reality through our senses. By suspending our self analysis and judgment being real invites a transparency and fullness of being with ourselves and one another on terms that are less defined by tradition, history, personality, persona or self-image. Reconnecting with our ground of presence in a way that is not determined or influenced by these constructs invites us into a fuller contact with reality. Here, existential reality is given its place in our immediate experience, offering us a more robust and transparent ground for meeting and experiencing life *as it is*.

With this invitation to connect with the real, initially on our terms, then on its terms, we uncover the first level of presence for letting go of whatever might be obscuring this ground. As we descend into the presence of the real, there is a discovery and settling into a more substantive ground of being than the personality and separate self. This reconnection with a more trusted

117

collective source of who we are facilitates a strengthening of awareness and awakens a courage to stand in solidarity with one another in this emerging space of individual and collective authentication. As we each increase our capacity to be with and orient from the real, this consolidates our presence at the level of our senses and inner bodies. Sensing into and orienting from the real gives each of us permission to rest more fully in our nature, in turn activating conditions that allow ourselves to be recalibrated ontologically by the real together.

In the second phase, there is a shift from an emphasis of uncovering and discovering to embodying and entraining with the real. When this ground is experienced on terms of what we always already are, our imperfections and shortcomings can be met and transmuted rather than judged, managed, avoided or recoiled from. Whatever tendencies or habits prevented us from being more fully present with situations in the past, at this point, the real provides a collective basis for discovering and then integrating our shared common ground for our journey into Primary Presence.

Being Witness

Following an immersion into the real, we relax into exploring the witness. A principle practice to move into engaging the second lifeworld is "surrendering into witnessing" (Gunnlaugson & Moze, 2013). In this phase of our journey, our attention shifts from identifying with and orienting from the real to relaxing into a place of noticing that we are "having" these experiences. Being witness takes place when we let go from the real and move into the experience of witnessing consciousness. Letting the real settle into the background of our awareness, it shifts into becoming part of the phenomenological context, which informs our exploration of witnessing awareness. Traditionally, witnessing our experience involves noticing the content of our awareness and the respective currents of thought, emotion and the variegated impulses and opinions that arise in our mind streams. The surrendering aspect invites a deeper continued exhalation from being real by further letting go of the familiar constructs that we hold in our experience. Surrendering into Witnessing involves initially noticing our immediate experience as it arises much like in awareness-based practices of meditation.

A guided process of offering pointing out instructions can be helpful to connect with the ever-present witness in our immediate experience. Becoming aware of our thoughts, feelings, and sensations as they arise releases us to being drawn deeper into the background of witnessing awareness that is noticing all of this. The nature of this experience tends to be freeing, in that it helps us relax our hold on identifying our experience or thinking as "ours." In being less identified with arising thought, feelings or sensations, there is also a tendency to become more detached. Surrendering into witnessing is more about becoming re-established inside the witness, not as a place for detached or non-attached seeing, but rather inside the subtle grounds of our more transcendent, released nature. Though this ground stands in contrast with the first lifeworld where we are more strongly immersed with the textures of the real, the invitation here is to let this dimension of our nature influence our way of being more directly and subtly together as we give ourselves the chance to discover a released experience of witnessing that is at once intimate, felt and subtly embodied.

The release from the gravitational hold and embeddedness in the real invites the witnessing dimension of our natures to unfold, helping us shift into an at once more distributed yet connected place. As we transition into making contact with witnessing awareness, this helps us discover a way of being together from this new expansive ground of presence. Witnessing helps us sustain a more fundamental suspension of our seeing or seeing our seeing. This mode of suspended seeing uncovers new perceptual grounds from which we can experience our immediate reality and experience from a distinct vantage point that again is paradoxically expansive yet connected to a shared ground of inter-being. Orienting from witnessing fosters a subtly embodied yet expansive quality of inter-being, which is essential in discovering the prospects of witnessing as a way of being—that is, an essential dimension of our natures.[5]

Witnessing infuses our ground of presence with spaciousness, ease, a curiosity for what is emerging, de-centered compassion, and other welcoming and releasing transpersonal qualities of attention and presence. Witnessing gives us a vivid, subtly embodied yet comparatively (to the real) more "impersonal" or "objective" access point to our thoughts and feelings. This is a marked contrast to the executive function of the everyday mind, superego and other psychological processes of the self that draw upon more survival-oriented action logics. As such, surrendering into witnessing drops us into the next level of presence, and prepares us for a deeper shift in our individual and collective identity. Released from the limiting conditions of the conventional sense of self and even to an extent, the real, we let go into experiencing a basis for being that has but is much less identified with these needs, helping us discover a new empowered vantage point and locus of identity in embodied witnessing awareness.

When listening and speaking arise from being witness, perception is drawn through a felt sense of unity with our own experience inside the ground of presence. This fosters a shared experience of intimate yet paradoxically less personal or attached terms of relating. Being witness offers us a more spacious canvas to be more fully as we are, further expanding the insights and realizations of the real, filling out who we are in a more distributed way. Exploring the subtle embodiment of witnessing awareness gives a qualitatively distinct access to reality and our transpersonal nature. As we attune our listening and speaking from this place, surrendering into witnessing offers a rich and complimentary vantage point to the wisdom and grounds of the real.

As we learn to access and orient from the witness, attention is freed and can be redeployed toward discerning new knowledge, learning and discoveries in novel ways. Where the former exploration of the real evoked a more unfiltered existential way of being and meeting reality, connecting to the Witness invites a sanctuary and release point for the self to grow into a fuller sense of its ground and nature. The witness interrupts the intensity of the real, helping us release our identification with the rawness of life in a way that is less threatening as this background takes hold and begins to infuse our perception directly from a more distributed and compassionate grounds. Here, being witness helps us discover a distinct form of relational and inner coherence that expands and deepens our sense of the nature of what is real, opening up an important ground level of presence from which to orient the presencing process from.

Being Essence

Transitioning from being witness, we are invited to reconnect within, and open into being essence. Relaxing our identification with witnessing awareness gives rise to the possibility to move into the next iteration of a more subtle and receptive way of letting go into connecting with our essential nature. Orienting as essence relaxes witnessing awareness into the background. At this junction point, we explore the next level of our being as essence.

By essence I am referring to a multi-dimensional flowing quality of presence that draws from the innermost place of being and relating. Inside being essence, witnessing awareness plays a supporting role in filling out our presence, as does the fierce yet vulnerable real. The capacity to embody and orient from the lifeworld of essence and to engage this dimension of presence opens up rich phenomenological grounds of relating. Connecting to our essence, we begin to uncover a subtle dimension of our being and presencing nature that has a timeless quality to it. Neither memory nor time dependent, our essence is in some sense impervious to time or how we experience ourselves in the world in time. As we arrive into our individual expression of essence, there is a reconnect with what is central to our most intimate sense of intrinsic purpose, drive and sense of what it means to be truly human for us. When our essence is diminished or underdeveloped, the inherent richness, depth and dynamism of who we are is not yet experienced.

Transitioning into being essence, our focus here is to bring our faculties into a coherent state of felt contact with our essential nature. In doing this, our particular embodiment of essence flows forth, speaking and interacting through us in a revelatory manner. As our individual expression of essence awakens into its relaxed and sometimes passionate expression, it is like an underground river or fountain that never ceases from flowing. When essence is contacted through the inner body and given the space to unfold in conversation, this dimension of our nature is free to flow forth from our in-the-moment contact with this deeper stream of intelligence. As the inherent dynamism of essence finds its way into expression, this opens us into a spontaneous and inner aligned perception of the essential nature of reality. The two are no longer separate at these depths. Orienting from our essential nature deepens the center of gravity of our presence.

The journey into being essence at this stage involves exploring phenomenological practices for activating our essential nature directly with our presencing nature in the field. The focus here is more on ontologically re-rooting and re-acclimating to this inner, shared dimension of essence and sensitizing ourselves to its nature as a ground from which we can access presence from. Unlike the spacious expansive Witness as a more fundamental aspect of who we are, essence offers a distinct quality of ground as this site of our innermost sense of experience is uncovered.

As mentioned, each lifeworld provides distinct grounds for exploring particular inflections and functions of presence. Engaging our arising experience from essence brings about key emergent conditions to access, embody, relate and inquire from this lifeworld directly. Where witnessing awareness supported the relaxation of our identification with our thoughts and emotions in our immediate experience into a more meta-aware state, essence awareness re-engages us with the subtler more intrinsic qualities of being.

Learning to connect, orient and articulate from the interface of essential presence shifts our center of gravity, bringing forth a distinct ontological resonance and sensemaking process. Through an essence-led discernment of *what is, what is arising* and our dynamic felt sense of this unfolding revelatory process, new ontological ground awaits our exploration and integration.

Being Source

Through the activation of these core dimensions of our individual and collective presencing nature, new presencing territory becomes available for both individual and mutual exploration. As we have briefly explored, each lifeworld becomes a site for activating a particular mode of presence that lies at the basis of a fundamental presencing way of being.

Having arrived into being source, we draw on a mode of being that is no longer constituted by our conditioned personality and socialized self. Descending into this final lifeworld, we explore establishing contact with the origin point of our moment-to-moment experience. When source is enacted in our perception directly, there is a re-orientation process from the very context and grounds from which we have come to know ourselves. Traditionally and as advocated for in the presencing literature, source is accessed primarily through intentional practices in solitude (Scharmer, 2007; Jaworski, 2012). In Dynamic Presencing, Source-based stillness informs presence directly as a way of being when engaging presencing in the context of conversation, inquiry and other forms of leadership.

Arriving into being source involves a final letting go from the core ground of essence. Here we draw from source as the fundamental not-yet-manifest domain of who we are as human beings and like the real, witness and essence, being source provides a distinct generative interface through which new sensemaking modes of being can be explored. Source represents the living and breathing origin point of our immediate experience and the underlying driving force of existence and life itself. As we uncover our ground in source, this fundamental dimension of our presencing nature opens us into direct contact with stillness. Letting ourselves go into being with and from the source dimension of reality re-connects us to this quiet still dynamism that's always already present, always listening for conditions to be more of itself through us. Exploring source directly opens new ontological possibilities for sensitizing leaders to source as an always present dimension of our experience—less a special or rarified place we go to or access in solitude or under special esoteric conditions.

In certain respects, the legacy of modernity in western culture has left us with a mostly disembodied fragmentary sense of what it means to really be, relate and know through to that place of source reconnection and co-enactment. Bhaskar (2013) elaborates:

The deep interior or fine structure of any moment of being. If you go into this deeply enough, if you just observe it, suspending all judgment, thought, emotional turbulence or anything else except that moment and, so observing, eventually you will experience identification with it, and the ground-state on which it depends, together with the love, intelligence, energy, bliss, etc. which characterizes it. The experience corresponds to what was believed by traditional religious theorists to be uniquely characteristic of religious experience, whereas I am arguing that it is characteristic of all moments of experience, aspects of being, even of the most ordinary sort, in their deep interior... So you can have the sort of experience that people normally only experience when listening to great music or possibly a moment of scientific inspiration, or certainly indeed through meditation or prayer, in any moment of life and in relation to anything. For anything to exist it must connect in some way to a ground-state and the cosmic envelope, and eventually through the power of your pure awareness, you will be able to access it.

Inside this experience of source lies an invitation to open into a more fundamental non-contingency and letting go of any remaining individual effort-ing to be someone, do something or get anywhere other than exactly wherever we find ourselves. Learning to connect with and rest inside source recalibrates our presencing nature and perceptual receptivity to directly being-with emergence from the inside out. In other words, from this place of source stillness, we begin to see into the heart of emergence itself. By connecting with this driver of emergence and allowing space to establish a relation with it helps us begin to engage with a kind of source-based being, which in turn gives rise to a source-based *seeing*, another way of describing presencing at the level of our perception.

Learning to be source returns us to establishing key ontological grounds for engaging our emerging, evolving self, world and kosmos. Connecting to source at the level of our being and presence unites us with the fundamental grounds of our experience. While the real connected us to our fierce yet vulnerable edge, the witness opened us into an expanded sense of self and relational field and essence reconnected us with our unique innermost sense of being, source activates a generative quality of presence that is at once in touch with the fullness and immediacy of what is here and the underlying formless dimension of reality. At this threshold, there is a spacious ground of stillness that is interfacing with what is moving into the present moment, i.e. the emerging future. Learning to occupy our presence from this location within our presencing nature puts us into contact with a locus of generativity that, the more we surrender into being it, opens us beyond what we had imagined possible in this or the next moment.

In this way, we begin to uncover new generative and actionable dimensions of source in our immediate experience at the very seat of our experience. The subtle act of doing this invites us into a form of creative service with engaging our emerging world and future, particularly as source becomes accessed as a discernable way of being. Connecting us to our primary groundless ground, source, contrary to certain wisdom traditions, neither lies exclusively within, and contrary to political philosophers and traditional activists, does not lie exclusively without either. As the distinctions of inside and outside dissolve, they give way into a more unitive experience of being at once present with what is emerging and the formless dimension underlying this movement.

In the context of our journey into the full ground of presence, source serves as an interface for accessing our core generative way of being that is uncovered in the depths at the very bottom of the U. Being source puts us in direct ontological participation with the void of stillness that informs and leads forth emergence. By establishing an inner basis for leading from within, being source restores and empowers a deeper collective sense of being intimately a part of the world and its emergent process. To the extent to which our ontological constitution can be recalibrated to this realization as a way of being, is the extent to which source intelligence can guide our leadership and actions in the world. Systems awareness is not enough; rather a leadership education must include how to effectively lead from the very interior source dimension of reality that gives rise to our world, culture and selves amidst this period. Being source, in re-connecting us with this deep dimension of who we are, opens up a new inner seat to engage presencing from.

With practice, familiarity, and the process of discovery, each of these lifeworlds eventually becomes an embodied *homeworld*, analogous to each state of presence with adequate practice becoming a more enduring stage. With each homeworld, a more agile, intelligent, receptive whole mode of orienting, feeling and thinking can emerge and inform the first journey of the Dynamic Presencing process as we transition into learning how to steward and lead from these inner regions of our experience.

Closing Reflections

This first Dynamic Presencing journey works with a phenomenological process of re-sensitizing our faculties of being to be more intimately and directly attuned with the emerging nature of self and reality directly. Learning to calibrate our ontological and sensemaking processes from these four foundational ground levels of presence develops a felt embodied basis for practitioners to experience presencing. This is indispensable to developing the capacity to attend more closely, granularly and in a felt-embodied manner to our overall presencing experience. With sufficient exposure and practice, each lifeworld opens us into a particular depth dimension of being, which has a specific baring and influence on the quality and depth of our presence-in-action. In turn, this helps us cultivate the staying power to engage presencing as a sustained mode of experiencing and leadership.

References

Boiral, O., Baron, C., Gunnlaugson, O. (2013). Environmental Leadership and Consciousness Development: A Case Study among Canadian SMEs. *Journal of Business Ethics*

De Quincey, C. (2000). Intersubjectivity: Exploring consciousness from the second person perspective. *Journal of Transpersonal Psychology, 32*(2), 135-155.

De Quincey, C. (2005). *Radical knowing: Understanding consciousness through relationship*. South Paris, ME: Park Street Press.

Gunnlaugson, O. (2015b). Dynamic Presencing: Illuminating New Territory at the Bottom of the U. *Integral Leadership Review*. Jan-Feb. 2015.

Gunnlaugson, O. (2014). *Invited Article*. Bohmian Dialogue: a Critical Retrospective of Bohm's Approach to Dialogue as a Practice of Collective Communication. *Journal of Dialogue Studies* 2(1), 25

Gunnlaugson, O., Vokey, D. (2014). Evolving a Public Language of Spirituality for Transforming Academic and Campus Life. *Innovations in Education and Teaching International*. 51(4)

Gunnlaugson, O. & Walker, W. (2013). Deep Presencing Leadership Coaching: Building Capacity for Sensing, Enacting and Embodying Emerging Selves and Futures in the Face of Organizational Crisis, In Gunnlaugson, O., Baron, C., Cayer, M. (2013). *Perspectives on Theory U: Insights from the Field*. IGI Global Press.

Gunnlaugson, O. & Scharmer, O. (2013). Presencing Theory U, In Gunnlaugson, O., Baron, C., Cayer, M. (2013). *Perspectives on Theory U: Insights from the Field*. IGI Global Press.

Gunnlaugson, O., Baron, C., Cayer, M. (2013). *Perspectives on Theory U: Insights from the Field*. IGI Global Press.

Gunnlaugson, O., Moze, M. B. (2012). Surrendering into Witnessing: A Foundational Practice for Building Collective Intelligence Capacity in Groups. *Journal of Integral Theory and Practice*. 7(3), 78-94.

Gunnlaugson, O. (2012). Fostering Conversational Leadership: Re-Visiting Barnett's Ontological Turn. *International Journal of Progressive Education*. 8(2), 49-59.

Gunnlaugson, O. (2011a). Advancing a Second-Person Contemplative Approach for Collective Wisdom and Leadership Development. *Journal of Transformative Education*. Sage Publications, 9(1), 134-156.

Gunnlaugson, O. (2011b). A Complexity Perspective on Presencing. *Complicity: International Journal of Complexity and Education*. 8(2), 1-23.

Gunnlaugson, O. & Moore, J. (2009). Dialogue Education in the Post-Secondary Classroom: Reflecting on Dialogue Processes from Two Higher Education Settings in North America. *Journal of Further and Higher Education.* Routledge (UK). 33(2).

Gunnlaugson, O. (2009). Establishing Second-Person Forms of Contemplative Education: An Inquiry into Four Conceptions of Intersubjectivity. *Integral Review*, Arina Press, 4(2), 23-56.

Gunnlaugson, O. (2008). Metatheoretical Prospects for the Field of Transformative Learning. *Journal of Transformative Education*, Sage Publications, 6(2), 124-135.

Gunnlaugson, O. (2007a). Revisioning Possibilities for How Groups Learn Together: Venturing an AQAL Model of Generative Dialogue. *Integral Review*, (3)1, 44-58.

Gunnlaugson, O. (2007b). Shedding Light upon the Underlying Forms of Transformative Learning Theory: Introducing Three Distinct Forms of Consciousness, *Journal of Transformative Education*, Sage Publications (4)2.

Gunnlaugson, O. (2006). Exploring Generative Dialogue as a Transformative Learning Practice within Adult & Higher Education Settings, *Journal of Adult and Continuing Education.* Scotland. (12)1, pp. 2-19.

Gunnlaugson, O. (2005). Toward Integrally-Informed Theories of Transformative Learning. *Journal of Transformative Education*, Sage Publications (3)4, pp. 369-398.

Gunnlaugson, O. (2004). Towards an Integral Education for the Ecozoic Era. *Journal of Transformative Education,* Sage Publications. (2)4, pp. 313-335

Jaworski, J. (2012). *Source: The Inner Path of Knowledge Creation.* Barrett-Koehler Publishers.

Peat, D. (2008). *Gentle Action: Bringing Creative Change to a Turbulent World.* Pari Publishing.

Rosch, E., & Scharmer, C. O. (1999). Primary knowing: When perception happens from the whole field (Interview with Eleanor Rosch). Retrieved January 23, 2015, from https://ai.wu.ac.at/~kaiser/birgit/Rosch-1999.pdf

Scharmer, C. O., & Kaufer, K. (2013) *Leading From the Emerging Future: From Ego-system to Eco-system Economies.* San Francisco, CA; Berrett-Koehler Publishers

Scharmer, C. O. (2007). *Theory U: Leading from the future as it emerges.* Cambridge, MA: Society for Organizational Learning.

Scharmer, C. O. (2000a). Presencing: Learning from the future as it emerges. *The Conference On Knowledge and Innovation*. Helsinki School of Economics, Finland, and the MIT Sloan School of Management.

Scharmer, C. O. (2000b). Conversation with Francisco Varela: Three Gestures of Becoming Aware.Retrieved January, 02, 2018, from http://www.iwp.jku.at/born/mpwfst/02/www.dialogonleadership. org/Varela.html

Senge, P., Scharmer, O., Jaworski, J., & Flowers, B. (2004). Presence: Human purpose and the field of the future. Society for Organizational Learning. Cambridge, MA: Society for Organizational Learning.

Warren, S. (1984). *The emergence of dialectical theory: Philosophy and political inquiry*. Chicago, IL: University of Chicago Press.

Wilber, K. (2006). *Integral Spirituality: A Startling New Role for Religion in the Modern and Postmodern World*. Integral Books: Shambhala.

CHAPTER 5

The Importance of Presencing in Creativity

Gareth Loudon and Gina Deininger

Introduction

Scharmer and Kaufer (2013) describe Theory U as a "framework for learning, leading, innovating, and profound systemic renewal" (p. 18). Our research has focused on the factors and processes affecting creativity and we believe that one of the key factors affecting creativity relates to the concept of presencing that we describe as a person's 'state of being' (Deininger, 2013). In this chapter, we share some of the research that we, and others, have undertaken into factors and processes affecting creativity and how they relate to the concepts of presencing and Theory U. We also present a new model for creativity, and explain why the ideas from presencing are at the heart of the model. Finally, we share some thoughts on what this means in practice for organisations who want to enhance the creativity of their staff. Throughout the chapter, we draw on the literature of presencing and Theory U (Scharmer & Kaufer, 2013; Scharmer, 2018) to support our arguments and view.

Scharmer and Kaufer (2013) highlight that we are facing significant global challenges that are ecological, social and spiritual

131

in nature, and that new ideas and approaches are needed. The World Economic Forum also describes similar global challenges and suggests we are entering a fourth industrial revolution (Schwab & Samans, 2016). To address these global challenges the World Economic Forum has listed creativity as one of the top three skills needed in the workforce by 2020, along with skills in complex problem solving and critical thinking. In fact, we would argue that complex problem solving is a skill based on a combination of skills in creativity and critical thinking. As creativity is necessary to help generate new ideas and solutions to meet the major global challenges that lie ahead, we think it is important to ask questions such as what do we really mean by creativity; what factors and processes affect creativity; and what practical things can be done to help creativity thrive in individuals, teams and organisations? These and other related questions are addressed throughout the chapter.

Background

Our experience of working with businesses suggests that there is often a lack of clarity concerning what creativity is. We define creativity as "the ability to come up with ideas or artefacts that are novel, valuable and substantive within a psychological or historical context" (Deininger, 2013, p. 39), i.e. new insights, ideas or things that are valuable and substantive either at a personal level or in a broader context.

Back in the 1920s, Wallas proposed a model for creativity consisting of five main stages: preparation, incubation, intimation, illumination or insight and verification (Wallas, 1926). This model is still recognised as the foundation for most modern-day models of creativity, and there are similarities between Wallas's model and Theory U. For example, the ideas in Theory U of using observation at the initial stages links to the preparation stage in Wallas's model; the importance of retreating and reflecting links to the stages of incubation, intimation and illumination; and the concept of acting in an instant and prototyping relates to Wallas's final verification stage. Wallas also talks about the role of the unconscious mind in the incubation stage and how a person gets a 'feeling' about a solution during the intimation stage, which has some resonance with the ideas of presencing.

More recently, one of the most popular creative processes used in industry is Design Thinking (Kelley & Kelley, 2013), and the process builds on some of the ideas from Wallas's creativity model. The Design Thinking process has four main stages: inspiration; synthesis; ideation/experimentation; and implementation. Again, the inspiration stage has strong similarities with the early stages of the Theory U process, encouraging observation, participation and empathic listening to gain new ideas and insights; the synthesis stage with the idea of retreating and reflecting; and the ideation/experimentation and implementation stages relating to the ideas of acting in an instant, prototyping and gaining quick feedback on ideas and concepts. However, one key difference between Design Thinking and Theory U is the importance Theory U places on the "interior condition" of the person undertaking the work (Scharmer, 2018, p. 7), and this is an area we have been particularly interested in our own research.

Back in the 1960s, Rhodes (1961) suggested that creativity is affected by four main factors (strands) with one of the factors focusing on the attributes of a person, including a person's intellect, personality, temperament, attitudes, behaviours, values and concept of self. Rhodes also highlighted the importance of motivation and perception in enabling creativity. Since that time, many researchers have conducted further research into the factors affecting creativity including the importance of intrinsic motivation and purpose (Ryan & Deci, 2000; Amabile & Kramer, 2011); attention and positive emotion (Isen, Daubman, & Nowicki, 1987; Csikszentmihalyi, 1996; Amabile, Barsade, Mueller & Staw, 2005; Davis, 2009); and the role of play and playfulness (Brown & Vaughan, 2010; Bateson & Martin, 2013).

State of Being and Dynamic Movement

Our research into the factors and processes affecting creativity suggests that there are two overarching factors, a person's

133

'state of being' and dynamic movement. We define a person's state of being as "the emotional, mental and physiological condition of a person" and dynamic movement as the "continuous motion of personal experience that is of a non-linear and spontaneous nature" (Deininger, 2013, pp. 35-38).

To help explore the relationship between a person's state of being and creativity we conducted experiments where we used Heart Rate Variability (HRV) as a psychophysiological measure of mental and physical health (Xhyheri, Manfrini, Mazzolini, Pizzi & Bugiardini, 2012; Kemp & Quintana, 2013). Our results found that people enter a distinct state while undertaking a creative activity that is characterised by high levels of attention and positive emotion (Loudon & Deininger, 2016; Loudon & Deininger, 2017). One consequence of having a positive emotion during high concentration is that it broadens the scope of attention (Rowe, Hirsh & Anderson, 2007; Fredrickson, 2013), and broadens "an individual's momentary thought-action repertoire" (Fredrickson, 2004, p. 1).

In another research study, we explored if people could improve their level of attention and relaxation (to help enhance their creativity) by getting real-time feedback on their mental, emotional and physiological state (Loudon, Zampelis and Deininger, 2017), i.e. paying attention to their attention. We did this by estimating a person's levels of attention and stress/relaxation in real-time using biofeedback of their heart rate variability (HRV) and presenting that information back to them visually on a screen. Our results showed that people could improve their level of attention and relaxation by using this biofeedback mechanism, i.e. by 'listening' to their state of being.

Our research suggests that a state of being that is conducive to creativity is one where a person is attentive and sensitive to the present moment but also to the future possibilities. Positive emotion is also important as it broadens the scope of attention to new possibilities. We use the term 'coherence' to describe the state of being conducive for creativity, where coherence is associated with "cohesiveness, openness and mental stillness" (Deininger, 2013, p. 35).

A key driver of creativity is intrinsic motivation (Amabile,

1988; Ryan & Deci, 2000). Ryan and Deci (2000) define intrinsic motivation as "the inherent tendency to seek out novelty and challenges, to extend and exercise one's capacities, to explore, and to learn" (p. 70). One of the key factors underlying intrinsic motivation is having a sense of purpose or meaning, i.e. being part of something beyond the self (Amabile, 1988; Ryan & Deci, 2000; Amabile & Kramer, 2011). A person's state of being is therefore affected by whether they are intrinsically motivated or not. Intrinsic motivation is also a key factor in supporting engagement and positive emotion.

We suggest that there are many similarities between our term coherence and the concept of presencing, and that both highlight the importance of the interior condition of the person. Scharmer explains that the root of the word presencing is "es" which means "to be" (Scharmer, 2018, p. 99). We also highlight that you need 'to be' creative to emphasize the importance of a person's state of being to creativity. Scharmer and Kaufer (2013) describe presencing as a combination of sensing, "feeling the future possibility", and presence, "the state of being in the present moment" (p. 19). We interpret this definition of presencing as including emotional, mental and physiological elements in a similar way to our own definition of state of being. Presencing emphasizes the primacy and quality of attention, and the importance of stillness, to "let go of the old and connect to the surrounding sphere of future potential" (Scharmer, 2018, p. 24). Scharmer and Kaufer (2013) also describe presencing in "which the circle of attention widens" (p. 20). We would argue that to allow attention to widen, this requires a positive emotion associated with the attention.

In addition to the idea of presencing, Theory U highlights the importance of curiosity and the primacy of intention (Scharmer, 2018, p. 80), particularly at the initial stages of the Theory U process (co-initiating). Theory U's description of intention aligns closely with the idea of intrinsic motivation and the importance it plays in encouraging curiosity and creativity.

As stated earlier, we believe that creativity is not only affected by a person's state of being but also by the "continuous motion of personal experience that is of a non-linear and spontaneous nature". That led us to develop a new model for creativity, called the LCD (Listen, Connect, Do) Model that puts a person's state of being and dynamic movement at its heart.

LCD Model for Creativity

The LCD model is based on the dynamic movement and interaction between three key activities that support creativity: listening, connecting and doing, with a person's state of being underpinning all activities. See Figure 1 below.

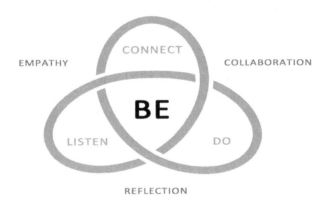

Figure 1. The LCD (Listen, Connect, Do) Model.

The LCD model of creativity has many similarities with Theory U and the idea of presencing, with a focus not just on what to do or how to do it, but also on a person's state of being during the creative process. Like Theory U, the LCD model puts the interior condition of the person at its heart. In addition, the activities of Listen, Connect and Do have strong similarities with Theory U's five movements of co-initiating; co-sensing; co-presencing; co-creating; and co-shaping (Scharmer, 2018). These are discussed below. However, we believe one of the key differences between the LCD model and Theory U relates to the linearity and spontaneity of the two processes. Theory U is presented as a more linear process, while the LCD model encourages a non-linear, dynamic movement between activities that can be spontaneous in nature.

The LCD model highlights the strong interrelationships between all activities using a trefoil knot – a non-trivial knot that is not possible to untie. The LCD model also suggests that you can start the creative process with any of the three activities. For example, you could start the creative process by playing around with a new (or existing) technology or concept to see what new ideas might result (i.e. the doing activity), or start by listening to key stakeholders about currently unmet needs.

We believe another difference between the LCD model and Theory U is that the LCD model emphasizes more directly that a person's state of coherence is important throughout all activities (listening, connecting and doing). This is not to say that Theory U does not support this, as Theory U emphasizes the central role of an "open heart", "open mind" and "open will" throughout the process (Scharmer, 2018, p. 25). However, Theory U also talks about a process of moving down the 'U' from downloading, seeing and sensing to presencing (with its clear focus on mental stillness and "letting go"), and puts prototyping as a subsequent activity. We believe that the concept of presencing (and our concept of coherence) is critical during all activities, including the prototyping activity. Below we describe each of the activities in the LCD model (Listen, Connect and Do) and reflect on the similarities and differences between these activities and the core elements of Theory U.

Listening

The listening activity of the LCD Model is about gaining inspiration and new ideas. It involves going to key places of interest and listening to what people have to say, observing what they do, and observing what they use. However, it is also about listening to our own selves, i.e. being self-aware of our own state of being. Key aspects of the listening activity include:

- Quality of attention: As highlighted above, attention is one of the key factors affecting creativity. The quality of attention is also affected by emotion, as positive emotion widens a person's attention and supports engagement with others. This combination of positive emotion and attention is critical for creativity as it creates an openness to new ideas; a willingness to engage and listen to others; and helps a person still their mind and focus on the present moment. Stilling the mind, through paying attention to the present moment, helps a person suspend judgement (at least temporarily), again enabling an openness to new ideas and perspectives.
- Empathic listening: Being able to understand the feelings, needs and concerns of others is important for creativity as such understanding can often provide new insights and inspiration for new ideas. Empathic listening is the bridge between the listening and connecting activities of the LCD model. Empathic listening requires a person to pay attention with positive emotion.
- Reflection: The bridge between the listening and doing activities is reflection. Reflection is about listening inwardly and paying attention to all the insights gained from exploring and playing with ideas, perhaps through physically making and testing prototypes. Again, the person's state of being is critical during reflection to reduce bias and to avoid limitations placed on the resultant creativity.
- Internal attention: It is often very difficult to suspend judgement, and we often narrow our scope of attention through our set of beliefs, and often look for evidence to support our existing views. Therefore, it is important to listen to and question our own mental thoughts, views and attitudes, as well as listening to our emotional and physiological state, to gain deeper insights into limitations we might be imposing, and consequently limiting the insights gained through listening.

There are many similarities between the listening activity of the LCD model and key aspects of Theory U. At a high level, the listening activity of the LCD model matches very closely with the first two movements of Theory U (co-initiating and co-sensing) where the person is encouraged to immerse themselves "in the places of most potential, in the places that matter most to the situation" (Scharmer & Kaufer, 2013, p. 21) through listening and observing.

Both models talk about the importance of the quality of attention and empathic listening, with Theory U emphasizing the importance of compassion and an open heart, and the LCD model highlighting the importance of positive emotion. Theory U also highlights the importance of "generative listening" that is "a space of deep attention that allows an emerging future possibility to land or manifest" (Scharmer & Kaufer, 2013, p. 147). We would argue that generative listening closely resembles our definition of coherence, i.e. cohesiveness, openness and mental stillness.

Both models refer to the importance of trying to suspend judgement, and both models also recognise that an awareness of one's own judgements sometimes only arise when you pay internal attention. For example, Theory U talks about the importance of "bending the beam of observation in order to see yourself" (Scharmer & Kaufer, 2013, p. 149). However, we would argue that the LCD model more directly emphasizes the importance of listening to one's whole state of being, including one's emotional, mental and physiological condition, to help uncover any issues that might limit creativity.

Another key difference is that the LCD model directly states that all listening activities should ideally be undertaken while in a state of coherence to maximise creativity, including empathic listening and reflection. In addition, the LCD model more clearly shows how the listening activity interacts with other key activities, including reflection on the making and testing of prototypes.

Connecting

There are several key aspects of the connecting activity in the LCD model. Firstly, the connecting activity implies connecting with key stakeholders in relation to the area of focus, to understand their needs, desires, behaviours, motivations, beliefs and values. Secondly, it implies capturing the ideas of key stakeholders throughout the creativity process, including their initial thoughts and ideas, as well as during the 'doing' activities. For example, key stakeholders could be involved in a co-creation process to ensure that ideas consider a range of perspectives, and in an evaluation of ideas and prototypes.

During the connecting activity, it is important to make sure that the creative process does not focus purely on connecting with key stakeholders, but also provides the opportunity to connect with people seemingly unrelated to the area of focus to gain new perspectives and to spark new insights and ideas. Again, it is important that the person's state of being is considered during the connecting activity to make sure that the person is open-minded and attentive when connecting with others and is self-aware of their own state of being to minimise biases and maximise creative insights.

Another aspect of the connecting activity relates to the connection of seemingly unrelated ideas and the exploration of a range of possibilities (called divergent thinking), rather than convergence towards one right answer (Guilford, 1950). Divergent thinking is recognised as a core component of creativity (Guilford, 1950; Kelley & Kelley, 2013).

The connecting activity could happen when the person is on his/her own or with others, but in both cases, it is important that they are attentive and open-minded during the connecting activity. Our research has shown that a person's level of divergent thinking is correlated with their psychophysiological state (Loudon & Deininger, 2016). Therefore, as highlighted in the listening activity, a person's creativity will be limited if they are not in a state of coherence while connecting with others or undertaking divergent thinking.

The bridge between the connecting and doing activities is collaboration, and therefore links to the ideas of co-creation as described in Theory U. When comparing the connecting activity of the LCD model with aspects of Theory U there are several commonalities. Firstly, presencing is also about connecting. The co-initiating and co-sensing stages (movements) of Theory U talk about the importance of connecting with (and listening to) stakeholders but also "seeing the system from the edges" (Scharmer, 2018, p. 139), suggesting that it is important to connect with people beyond core stakeholders. In addition, Scharmer (2018) highlights that Theory U integrates ideas from Design Thinking into the co-creating process. This implies that techniques such as divergent thinking are used. However, we would argue that the LCD model highlights more strongly the importance of connecting with people seemingly unrelated to the area of focus to bring in new ideas and increase the chance of more creative solutions. In addition, we believe that it is important to highlight the power of divergent thinking to help generate a range of new ideas, as adults are often trained to find a single right answer (Wujec, 2010).

Doing

The doing activity of the LCD model focuses on exploring, experimenting, making, experiencing and most importantly playing, to generate new ideas of value. As with the listening and connecting activities, it is important that people be in a state of coherence while doing.

The doing activity incorporates elements of divergent and convergent thinking. Sometimes it is important to develop a variety of concepts in parallel (i.e. divergent thinking) and to have a broad scope of attention. This requires the person to be open-minded to a range of different ideas and to allow for the possible connection of seemingly unrelated ideas. At other times, it is about narrowing down options through critical thinking, selection and evaluation to develop refined ideas and concepts (i.e. convergent thinking).

It is important to note that an iterative process of prototyping and testing does not necessarily lead to an exploration of a variety of concepts (Dow, Heddleston & Klemmer, 2009), as people often start with a narrow focus of attention while prototyping. This results in people selecting an initial idea too early, and then iterating to improve that one (perhaps poor quality) initial idea.

Schrage (1999) highlights the importance of integrating play into the creative process, to encourage improvisation and to explore possibilities, particularly while prototyping. Gordon (2008) suggests that play is "highly purposeful, though usually not toward any explicit goals" and that it's "purpose is to generate more possibilities" (p. 14). Bateson and Martin (2013) argue that play "enables the individual to escape from local optima and discover better solutions" (p. 5). Therefore, play links to the idea of broadening the scope of attention. Brown and Vaughan (2010) describe play as being an altered state, where key attributes of play include joy; engagement; freedom; safety; gaining immediate feedback on one's actions; no worry of failure; and self-consciousness disappearing (Lieberman, 1977; Gordon, 2008; Brown & Vaughan, 2010). Play is also a practical example of intrinsic motivation in action.

Our own research found that play helps creative problem solving, even when play is not related to the problem at hand (Loudon, Deininger & Gordon, 2012), suggesting that a person's state of being during play may be an important factor. In addition, we found that people's natural tendency is to want to interact and play with their external environment to help solve complex problems (Deininger, Loudon & Norman, 2012), i.e. to use a combination of mental, emotional and physical skills.

We believe that play is by definition, a natural way of exploring, experimenting, making and experiencing while in a state of coherence. Bateson and Martin (2013) also argue that "new forms of behaviour and new modes of thought frequently derive from play and especially from playful play" (p. 4). Play also enables the exploration of ideas in a non-linear manner. Therefore, play is a key part of the 'doing' activity in the LCD model.

It is important to note that play only happens in a safe environment; therefore it is important to make sure that the appropriate social and physical environment is created to allow play and creativity to thrive. The setting of boundaries is also important for creating a safe space for idea generation, play and exploration. Sometimes, making the area of exploration too wide and open can create anxiety for people, i.e. it affects their state of being (Loudon, 2018). The same holds true for timescales. With too open-ended timescales, people can lose motivation and focus.

One of the biggest barriers to creativity is fear of failure (Kelley & Kelley, 2013). We believe that a playful exploration of ideas, as advocated by the LCD model, is a way of reducing the worry of failure, gaining immediate feedback on one's actions and encouraging further experimentation. This dynamic interplay of the LCD activities also enables small wins to take place and for people to build creative confidence. In addition, creative confidence is built by conscious reflection, and recognizing and acknowledging those small wins.

The doing activity of the LCD model has several commonalities with the co-creating stage (movement) of Theory U. For example, Theory U and the LCD model both highlight the importance of 'learning by doing' through co-creating and using prototypes for exploration. Both models also talk about the importance of creating a range of prototypes to explore ideas rather than focusing on just developing one possible solution. In addition, they highlight the importance of iterating through a process of prototyping and testing to develop and refine ideas. Consequently, both models address the issue of overcoming fear and building creative confidence through small wins.

However, there are differences between the two models. In our opinion, the LCD model more directly emphasizes the importance of a person being in a state of coherence during the doing activity. In addition, the LCD model suggests that play is a natural way of exploring, experimenting, making and experiencing while in a state of coherence. The LCD model also highlights the importance of setting boundaries to create a safe place to play and generate ideas. While the LCD model focuses more on the power of play and the dynamic movement between all activities to help build creative confidence and overcome fears; Theory U focuses more on the importance of perseverance and courage to overcome voices of doubt, judgement, cynicism and fear when leading change.

On reflection, perhaps both models can learn from each other. We would argue that play should be embedded as a key activity within Theory U, and perhaps the importance of perseverance and courage needs to be emphasized more in the LCD model.

Practical steps for organisations

If we are to address the significant global challenges that currently exist, organisations need to play their part in coming up with ideas that are novel, valuable and substantive, i.e. organisations need to be creative. In the final part of this chapter, we share some thoughts on practical steps organisations can take to enhance the creativity of their staff, their teams and their organisation as a whole, and highlight how our suggestions map to the practical steps already described in Theory U.

Firstly, it is important to note that one of the main barriers to creativity is the fear of change. Therefore, the overarching process we would recommend to help employees overcome this fear of change is to follow the Theory U process. In addition, we would recommend that all employees participate in training workshops on creativity, so that they become fully aware of the basic factors and processes affecting creativity, including: the importance of an employee's state of being; why the different activities (including the dynamic movement between activities), as described above, are important for enhancing creativity; and to learn how to implement the activities. With that said, we have broken down our additional suggestions into three main areas:

1. Clarifying what creativity is and its importance to the organisation.
2. Motivation and organisational structure.
3. Giving time and space for creativity to thrive.

Clarifying what creativity is and its importance to the organisation

As we stated at the beginning of the chapter, our experience is that there is often confusion amongst employees inside organisations (including managers) on what creativity is and its importance. For example, creativity is often seen by employees as being related to the creative industries and arts based subjects, and therefore not relevant to them; or it is narrowly defined as only being about problem solving in relation to improving the productivity or efficiency of the organisation; or that employees see creativity as being synonymous with the R&D department or the role of management and therefore something they do not need to engage with. Therefore, one of the first steps we would recommend is for organisations to make sure there is a clear and agreed understanding amongst all employees of what creativity is for them, whether that includes improving products or services; exploring new markets; developing new products or services; improving productivity and efficiency; being more sustainable; increasing the well-being of staff; or giving more back to the community. In addition, that every employee understands that they can (and should) play a part in enhancing the creativity of the organisation.

As highlighted above, one of the key factors that drives creativity is intrinsic motivation, and one of the main factors affecting intrinsic motivation is having a sense of purpose. Therefore, an important part of the clarification of what creativity is and its importance to the organisation is the clarity of the organisation's purpose. To help gain clarity on the organisation's purpose it is important to 'listen' to the employees and have them contribute to the understanding, rather than take a top down approach. As Theory U highlights, the "quality of the results in any kind of socioeconomic system is a function of the awareness that people in the system are operating from" (Scharmer & Kaufer, 2013, p. 20). If employees are aware of the purpose of the organisation, and that purpose is in line with their own sense of purpose, it is more likely to get employees engaging, making positive contributions and being open-minded to change. These ideas also link to the starting point of the Theory U process (co-initiating) where the focus is on "uncovering common intention" (Scharmer, 2018, p. 78), including getting staff to listen to what intrinsically motivates them.

Motivation and organisational structure

An employee's intrinsic motivation (and their state of being) is not only affected by the organisation's overall purpose, but by what role they play inside the organisation; the autonomy they have; and the opportunities they have to improve their skills. Employees want to undertake work that is interesting and meaningful to them (Amabile & Kramer, 2011). Therefore, to enhance the creativity of employees, organisations need to understand what motivates individual employees to explore how to maximise their talents, skills and interests. If employees are intrinsically motivated, it is likely to have a positive impact on their state of being, and consequently help increase their curiosity, quality of attention, and creativity. As Theory U highlights, "We cannot transform the behavior of systems unless we transform the quality of attention that people apply to their actions within those systems, both individually and collectively" (Scharmer & Kaufer, 2013, p. 19).

One way of doing this is by running a series of exercises to help employees understand more about their personality type; their natural preferences for working; and what motivates them. Intrinsically motivated employees are more likely to have higher levels of engagement and positive emotion (other key factors affecting creativity). The results of running such exercises might highlight that some employees' skills, talents and interests are not being maximised because of where they fit inside the organisation or because of the rigid structure of the organisation. Therefore, another key step might be to look at moving some employees into different roles or to create a more flexible structure that allows employees to explore ideas outside of their main remit, including collaboration with others from different departments or organisations.

Another area for organisations to analyse is the processes they have in place to support creativity. Our LCD model of creativity is a non-linear and spontaneous process that requires a range of activities including listening, observing, connecting, empathising, experimenting, playing, collaborating, co-creating and reflecting. Often strict linear processes exist inside organisations because of the desire to minimize risks when doing something new. However, the downside of strict linear processes is that they will likely restrict creativity, as sometimes it is important to allow employees to explore a range of ideas in parallel before deciding on the best ones to focus on (as also advocated by Theory U). Linear processes also limit the rapid iteration of ideas or the need for a change of direction. Implementing a non-linear process, as described in the LCD model, will require organisations to put more trust in employees. A non-linear process can also be managed by setting clear boundaries and by making sure that employees are responsible and accountable for their actions. This links to the importance of building confidence, courage and resilience in employees with regards to creativity.

Giving time and space for creativity to thrive

Confidence is built (and fears overcome) by experimenting, playing with ideas, prototyping, getting feedback, making mistakes, and having small wins (as described in Theory U and the LCD model). Such an approach also improves the skills of employees. Therefore, employees need permission, time and resources to explore. However, the most common feedback we get when running creativity workshops with organisations (particularly smaller organisations) is that they do not feel they have the time or resources to be creative. One way of overcoming this possible barrier is to get senior management to reflect on how they can stay competitive, as this always requires new ideas and solutions. The result is often a recognition that permission, time and resources are necessary.

As highlighted in both Theory U and the LCD model, a key element for creativity to thrive inside an organisation is making connections with others to gain new ideas and insights – and this requires time. This includes making new connections inside the organisation; gaining a deeper understanding of customers' needs and desires; gaining knowledge of new ways of working and new technologies; and making new connections with other businesses. Therefore, employees should be encouraged, and

147

given time, to get out of the office and make new connections. This includes going out into the field to meet existing or potential customers, but also creating a social and physical environmental inside the organisation that encourages collaboration and more serendipitous connections. This can be done through the effective design of spaces (Groves & Marlow, 2016). Separate, isolated departments or organisations significantly restrict creativity and can create what Scharmer (2018) calls "an architecture of separation" (p. 31). However, as the LCD model and Theory U highlight, it is not just about connecting with others, it is the way you connect with others. Theory U talks about the importance of compassion, empathy, open-mindedness and the quality of attention when connecting with others, particularly when connecting with people who are from different backgrounds or have different perspectives. Similarly, the LCD model talks about the suspension of judgement and the importance of being in a state of coherence when connecting with others.

One of the new ways companies are enhancing their connections, and recognising the importance of a person's state of being while connecting, is by joining coworking spaces. Coworking is a model of working that not only encourages making new connections, but is also based on a set of core values including the importance of openness and the free sharing of ideas; collaboration, including the creation of shared values by cooperating with others; sustainability; accessibility; and community (Kwiatkowski & Buczynski, 2011). Normally, coworking spaces have a diverse range of companies and freelancers as part of their community and the spaces are designed specifically to encourage collaboration and interaction. They also have community managers to help facilitate new connections. The coworking model is a good example of a social system that supports what Scharmer (2018) calls "the cycle of presencing" representing "co-creation and social warmth", as compared with other social systems (organisations) that support "the cycle of absencing", representing disconnection and distrust (p. 31). As Groves and Marlow (2016) highlight, "coworking is fast becoming a symbol of the zeitgeist of a shift from fixed linear command-and-control working to community-based creative collaboration" (p. 208)

Small organisations might want to consider relocating their operations to coworking spaces to enhance their connections, and to be part of a community that fosters creative confidence, supports open-mindedness, creates a positive atmosphere, and has an environment that is conducive to sparking new ideas and opportunities. Larger organisations might also want to allow and encourage their employees to spend a period of time based at coworking spaces to gain new insights and make new connections (Fuzi, Clifton & Loudon, 2014). It might also help improve their emotional, mental and physiological condition, i.e. their state of being.

Another important element for creativity to thrive is to allow employees time for reflection and mental stillness - a key part of Theory U and presencing, and the heart of the LCD model. However, this does not often happen, as employees feel pressure to be seen to be busy - often sitting at their office desk behind their computer. A way to address this issue is to ask all employees (particularly senior management) when and where they have had their best creative ideas. Our experience is that you rarely, if ever, get the answer of sitting at their office desk, and are more likely to hear: while out walking in nature; talking to customers or people from a different area; or while lying in bed at night. This is because these are periods of quality attention, without distraction, and without high levels of stress. When there is value given to the generation of creative ideas and recognition that the best ideas come in such situations, there is usually more willingness to allow (even encourage) employees to have more time and space for quiet reflection. Theory U encourages people to take time during the day for quiet reflection including "intentional silence" (Scharmer, 2018, p. 82), and we would encourage this too. In addition, we would encourage organisations to allow employees to work from home for part of the week; to create a quiet space for reflection inside the office; and allow employees time to take a walk outside during work hours. Theory U's five-day leadership programme formally has a "half-day silence-in-nature practice" (Scharmer, 2018, p. 101) as it recognises the importance of creating the conditions to support presencing.

The final area where permission, time and space is needed

relates to the importance of playing, prototyping, experimentation and testing of new ideas and concepts. Play is a critical part of the creative process as it is a natural way people can get into a state of coherence while exploring new ideas and possibilities. It is therefore a powerful tool for overcoming what Theory U calls the three enemies of judgement, cynicism and fear. Groves' study of some of the most creative companies around the world found that they all have spaces for employees to play (Groves, Knight & Denison, 2010). The key is to create safe spaces for employees to play and explore with clear boundaries put in place to minimise risks. All organisations should consider creating spaces for play and experimentation, but also explore how collaborations with universities or with other making spaces such as Fab Labs (MIT, 2018) might facilitate the exploration of new ideas more effectively.

Summary

Scharmer and Kaufer (2013) suggest that we should be "attending to the crack" (p. 23), i.e. paying attention to the future opportunities and challenges. We agree with this, and believe that creativity is crucial to address the major global challenges that lie ahead.

Our work has focused on understanding the factors and processes affecting creativity through a combination of theory and practice, with the development of a new model for creativity that puts dynamic movement and a person's state of being at its core. Our research suggests that it is important for a person to be in a state of coherence (i.e. a state of cohesiveness, openness and mental stillness) to maximise their creativity. Our idea of coherence seems to match very closely with the concept of presencing. In addition, the core activities that we see as crucial in supporting creativity (listening, connecting and doing), closely match the core activities (movements) of Theory U.

However, there are some differences between Theory U and our LCD model of creativity. For example, our research suggests that creativity is a non-linear and spontaneous process. Even though iteration is important to Theory U and elements of non-linearity are presented, Theory U implies a more linear process, with a process of moving down, and then back up the 'U'. Perhaps this is because Theory U is a framework and process for leading change rather than a model specifically for creativity. Nevertheless, we think there are opportunities to explore how Theory U could be extended to incorporate some of the ideas from our creativity model - and opportunities for us to learn from all the developments of Theory U. For example, we think that the idea of presencing (or what we call coherence) could be at the heart of all Theory U activities, whether that is listening, observing, connecting, making, collaborating or reflecting. It is often implied in Theory U that this is the case, but we believe it could be made more explicit. This also relates to the idea of play, as when people play, they explore new ideas and possibilities while in a state of coherence (presencing). We see play as an important element for creativity and Theory U. Therefore, we think that play could be integrated more formally into Theory U. As Scharmer and Kaufer (2013) already say, "the future shows up first in our feelings and through our hands, not in our abstract analysis" (p. 23).

References

Amabile, T.M. (1988). A model of creativity and innovation in organizations. *Research in organizational behavior, 10*(1), 123-167.

Amabile, T.M., Barsade, S.G., Mueller, J.S., & Staw, B.M. (2005). Affect and creativity at work. *Administrative science quarterly, 50*(3), 367-403.

Amabile, T., & Kramer, S. (2011). *The Progress Principle*, Harvard Business Press.

Bateson, P., & Martin, P. (2013). *Play, playfulness, creativity and innovation*. Cambridge, UK: Cambridge University Press.

Brown, S., & Vaughan, C. (2010). *Play: How It Shapes the Brain, Opens the Imagination, and Invigorates the Soul*, J P Tarcher/Penguin Putnam.

Csíkszentmihályi, M. (1996). *Creativity: Flow and the Psychology of Discovery and Invention*. New York: Harper Collins.

Davis, M. A. (2009). Understanding the relationship between mood and creativity: A meta-analysis. *Organizational Behavior and Human Decision Processes, 108*, 25-38.

Deininger, G.M. (2013). *Does State of Being and Dynamic Movement have a relationship with Creativity?* Ph.D. Thesis. Cardiff Metropolitan University, Cardiff, UK.

Deininger, G.M., Loudon, G.H., & Norman, S. (2012). Modal Preferences in Creative Problem Solving, *Cognitive Processing, 13* (1), 147-150.

Dow, S. P., Heddleston, K., & Klemmer, S. R. (2009). The efficacy of prototyping under time constraints. In *Proceedings of the seventh ACM conference on Creativity and cognition*, 165-174.

Fredrickson, B.L. (2004). The broaden-and-build theory of positive emotions. *Philosophical Transactions of the Royal Society B: Biological Sciences, 359*(1449), 1367.

Fredrickson, B.L. (2013). Positive emotions broaden and build. In *Advances in experimental social psychology*, 47, 1-53.

Fuzi, A., Clifton, N., & Loudon, G.H. (2014). New in-house organizational spaces that support creativity and innovation: the co-working space, *R&D Management Conference*, Stuttgart, June.

Gordon, G. (2008). What is Play? In Search of a Universal Definition. In Kuschner, D.S. (ed.) *From children to red hatters: diverse images and issues of play, Play and Culture Studies*, 8, 1-15.

Guilford, J.P. (1950). Creativity. *American Psychologist, 5*, 444-454.

Isen, A.M., Daubman, K.A., & Nowicki, G.P. (1987). Positive affect facilitates creative problem solving. *Journal of personality and social psychology, 52*(6), 1122.

Groves, K., Knight, W., & Denison, E. (2010). *I Wish I Worked There!*, John Wiley & Sons.

Groves, K., & Marlow, O. (2016). *Spaces for Innovation: The Design and Science of Inspiring Environments*, Frame Publishers.

Kelley, T., & Kelley, D. (2013). *Creative Confidence: Unleashing the Creative Potential Within Us All*, New York: Harper Collins.

Kemp, A.H., & Quintana, D.S. (2013). The relationship between mental and physical health: Insights from the study of heart rate variability. *International Journal of Psychophysiology, 89*, 296–304.

Kwiatkowski, A., & Buczynski, B. (2011). *Coworking: How freelancers escape the coffee shop office*. Fort Collins.

Lieberman, J.N. (1977). *Playfulness: its relationship to imagination and creativity*. New York: Academic Press.

Loudon, G. (2018). Experiences of running a 'Play and Creativity' module in a School of Art & Design, In James, A. and Nerantzi, C. (Eds.),

The Power of Play in HE: Creativity in Tertiary Learning, Palgrave Macmillan (IN PRESS).

Loudon, G., & Deininger, G. (2016). The Physiological Response during Divergent Thinking. *Journal of Behavioral and Brain Science, 6*, 28-37.

Loudon, G., & Deininger, G. (2017). The Physiological Response to drawing and its relation to attention and relaxation. *Journal of Behavioral and Brain Science, 7*, 111-124.

Loudon, G.H., Deininger, G.M., & Gordon, B.S. (2012). Play, Autonomy and the Creative Process. In: Duffy, A., Nagai, Y., Taura, T. (Eds.), *Proceedings of the 2nd International Conference on Design Creativity*, The Design Society, UK. 87-96.

Loudon, G., Zampelis, D., & Deininger, G. (2017). Using Real-time Biofeedback of Heart Rate Variability Measures to Track and Help Improve Levels of Attention and Relaxation. In *Proceedings of the 2017 ACM SIGCHI Conference on Creativity and Cognition*. 348-355.

MIT (2018). *MIT Fab Lab* [online]. Accessed at: http://fab.cba.mit.edu [Accessed: 15th April 2018].

Rhodes, M. (1961). An analysis of creativity. *The Phi Delta Kappan, 42*(7), 305-310.

Rowe, G., Hirsh, J.B., & Anderson, A.K. (2007). Positive affect increases the breadth of attentional selection. *Proceedings of the National Academy of Sciences, 104*(1), 383-388.

Ryan, R.M., & Deci, E.L. (2000). Self-Determination Theory and the Facilitation of Intrinsic Motivation, Social Development, and Well-Being, *American Psychologist*, 55(1), 68-78.

Scharmer, C.O. (2018). *The Essentials of Theory U: Core Principles and Applications*. Berrett-Koehler Publishers.

Scharmer, C.O., & Kaufer, K. (2013). *Leading from the emerging future: From ego-system to eco-system economies*. Berrett-Koehler Publishers.

Schrage, M.D. (1999). *Serious Play: How the World's Best Companies Simulate to Innovate*. Harvard Business School Press.

Schwab, K., & Samans, R. (2016). *The Future of Jobs. Employment, Skills and Workforce Strategy for the Fourth Industrial Revolution*. World Economic Forum.

Wallas, G. (1926). *The Art of Thought*, New York: Harcourt Brace.

Wujec, T. (2010, February). *Build a tower, build a team*. Available at: https://www.ted.com/talks/tom_wujec_build_a_tower

Xhyheri, B., Manfrini, O., Mazzolini, M., Pizzi, C., & Bugiardini, R. (2012). Heart Rate Variability Today. *Progress in Cardiovascular Diseases, 55*, 321–331

CHAPTER 6

Earthrise: On the interplay of States and Structures in Theory U

By Karsten Skipper

"When you see the Earth from the moon, you don´t see any divisions there are no nations or states. This might be the symbol for the new mythology to come."

Joseph Campbell

As United Nations Secretary-General António Guterres rounded off 2017 by issuing a red alert for the world, it should be apparent to most people that we live in a time of exceptional challenges – and possibilities – for humanity and for the planet. Scientists warn us that within the next decades the rapid destruction of the environment could spin out of control and lead to a fundamental altering of life conditions and a drastic decrease in biodiversity (Ceballos, 2017). Or, we could lay the foundation for a new way of living in balance with the ecosystem, where a stable population of perhaps 9-10 billion people in a thriving ecosystem can start believing that the one planet which we share, is enough for all.

The work and ideas presented here rest on the understanding that this situation of crisis and possibility form a central impetus – and thus a common ground – for both Theory U and the

155

various models in human development theory that map out structural stages of development beyond Piaget's formal operational level of cognition, the level that seems to have been the ideal of maturity in the modern, industrial era (Cook-Greuter, 2013, p. 19. Wilber, 1995).

When Otto Scharmer says that we have "entered an age of disruption" (Scharmer & Kaufer, 2013, p. 293) and talks about the need to "turn the beam of attention back onto the observer – helping a system to see itself," he may well be describing Robert Kegan's late fourth order of consciousness, the stage of development at which we can turn our attention on the system and start to act upon the system of which we are a part (Kegan, 1994). Kegan suggests that this capacity may be the way in which evolution is trying to find a solution for the disastrous side-effects of the modern, industrial era. And thus, echoing Scharmer's call to support "vertical literacy" (Scharmer, 2018a), he points out that: "there may be no more important thing to do" than supporting people in their development (Kegan, 2013, 16.20).

In the description of transition from ego- to eco-system awareness Theory U has already incorporated structural stages of development to some degree, while remaining centered around action learning and the essentially phenomenological practice of presencing. I believe that Theory U could benefit from integrating more of the insights from structural human development models, particularly when it comes to self-development and capacity building for leaders and facilitators[6]

For this integration to be successful however, it is important to be clear about the relationship and potential tension between phenomenological approaches and structural approaches. Theory U and structural human development theories are on common ground, when it comes to emphasizing the awareness aspect of dealing with social, ecological and spiritual/psychological issues at global level, and yet, I believe there is a good reason why integrating the insights of structural development with presencing and Theory U is still, to a large extend, incomplete. In a way, we are facing the same fundamental dilemma that Kierkegaard once pointed out:

> It is perfectly true, as the philosophers say, that life has to be understood backwards. But in that one forgets the other proposition, that it has to be lived forwards. This proposition, the more it is thought through, ends in that life, in the temporal, is never really understood, precisely because there is never a moment in which I can be fully at peace to assume the position: backwards. (Kierkegaard,1843. Authors translation).

Developmental theories primarily obtain their data by turning backwards and attempting to spot structures that are laid down in the past and that shape the ways in which we perceive the present. As facilitators using presencing we do the opposite and let go into the present moment sensing forward to catch a glimpse of the future and bring it to the present. As Kierkegaard knew, we cannot live life in a backward position. The present is much too alive to let us do so. As activists, leaders or facilitators we might ask what good, this structural preoccupation with the past could possibly do, when what we want is to presence the emerging future!? Wouldn't that just add unnecessary complexity and invite downloading old ideas and preconceptions?

Instead of choosing between a backward-facing, reflective path or a forward-facing path of action, we might note that the capacity to deal with complex situations with an "in-the-moment immediacy" is a key aspect of the later levels of development (Torbert, 2004, p.102). This immediacy is not a matter of getting lost in the present and forgetting all about the past, but is connected with developing a sense of time, where past and future are experienced as aspects of the living present (Wilber, 1980, p. 58). This means that formulating structural perspectives in a more present-centered language and doing presencing with a clearer awareness of how the structures of the past are present in this and every moment – although challenging – may be a perfect way to train and invite eco-system awareness.

This type of training takes time. The approach presented at the end of this chapter requires long-term, in depth self-development work – something not achieved in a single training session. Longer periods of time and a setting that offers peace for deeper inquiry are required for the structural details to become more than external labels and begin to enter our experience of the living present.[7]

States and structures

What distinguishes *states* and *structures* of consciousness is that our states of mind – such as waking, dreaming and deep sleep, open mind, open heart and open will, or altered states like elation, anger and intoxication – describe a quality or tone of our immediate awareness and as such they may come and go in no fixed order. Structures of consciousness (composed of what is variously known as orders, stages, levels, waves) on the other hand, are meaningful abstract patterns in the myriad ways we perceive the world. The structural patterns are found through observing many people over extended periods of time and no person fits the structural descriptions perfectly.

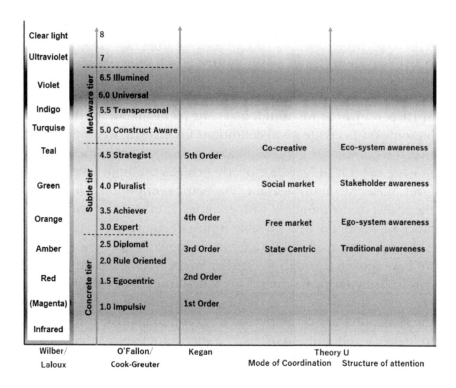

Figure 1: Four Models of Development

Structures are not directly experienced but inferred and they emerge over time somewhat like if the states were dripping water in a cave and the structures were stalagmites growing from the floor and upwards. Just as a stalagmite must start from the floor and grow upwards, the structures emerge in a particular order, since every structure builds upon, expands, and in a sense, reinterprets the previous structures. Structures are said to transcend and include previous structures in a way that has sometimes been likened to Russian dolls (Cook-Greuter, 2013, p. 8). Examples of structures and their sequence of emergence can be seen in the four models of development represented in Figure 1.

Once a structure has emerged, the earlier structures remain accessible and this means that if we look at what structures are active in a particular situation, we often see that the process jumps up and down the whole system of available structures according to changing needs and in no particular order. At the heart of structural developmental thinking – and indeed of presencing – is a basic respect for the natural process as it unfolds. This means that facilitating development is not about pulling or manipulating the person or group towards higher levels (Cook-Greuter, 2010, p. 5). Just as we cannot make the plants in our garden grow but only try to create good conditions for growth, we understand that the criteria for good facilitation are not what comes up but how we meet it. Regardless of what comes up, high level or low level, pleasant or unpleasant, popular or unpopular, by facing the reality of the moment, with openness, authenticity and acceptance we invite the best possible future to emerge.

Although later levels imply a greater range of experience, since we have moved through the earlier levels, later levels are not intrinsically better or happier. The added complexity of later levels means that more can go wrong. Over time we would expect the facilitation to aid the person or group to mature and grow to higher levels, but importantly, a successful process might consolidate the level that the system is already at or strengthen an earlier level in a way that is needed for the system to better align itself with the reality at hand.

States and Structures in Theory U

When we look at the basic movement through Open mind, Open heart and Open will, one of the ways it is used is as a description of universal states with reference to various contemplative traditions. We see examples of this in Scharmer's conversations with Varela (Varela & Scharmer, 2000) and Wilber (Wilber & Scharmer, 2004). These basic states are universal, in the sense that they are not tied to specific levels of development, but can occur at any level of development. Other elements in Theory U, particularly the movement from ego-system to eco-system awareness that make "systems become aware of themselves" would seem to require certain developmental capacities. These are explicitly linked to levels in the structure of awareness in the social evolution (Scharmer and Kaufer, 2013, p. 148). In this sense, they are stage specific.[8]

Clarifying the distinction and understanding the interplay of states and structures in development is immensely valuable to us when trying to achieve what Scharmer calls "vertical literacy" (Scharmer, 2018a). This new ideal for education, beyond the level of maturity that shaped modern society is a level where, as Scharmer formulates it: we naturally understand that *"the issues outside are a mirror of the issues inside"* (Scharmer's emphasis). If we are used to noticing the state shifts involved in going through the U from a specific structural level, we might not meet the process appropriately with groups or individuals at other levels. Since Theory U seems to stress the structural transition from ego- to eco-system awareness, this might give rise to concerns regarding the extent of the applicability of Theory U. As Jonathan Reams (2007, p. 255) put it: "Is this another case of the implicit curriculum making demands that place people "in over their heads?" Can this lead to presencing and the U theory being limited to an elite spectrum of the population such as the so-called "cultural creatives?""

The expression "In over our heads" is a reference to developmentalist Robert Kegan's book by this title (Kegan, 1994) and alludes to the general understanding in developmental studies that intervention and teaching has little effect if it is not adjusted to the developmental level of the receiver (Cook-Greuter, 2013, p. 8).[9]

Although much has happened in the preceding ten years, I think Reams is still right that "there is further work to be done here to clarify and strengthen how the U process deals with these issues" (Reams, 2007, p. 256). He suggests approaching this through "a distinction between structural stages (relating to relevant action-logics as centers of gravity) and state stages (relating to this aspect of the field of attention)" (Reams, 2007, p. 256).

I will see to do just this, although I will focus on the STAGES model instead of Bill Torbert's Action Inquiry, suggested by Reams.[10] And I will begin by looking at the structural description of developing from ego-system to eco-system awareness.

Ego- to eco-system awareness

Ego-system awareness is the modern ideal of maturity. This ideal rests to a large degree on the paradigm laid out by the philosophers of Enlightenment in the 18th century and relies upon the idea that we all have access to a universal reason. And thus, to Immanuel Kant, enlightenment meant, to step out of "self-imposed immaturity" of blindly following the authority of others and rely on our own reason. "Sapere aude! 'Have courage to use your own reason!'- that is the motto of enlightenment," Kant famously declared in the opening of his essay, "Answering the question: What is enlightenment?" from 1784.

The modern autonomous ego celebrated by Kant, is the self at the Achiever level in the Cook-Greuter/Bill Torbert model of ego development and corresponds to the level of Jean Piget's formal operational cognition. Susanna Cook-Greuter describes it this way: "By most modern expectations, fully functional adults see and treat reality as something preexistent and external to themselves made up of permanent, well-defined objects that can be analyzed, investigated, and controlled for our benefit. This view is based on a maximal separation between subject and object, thinker and thought. It epitomizes the traditional scientific frame of mind that is concerned with measurement, prediction, and control. It also represents the goal of much of Western socialization and schooling." (Cook-Greuter, 2013, p. 19).

In Theory U, the Ego level is the second of four levels in the evolution of the "logics or paradigms" of modern economic thought (Sharmer and Kaufer, 2013, p. 13). As shown in Figure 1 these four levels are preceded by a single level that represents the entire premodern spectrum of development. This makes sense to the extent that we are looking at the development of outer systems through which the levels of awareness have expressed themselves. The levels 1.0 to 4.0, on which Scharmer and Kaufer focus, should cover the types of organizations we need to keep in mind when working to transform the global economy of today. Although, arguably, it would have made a more complete picture to include Laloux's Impulsive-Red (O'Fallon's 1.5, Egocentric) organization, exemplified by criminal groups that operate through violence (Laloux, 2014, p. 17).

The four levels, plus the premodern level, are labeled with reference to an outer, systemic development (Wilber's lower right quadrant (Wilber, 1995)), and subtitled with an inner, awareness aspect. People familiar with the work of Ken Wilber and his summaries of developmental stages (Wilber, 2006) and Frederic Laloux' later work (Laloux, 2014, 2016), would naturally make a rough correlation between 0.0, *premodern awareness*, and the premodern stages of Wilber/Laloux up to and including Red. Likewise, the stages; 1.0, *Traditional Awareness*, 2.0, *Ego-Centric Awareness*, 3.0, *Stakeholder-Centric Awareness* and 4.0, *Eco-Centric Awareness*, would appear to correspond to Wilber/Laloux's stages Amber, Orange, Green, Teal, respectively. (These correlations are indicated in figure 1).

With the insights from developmental theory in mind, it is important to note that while the outer organizations, and systems expressing earlier levels, need to be changed, the earlier levels remain active. The older systems should as Scharmer (2018a) put it, be "mitigated" and aligned with eco-system awareness, but the earlier levels of awareness remain as integral parts of the whole system, the organizations, and within each of us. The description of structural development that is currently integrated in Theory U may be adequate for categorizing organizations and concrete systems but compared to other models of human structural development it lacks precision in the early spectrum of development. We should expect this to affect fieldwork and self-development, since those early levels do not go away and they are the very voices we need to bring into the dialog when exploring how to implement later level ideals of global awareness and sustainability.

Development as increase in the number of perspectives available

An essential aspect of structural development is the increasing capacity to take perspectives. The progressive rise in the number of perspectives that are available at a given stage, and how this affects meaning making is thoroughly elucidated in Cook-Greuter's model of ego-development and in Terri O'Fallon's further developed version, the STAGES model. Increasing perspective taking capacity could be said to form the very spine of these models, and the levels in the STAGES model are numbered according to the number of perspective-stages available. In terms of perspective taking, the transition from ego- to eco-system awareness, described by Theory U may be expressed as the move from late 3rd person perspective (pp), (in the STAGES model called 3.5 Achiever or simply 3.5), to late 4th pp (4.5 Strategist), or later.

To understand what this means let us briefly look at the development of perspective taking.

As we embark on the journey of life, we are bound to a single perspective. At first in a highly undifferentiated way (1.0 Impulsive) and only gradually do we learn to differentiate between self and others (1.5 Egocentric). Having access to only our own perspective means we are *egocentric*. Only later, when we learn to take a 2nd pp, we can take the perspective of others, which opens a new sense of 'we' and means that we now have access to a much clearer sense of what others want from us and can start to learn the rules and the roles of the 'we' to which we belong. Until we can take a 3rd pp. whenever we encounter a set of rules or values, we can only evaluate them by using the concrete values and rules of the 'we' that we identify with as the unquestionable blueprint. This means that the level of the 2nd pp. we are *ethnocentric* and conventional.

Taking the 3rd pp means it is now possible to look at and compare views, not just using the set of rules we have learned, but from the point of view of an objective, outside observer. This is the foundation for ego-system awareness in Scharmer and Kaufer's sense, and the basis of both modern science and universal human rights. As we will explore in more detail later, this level requires, and progressively strengthens, a new ability to focus attention on subtle ideas and thoughts, bringing new abstract con-

164

cepts and enabling us to imagine entirely new future scenarios and plan accordingly.

With the 4th pp the subtle focused attention of the 3rd pp widens out and allows us to become aware of the subtle contexts of our 3rd pp. This contextualizing makes us aware of the limitations and relativity of the 'objective' observations of the 3rd pp and in this landscape of multiple, alternative 3rd pp's we learn to look through and empathize with entire paradigms or world views (not just other individual perspectives on concrete rules and situations as with the 2nd pp). The early 4th pp (4.0, pluralist) parallels Scharmer and Kaufers stakeholder-Centric Awareness and at this level we do not easily prioritize within this new and highly complex field view. This comes with the late 4th pp (4.5, Strategist) where we find a new level of detachment in relation to the complex subtle systems we are part of and this gives us a new creative freedom to act upon and influence the field.

If we look at the organizing principles in Scharmer and Kaufer's "Matrix of Social Evolution" (2013, p. 148) through the lens of perspective-taking, the 2nd pp opens the landscape of the actual, concrete We-spaces of which we are a part. Here we learn to navigate the rules and roles of our group. If we have no access to a 3rd pp from which to evaluate these rules and roles, we invariably identify with the values and ways of the group we feel most connected to and apply them as the universal and unquestionable blueprint in all situations. The result is the rigid hierarchy that is the hallmark of the late 2nd pp (2.5, Conformist) and pointed to as *"centralized control: organized around hierarchy"* by Scharmer and Kaufer. With the 3rd pp we look to extract what 'objectively' works best. The organization is machinelike and *"divisionalized: organized around differentiation"*, which means that hierarchies of the late 3rd pp (3.5, Achiever) are based on expertise and competition and therefore way more flexible than at 2.5. As the 4th pp widens our perception we become aware that stakeholders cannot be treated in a monological, purely objectifying manner, as if they were unchanging parts in a machine. Their voices need to be heard and engaged in ongoing dialog. Thus, the organizational level is *"distributed/networked: organizing around interest groups"*.

The level of the late 4th pp (4.5, Strategist) has been held out as a turning point in human development and as the first truly integral level. Ken Wilber (2001, p. 11) popularized Clare Graves' notion of a "momentous leap" in development that marked the shift to second tier, in the models of Graves and in Spiral Dynamics (Beck & Cowan, 1996) as well as in Wilber's current summary of numerous developmental models. In recent years this conception has received new attention in the field of organizational development through Frederic Laloux' work on the notion of teal organizations (In figure 1, teal is the color ascribed to 4.5, Strategist in Wilber's system).

The main reason for the emphasis on this level is that with the maturing of the 4th pp, the vertical dimension through which these developmental levels unfold, can be seen for the first time. At the early 4th pp we are still new to the fluid landscape of the various paradigms and worldviews of the field and cannot easily prioritize and act upon the field in a conscious way. But with late 4th pp there is more freedom and agency and subtle meta-patterns like the development of awareness can be identified and used and modified in accordance with the situation. This is where Scharmer and Kaufer talk of the organization as *eco-system: organizing around what emerges*. A key feature of this level is a new attitude of vertical inclusion that allows us to deal with the field as it is. The various logics and levels involved in a situation are met at their own level, in contrast to what happens at previous levels where we still have our own level of development in the blind spot and therefore unconsciously assume that everybody should really see things from our level.[11]

In the STAGES model, the "momentous leap" takes place in the shift from 4th to 5th pp. As we shall examine in more detail, later in this chapter, at this level we not only understand the subtle grammar of contexts that shape the field, we start to shift our identity to an even subtler place of witnessing, from where the constructed nature of reality, and our own moment to moment role in this construction starts to dawn on us.

Although few people develop past the 4th pp[12], the Cook-Greuter model includes the 5th pp. Terri O'Fallon has found evidence of a 6th pp and her STAGES model even includes the possibility of 7th and 8th pp. Fascinating as these frontiers of human development might be, it should be remembered that our models are limited by the language of their time and by the levels at which they are read and used. Thin evidence at very late levels might therefore have limited predictive value regarding future large-scale changes. And while the models created by pioneers like James Mark Baldwin and Aurobindo Ghose about a century ago do resemble the models we use today to some degree, I find it unlikely that the models of today will be of much use a hundred years from now, when we consider that development appears to be accelerating. At any rate, for the purpose of our exploration, we will keep our focus with the 4th and 5th pp.

What I'm suggesting through this brief overview of structural development is that the future we are trying to bring to the present could be described as the turning point from 4.5 (Strategist) to 5.0 (Construct Aware). 4.5 allows us to understand both the cultural complexity of the planet and our interpenetrative relationship with its biosphere in complex systemic and autopoietic terms. 5.0 connects this understanding to our immediate moment to moment awareness. I believe this is the level of perception from where a truly global awareness could emerge – and is emerging. Although the shift from 2nd pp to 3rd pp is in many ways a move from *ethnocentric* to *universal*, this level of the modern ego "produces" as Scharmer would put it, "results that nobody wants" and historically it has proven to be *anthropocentric* – centered around humans and not around the planetary eco-system that is now forcing its way to the foreground of our attention. The first truly globe-centered or *Earth-centric* awareness matures with the 4th pp.

We can now see how the universal and the stage specific aspects of Theory U may be viewed as two sides of the same coin: on the one hand we desperately need to renew our economic, social and organizational systems in a way that embodies a truly Earth-centered awareness – this is the stage specific process of ego to eco. On the other hand, if this is not to be just another beautiful, Utopian idea, with no grounding, this can only be achieved through an attitude of stewardship and care for all levels of development, both within ourselves and in our work and co-operation with others.

With this preliminary clarification of structures and states in Theory U in place, we will now take a closer look at the interplay of structures and states, as portrayed by the STAGES model, to see how this might strengthen both accuracy and breadth in the application of Theory U and presencing.

The Stages model of Development

The STAGES model was developed by Terri O'Fallon and is the third generation of developmental models following the tradition of Jean Loevinger and Sussane Cook-Greuter. These models describe ego-development based on very extensive empirical research gathered through sentence completion tests (Cook-Greuter, 2013. O'Fallon, 2013).

Although the levels and their labels are very similar to the sequence used by Cook-Greuter (and adapted from Bill Torbert), the logic of development and the interrelation between the stages is described in a very different way than in Cook-Greuter's model. According to O´Fallon and Barta (2016, p. 4) the model has taken "a significant detour from the developmental approaches of the past." and it is this detour that makes it especially interesting in the present context.

In her reinterpretation of the previous model, O'Fallon has explicitly tried to incorporate key elements of Ken Wilber's meta-model, the AQAL. Importantly, she also tries to bring the description of the abstract *Structures* closer to the phenomenologically observable *states* and the senses. By doing this, she is essentially taking the language and the level of description from the backward facing, analytical and somewhat disembodied view of earlier structural models and brings it closer to the present moment and the forward position of lived life – to use Kierkegaard's image.

It is still too early to pass any kind of final judgement about how successful this reformulation is, but as we will see, the patterns identified by O'Fallon seem to correspond remarkably well with the experiences and technologies of transformation that are paradigmatic to Theory U, and it also provides very detailed support for further upgrading self-development and capacity building. In recent years, O'Fallon and her brother, Kim Barta, who is a psychotherapist, have started developing a method of on-the-fly assessment (Barta, 2017). This method allows therapists and coaches to determine the level, or levels, from which a client is expressing him or her-self as the session progresses and to adjust their interventions accordingly. The first proper education program launched in Martz 2018. If it turns out that the claims implicit in this approach can be further validated, there is no reason why it should not be applicable when facilitating a U-process in a group or an individual.

Tiers as upshifts or overtones

The first aspect of the STAGES model that I would like focus on is not the levels, but the tiers of development. I'm sorry to have to introduce this new distinction in an already complex discussion, but the tiers are in many ways as fundamental in the STAGES model as the levels. And as we will see, this addition to the lineage of structural models of human development, is particularly instrumental in moving us beyond the limitations of traditional, linear ladder or Russian doll metaphors of development, and opening the way to a more in-the-moment oriented integration of states and structures in the context of Theory U.

A tier represents a step, or a kind of meta-level, within a larger pattern of development. In the case of STAGES, each tier comprises four levels of development, and each tier is regarded as an "upshift" – or as I like to think of it, an overtone – of the former tier. Levels 1.0 to 2.5 make up the first, or "concrete tier" and levels 3.0 to 4.5 make up a subtler upshift of these levels, comprising the "Subtle" tier. This is followed by the even subtler "Met-Aware" tier and O'Fallon speculates that a forth tier, the "Nondual" tier might succeed that. In figure 2, The Butterfly diagram or the Breath and Heartbeat of development I have tried to represent the four fundamental phases as they iterate through the subtler and subtler tiers. (Note that the relationship between the three tiers is not meant to be accurately represented here. This would require a third axis.).

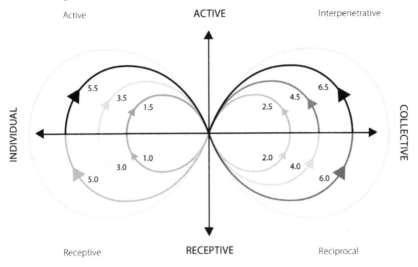

Figure 2. The Butterfly diagram - Breath and Heartbeat of development.

Before I move on to explaining the phases of the fundamental iteration patterns and the dynamics of upshifts through the tiers, let me start by noting that part of what makes this particularly interesting with regards to Theory U, is that not only does the central notion of a transformation from ego-system to eco-system awareness coincide with the development of the subtle tier, but the primary technologies of social change, namely the four levels of listening and conversation, also bear striking resemblance to the four phased pattern that STAGES identifies as fundamental to development.

More than simply assigning Theory U its place within the larger developmental map, this broadens our understanding of why Theory U seems to work so well and helps to situate the change processes that we encounter in the 3rd and 4th perspective (ego- to eco-systems awareness) in their living relation to earlier development through 1st and 2nd pps – the ground tone of development, so to speak. This gives us a detailed language for addressing issues concerning the foundation for ego- to eco-development and makes it easier to see what basic sense-based awareness-capacities of earlier levels might support these later transformations.

Concrete, Subtle and MetAware

In using the situational assessment practice developed through the STAGES model, focus is not primarily on determining the center of gravity or the latest stage available in a person or a group, but on tracking the process as it unfolds. One of the key factors in this is noticing the types of objects that are being related to. At the concrete tier only concrete objects are available. This includes what O'Fallon calls "subtle inner sensations of concrete objects", so if you imagine a concrete object, like a tree, this is a subtle sensation of a concrete object, and therefore we are in the concrete tier. The 2nd pp gives access to new concrete objects like concrete rules and roles, but there are no subtle objects before the subtle tier arrives with the 3rd pp.

O'Fallon follows Wilber's understanding that the concrete, subtle and very subtle or causal states are available at any stage[13]. However, since there are only concrete objects at the levels of the concrete tier, any state experience from opening through the U can only be interpreted as concrete at these stages. For example: like many children, as a child I had imaginary friends whom I would visit by closing my eye and imagine that I fell through a tunnel of colored light. To me they were actual concrete beings who lived in an actual world behind [a] wall at the end of the universe. But here on Earth they could only be seen through my imagination – i.e. through subtle sensations of concrete objects.

O'Fallon tries to describe developmental structure in terms of our senses growing up. She does this by defining senses broadly as "any channel through which distinctions are made" (O'Fallon, 2013, p. 2). In the subtle tier, we start having "subtle sensations of subtle object". Enabled by the 3rd pp (and later the 4th pp), we start to look at our own thoughts, feel our own feelings and see our seeing. This might involve any combination of subtle sensations such as feeling thoughts (kinesthesia/proprioception of inner auditory sensations) or thinking about our feelings (auditory sensation of kinesthesia/proprioception) and so on. This gives rise to new subtle objects like complex thoughts and feelings, for example ideas about the future as something novel and not just a direct repetition or projection of the past. As subtle tier development proceeds into the 4th pp. still more complex subtle objects will emerge, like interpretations, judgments, projections and social constructions.

With the 5th pp. the MetAware tier emerges. This is defined by causal or very subtle objects like awareness of awareness which in turn create the foundation for a new very subtle identity (5.0, Construct-aware and beyond). From here it is possible to look at subtle constructions, including one's own subtle self and its subtle collective context, with a whole new level of clarity.

In summary, profound U processes may take place at any level of development. Paying attention to the type of objects in play, help to determine what tier is active and this helps to meet the process appropriately.

Iterating patterns of development

Before I can return to Theory U and explain how the structural insight may impact our understanding of field-work and self-development, we need to go into more detail regarding the interplay of structure and states suggested by the STAGES model.

The butterfly-like double loop pattern that iterates through the tiers of development may be described as a combination of two separate motions or polar drives of development. The first is an oscillation between receptive and active phases within each perspective, depicted in figure 2 as the downward and upward vertical axis. The levels with a number ending on .0, are receptive while the levels ending with .5 are active. The receptive stage is the early phase of learning to take a new perspective, becoming aware of the new objects and not yet being clear about the border between the new self and the new object life space. As we become clearer about the outside and inside of our new self, we swing into the active phase of the perspective. We move from being "had by" the view to "having" the view as we actively begin to expand our control of the corresponding world space.

The second pattern is the alternation between foregrounding the individual and the collective, as shown by the horizontal axis in figure 2. The uneven stages 1, 3, 5… tend to foreground the individual aspect of the world space and the even stages 2, 4, 6… foreground the collective. Together these two patterns make up the double loop motion in figure 2, that repeats every four levels and make up a tier of development.

According to the STAGES the four levels comprising a tier, may also be viewed in relation to four phases that make up a fundamental learning-sequence. The learning-sequence is a description of the stage-like steps through which access to a state is stabilized. Unlike proper structural levels (structure-stages) the sequence of these state-stages is not necessarily as fixed. For example, it might be possible to have peek-experiences of a later state-stage without having stabilized the previous stage.

This learning-sequence or "pattern of states" is an attempt to capture the process through which states turn into structural levels (or stages in the usual terminology of STAGES). O'Fallon describes it like this: "First, a state is an uninvited accident, which happens to you (receptive). The second phase is the attempt to get back to the state again by engaging in a practice, which makes you more prone to access this state again (active). Next, one can rest in the state at will but can't maintain it in one's ordinary life (reciprocal), and lastly, the state becomes a stage and is so ordinary that it operates out of consciousness (active-interpenetrative)" (O'Fallon, 2013, p. 8).

Looking at the concrete tier, we see how this process of the gradual stabilizing of states with concrete objects, results in the four levels of the concrete tier emerging in sequence:

1.0 Impulsive is a *receptive* individual stage in the concrete tier, where we are inside our own individual experience, and only gradually getting to know, the boundaries of our own concrete self. We learn by copying.

1.5 Egocentric is an *active* individual stage in the concrete tier. This is described as an "either/or-stage" with one way seeing. We now have a clearer sense of self and other but can't jet see things from the point of view of others. We are actively expanding our range and control of our concrete surroundings. Moving across to the collective side of figure 2, which is a slightly bigger jump than from 1.0 to 1.5, we now get to:

2.0 Rule Oriented. This third phase is *reciprocal* (receptive collective), which means it's a "both and-stage". I can see things from your perspective and see you seeing me back, and we can form a genuine we, where we are not just "talking at" each other, but also "with" each other. Taking 2nd pp means we can start to learn the common rules and roles, but as with all early perspectives (the receptive, .0s), we do not easily prioritize, which means it's difficult to have an overview of the rules and know which ones are most important. As we were "had by" the physical sensations and impulses at 1.0, here we are "had by" the new relationships and rules.

2.5 Conformist is the *interpenetrative* (active collective) phase of the concrete tier. Here we begin to be at home with the rules and roles of the collective and gain a new agency as we "have" the rules, rather than being "had by" the rules. I internalize (introject) the rules and project them onto others, so at this level individual and collective - I and the group - interpenetrate and become one through the rules.

As we move through these same four phases of receptive, active, reciprocal and interpenetrative in the subtle tier, we find that they express themselves differently, and yet they are also clearly recognizable in the new subtle upshifts or overtones of the concrete tier. To move into the subtle tier means we have the concrete tier in place to a reasonably functional degree, and that sensing and acting in the world of concrete objects, including rules and roles has become second nature. As new subtler objects emerge, we keep unfolding in the concrete world and it is important for healthy development and wellbeing, that we stay grounded in a living contact to the concrete tier, which is continually reinterpreted through the emerging later levels.

Indispensable states in structural development

In a moment we will proceed to look at the iterating patterns as they express themselves in the world of subtle objects. As already suggested, the subtle tier and the unfolding of the 3rd and 4th pp. is essentially the landscape in which Scharmer's movement from ego to eco takes place. But first I will briefly mention an example of how O'Fallon's attention to the senses and development of basic perception helps to reveal the importance of the early levels of development and the unbroken chain of evolving capacities that form the basis of the ego- to eco- transition. O'Fallon identifies a set of states that emerge in a sequences and are essential in overall development. These are: "1) concrete sensory states, 2) subtle internal sensory states, 3) focused attention (concentration), 4) awareness, 5) awareness of awareness 6) non-dual, and 7) awakening" (O'Fallon, 2013, p. 8-9). We might develop these state capacities at any stage. That doesn't necessarily bring us to the next structural stage. But without developing these states to some degree, certain stages cannot emerge. For example, we cannot develop subtle internal states, like visualizing an object that is not present, before we are able to experience concrete objects, and subtle internal states are necessary for developing access to another person's point of view – 2nd pp (2.0 Rule Oriented and 2.5 Conformist). While this may seem obvious, the role of visualization in relation to basic learning like reading and writing is often forgotten. As we move further down the list, the connections may not be immediately obvious, and becoming aware of them is extremely valuable for anyone who wishes to cultivate development.

Moving on to the third state in the sequence; focused attention or concentration is claimed to be the entry ticket to 3rd pp (3.0 Expert and 3.5 Achiever). At 1st pp we have no power over our attention. It is simply taken by objects that seem interesting or threatening. At 2nd pp our ability to concentrate depends on the outer authority or the internalized rules of the we-space that we identify with. The 3rd pp and the ability to look at the concrete values, rules, and roles of the 2nd pp relies on a certain ability to focus attention at will – independently of the 2nd pp context.

Next, a certain capacity for *awareness* is identified as the pre-requisite for moving into the 4th pp (4.0 Pluralist and 4.5 Strategist). The capacity to zoom out from the more exclusive focused attention that is favored at 3.5 Achiever, brings a wider (field-) awareness to the fore, and this enables the subtle collective contexts to enter as the new object domain at these levels. This shift is an example of another important principle, sometimes described by O'Fallon as the rocking chair of attention and awareness (O'Fallon, 2014): The capacity for attention gradually increases through the otherwise diffuse receptive phase and peaks in the active phase only to recede in exchange for awareness during the reciprocal phase. Attention resurfaces in the interpenetrative phase, where we learn to balance and integrate attention and awareness.

To finish the sequence of indispensable states, O'Fallon links "non-dual" and "awakening states" to very late levels where these capacities are necessary, but the last connection we will mention in this context is that some degree of awareness of awareness is necessary to enter 5.0 Construct Aware and stabilizes during the MetAware tier. Awareness of awareness means that the subtle field of awareness can be looked at from a state of very subtle/causal witnessing, and this is the prerequisite for the shift of identification that marks the beginning of the MetAware tier: from a subtle role that is constructed by the subtle collective field to awareness itself.

The sequence of indispensable states is a good example of how STAGES may lend valuable insights to support the task of creating systems of learning and education that support the vertical dimension of development.

Unfolding the subtle tier

When we first awaken to the 3rd pp (3.0, Expert) we become aware of subtle objects, such as thoughts about thinking and seeing our seeing, i.e. we can look at our inner images and thoughts (inner auditory sensations) about the concrete world. Since this is a new landscape, we are passively/*receptive*ly taking it in. We gradually learn to focus our attention on these new objects, but at this point we do not yet have a clear distinction between inside and outside, meaning we do not yet see others as having their own subtle object experience. As we move into the *active* phase of the 3rd pp, (3.5, Achiever), we get better at focusing our attention on the subtle object, increasing our sense of control and with a clear sense of self and other in the subtle, where - as opposed to what was the case in the concrete tier - a person is not solely identified by his or her concrete appearance or concrete role or position.

As mentioned, the unfolding of a 3rd pp is the basis of the modern scientific ideal of objective truth and of universal human rights. Notice that even though with the mature 3rd pp (3.5) we recognize others as subtle individuals, with their own subtle interiors, we do not yet have the awareness that others see our subtle selves back. The subtle collective does not emerge until we are able to take a 4th pp, and this means that up until that point our sense of the collective is still concrete. In other words, we experience the collective as a sum of individuals with subtle interiors, but the synergy aspect of minds and hearts meeting to form a we-space that is greater than its parts is not within our horizon.

With the 4th pp we sense that the objectivity of the 3rd person perspective is not the final and complete truth. When we look at each other from this new subtle openness or sense of relativity, we realize that the other can see our subtle selves back, and with this the *reciprocity* (receptive-collective) that characterizes 4.0 Pluralist has emerged. In the opening of the subtle meeting, the new we-space is experienced as something that is prior to or more real than the subtle self that at this point is much more flexible than at 3.5.

Through exploring the subtle roles in ourselves and others as they are formed and changed by the newly emerged subtle collective, we gradually move from being 'had by' to 'having' the experience of reciprocity – we start acting upon or constructing the system, rather than being passively constructed by it. This marks our entry into the late 4th pp, (4.5, Strategist) and the phase of *interpenetration* (active-collective).

In the work of Wilber, 4.0, Pluralist (Wilber's Green) has often been accused of denying hierarchy. But it is worth noting that in the STAGES model, all receptive stages tend to let hierarchy slip into the background, because they do not easily prioritize within their new object-space. At 3.0, Expert for example, we do not yet have a steady capacity to focus on subtle objects like our abstract ideas, our future and our goals and tend to hold on to all our ideas and gather understanding in the specific area that we happen to be concerned about. At 4.0 we are so absorbed in exploring our new subtle relations and cannot yet take an outside view of the subtle collective. 4.5 is a new active stage, like 3.5, and here we expand our sense of mastery and control in the subtle collective and experience a sense of unity as *interpenetrated* by the subtle projections that we now recognize. We can now prioritize within the subtle collective and thus operate with fluid hierarchies or "actualization hierarchies" (Laloux, 2014, p. 69), in accordance with whatever the situation calls for.

Levels of listening and conversation

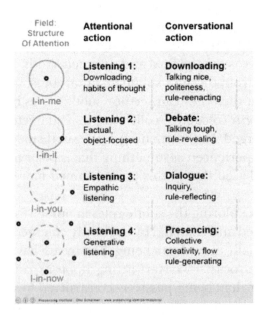

Figure 3: Levels of Listening and Conversation

Introducing the levels of conversation to students of the U.lab online education program, Otto Scharmer says he believes he has only ever seen the four different patterns of conversation, namely: Downloading (talking nice), Debate (talking tough), Dialogue (reflective inquiry), and Collective creativity (generative flow). These four levels of conversation correspond to the four levels of listening, and each level is connected to a specific "structure of attention" in relation to the field. These three aspects and the four levels are shown in figure 3. Notice the similarities with the four phases of moving through a tier of development, spotted by O'Fallon and shown in the butterfly motion of figure 2: First we are inside our small bubble of perception where one's own ideas tend to filter the emerging (subtle) world. Then we shift to an *active* mode (technically, the *outside* of the 3rd pp) and come out to expand our understanding in a comparing and choosing fashion that O'Fallon describes as "either, or". In the third, *reciprocal* phase we explore the landscape of collective flow in an including "both, and" mode, and finally, with the *interpenetrative* phase, we gain a new freedom to be ourselves and hear our own sense of direction, through the spellbinding and seductive sense of flow in the collective.

I believe the four categories identified by Scharmer and O'Fallon's learning sequence are versions of the same universal pattern in human transformation processes. This is supported when we note that not only has this pattern been observed and described independently by O´Fallon and Scharmer, it is also clearly recognizable in Arnold Mindell's Process Work[14] and shows interesting resemblances to Stanislav Grof's four Basic Perinatal Matrices (BPMs) (Groff, 1990).

The breath and heartbeat of development

I think of the recurring double-loop motion as the breath and heartbeat of development because this simple figure seems to represent a pattern of transformation that may well be even more fundamental than the spectrum of development covered by the STAGES model. Since evolution didn't start with the human spectrum of development, why shouldn't the fundamental divers of development assumed in the STAGES model have some kind correlation to the more instinctive or biological layers of development? Even if respiration and heartbeat are merely metaphors, they may serve as a reminder of the bio-sphere connection involved in sensing from the field.

The heart is widely associated with connecting deeply with oneself and others, and thus the heartbeat seems an appropriate metaphor for individual-collective driver of development (the left right movement in the Butterfly diagram, figure 2). Similarly, with respiration, O'Fallon connects the receptive-active pattern in STAGES with the alternation between being "inside" and "outside" the basic perspective of the level. Breathing continually connects inside and outside. Paying attention to the breath is a universal aspect of various paths of transformation and self-discovery, including the traditional mindfulness practices that inspired the U process (Varela & scharmer, 2000). Opening our lungs to the life-giving oxygen of the surrounding atmosphere is perhaps more than a metaphor for the receptive phases of development and the shifts of redirecting and letting go of the known and opening ourselves to the question of who we really are. Likewise, throughout the martial arts the outbreath is universally associated with expression and dynamic forceful movements, and thus a precious friend when we "act in an instance" and begin to enact and embody our deeper work.

Focusing on this universal learning pattern gives us a very smooth way of integrating Theory U and STAGES. The first expansion of Theory U that this approach brings forward is the distinction between concrete and subtle expressions of a universal learning pattern. In the following, I offer some suggestions as to how Scharmer's four levels and their "structures of attention" (figure 3) may be adjusted and refined in terms of their ground- and overtones as seen in the butterfly model.

Ground- and overtones of the field

As noted earlier, the U process points to a universal experience of state change that we expect to find at any level. Nevertheless, the movement through the subtle tier - from ego to eco - appears to be paradigmatic to Theory U. What the STAGES model adds is essentially a possibility of distinguishing the concrete, subtle, and very subtle (MetAware) expressions of Scharmer's four levels. This is useful because it allows people working with these levels to gauge the levels of development that -are activated in a given situation and adjust their response accordingly.

An essential point here is that when Scharmer emphasizes that we are not trying to eliminate the first three levels in exchange for the fourth, but rather to use the whole scale more fluently to enhance transformation, he is voicing the vertical inclusion, characteristic of 4.5, Strategist (Eco-system awareness) and later levels. This vertical inclusion is incomplete without the tools to include and distinguish the full spectrum. This not only affects work outside the subtle spectrum of developments but also our ability to heal and enhance transformation at any level, since healthy expressions of the concrete levels provide the energy and momentum for the subtler upshifts.

I-In-Me, ground- and overtones

We tend to use 'downloading' in a somewhat derogatory fashion, as a catch-all phrase for being closed off to perceptions that do not fit preconceived ideas. In this sense, every level until and partly including 3.0 (Expert) arguably fit the bill since experience of an actual future – in the sense of something that brings entirely new possibilities – emerges with the unfolding of the 3rd pp. However, the STAGES model correlates the I-In-Me-like receptive-individual structure of attention with the uneven numbered .0 levels, 1.0, 3,0 and 5.0.

Paradoxically these levels are wide open and indeed *receptive*, while at the same time appearing uncontactable and closed to their surroundings. This is because they are exposed to new types of objects and still can't orientate themselves skillfully and consistently in this new arena. Thus:

Though Experts (3.0) tend so see things only from their own perspective, they have the capacity to think about what they would do if they were in the other's situation and to *try* to take the other's perspective. The limitation is that when they try to do these things, they can't see that they are still coming from their own perspective when they do this (they can't "see" or consider that their own perspective affects the process). The outcome is that they argue from a single perspective, their own, on both "sides". (O'Fallon, 2017)

Similarly, Scharmer describes the first level of listening like this: "I pay attention to what I already know. It's like projecting my own slides on the wall" (Scharmer, 2015, 2:28). "The outcome is; we reconfirm what we already know" (3:12).

The ground tone or downshift of this level is 1.0 (Impulsive), which is marked by a state of concrete receptivity or as we might put it, a concrete I-in-Me structure of attention. Here we are absorbed in taking in concrete reality without distinguishing self and other. In a sense, we are downloading concrete reality and reacting without any kind of suspension of the automatic 'judgement' - knee jerk instinct in this case - dictated by our immediate needs. This is the developmental level of an infant. In adults, the receptive first pp. is normally integrated and held in context by later structures but might also show up as unconscious shadow material, perhaps as an underlying sense that someone should just magically know my every need and immediately fulfill it. If we sense that this is present in the field, it might be wise to address these needs and try to create a safe environment where taboos around having these basic needs may be lifted, and the misplaced responsibility for fulfilling them may be brought home.

The potential in this state is a basic sense of safety, a sense that "I'm ok as I am", and it is ok to have needs, be vulnerable, and not know. This opens a window for us to start to explore at our own pace and style, which naturally takes us to the next phase of the basic learning pattern. I-In-Me in the sense of resting in -oneself is after all a healthy foundation for developing and not a thing to be gotten rid of.

I-In-It, ground- and overtones

At this level we can hear facts that contradict our view. "We notice what's different, we access open mind, and the outcome is that we notice disconfirming data" (Scharmer, 2015, 3:26).

With the usual four levels of listening and debate, we are bound to conflate the openminded debate style of 3.5, Achiever, where we acknowledge differences, with the tough and even abusive attitude of 1.5 Egocentric. At 3.5 we seek out differences to determine the truth. At 1.5 we seek them out to eliminate opposition. Although the difference is substantial, it may be evasive since 1.5 may come in highly advanced versions, and 3.5 may often come with various degrees of implicit 1.5 shadow material. Although both of these levels are individualistic, the former is universal and supports democracy and human rights, whereas the latter is egocentric, and "what's in it for me" is the bottom line. If in doubt we might explore and challenge the position of the subtle roles, persons, or groups in question to find out whether or not they are willing to set aside social expectations and rules of conduct to get their way.

1.5 expressions are challenging by nature, but like their overtone at 3.5 they are highly dynamic, and the innate tendency to explore the edge tends to keep us from falling asleep. It's important for 1.5 to be met and matched and to have clear boundaries, which might not happen if we allow uncertainty about whether we are dealing with 3.5 or 1.5.

Once we have addressed potential 1.5 elements, the quality of 3.5 will likely stand out clearer. Scharmer describes the I-In-It attitude (3.5) through the example of Charles Darwin who kept a diary of things that *didn't* fit with his beliefs. If allowed to unfold, this attitude of open-mindedness will naturally take us in the direction of the next level, the I-In-You.

I-In-You, groundtone and overtone

(Scharmer, 2015, 5:57) "Listening begins to happen from the field or from the other person". The shift in atmosphere as we move from I-In-It to I-In-You is palpable and should be recognizable to most people. It is the shift from foregrounding the individual to foregrounding the collective. Parents and people working with children notice when the I-in-You capacity emerges (often around the age of 4 years), and kids go from parallel play to playing *with* each other. Similarly, when grown-ups are together, this is the shift from talking *at* each other to talking *with* each other.

It is important to notice whether this shift is expressed solely in relation to the concrete situation or whether the person or group also has access to the overtone expression at 4.0. At 4.0 we are context aware and experience our own internal collective. At 2.0 these advanced subtle objects are simply not available. This means that bonding through dyad or group activities (such as through sports or in the various forms of Social Presencing Theater) may create a strong sense of collective flow and togetherness, but if 4.0 is not available this experiencing-through-the-other will not give rise to a conscious experience of new parts of ourselves (subtle subpersonalities), and it will not make us understand new aspects of how the subtle context (such as unexpressed or informal roles and rank in the subtle field or culture) creates certain outcomes.

A likely scenario is having a strong base in the 3.5 expressions of I-In-It and little or no access to 4.0. If the shift to I-In-You expresses itself at 4.0, it will most likely be accompanied by an appetite for further exploration and an appreciation of how we need mutual interaction to grow. If it only expresses itself at 2.0., it might be more like: "This was fun. Perhaps we should do something like this more often.". Both are fine, but noticing to what degree 4.0 is available will allow a facilitator to intervene and plan further steps more accurately.

I-In-Now, groundtone and overtone

"You know whether or not you are operating on level 4 listening when you watch your level of energy and when you watch whether or not your sense of self - your sense of identity - has shifted a little bit towards the person who you really are, and whom you are moving towards" (Scharmer, 2015, 7:08).

In the video from which this quote is taken, Scharmer says that this is the truly new level, whereas all the levels before this are commonly known. The danger revealed through the lens of the STAGES model is not so much conflating ground- and overtone, but rather missing their structural similarities and thus an important opportunity to integrate the concrete tier and the subtle tier. In this age of globalization, we often notice 2.5 when it shows up as a reactive and contracting stance in opposition to later levels. 2.5 (Conformist) is ethnocentric, often fundamentalist, and tends to idealize the distant past. Surely a frame of mind that makes downloading the pregiven ideas from the past its highest virtue could not be further from the generative listening and presencing the future as it emerges, whichTheory U aims for?

Nevertheless, the STAGES model points to the structural similarity of 2.5 (Conformist) and 4.5 (Strategist) through their common pattern of interpenetration. 2.5 is the interpenetration of the polar opposites of the concrete individual and the concrete collective through concrete rules. 4.5 is the interpenetration of the polar opposites of the subtle individual vs. the subtle collective through the understanding of subtle projections. At 2.5 we can follow and apply the rules even if they are against our own interest (1.5) or the interest of people we connect with (2.0). At 4.5 we can act upon the collective field that we are part of without reverting to narrow individual goals (3.5) or being swallowed by the sense of powerlessly being constructed by the collective (4.0) because we understand that whatever we perceive *out there* is in some sense *in us* and vice versa.

Common to the ground- and overtone expressions of the I-In-Now state experience is the sense of alignment with something that is both beyond me and makes me a better version of myself as it connects me with the whole. In the concrete version, I align with a concrete truth that empowers me and shows me my right place in relation to the concrete society or group. In the subtle overtone, I might align with the source, the energy level tends to rise, and as we heard Scharmer put it: "your sense of self

[...] has shifted a little bit towards the person who you really are, and whom you are moving towards". In both cases, there is the paradoxical sense of letting go of yourself and being empowered.

Acknowledging these similarities help to deal more skillfully with 2.5 (Conformist) expressions and appreciate the strength of operating from healthy core values (2.5). It also makes it easier to see how 4.5 (Strategist) may tend toward subtle forms of fundamentalism, overly identifying with its own subtle 'crusade' and sometimes comes with a somewhat sanitized air of control, owing to the fact that at this level we understand projections and naturally embrace self-development but do not yet have the in-the-moment transparency of 5.0 (Construct Aware).

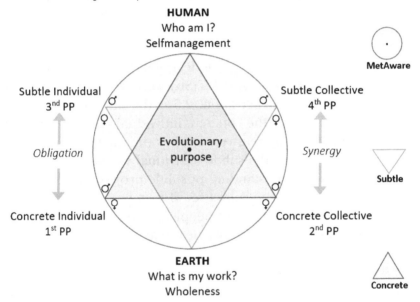

Figure 4: The Inner Compass of Stewardship

The ground- and over-tones of the fundamental learning sequence is an example of how the STAGES model invites working with developmental dynamics that are not limited to the linear, hierarchical sequence of the traditional Russian doll image of structural development. The butterfly diagram (figure 2) is meant to draw out a more mandalic image of development better suited for the phenomenological field-oriented approaches. Another way of doing this is suggested in the *Inner Compass of Stewardship* (figure 4).

This model is particularly suited for grounding our work in the mature 4th pp or later. As mentioned, this is where vertical inclusion of other levels emerges, and through understanding the mechanisms of projection, we understand the symmetry of inside and outside. We are the field, and the field is us. Determining the developmental level of a group or an individual has its merits, but when we aim to cultivate eco-system awareness in a living situation, it is often more interesting to ask ourselves how the full spectrum of previous levels represent and express themselves – or even how they *do not* express themselves. By acquaintance with the levels within ourselves, we develop a sense of the state of the levels in the field and vice versa. When we develop our capacity to gauge the climate and accessibility of the various levels, we develop an Inner Compass that helps us navigate transformation processes and find our way around the various divides, shadow areas and hot spots in the field.

The three divides revisited

A global society based on eco-system awareness (4.5 or higher) would not require that everybody, or even a majority, has access to 4.5 capacities, merely that 4.5 is expressed sufficiently to reinterpret, shape, and influence the way that earlier levels are expressed. When this is the case, the compatibility of each level with the whole system is enhanced, and the flow of energy, emotion, and information between each level and the whole system is maintained. Scharmer appears to hint at this important vertical dynamic when he says that the new upgraded system needs to "mitigate" the old systems (2018).

The Inner Compass of Stewardship clarifies the distinction between eco-system awareness in the narrow sense of 4.5 or higher and a wider sense where eco-system awareness prevails as an organizing principle for the system as a whole. It gives a visual image of the fundamental balances of an integrated system such as derived from the STAGES model. Consequently, we may also use it to distinguish some of the ways that the flow of the system might be divided or out of balance. The major imbalances relate to the three basic drivers of development, assumed in the STAGES model. I will discuss these imbalances and suggest how they might be seen as deeper structural aspects, relating to and elaborating upon Scharmer and Kaufers' concept of the "three divides" (2013, p. 4), a concept through which they sum up the various symptoms of our current crisis.

The balance between individual and collective is represented by the left and right sides of the model (this is the 'heartbeat of development' in the Butterfly diagram (figure 2)). Since 1st and 3rd pps foreground the individual while 2nd and 3rd pps foreground the collective, a group or an individual might orientate themselves more towards either side. This is not necessarily a problem, but an unhealthy divide between the individual and the collective might give rise to the symptoms described by Scharmer as the social divide – the divide between self and other. As noted, the emphasis on a shift from ego- to eco-system awareness regards the development from an exclusive individual 3rd pp to a 4th pp. The Inner Compass shows that this individual-collective imbalance in the subtle tier (the invers, green triangle) has a corresponding concrete version in the imbalance between 1st pp. and 2nd pp (the red, base-down triangle). This concrete social divide occurs whenever traditional authorities and values (2nd pp), loose their ability to integrate and check egocentric needs and impulses (1st pp). For example, when a value and identity crisis in traditional religious communities (2.5) results in youth crime and gang violence (1.5), or when farmers (at 2.5) get frustrated with politicians that favor animal rights (from 4.0) and take matters into their own hands (1.5) by illegally shooting wolves.

Another type of potential imbalance regards the receptive-active driver of development, represented by the feminine and masculine symbols at each of the four pp points in the model (this is the 'breath of development' in the Butterfly diagram (Figure 2)). Developmentally, we might move through the perspectives with a preference for either receptive or active states. The fluidity of the natural inhalation and exhalation between receptive and active affects the dynamic of reorientation and expression in each new object domain throughout our development. If we consider Scharmers' Brian Arthur-inspired formulation of the basic U-process: "observe, observe, observe; retreat and reflect: allow the inner knowing to emerge; act in an instant" (2009, xiv), we see how this vital balance is in fact related to Scharmers' spiritual/psychological divide – which he also describes as the divide between self and Self. In the early phase of each new perspective, we are exposed to new types of objects and "observe, observe, observe", before eventually moving into an active phase where we begin to find our new expression and start trusting and exploring new flavors of intention. The Inner Compass shows four manifestations and thus four entry points to working with this balance. At the 1st pp related to basic needs and impulses, at 2nd pp to the narratives, rules and values of the concrete collective, in the 3rd pp to the subtle sense of our future goals and possibilities, and at 4th pp to the dynamics of the inner and outer collectives and our relation to our subtle contexts. At each of these developmental junctions, we essentially reformulate our deeper Selves into new active selves, and as we mature, the four perspectives remain as both the windows and channels of expression of our psychological and spiritual sense of attunement.

A third type of balance, and thus a potential source of imbalance or divide, is the vertical integration across tiers. Vertical integration connects the later aspects of our development with our earlier developmental base and ultimately with our evolutionary past as a species. For this reason, developmental divides or imbalances in the integration of tiers could be viewed as structural developmental counterparts of Scharmer's ecological divide – the divide between self and nature.

In the STAGES model, the transition from one tier to another is a more complicated and potentially difficult transition because it involves a shift in relation to all three of the fundamental aspects of development: 1) the active-receptive(-reciprocal-interpenetrative), 2) the individual-collective and 3) the types of objects (concrete, subtle, and MetAware). For the purpose of this discussion, we will focus on the integration of the concrete and the subtle tiers.[15]

Theory U specifically addresses the field of current economics, and in that context, it is natural to emphasize the divide between 3rd pp liberalistic, individualistic forces and the egalitarian whole system orientations of 4th pp, but arguably the single biggest challenge of our time is not the transition of ego (3.5) to eco (4.5), but vertical integration of the concrete and subtle within the wider horizon of awareness (MetAware/very subtle). Thus for example, the negative meta-trends singled out by Scharmer recently (2018b) - post truth, post democracy, post planet - are not primarily examples of ego-system awareness (3rd pp) getting out of hand, but lower 1st and 2nd pps that have come out of resonance with the emerging overtones and are consequently now high-jacking political and cultural agendas on a large scale. An obvious example is the presidency of Donald Trump, who seems to operate largely from egocentric (1st pp) and ethnocentric (2nd pp) levels and whose popularity, as Wilber has pointed out (2017), may well spring from his being first and foremost anti-4.0 (anti-green in Wilber's terminology).

Half a century after the students' uprisings of '68 and the birth of the modern environmental movement, the cultural elite at 4th pp and beyond has largely failed to inspire sufficient change to convince the majority of their fundamental values and world views. Scharmer touches upon this when addressing what he calls the knowing-doing gap:

> We can interpret the current global surge of terrorism, fundamentalism, xenophobia, Trumpism, and autocracy as expressions of the *same* underlying phenomenon: the *missing capacity* as a society to respond to challenges in generative ways, by evolving ourselves "vertically," by upgrading the way we listen and attend, the way we converse and think, and the way we organize and coordinate in the context of larger systems(2018a).

The developmental approach expands our understanding of the developmental - inner - aspects of this "upgrade" and makes it clear that it is not just a matter of getting more people and organizations to operate from eco system awareness (4.5), but also of upgrading the outlook and behavior of the earlier levels to maximize vertical integration.

Two forces of vertical integration and eco-system healing

I have tried to incorporate a reminder of these two kinds of upgrade in the Inner Compass of Stewardship (figure 3) though the interlocking triangles representing the concrete and subtle tiers of development. The upward and downward points represent two forces of vertical integration. The keywords at the top, bottom, and center points may serve as inspiration for contemplations and explorations that aid the natural process of vertical integration of the tiers[16].

Upwards pointing, red triangle - concrete tier: Once the subtle tier has emerged, the concrete tier continues to evolve in response to the ongoing quest to understand the nature of the new subtle interiority. A cultural keystone in this process is the concept of the human being, archetypically represented through Leonardo da Vinci's iconic drawing, Vitruvian man, and associated with the ideas of humanity and universal human rights. The corresponding driving force of upwards development relates to the core question, "Who am I?". On a personal and organizational level, this aspect of development may be accessed through exploring the topic of self-management, as exemplified in the writings of Laloux (2014, 2016).

Inverse, green triangle - subtle tier: The innate pull of subtle tier development (its omega point) is the urge to overcome the tension between the experience of our unique subtle interiority (that emerged at 3.0) and the sense of exteriority resulting from our development through the concrete tier. A cultural keystone in this process is the view of the Earth from space and associated ideas expressed by the modern environmental movement, by the founders of the UN, in Jeremy Rifkin's concept of biosphere consciousness etc. The core question that evokes this inner pull is "What is my work?" Accessing this aspect of development on a

191

personal and organizational level may be done through exploring wholeness (Laloux, 2014, 2016).

To understand the use of these forces and the related concept of keystones of development, it is useful to understand the way STAGES might inspire us to use gestures, keywords, situations, and key-events or keystones to weave vertical connections. I will start with gestures as used in Social Presencing Theater.

Social Presencing Theater and STAGES

Working with transformation across developmental tiers requires activating universal state changes (as we do in presencing) and adapting the way we frame the process in accordance with the developmental levels available. In that connection, it is worth noting how elegantly and simply, Social Presencing Theater (SPT) follows the basic drivers of development and gives them a body-based expression. The fact that SPT and STAGES correspond on this fundamental level makes it a valuable example of how vertical integration may be enhanced.

SPT is practiced through a basic alternation between pauses and simple spontaneous movements. This perfectly mirrors the receptive-active driver of development (the breath of development in the butterfly-diagram). In one of the simplest forms of SPT, the "duet", two people alternate their pauses and movements to make a silent conversation. This is one of the simplest possible ways to model reciprocity and practice the individual-collective driver of development (the heartbeat of development in the butterfly-diagram).

Another form of SPT, "Village", expands these aspects to groups, and "Stuck" applies them to explore a specific problem. In the more complex practice of "4-D mapping", an issue is explored through having people on the floor sculpting stakeholders and their emerging future. But along with the concrete roles involved, representatives of the marginalized, the future generations and nature are brought into the exploration. This effectively creates a situation of co-sensing, and when the group subsequently debriefs and makes sense of the experience, they create what Scharmer calls "a collective language of shared perception" (2015b).

Again, this is a model example of cross-tier (vertical) integration emphasized through the third aspect of development in the STAGES model. But the developmental angel of STAGES also makes it clear that this "collective language" doesn't necessarily mean "shared perception". The shared language created around the concrete situation might in fact allow expressions from different levels, with different perceptions, to unfold around the shared situation. People expressing themselves from different levels tend to choose different words, but even the same words, used in the same situation, might point to different perceptions.

As we found with the four structures of attention, the example of SPT confirms that Theory U and STAGES are in touch with the same fundamental dynamics of transformation. This correspondence makes it clear how the STAGES model might help us unpack the gestures and shared experience gained through SPT and maximize full spectrum vertical integration.

Just as gestures in SPT may create vertical integration, by making a shared point of reference that may be experienced and interpreted differently at different levels, specific words, situations, and large events may serve to facilitate vertical integration or identify divides in the field. Scharmers' writings clearly show his exceptional capacity to catch and utilize such key situations and key events like his personal account of the fire that obliterated his childhood home (2009, p. 23), the fall of the Berlin Wall (2009, 119), Nine-eleven (2015c), and the election of Donald Trump (2016b). These kinds of situations and events are strong enough to alter the way we perceive things. Interpretations based on the past seem to collide with a future that would have it otherwise. They have a type of symbolic power that Scharmer appears to have a talent for using. STAGES may indicate how this ability could be deliberately trained.

The meeting of past and future

Several years ago, I saw Scharmer present the essence of Theory U at the University of Aarhus. The one thing that stood out clearest from his presentation was his notion that in this and every moment, what we are is really a meeting between two people: The person we are as a result of our past and how we have negotiated it, and the person who is our own greatest potential, as it arrives from the future.

Scharmer's image of the arriving future brings to mind the contrasting image of the "Angel of History" from Walter Benjamin's interpretation (1940) of a painting by Paul Klee. Facing toward the past and staring at the ever-growing pile of debris from continuous catastrophe, the angel of history is powerlessly hurled backwards into the future by a storm. The angel wants to stay to help and heal, but it can't because its wings are caught by the storm we call progress.

I have no doubt Benjamin's bleak image accurately captures a very real experience of powerlessness, not just for Benjamin and countless others in 1940 when he wrote it, but also for multitudes of people today, who are caught in what Dominique Moïsi (2010) labeled the "culture of despair". I do not see Scharmer's alternative description of time as a denial of this experience but as a powerful antidote that to me captures the uplifting and empowering spirit of the Theory U movement.

In this chapter I have tried to bring about a theoretical meeting between the backward facing structural approach and the forward facing phenomenological orientation of presencing by combining Theory U and STAGES. *The Inner Compass of Stewardship* (figure 4) may be viewed as a matrix of the present as the arena of a meeting between the future arriving from the center and the structural patterns or tendencies of the past at the rim. The figure particularly emphasizes the vertical integration of the concrete and subtle tiers of development. Vertical integration, in itself a kind of meeting between past and future, is perhaps the main point that arises from incorporating STAGES into Theory U.

Conclusion and closing remarks

We have come to the close of the present exploration. In regard to the integration of STAGES in Theory U and presencing, I see this as a theoretical exploration and an early prototype. More experience with applying these ideas is needed to make it truly useful and see what really works on a practical level.

I started by noting the common ground of structural developmental models and Theory U, but also the inherent difference and possible tension between the phenomenological and 'forward-facing' approach of presencing and the 'backward-facing' orientation of structural development studies. My discussion focused on the STAGES model because Terri O'Fallon's efforts to base her description of structural development on the senses (as well as the recent application of the model in psychotherapy and coaching) appear to address this possible tension.

When I compared the STAGES model and other structural models of human development with already incorporated structural levels of development used in Theory U, I found that they correspond well, but also that there is a lack of precision when we move outside the levels described as ego- to eco- systems awareness by Theory U (and roughly covering the subtle tier of development in STAGES). Theory U might benefit by upgrading and refining its description, particularly of the earlier levels of development. Centering its description narrowly around the development from ego system awareness to eco system awareness could limit the applicability of Theory U when it comes to people, organizations, and societies that are centered at earlier levels, but perhaps more importantly this limitation in vertical inclusion also makes it harder to notice and engage these earlier levels as they express themselves in the individuals and groups that do have access to later development.

While it is hardly surprising that STAGES presents more levels of development than those already used in Theory U, the most important discovery made through my comparison was that one of the major approaches to transformation used by Theory U, namely through noticing the 'structures of attention' and the associated 'levels of listening' and 'levels of conversation', correspond closely to the 'basic learning sequence' or 'pattern of states' that iterate through the levels of development according to the STAGES model.

Assuming that these patterns are in fact the same universal learning pattern gives us an in-the-moment approach to increasing the granularity of working with the field in Theory U and presencing. Based on insights of the STAGES model, I have presented two examples of non-linear or mandalic representations of the dynamics between structural levels, the butterfly diagram (figure 2) and the Inner Compass of Stewardship (figure 4) and used them to suggest how we can distinguish between upshifts and downshifts (overtones and ground-tones) of the four structures of attention and how the basic dynamics development assumed in the STAGES model expands our understanding of the developmental aspects of major imbalances such as Scharmer and Kaufer's 'tree divides'.

I particularly focused on the aspects of vertical inclusion and vertical integration across the concrete and subtle tiers of development since the deeper understanding of the earlier levels of development (from STAGES) widens our attention from a somewhat exclusive emphasis on the tension between ego (3.5) and eco (4.5) to include the arguably more fundamental tension between the concrete and subtle tiers of development.

I also looked at Social Presencing Theater (SPT) through the lens of the STAGES model and discussed how using gestures in SPT enhances vertical integration by providing a shared point of reference that allows for a sliding scale of interpretations across different levels of development. I suggested that the same is true not just for gestures, but that we may also use keywords, key situations and historic events (or keystones of development) to gauge and engage the developmental levels in any given situation. As an example, I mention how Scharmer frequently uses key situations and, in connection with the Inner Compass of Stewardship, I point to our view of the Earth from outer space as an example of a keystone that is particularly instrumental in integrating later (subtle tier) and earlier (concrete tier) levels of development.

Through Google Earth, virtually everyone has access to the experience of fluidly zooming-out from local through regional landscapes to the image of Earth floating in space. And, as Campbell reminds us, there are no divisions in the wholeness of Earth when seen from outer space. We still do not have the same fluidity when it comes to zooming in from our subtle (4th person) perspectives of interconnection with the global (eco-)system to our concrete hopes, fears, and values. The subtle ideas about how our present challenges may lead us to a new way of co-existing with each other and with nature are not easily translated to our concrete belief systems. It may seem more plausible to the large parts of the world population, still centered around concrete levels of development, that if problems are caused by for example the growing population, nature (or God) will eventually fix the problem in a concrete manner, by reducing population again. We need alternative concrete examples to inspire hope and stop knee-jerk survival modes from increasing the divides.

The integration of Theory U and STAGES proposed here is new territory. I hope that others will be inspired to join the exploration and help to bring about the needed experience to further develop the language, models, and methods for this work. One of the challenges we face is that understanding and applying the structural approach requires intensive training. Though presencing, it is relatively easy to get an experience of state changes, but a deeper acquaintance with the developmental structures in oneself takes longer and requires peer training.

In further developing this approach to Theory U, it would seem helpful to work with SPT (or similar body-based approaches) and an interesting avenue of future exploration might be how the sequence of indispensable states proposed in the STAGES model could be used to develop more effective and precise modes of vertical transformation and integration.[17]

References

Barta, K. (2017). Five Ways that STAGES Can Improve Therapy and Coaching. Retrieved from: https://www.stagesinternational.com/5-ways-stages-can-improve-therapy-and-coaching/

Barta, K. & O'Fallon, T. (2016). Shadow to Spirit: A Developmental Exploration. Retrieved from: https://www.stagesinternational.com/shadow-to-spirit-a-developmental-exploration/.

Beck, D. E. & Cowan, C. (1996). *Spiral Dynamics. Mastering Values, Leadership, and Change*. Blackwell Business, Oxford, UK.

Benjamin, walter (1940). Kvote from: https://en.wikipedia.org/wiki/Angelus_Novus Campbell, J. & Moyers, B. (1988). *The Power of Myth*. Doubleday, New York.

Ceballos, G. et. Al. (2017). Biological annihilation via the ongoing sixth mass extinction signaled by vertebrate population losses and declines. Retrieved from: http://www.pnas.org/content/114/30/E6089.full.pdf

Clarke, A. (1997). *3001: The final Odyssey*. Voyager Books, United Kingdom.

Cook-Greuter, S. (2013). Nine Levels Of Increasing Embrace In Ego Development: A Full-Spectrum Theory Of Vertical Growth And Meaning Making. Retrieved from: http://www.cook-greuter.com

Esbjörn-Hagens, S. & Zimmerman, M. E. (2011). *Integral Ecology. Uniting Multiple Perspectives on the Natural World*. Integral Books.

Fitch, J & O'Fallon, T. (2014). Theory U Applied in Transformative Development. 114-127. In Gunnlaugson et al. *Perspectives on Theory U: Insights from the Field*. EGI Global, United States of America.

Grof, S. (1990). *THE HOLOTROPIC MIND: The Three Levels of Human Consciousness and How They Shape Our Lives*. HarperSanFrancisco, HarperCollins.

Hildebrandt, S & Stubberup, M. (2015). *Sustainable Leadership – Leadership from the Heart*. Copenhagen Press.

Kegan, R. L. (1994). *In over our heads: The mental demands of modern life.* Cambridge. Cambridge: Harvard University Press.

Kegan, R. (2013): The Further Reaches of Adult Development - Robert Kegan. Retrieved from: https://www.youtube.com/watch?v=BoasM4cCHBc&t=913s

Kierkegaard, S. (1843). Journals IV A 164. Retrieved from: http://teol.ku.dk/skc/sab/citater/#livetforst%C3%A5sforfra

Laloux, F. (2014). *Reinventing Organizations. A Guide to Creating Organizations Inspired by the Next Stage of Human Consciousness*. Nelson

Parker.

Laloux, F. (2016). *Reinventing Organizations. An Illustrated Invitation to Join the Conversation on Next-Stage Organizations.* Nelson Parker.

Mindell, A. (2002). *Dreaming While Awake: Techniques for 24-Hour Lucid.* Hampton Roads Publishing.

Mindell, A. (2017). Conflict: Phases, Forums, and Solutions for our dreams and body, organizations, governments, and planet. World Tao Press.

Moïsi, D. (2010). *The Geopolitics of Emotion: How Cultures of Fear, Humiliation, and Hope are Reshaping the World.* Anchor.

O'Fallon, T. (2010). The Collapse of the Wilber Combs Matrix: The Interpenetration of the State and Structure Stages. Retrieved from: www.pacificintegral.com

O'Fallon, T. (2011). StAGES: growing up is waking up--interpenetrating quadrants, states and structures. Pacific Integral. Retrieved from: www.pacificintegral.com

O'Fallon, T. (2013). The Senses: demystifying awakening. Paper presented at the Integral Theory Conference, 2013, San Francisco CA.

O'Fallon, T. (2014). Growing up and waking up – the natural unfolding of states and stages. Interview with James Alexander Anfinsen. Retrieved from: http://www.levevei.no/2014/01/episode-91-growing-up-and-waking-up-the-natural-unfolding-of-states-and-stages/

Ream, J. (2007). Illuminating the Blind Spot: An Overview and Response to Theory U. *Integral Review* 5, 2007, 240-259 Terri O'Fallon, Tom Murray, Geoff Fitch, Kim Barta, and John Kesler (2017). 8/31 – A Response to Critiques of the STAGES Developmental Model. *Integral Leadership Review, August-November.*

Scharmer, O. (2009). *Theory U. Leading from the Future as it Emerges.* Berret-Koehler Publishers, Inc. San Francisco.

Scharmer, O. (2015): Otto Scharmer on the four levels of listening. Retrieved from: https://www.youtube.com/watch?v=eLfXpRkVZaI

Scharmer, O. (2015b): U.lab 1x: 4D mapping (part 1). Retrieved from: https://www.presencing.org/#/aboutus/spt

Scharmer, O. (2015c). Paris: Shifting the Heart of the Collective, *Huffingtonpost.com.* Retrieved from: https://www.huffingtonpost.com/otto-scharmer/parisshifting-the-heart-o_b_8591364.html

Scharmer, O. (2016a): Ego System to Eco System Economies. Talks at Google. Retrieved from: https://www.youtube.com/watch?v=RftTYFU4DTw

Scharmer, O. (2016b). 2017—Trump—Are We Ready To Rise? *Huffingtonpost.com*.
Retrieved from: https://www.huffingtonpost.com/entry/2017trumpare-we-ready-to-rise_us_5861ea62e-4b014e7c72eddf2

Scharmer, O. (2017): Levels of conversation (Pt 2). U.lab, module 2

Scharmer, O. (2018a). Education is the kindling of a flame: How to reinvent the 21st-century university, *Huffingtonpost.com*.
Retrieved from: https://www.huffingtonpost.com/entry/education-is-the-kindling-of-a-flame-how-to-reinvent_us_5a4ffec5e4b0ee59d41c0a9f

Scharmer, O. (2018b). Otto Scharmer - Book Launch Webinar from Presencing Institute on Vimeo. Retrieved from: http://book.ottoscharmer.com

Senge, P. (2008). *The Power of Presence*. (Audio Cd). Sounds True.

Senge, P et Al. (2004). *Presence. Human Purpose and the Field of the Future*. Crown Buisness, New York.

Torbert, B. et Al. (2004). *Action Inquiry. The Secret of Timely and Transforming Leadership*. Berret-Koehler Publishers, Inc.

Varela, F. & Scharmer, O (2000). Three Gestures of Becoming Aware. Conversation with Francisco Varela January 12, 2000, Paris. https://www.presencing.com/sites/default/files/page-files/Varela-2000.pdf

Wilber, K. (1980). The Atman Project. A Transpersonal View of Human Development. Quest Books, USA.

Wilber, K. (1990). *Eye to Eye. The Quest for the New Paradigm*. Boston: Shambhala. Massachusetts, USA.

Wilber, K. (1995). *Sex, ecology, and spirituality: the spirit of evolution*. Boston: Shambhala. Massachusetts, USA.

Wilber, K. (2001). *A Theory of Everything. An integral vision for business, politics, science and spirituality*. Boston: Shambhala. Massachusetts, USA.

Wilber, K. (2006). *Integral spirituality: a startling new role for religion in the modern and postmodern world*. Boston: Shambhala. Massachusetts, USA.

Wilber, K. (2017). *Trump and a Post-Truth World*. Shambhala.

Wilber, K. and Scharmer, O. (2004): Mapping the Integral U A Conversation between Ken Wilber, Otto Scharmer. Retrieved from: http://www.unikat.at/wilber-scharmer-2003.pdf

From Social Technology to Technologies of the Self to Larger Scale Social Technology

Tom Karp

Introduction

"Change will not come if we wait for some other person or some other time. We are the ones we've been waiting for. We are the change that we seek". US President Barack Obama said this in his Super Tuesday Speech on 5 February 2008, a year before being elected to his first presidential term. Theory U is designed to help leaders and change agents to be 'the change they seek' by breaking away from unproductive patterns of behaviour that lock them into ineffective patterns of decision-making. Theory U thus proposes that the quality of the results created in any kind of social system is a function of the quality of the awareness, attention or consciousness with which the participants in the system operate. Consequently, one of the premises of the theory is that the actions of leaders and change agents depend not on what they do or how they do it but on the source from which they operate. The essence is that people cannot transform the behaviour of systems unless they transform the quality of the awareness and attention that they apply to their actions within these systems. Therefore, in this chapter, I will argue that it is difficult to implement deeper change without those involved in the change processes also undergoing change. Consequently, it is not enough to implement change processes at the group level and on a larger scale; individuals also need to implement personal change processes. These processes can be carried out parallel to large-scale change, but they can also occur both before and after a U process. In many cases, leaders and change agents know what they need to do to realize change, but they encounter barriers that prevent them from doing what they need to do. These barriers must be minimized in order to carry out change. Although Scharmer (2007) discusses this topic somewhat, such barriers are nevertheless a blind spot in Theory U.

Theory U deals with the type of leadership needed to implement change. The literature in the field of leadership and change is full of normative recipes and models for what leaders and change agents should do. However, there are many indications that they often do not act as they should, and that there is a difference between rhetoric and reality (Alvesson et al., 2017; Birkinshaw, 2013; Hogan, 2006; Hogan & Kaiser, 2005; Gallup, 2013; Karp 2013; TUC, 2008; Telfer, 2013; Tengblad 2012; Ennova, 2013; 2015). Therefore, it is important to address not what leaders and change agents should do to bring about changes but rather what prevents them from bringing about the changes they wish to make, as well as how to overcome these obstructions. This is because Theory U is a social technology outlining what people ought to do. To succeed with the process, it is necessary for participants to suspend their voices of judgement, cynicism and fear, Scharmer argues (2007). However, these voices are only a part of the picture. In order to understand what prevents people from doing what they should be doing, we need to investigate the phenomenon more thoroughly. We need to combine our research on social technologies with what French philosopher Michel Foucault calls 'technologies of the self' (1988). These are the practices and methods learned and employed by individuals that enable them to manage and change their own lives and ways of being. Then we need to understand large-scale technologies for change and discuss what is required to better integrate the individual, group and systemic levels, a move from what I will call Small U to Big U processes. Therefore, in this chapter, I will develop arguments that may contribute to the further development and application of Theory U.

A Road Less Travelled

Literature on leadership and change has generally focused on describing what leaders and change agents ought to do, not what they actually do. However, there are some notable exceptions, such as Alvesson et al. (2017), Birkinshaw (2013) and Pfeffer (2015). They argue that external pressures may force organisations to act in particular ways that make change and leadership efforts irrelevant, marginal or impossible. These forces may range from broader economic, legal and societal constraints to more specific forces, such as industry-specific parameters, market pressures, customer demands, supplier constraints or competitive pressures. Internal organisational conditions such as hierarchy, bureaucracy, internal politics, power struggles and system restraints also limit the scope for maneuver, and lack of competence may undermine change initiatives and leadership attempts. In addition, leaders and change agents may not be capable of doing what is required of them due to their own biases and weaknesses. As a result, leading change as prescribed in much of the literature is, in general, a road less travelled. Scharmer asks why. Why is it that, even if people are aware of this deeper process of knowing, it does not always happen in the context of larger systems? Scharmer (2007) gives part of the answer himself and points to three obvious barriers: judgement, cynicism and fear.

The principles of Theory U are most likely well-known to readers of this chapter. At the core of the theory is *presencing*, which is a key stage in the change process with five central movements. In that process, at the bottom of the U, lies an inner gate that requires people to drop everything that is not essential. This process of letting go of the old ego and letting come the highest future possibility of the self establishes a connection to new knowledge. This knowledge is the essence of *presencing*. Once a person or a group crosses this presencing threshold, a deeper order of change is underway. New knowledge and insights begin to emerge, and individual members and the group as a whole may begin to operate with a heightened level of energy and a sense of future possibility. Theory U now constitutes a body of praxis, and many researchers and practitioners have gathered experiences and insights from working with the theory. Key attributes include possible linkages of the consciousness of teams with the results of their work, whole system planning processes, vision-oriented policy making, individual and organisational development and a social technology that may contribute to conflict resolution and social engineering. The theory and its premises have been extensively discussed by Scharmer and colleagues (Scharmer, 2007; 2009; Senge et al., 2005), as well as by a growing community of academics and practitioners (e.g. Gunnlaugson et al., 2014).

Common criticisms of the theory are that it is strictly normative without sufficient empirical backing; that it does not present anything that is not covered in leadership techniques and processes such as mental stillness, active listening, reflection, idea generation, and prototyping; and that the 'soft', qualitative, quasi-spiritual language is off-putting to some. On a more social level, Theory U may also be criticised for being somewhat naive and assuming that people are without agendas. Another criticism is that it is challenging to create this kind of social field within a group whose minds, hearts and wills are not sufficiently open. However, a much greater challenge is to transfer such insight, commitment and change momentum into other systems, institutions, and society at large, other than the those participating in the process, in order to succeed with change at more macro levels. Theory U may lead groups to powerful experiences of great interpersonal connectedness, openness, creativity, will and wisdom. However, sustaining such positive effects beyond the group remains an ongoing challenge for those seeking to facilitate change in large systems. Scharmer are not unaware of this challenge (2007, p. 269).

A Momentous Challenge

In the recent book *Perspectives on Theory U* (Gunnlaugson et al., 2014), researchers and practitioners who have gathered insights on working with the theory discuss how to better apply it. For instance, Hardman and Hardman (2014) suggest that organisations and individuals may free up a more effective range of human faculties by using contemplative practices of purposeful meditation. Southern (2014) proposes exploring the nature of relational beings and encounters, a process which she calls *being in care*, in order to achieve transformational learning and change. Darsø (2014) advocates that leaders must reconnect with their authentic selves, and Hays (2014) discusses how teams can overcome counterproductive thought patterns and habits while achieving collective presence, authenticity, reflection and team learning. These suggestions are constructive, but they represent normative models that place significant demands on individuals and their ability to operate in groups, be present, put their own interests aside and acquire new insights. For many organisations, groups and individuals, these difficult-to-access processes may not be easy to apply in everyday life, especially within an organisation in which power, influence, emotions, needs and cognitive processing errors permeate interpersonal interactions. For most people, meditating, maintaining in-depth relationships, being authentic and engaging in collective learning are difficult tasks and may be somewhat distant from the realities of their everyday working lives. It is certainly possible to create processes and social fields in which such processes predominate, but it is not easy to achieve transfer from such constructed processual fields to larger systems in need of change.

One of the more interesting contributions in the above-mentioned book is from Cox (2014), who argues that if we want to understand what drives the behaviour of leaders and change agents, we need to look into underlying mental activity and explore its causes: the conflicts, defensive behaviours, tensions and anxieties. Disciplines such as psychodynamics, psychoanalysis, psychotherapy, developmental psychology and neuropsychology contribute to such understanding (e.g. Bowlby, 1969; Emde,

1981; Erikson, 1963; Kagan & Moss, 1983; Lichtenberg, 1991; McDougall, 1985; Mahler et al., 1975; Winnicott, 1975). The premises of such disciplines are that a considerable portion of the regulation of people's behaviour takes place outside the domain of conscious awareness. This gives rise to defensive reactions, innate response patterns, and scripts that have outlived their effectiveness. The implication of this somewhat darker side of human behaviour is that people often misperceive situations and conversations and act in inappropriate ways. Cox (2014) claims that unawareness prevents people from engaging at deeper levels in the social processes put forward by Theory U.

This unawareness is what Cox calls a psychosocial immune system, which is created to protect and preserve people's belonging and standing in groups on which they depend. The immune system protects people's awareness by keeping from it those feelings that they may find too threatening, embarrassing or shameful to expose to others. This needs to be dealt with in order to benefit from the U process. Even though participants in an organisation may desire a more open social field, they may also avoid experiences that might expose them to vulnerability. Such experiences can include emotional openness, trust, bonds, dependencies, mistakes, interpersonal safety, limits, ignorance, strengths and weaknesses. The need to avoid such feelings may drive a group to maintain the status quo of what can and cannot be talked about. Scharmer (2007) states that being willing to risk the experience of interpersonal vulnerability is a necessary condition for creating the type of social field required by Theory U. In social fields, risks such as loss of value in others' eyes, loss of power, loss of status and loss of group membership tend to govern interactions between group members. In other words, people need to have the capacity to be emotionally vulnerable, to transcend negative emotions and needs, as well as have insight into their own inner lives, in order to fully participate.

This is challenging. From a psychodynamic perspective, this may be related to Freud's (1923) most enduring idea about the 'battle' between the conscious and unconscious minds. A primary assumption of Freudian theory is that the unconscious mind governs behaviour to a greater degree than people suspect. Indeed, the goal of psychoanalysis is to make the unconscious conscious. Cox's solution to this challenge follows such a tradition, and he suggests a collective reflective practice by which the unconscious is made conscious. He recommends that groups talk about degree of openness, social safety within the group, degree of authenticity and inclusiveness and how to deal with conflicts and defensiveness. The purpose is to be aware collectively of inner thoughts and feelings. But as Cox points out, circumstances such as political and hierarchical realities may rule out such collective openness for many groups, and, even if they are removed, many groups will not see the value of taking on such collective challenges since the social risks are still present (even if they are talked about).

People's Inner Forces

Psychodynamics focuses primarily on dysfunctional behaviour, but people are also driven by positive psychological processes such as hopes, dreams, ambitions, growth, learning and development. Behaviour, value systems, assumptions, mental maps and thought patterns can be deliberately influenced and changed. People can choose to focus on their potential instead of their limitations, on positive elements instead of errors and on the present and the future instead of the past. Let us therefore apply a broader range of psychological mechanisms to understand change and the role of individuals in change processes by using disciplines such as behavioural psychology, cognitive psychology, humanistic psychology and positive psychology, and by studying people's inner lives and the connection to Theory U.

Individuals have inner lives, populated by beliefs, priorities, aspirations, needs, values and fears. These interior elements vary from one person to the next, directing people to take different actions. Boaz and Fox (2014) claim, like Scharmer, that leaders and change agents must understand and manage themselves and their inner conditions in order to bring about change. This involves being aware of what drives thinking and behaviour, what one may call modes of operating, so people are able to understand what makes them act as they do. There are two dimensions relevant to the U process that are particularly interesting. They concern the development of what Boaz and Fox call profile awareness and state awareness. An individual's profile awareness, or awareness of self (which is the term we will use throughout this chapter), concerns them being able to recognise their habits, thoughts, emotions, will and behaviour and how these influence various situations throughout their lifetimes. This also concerns the patterns that shape their personalities and which say something about who they are and what they stand for. The other dimension that affects a leader or a change agent's ability to change is what Boaz and Fox call state awareness. This is the recognition of what drives or holds them back at the moments when they take action. State awareness involves real-time perception of a wide range of inner experiences and their impact on people's behaviour which we, for the purpose of this chapter, will divide in two categories: what drives people towards action and what holds them back. State awareness, and subsequent action, may thus be regarded as an inner battle that drives leaders and change agents towards action versus what holds them back. Let us explore these in more detail.

Awareness of Self

People commonly use labels to describe their personality profiles, such as 'I'm outgoing'. The purpose of such simplified labels is to understand ourselves. Our self-understanding is obviously shaped by social interaction, culture and surroundings. William James described the self in his *The Principles of Psychology* (1890) as the sum of an individual's mental processes. Today we know that each individual neuron in our brains cannot be imagined as possessing self-will or consciousness. Yet, together with billions of others, they become more; they create awareness. Science has not yet been able to show how this occurs, but what we do know is that people develop themselves through a process of construction and reconstruction based on interpretations of their own experiences. What people say to themselves and the labels they give themselves are thus central.

The self is constructed by the stories people tell themselves about themselves. The unifying dimension is the understanding and the story of oneself, not as a fixed construction but rather as a process. It exists through language as a continuous, changeable self-understanding. Individuals get to know themselves, what drives them and what holds them back; they get under the surface. Binney and colleagues (2012) studied leaders in a number of European companies. When the leaders were put to the test, they asked themselves questions such as 'Will it go well? Do I have the knowledge I need? What are my limits? Will I get through this?' It was the leaders' ability to deal with their darker sides that was tested. Typical examples were the need to prove something, such as that they were competent, or the desire to receive recognition from others. However, there were also those who were driven by fear of rejection, or who were self-critical, demanding too much of themselves as well as others. In addition, some needed to take risks and experience excitement. Being aware of the darker domains of their lives meant that the leaders were better able to deal with situations and the people they managed, the researchers claimed (Binney, 2012).

Lack of self-awareness could result in leaders not being in touch with their feelings, thoughts and behaviour, which could lead them to withdraw from demanding interpersonal interactions (Karp, 2016). Neisser (1993; 1994) thus argues that self-insight is central. Self-insight is a state in which one is self-aware, that is, aware of one's own thoughts, feelings, will and behaviour (Crisp & Turner, 2010; Franzoi, 1996). Our selves are hence in part socially and biologically constituted; nevertheless, most people need to know that they are themselves and that what makes them *them* is a crucial question. This concerns who people are; what qualities, resources or abilities they have; their strengths, weaknesses and limitations; how they develop relationships, how they learn, how they get what they want, how they deal with opposition and difficulties and what they want to do with their lives. People develop by constructing and reconstructing themselves based on an ongoing process of interpreting and re-interpreting their experiences. A person's awareness of his or her self helps facilitate knowing themselves and their patterns. 'Know your-self', says Socrates. In the *Faidon* dialogue, he claims that the un-examined life is not worth living; examining both oneself and others is the best a person can do (Plato, 2007). The same goes for those who seek to change. Increasing awareness of self is a de-manding, long-term project, and there is not necessarily a cor-relation between increased awareness and better downloading, seeing, sensing, presencing, crystallizing, prototyping and per-forming, as set forth by the U process. But knowing oneself may enable leaders and change agents to work better in social fields such as U processes and thus increase the probability that such processes will result in long-term effects when change initiatives are implemented.

Awareness and Regulation of State

State awareness is the recognition of what is driving people in the moments when they take action. In common parlance, peo-ple use the phrase 'state of mind' to describe this, but the term 'state' is used to refer to more than the thoughts in people's minds. Holistic psychologists (e.g. Wilber, 2000) refers to state as consciousness, combining cognitive, moral, interpersonal, spiri-tual and affective conditions with body, mind, soul and spiritual perspectives. In this chapter, we will limit ourselves to address cognitive, interpersonal and affective conditions of the mind. We will also argue that a state is a mental condition in which the qual-ities of a state are relatively constant, even though the state itself may be dynamic. The state affects a leader or a change agent's actions. Being aware of the conditions that make people act as well as hold them back is state awareness. Awareness is also the starting point to influence the state: to regulate oneself so one acts in line with what one wants.

We can divide these states into two parts: forces that drive leaders and change agents forward and push them into action and forces that hold them back so they are unable to accommo-date new knowledge or take action as required. A *future time per-spective* is awareness of what drives one forward instead of focusing on the past. Studies have concluded that personal strategies that include a future time perspective and an instrumental approach to what people do correlate with individuals achieving their goals (Gjesme, 1996). Studies have also concluded that using both short-term and long-term goals can improve self-confidence, learning and performance of individual tasks (de Volder & Lens, 1982; Bandura & Schunk, 1981; Kirschenbaum & Humprey, 1981). Research findings also support the importance of being committed to something, creating a psychological contract between oneself and what one aims to achieve; for example, a goal can have a value in itself. It can also increase the chances of completing a goal (Alexander, 2005). The process of commitment is therefore sometimes seen as more important than the actual ambition (Jaros, 2010).

People are also driven by needs. Since Maslow developed his theory of human needs in 1943, many researchers have provided new contributions (e.g. Hogan, 1982; Max-Neff 1991; Deci & Ryan, 2000; Reiss, 2004; Sheldon, 2004). Needs such as autonomy, competence and relationships are important, and findings indicate that needs are not a question of either/or: people have different needs as parts of their personalities (Sheldon, 2004). Needs affect behaviour, and the underlying factor is motivation. Motivation explains why people choose one thing rather than something else, and it affects the intensity and endurance of actions. People are commonly motivated when they help other people grow; they want to be of benefit to others, and contribute to something greater than themselves, which is called prosocial motivation (Grant & Berg, 2012). Having a purpose may address such motivation. A purpose includes a meaning dimension that cannot necessarily be defined in time. Additionally, the prospect of mastery drives people (Pink, 2009). Bandura (1977) has shown that people's subjective feelings of mastery are important for their ability to reach their goals and keep going when they are solving difficult tasks.

It is important to understand what drives you forward if you aim to lead or change. Another, and probably more important aspect in demanding change processes, is considering what keeps people from doing what they should do, something Cox (2014) also discusses. Needless to say, awareness and regulation of state are harder to master than awareness of self. 'To live is to war with trolls', according to Norwegian author Henrik Ibsen (1906). Leaders and change agents will not be able to participate fully in open social fields, as required by Theory U, if they do not learn to deal with their weaknesses. It is often what people consider to be their flaws that makes them whole as human beings and capable of performing challenging tasks. Let us therefore discuss some of the forces that frequently keep people from doing what they should be doing.

Forces Holding People Back

One obvious candidate is destructive or unproductive thoughts. Within cognitive psychology, researchers argue that one can influence one's thought patterns by attempting to understand what holds them back and then making efforts to change this. Burns (1999) recommends finding the thoughts that induce negative feelings and then creating other thought patterns that over time can replace the negative thoughts. This is the essence of cognitive techniques that are regarded by many as effective (Berge & Repål, 2008). They are also easily accessible, research-based and can show good results (Lunde, 2008), even though they may be criticised for simplification (de Charms, 1968).

Often, when people make decisions, they unconsciously try to maximize positive emotions and minimize negative ones (Grinde, 2014). Emotions contain a cognitive processing of the body's signals (Damasio, 1999). They are not just hormonal impulses; they are based on assumptions of what will happen (Lehrer, 2009). The purpose of changing thought patterns is thus not to suppress feelings but to become aware of them. 'Expose the trolls to the sunlight and they will burst' is a saying in psychotherapy. Negative feelings have had a bad reputation, but these are important for people's functioning (Gullestad & Killingmo, 2005). Repressing negative feelings increases the probability of destructive actions. Pain, fear and other difficult feelings, as Cox (2014) discusses, have a purpose: they help people deal with social or physical dangers. Suppression mechanisms prevent individuals from understanding and mastering emotions, and they keep them from dealing with difficult situations, people and tasks. Better state awareness therefore requires avoiding using suppression mechanisms, instead focusing on becoming aware of, expressing and using feelings as effectively as possible (Monsen & Monsen, 1999). This increases the probability that people participating in demanding U processes will not withdraw from difficult discussions, close themselves off, or use destructive behaviours. In addition, it will also help leaders and change agents be in touch with their needs. The root of many physical and mental disorders is that important needs have not been fulfilled. When needs are not taken care of, negative and eventually overwhelming emotions can develop, which can give rise to a wide range of ailments and symptoms. People are drawn to situations or people who can fulfil their most pressing needs, and they avoid situations or people that hinder fulfilment (Grinde, 2014).

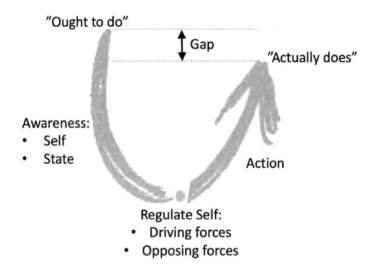

"Small U": Technologies of the Self

Figure 1.0: Small U: Technologies of the Self

Awareness of state is thus used to gain a deeper understanding of what drives leaders and change agents towards action, what holds them back, and to regulate such forces (Figure 1). Driving forces can neutralise the forces holding people back. A compelling vision, an ambitious goal, a commitment, a need to make a difference, the desire for a better world and a search for meaning may reduce restraining forces, such as fear, anxiety, cynicism and social risks. It may improve the probability of people crossing the threshold, which is the ambition in Theory U. In addition, knowing oneself and accepting some of the restraining forces may reduce their impact. And if one goes a step further, working with strategies that reduce the influence of unproductive thought patterns, destructive beliefs, restraining emotions, defence mechanisms and unhealthy needs may lead to more productive patterns of behaviour for leaders and change agents, both in daily life and when they are engaged in demanding processes, such as the U field. Being conscious of one's state and influencing this is demanding, but may be necessary to create change. 'Everyone thinks of changing the world, but no one thinks of changing himself', wrote the renowned Russian novelist Leo Tolstoy (1886). Individuals and groups need to change their individual thinking and behaviour to achieve change at the system level. Larger systemic changes will most likely not occur if no groups, teams or individuals change (Karp, 2014; Whelan-Berry et al., 2003). A premise for U theory work is therefore that individuals participating in the process are able to change themselves so they can absorb the knowledge they need, discuss it openly with others and then turn it into action.

Larger Scale Social Technology

As argued herein, it is often the case, both in life in general and in demanding change processes in particular, that there is a gap between what people should do and what they actually do, even if they have achieved collective learning and new insight. It is this gap between ideals and reality that many leaders and change agents need to deal with, the gap between the forces that push them into action and those that hold them back. It is a movement in theory and practice, from social technologies to technologies of the self. In order to create the social field prescribed by Theory U, which in turn gives rise to collective learning and the change desired, leaders and change agents need to understand how to influence the dynamics of change within their own lives. In order to spread change into something more than a single event that creates something good for those who participate, change management work must be consciously done to influence the system that is to be changed. This concerns working with large-scale social technology, what we will call the Big U.

It is beyond the scope of this chapter to discuss in depth the field of change management; however, some considerations relevant to Theory U are worth mentioning. First of all, the overall results in the field of change management are disappointing.

Studies show that change initiatives often do not deliver what is expected (IBM, 2004; Burke & Biggart, 1997; Kotter, 1995; Turner & Crawford, 1988; Prosci, 2005; Fine, Hansen & Roggenhofer, 2008; Clegg & Walsh, 2004; Kramer et al., 2004; Nguyen & Kleiner, 2003). We often assume that people act rationally and that organisational systems essentially process cognitively. With respect to Theory U, Peschl and Fundneider (2014) discuss how a new kind of cognition and epistemology is necessary to achieve U processes as 'learning from the future' and 'listening to the future'. They argue that this will involve a new set of cognitive abilities, attitudes and epistemological virtues. However, how people develop such new cognitive capabilities is difficult to understand. More importantly, organisations and individuals process at levels other than the cognitive. Alvesson and Spicer (2012) point to the limits of rationality and knowledge in organisational systems, which they claim is due to power and internal politics. These are the symbolic aspects of organisational life that are emphasised in daily activities instead of substance. The manipulation of symbols and exercise of power blocks communication and action, they claim. Therefore, when change initiatives are implemented, it is reflection and assessment that are necessary when leaders and change agents need to see progress. As Machiavelli wrote in his political treatise *The Prince* more than 500 years ago (Machiavelli, 1985, p. 13), 'It must be remembered that there is nothing more difficult to plan, more doubtful of success, nor more dangerous to manage than a new system. For the initiator has the enmity of all who would profit by the preservation of the old institution and merely lukewarm defenders in those who gain by the new ones.'

Executing large-scale social technology is thus a complex endeavour. Human factors are variable parameters when changes are made on a system level (Brunsson, 2000). Organisational processes are thus important, both to create interaction, cooperation and learning and to create the necessary arenas for conflicts and negotiations that need to be played out. The literature usually prescribes ideal ways to change systems but fails to describe what actually happens. It is not unusual that change processes are described in the literature as streamlined and with a kind of linearity that is often reflected in metaphors and figures used to describe change over time. However, reality is often far removed from such ideals. Change processes are commonly unstructured, random, without involvement from key stakeholders and without the necessary time, space, budget and resources to go into depth when required (Karp, 2014). This is due to a lack of understanding of both scope and the fact that plans, analyses and models often are unable to capture complex processes, structures and contexts. It is difficult to understand cause-effect relationships: there is uncertainty, and there are many layers and unexpected factors that emerge. MacKay and Chia therefore advocate a 'perspective on processes of change that emphasises process [as] constantly moving, frequently messy, rarely controllable, and often unpredictable' (2013, p. 226).

In other words, change initiatives move in unplanned directions. Leaders and change agents may therefore find it demanding to implement changes. It might also be risky to their careers, and they thus some spend time protecting themselves to ensure their own organisational survival instead of tackling difficult change processes. Change initiatives that challenge an established system may also meet resistance when threatening people's power bases, social structures and identities. One common criticism is therefore that the dynamics of power are considered too lightly when an attempt is made to implement change (Karp & Lægreid, 2014). Bourdieu (1977) was concerned with how power relations worked behind the scenes in systems. Instability, insecurity and resistance are the framework conditions for change, and the leader and change agent's ability to deal with resistance is often important. Change contains friction and is best managed when it is confronted (Karp, 2010). When systems are changing, the act of taking leadership, the use of power, creating processes that involve people, negotiating and standing in opposition often drive initiatives forward (Karp, 2014). This is not leadership in the form of grandiose, visionary, strategic, two-steps-in-front-of-all-others action; it is a messy practice in which turbulence, insecurity, opposition and a wide range of event-driven problems are the rule, not the exception. The processes, power, ownership, psychological contracts and social structures are thus important (Figure 2).

"Big U":
Large Scale Social Technology for Change

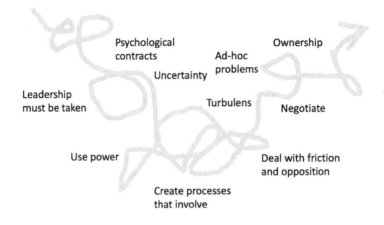

Figure 2: Big U: Large-Scale Social Technology for Change

Discussion

Theory U has promoted much innovative thinking within the fields of leadership and change management and consists of an entire community that both conducts research and applies the theory when working with change. To further expand this thinking and framework, Theory U should include micro and macro levels, as well as acknowledgement that insight and knowledge into the future are not necessarily sufficient to create large-scale systemic change. One route towards new theory development, as well as empirical testing, is to adopt pragmatic perspectives. Pragmatism will add the premise that practical action should be prioritised over theory and that experience should be prioritised over principle. Another perspective that may add fresh light is that of processual ontology, which has time and movement as its focus. Given a process ontology, reality is understood as events, experiences, expectations, and changes that direct attention toward tensions, contradictions, paradoxes and dialectics when changes are made. Thus, change is not a result of sequential steps, either linear or U-shaped, but multiple links between substance, context and politics in systems played out over time. A processual framework thus emphasises time, timing, power plays and internal politics staged as negotiations, conflicts, opposition and friction that occur at various levels inside and outside of a system when it changes (Pettigrew, 1985; Dawson, 2003).

Knowledge does not necessarily reflect an objective, agenda-free reality but is co-created as a result of ongoing processes between people, negotiated through an adopted order as a result of interaction. The system alternates between states of stability and instability, and adopted order and movement is the result of the overall interaction in the system (Stacey, 2000). Interaction is characterised by discussions, negotiations, internal politics and a struggle for the control of resources. Leaders, change agents or other individuals who possess resources may influence others if they have the legitimacy and are willing to deal with difficult issues, people and situations (Karp, 2010). Changing systems are thus arenas for discourse and practices, temporary and unstable adaptive practice communities tied together by actions and interactions, but also by competition, opposition and conflicts. Stability and change are created by conflicts and a temporary balance of power. Stability arises when these forces are in balance; change arises when there is an imbalance. There is no guarantee that the system moves towards an adopted order; groups with conflicting agendas can overcome the dominant constellation and key stakeholders. It is the re-occurring, discontinuous processes of confrontation, opposition, discussion and conflict that form the system (Van de Ven & Poole, 1995). Working with systemic change therefore requires work on Big U, U, and Small U process levels: large-scale social technology, social technology and technologies of the self (Figure 3).

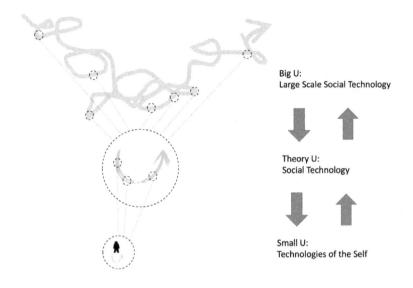

Big U:
Large Scale Social Technology

Theory U:
Social Technology

Small U:
Technologies of the Self

Figure 3: Working with Big U, U and Small U processes

Conclusion

Theory U may be developed in both time and space, both vertically and horizontally, encompassing systemic, group and individual levels. On the level of large-scale systemic change, where processes are permeated by variables such as leadership, power dynamics, uncertainty, psychological contracts, negotiations, friction and resistance, new theoretical development should take this into account. Thus, Theory U should acknowledge the fact that organisations are communities in which discourse and power often characterise their members' interactions in change processes. In addition, the theory should better address processual variables such as context, situation, sequence, timing and interpersonal processes. Explanatory linear models should be supplemented with the 'messiness' of change and learning. This involves acknowledging that factors at macro and meso levels affect insight, knowledge and cognition, as well as interaction and interpersonal learning. Identity, feelings, needs, power and processes are important. This means that linear understandings seldom have sufficient force of predication to explain what is happening when people and systems change. It is often the case that individuals must change in order for systems to change, and actions, movement and change at an individual level come together to create the aggregate systemic change.

Consequently, in this chapter, I have argued that leaders', change agents' and individuals' ability to be self-aware and regulate their inner forces that work both for and against action is the factor that enables them to be more receptive to new knowledge and to act in accordance with it. Among other things, this requires individuals to overcome obstructive forces and personal barriers. Having said this, it is important to emphasise that the ambitions set forth in Theory U are both important and relevant. The need for what Scharmer (2007, p. 443) calls 'global presencing' in action is greater than ever. But if Theory U is to evolve from being a mere processual tool to a theory for full-scale systemic change, it requires the addition of both new theoretical developments and empirical evidence to create better tools for leaders and change agents. Change is an important field, and Theory U is an important tool. Change fascinates, inspires, mobilises and terrifies. Nearly 2000 years ago, the Roman emperor Marcus Aurelius reflected on the phenomenon of change: he thought it was wrong to work against change, since it was a 'natural entity'. Aurelius was inspired by the Ancient Greek philosopher Heraclitus, who believed that reality had to be understood as a process. To quote Aurelius, 'The tides of change continually renew the universe, just as the unstoppable river of time continually refreshes what is eternal' (2006, p. 107). We must hope that further developments and new experiences with Scharmer's ideas may bring renewal to the universe. It is certainly necessary.

References

Alexander, E. D. (2005). The rule of three: A unified theory of leadership. Business Strategy Review, Special report: Leadership.

Alvesson, M. & Spicer, A. (2012). A stupidity-based theory of organizations. Journal of Management Studies, 49(7), 1194–1220.

Alvesson, M., Blom, M. & Sveningsson, S. (2017). Reflexive Leadership. Organising in an imperfect world. London: Sage.

Aurelius, M. (1976/2006). Meditations. (M. Hammond, Trans.). New York, NY: Penguin Classics.

Bandura, A. (1977). Social learning theory. Englewood Cliffs, New Jersey: Prentice-Hall.

Bandura, A. & Schunk, D. H. (1981). Cultivating competence, self-efficacy, and intrinsic interest through proximal self- motivation. Journal of Personality and Social Psychology 41, 586–598.

Berge, T. & Repål, A. (2008), (eds.). Håndbok i kognitiv terapi. Oslo: Gyldendal Akademisk Forlag.

Binney, G., Williams, C. & Wilke, G. (2012). Living leadership. A practical guide for ordinary heroes (3rd ed.). Harlow: Pearson.

Birkinshaw, J. (2013). Becoming a better boss. Why good management is so difficult. Chichester: John Wiley & Sons.

Boaz, N. & Fox, E. (2014). Change leader, change thyself. McKinsey Quarterly, March 2014.

Bourdieu, P. (1977). Outline theory of practice. Cambridge: Cambridge University Press.

Bowlby, J. (1969). Attachment and loss. New York, NY: Basic Books.

Brunsson, N. (2000). The irrational organization. Irrationality as a basis for organizational action and change. Bergen: Fagbokforlaget.

Burke, W. W. & Biggart, N. W. (1997). Interorganizational relations. In D. Druckman, J. E. Singer & H. Van Cott (Eds.), Enhancing organizational performance (pp. 120–149). Washington, DC: National Academy Press.

Burns, D.D. (1999). The feeling good handbook. New York, NY: Penguin Group.

Clegg, C. & Walsh, S. (2004). Change management: Time for a change! European Journal of Work and Organizational Psychology 13, 217–239.

Cox, L. D. (2014). Presencing our absencing: A collective reflective practice using Scharmer's "U" model. In O. Gunnlaugson, C. Baron & M. Cayer (Eds.), Perspectives on Theory U. Insights from the field (pp. 29 - 47). Hershey: IGI Global.

Crisp, R. J. & Turner, R. N. (2010). Essential social psychology. London: Sage.

Damasio, A. (1999). The feeling of what happens. San Diego: Harcourt.

Darsø, L. (2014). Setting the context for transformation towards authentic leadership and co-creation. In O. Gunnlaugson, C. Baron & M. Cayer (Eds.), Perspectives on Theory U. Insights from the field (pp. 97-113). Hershey: IGI Global.

Dawson, P. (2003). Reshaping change: A processual perspective. London: Routledge. de Charms, R. (1968). Personal causation. The internal affective determinants of behavior. New York, NY: Academic Press. de Volder, M. L. & Lens, W. (1982). Academic achievement and future time perspective as a cognitive-motivational concept. Journal of Personality and Social Psychology 42, 566–571.

Emde, R. N. (1981). Changing models of infancy and the nature of early development: Remodelling the foundation. Journal of American Psychoanalytical Association, 29, 179-219.

Ennova (2013). European Employee Index 2013. Norge 2013, 14. årgang.

Ennova (2015). Global Employee and Leadership Index 2015. Norge 2015, 16. årgang.

Erikson, E. H. (1963). Childhood and society. New York, NY: Norton.

Fine, D., Hansen, M. A. & Roggenhofer, S. (2008). From lean to lasting: Making operational improvements stick. The McKinsey Quarterly, November 2008.

Franzoi, S.L. (1996). The self. In S.L. Franzoi (Ed.), Social psychology. Iowa: Brown & Benchmark.

Freud, S. (1923). The ego and the id. SE, 19, 1-66.

Foucault, M. (1998). Technologies of the self. In L.H. Martin, H. Gutman og P.H. Hutton (ed.) Technologies of the self: a seminar with Michel Foucault. Amherst, Massachusetts: University of Massachusetts Press.

Gallup (2013). The state of the American workplace: Employee engagement insights for U.S. business leaders. Retrieved from www.gallup.com/services/176708/state-american-workplace.aspx.

Gjesme, T. (1996). Future time orientation and motivation. In T. Gjesme & R. Nygård (Eds.), Advances in motivation (pp. 210-224). Boston, MA: Scandinavian University Press.

Grant, A. & Berg, J. M. (2012). Prosocial motivation at work: When, why, and how making a difference makes a difference. In K. S. Cameron & G. M. Spreitzer (Eds.) The Oxford handbook of positive organizational scholarship(pp. 28-44). Oxford: Oxford University Press.

Grinde, B. (2014). Bevissthet. Forstå hjernen og få et bedre liv. Oslo:

Spartacus.

Gullestad, S.E. & Killingmo, B. (2005). Underteksten. Psykoanalytisk teori i praksis. Oslo: Universitetsforlaget.

Gunnlaugson, O., Baron, C. & Cayer, M. (2014). Perspectives on Theory U. Insights from the field.

Hersey: IGI Global.

Hardman, J. & Hardman, P. (2014). Travelling the U: Contemplative practices for consciousness development for corporate social trans-formation. In O. Gunnlaugson, C. Baron & M. Cayer (Eds.), Perspectives on Theory U. Insights from the field (pp. 1-13). Hershey: IGI Global.

Hays, J. (2014). Theory U and team performance: Presence, participa-tion, and productivity. In O.

Gunnlaugson, C. Baron & M. Cayer (Eds.), Perspectives on Theory U. Insights from the field (pp. 138-160). Hershey: IGI Global.

Hogan, R. (1982). A socioanalytical theory of personality In M. Page (Ed.) Nebraska symposium on motivation (Vol. 30). Personality: Current theory and research. Lincoln, NE: University of Nebraska Press.

Hogan, R. (2006). Personality and the fate of organizations. Hillsdale, New Jersey: Erlbaum.

Hogan, R. & Kaiser, R. (2005). What we know about leadership. Review of General Psychology 9, 169-180.

IBM Business Consulting Services (2004). Your turn: The global CEO study 2004. Retrieved from www.05.ibm.com/se/news/publications/ IBM_CEO_04_Survey_All_F2.pdf.

Ibsen, H. (1906). Samlede Verker, Bind IV. København: Gyldendalske Boghandels Forlag (F. Hegel & Søn).

James, W. (1918). The principles of psychology. New York, NY: Holt.

Jaros, S. (2010). Commitment to organizational change: A critical re-view. Journal of Change Management 10(1), 79–108.

Jung, C. G. (1962). Symbols of transformation: An analysis of the pre-lude to a case of schizophrenia (Vol. 2). New York, NY: Harper & Brothers.

Kagan, J. & Moss, A. H. (1983). Birth to maturity. A study in psycholog-ical development. New Haven, CT: Yale University Press.

Karp, T. (2010). Ledelse i sannhetens øyeblikk. Om det å ta lederskap. Oslo. Cappelen Damm Akademisk.

Karp, T. (2013). Studying subtle acts of leadership. Leadership, 9(1), 3–22.

Karp, T. (2014). Endring i organisasjoner. Ideologi, teori og praksis.

Oslo. Cappelen Damm Akademisk.

Karp, T. & Lægreid, L. (2014). Leading from the source: Exploring the bottom of the U. In O. Gunnlaugson, C. Baron & M. Cayer (Eds.), Perspectives on Theory U. Insights from the field (pp. 14-28). Hershey: IGI Global.

Karp. T. (2016). Til meg selv. Om selvledelse. Oslo: Cappelen Damm Akademisk.

Kirschenbaum, D.S. & Humphrey, L.L. (1981). Specificity of planning in adult self-control: An applied investigation. Journal of Personality and Social Psychology 40, 941–950.

Kotter, J. P. (1995). Leading change: Why transformation efforts fail. Harvard Business Review 73(2), 59–67.

Kramer, M. W., Dougherty, D. S. & Pierce, T. A. (2004). Managing uncertainty during a corporate acquisition: A longitudinal study of communication during airline acquisition. Human Communication Research, 30, 71–101.

Lehrer, J. (2009). The decisive moment. How the brain makes up its mind. Edinburgh: Canongate Books.

Lewin, K. (1951). Field theory in social science. New York, NY: Harper & Row.

Lichtenberg, J. D. (1991). Psychoanalysis and infant research. New York, NY: Lawrence Earlbaum.

Lunde, L-H. (2008). Vanskelig å legge fra seg. Tidsskrift for Norsk Psykologforening 45(12), 1525-1527.

MacKay, R. B. & Chia, R. (2013). Choice, chance and unintended consequences in strategic change: A process understanding of the rise and fall of Northco Automotive. Academy of Management Journal, 56(1), 208–230.

Machiavelli, N. (1985). The Prince. (H. Mansfield, Trans). Chicago, IL: University of Chicago Press.

Mahler, M. S., Pine, F. & Bergman, A. (1975). The psychological birth of the human infant. New York, NY: Basic Books.

McDougall, J. (1985). Theaters of the mind. New York, NY: Basic Books.

Metzinger, T. (2009). The ego tunnel: The science of the mind and the myth of the self. New York, NY: Basic Books.

Monsen, J. & Monsen, K. (1999). Affect and affect consciousness: A psychotherapy model integrating Silvan Tomkins's affect- and script theory within the framework of self-psychology. In A. Goldberg (Ed.) Progress in self psychology (Vol. 15). Hillsdale: The Analytic Press.

Monsen, J. T. & Solbakken, O. A. (2013). Affektintegrasjon og nivåer av mental representasjon: Fokus for terapeutisk intervensjon i Affektbevissthetsmodellen. Tidsskrift for norsk psykologforening 50(8), 740-752.

Neisser, U. (1993). The perceived self. Cambridge: Cambridge University Press.

Neisser, U. (1994). Self-perception and self-knowledge. Psyke & Logos 15, 392-407.

Nguyen, H. & Kleiner, B. H. (2003). The effective management of mergers. Leadership & Organizational Development Journal, 24, 447–454.

Peschl, M. F. & Fundneider, T. (2014). Theory U and emergent innovation: Presencing as a method of bringing forth profoundly new knowledge and realities. In O. Gunnlaugson, C. Baron & M. Cayer (Eds.), Perspectives on Theory U. Insights from the field (pp. 207-233). Hershey: IGI Global.

Pettigrew, A, M. (1985). Examining change in the long-term context of culture and politics. In J. Pennings & Associates (Eds.), Organizational strategy and change (pp. 269–318). San Francisco, CA: Jossey-Bass.

Pfeffer, J. (2015). Leadership BS. Fixing workplaces and careers. One truth at a time. New York, NY: HarperCollins.

Pink, D. (2009). Drive. The surprising truth about what motivates us. New York, NY: Riverhead Books.

Plato (2007). Crito. (C. Woods & R. Pack, Trans.). http://dx.doi.org/10.2139/ssrn.1023145

Prosci (2005). Best practices in change management. Retrieved from www.change-management.com/best-practices-report.htm

Reiss, S. (2004). Multifaceted nature of intrinsic motivation: The theory of 16 basic desires. Review of General Psychology 8(3), 179–193.

Ryan, R. & Deci, E. (2000). Self-determination theory and the facilitation of intrinsic motivation, social development, and well-being. American Psychologist 55, 68-78.

Scharmer, C. O. (2007). Theory U. Leading from the future as it emerges. Cambridge, MA: The Society for Organizational Learning, Inc.

Scharmer, C. O. (2009). Theory U. Leading from the future as it emerges. Oakland: Berrett-Koehler Publishers.

Senge, P., Scharmer, C. O., Jaworski, J. & Flower, B. S. (2005). Presence: An exploration of profound change in people, organizations, and society. New York, NY: Doubleday.

Sheldon, K. M. (2004). The psychology of optimal being: An integrated, multi-level perspective. Mahwah, New Jersey: Erlbaum.

Southern, N. (2014). Presencing as being in care: Extending Theory U through a relational framework. In O. Gunnlaugson, C. Baron & M. Cayer (Eds.), Perspectives on Theory U. Insights from the field (pp. 61-76). Hershey: IGI Global.

Stacey, R. D. (2000). Strategic management and organizational dynamics. The challenge of complexity. London: Financial Times—Prentice-Hall.

Telfer, J. (2013). Bosses behaving badly. Training Journal, March 2013, 44-48.

Tengblad, S. (Ed.). (2012). The work of managers. Towards a practice theory of management. Oxford: Oxford University Press.

Tolstoy, L. (1886/2005). The power of darkness. Whitefish, Montana: Kessinger Publishing

TUC (2008). What do workers want? YouGov poll for the TUC, August 2008.

Turner, D. & Crawford, M. (1998). Change power: Capabilities that drive corporate renewal. NSW: Business and Professional Publishing.

Van de Ven, A. H. & Poole, M. S. (1995). Explaining development and change in organizations. Academy of Management Review, 20(3), 510–540.

Whelan-Berry, K. S., Gordon, J. R. & Hinings, C. R. (2003). Strengthening organizational change processes: Recommendations and implications from multilevel analysis. Journal of Applied Behavioral Science, 39, 186–207.

Wilber, K. (2000). Integral psychology. Consciousness, spirit, psychology, therapy. Boston, MA: Shambhala.

Winnicott, D. W. (1975). Through paediatrics to psychoanalysis. New York, NY: Basic Books.

CHAPTER 8:

Deep Listening at the Eye of the Needle:

Music Improvisation & Co-creation In the Social Field of Presencing

Bobby Ricketts

Introduction: How Does What Happen?

An initial exploration of Theory U began by correlating collective, improvisational music performance with the framework; doing so provided language and terminology which had been lacking in prior conversations with organizational leaders. As my familiarity with the U journey increased, I began working in the opposite direction, attempting to position Theory U within the improvisational journeys I have lived and breathed for, over the past several decades. From this perspective, additional co-creative nuances that weren't necessarily evident in the framework or its explanations came to light in the musical sphere. Wondering why this might be so, I took the opportunity to view a streamed Presencing session to observe the proceedings. Seconds into the video, I was struck by one significant difference that hadn't occurred to me previously: the slowness of interaction. Whereas at mastery level, improvising musicians co-create instantaneously.

Two very different domains, true. Yet I was moved to examine more closely what happens - and how - when my colleagues and I create music, limiting the context of my inquiry to Theory U in general, and Presencing in particular. What follows are a series of reflective narratives and analyses concerning musical experiences and observations, which I hope will contribute to the Presencing conversation and inspire further inquiry regarding alternative inroads to Presencing and the Generative Field. In offering these perspectives, I make several assertions which I'll do my best to ground rationally throughout the chapter. A sampling:

- Masterful music improvisors demonstrate fluid ease of access to the generative field of co-creation (i.e., Theory U Field 4) with an agility which for (non-music) organizational cultures seems atypical;
- Within this generative social field, and at the threshold to an emerging, uncertain future, masterful music improvisors seem consistently able to co-create artful outcomes in real-time;
- A particular attentional quality in listening, which I refer to as Deep Listening, is a significant factor in enabling such artful, co-creative outcomes;
- Masterful music improvisors exhibit an ability to maintain, sustain, and deepen conscious awareness in the present moment, utilizing Deep Listening as a means to inform generative action through which real-time, artful co-creations emerge;
- Temporal Orientation facilitates masterful music improvisors' ability to direct and control consciousness in the present, and explore a more profound, sustained attentional listening awareness;
- Deep Listening provides abundant opportunities for learning, and, non-musicians can develop Deep Listening expertise.

The sum implication being that an examination of these particular qualities (and others) of improvisational music performance may serve to help expand, develop, or extend Presencing ability.

To the improvisational mindset, any framework is merely a point of departure.

Emergence through Coincidence

"Extended engagement in domain-related activities is necessary to attain expert performance in that domain. Most masters across domains emphasize the role of motivation, concentration, and the willingness to work hard on improving performance, as a factor in achieving mastery.[18] "

In retrospect, I see my life in music as progressing through three stages: Education, Application, and Emergence. This journey, spanning four decades, has been supported by continued reflection and self-study, consistent, deliberate practice within a variety of skill sets, and at a later stage in life, enrollment in graduate school, to study transformative processes more closely.

Stage 1 (Education) was centered around studies at Berklee College of Music in Boston after a period of success as an award-winning high school musician. While in college, I also worked as a freelance musician, often under the tutelage of my teachers, mentors, and older, more experienced musicians. It was an extended period of paying dues, learning the ropes, and allowing the rich legacy of musical icons before me to guide my aspirations. With experience came opportunity, bringing coveted engagements in jazz clubs and concert performances with various music groups. After relocating to Copenhagen, Denmark, the club and concert dates continued, now throughout the Scandinavian region, along with theater contracts, studio recording sessions, and performance engagements in television house bands.

Stage 2 (Application) ensued about ten years later, when I began to implement my learning up until that point more intentionally. As an entrepreneurial musician and independent business owner, I started to take responsibility for my career path and its outcomes. During this period, I served as a musical director and production executive for television and as a music producer with my own recording studio, fulfilling the needs of clients by composing and producing TV, documentary, and corporate presentation soundtracks. I also started a record label. This stage of my life involved more in-depth research and inquiry into music and the business of music, trial & error, increased risk-taking, and a more outward focus in life, searching for inspirational sources outside the realm of music.

Stage 3 (Emergence), began roughly fifteen years later and was all about freedom and emergence. I had embodied the full range of experiences and influences to which I had been exposed and started to zero in on a higher musical purpose. I returned once again to composing, recording, and performing my own material, something that hadn't previously been a primary pursuit, was able to cultivate an international audience for my music and began touring the world as a solo artist. This was an intense, highly rewarding period of life lessons while manifesting the dreams of my youth. I sensed a personal transformation from seeking the validation of what "they" say, to trusting an independent, internal frame of reference regarding the world and my place in it. The theme of this stage became personal growth and life experience from the bizarre to the beautiful; knowledge of, and learning from, world cultures beyond the Western-oriented, and increased spiritual and social awareness, self-discipline, and focus. I became more proficient as an instrumentalist than I had ever been at any point in my life. As my level of mastery increased, my ability for musical improvisation became more intuitive. The saxophone ceased to be a resistant, mechanical object and became a facilitative tool for effortless musical expression.

This longitudinal progression unfolded through coincidence and intuitive decision-making rather than by conscious, strategic design, as a result of constant immersion and activity in the music domain. Surprisingly, and here, interpreting "performance" as an ability to execute, I now track a correlation to a movement typical of the three phases in traditional theories of skill acquisition: (1) an initial "cognitive" phase of learning the underlying structure of an activity, and clear feedback regarding what aspects must be attended to, (2) an "associative" phase where an acceptable (in this case, professional) level of performance is attained, and (3) a third, "autonomous" phase, where the goal is typically to achieve effortless performance, and where expert performance continues to improve as a function of increased experience and deliberate practice.[19]

During my "emergent" third stage I began to notice, and eventually sought to explore, the beneficial powers of transformation which music holds. The more deeply I explored music performance mastery with the objective of achieving profound interpersonal connections with the audiences and musicians I encountered throughout my travels across North America, Europe, Asia, Africa, and the Middle East, the more I began to realize that there are no boundaries between music and life. The more I engaged and interacted with attendees of the master classes and seminars I was called upon to conduct while on performance tours, the more I became drawn toward facilitating cultural and social change via a musical and/or music improvisational perspective. I felt concern for the greater "We" - something which expressed itself through the search for a connection between artistic expression and the human condition. Wishing to connect the dots, I enrolled in graduate school to study critical and creative thinking, and transformational change processes.

As my career span seems to confirm, achieving, maintaining, and extending mastery in more complex domains is something that requires persistence over the long term, intention, and the cultivation of favorable practices that result in a consistent level of performance relative to a social field of masterful peers. Perhaps the real prize isn't mastery itself but the sense of 'knowing' that reveals itself along the journey. I register that my decisions have now become more deliberate, not in a strategic understanding of the word, but rather, as if determined by purposeful, meaningful navigation in what feels like a movement toward a higher Self. Conceivably, I find myself at the advent of a fourth stage, something beyond what I can perceive from my present vantage point. As such, an exploration into the expansion of Presencing capabilities as a means to engage the emerging future is as much a deeply invested personal journey, as it is a mission to share and exchange ideas with others.

Jazz Leadership & Learning

Jazz music as a genre, with its inherent components of improvisation and collaboration, has been recognized and leveraged as a useful tool for international diplomacy (e.g., through promoting understanding, tolerance, and cooperation between nations – which arguably, are beneficial, co-creative social outcomes) by the U.S. State Dept. since 1956. As an Arts Envoy of the U.S. State Dept. from 2010 until the present, I've had numerous opportunities to design and facilitate programs that leverage music-making, creativity, and dialogue to promote cultural understanding between nations.

Eminent jazz creators have provided a model of mastery comprised of beneficial musical habits, practices, and ways of being which are ingrained in the culture shared by improvising musicians. Throughout the history of jazz music, such eminent creators in the domain have pointed to a deeper capacity for listening as a driver for the artful outcomes produced. Ear training courses are a core component of musical training at the higher education level and help student musicians develop aural skills. Furthermore, participation in music ensemble performance activities in general fosters a heightened capacity for collaboration and teamwork.[20] As a musician, it falls naturally to connect models for achieving mastery, skill in perceiving meaning through listening, and a capacity for collaboration, as a scaffolding upon which to build Presencing ability.

Michael Jones (Artful Leadership; From Performance to Presence), Frank J. Barrett (Leadership Lessons from Jazz), Karl E. Weick (Improvisation as a Mindset for Organizational Analysis), et al. observe organizational leadership through a jazz improvisation lens; indeed, there are a myriad of scholars or writers examining just about any aspect of human life through a musical, jazz, or improvisational lens. Michael Jones seems inspired by certain

Theory U concepts, although, to the best of my knowledge, he doesn't mention Theory U directly in his writing.

The novel or original in my ideas relative to the work of others may be that I attempt to correlate my views with the Theory U framework itself. In doing so, the unique aspect may be, the ideas conveyed for the most part are my personal perspectives drawn from extensive practice and action research within the music domain. Scharmer's own incorporation of descriptive musical terminology in Theory U, such as 'play', 'listen', 'flow', 'in-tune', 'performing', et al. invites parallels to be drawn between Theory U and the music domain.

From the Inside Out

The perspectives put forth in this writing are based on an expansive, international, multi-cultural sample of experience. After roughly eight thousand-plus engagements (and counting) over some forty-odd years, interacting with world-class musicians on five continents in the process, noticeable patterns do emerge for the inquisitive eye and ear. During the past twelve years, I've journaled my reflections of numerous experiences, with particular attention focused during the past four years on a correlation between the "U" journey and the improvising musician's co-creative journey.

As a point of departure in this chapter, I begin at the core of the matter, so to speak, endeavoring to deconstruct personal experience and observation. I focus on how a particular attentional quality in listening, which I refer to as Deep Listening, is both a significant factor in enabling artful, co-creative outcomes and an ability that may be leveraged as a means to facilitate beneficial outcomes in social presencing contexts.

Accordingly, this writing will not address the entire Theory U framework but instead focus on a sub-section of the "U" movement where I observe (experience, perceive) Deep Listening taking place. That is, from "the eye of the needle" and beyond, with consideration given to how parallels drawn from a musical improvisation perspective may serve to expand, clarify, or elucidate inroads to the phenomenon of Presencing which takes place in the Theory U framework's generative Field 4.

The Social Technology Context

Theory U addresses the core question that underlies its theory and methodology: What is required in order to learn and act from the future as it emerges? Experienced Theory U and Presencing practitioners for whom this writing is intended, will, of course, be familiar with the dynamics of Otto Scharmer's entire framework. Nonetheless, I'd like to highlight certain features of the social technology as being relevant to this discussion, particularly (in Otto Scharmer's words):

- The Theory U proposition that the quality of outcomes is a result of the quality of awareness, attention or consciousness from which the participants in a socioeconomic system operate;
- Theory U's differentiation between four levels of awareness, suggesting that learning from the emerging future requires an intimate relationship with the fourth level, a deeper source of knowing called "Presencing";
- "Presencing" which combines the words "sensing" and "presence" to signify a state of being in the present moment, sensing and actualizing one's highest future possibility. A distinction exists between sensing - acting from the current whole - and "presencing". i.e. operating from the emerging future whole;
- The Generative Field, i.e. the social field where Presencing takes place, and from which a profound sense of connection and collective creation emerge, signified by two long-term outcomes: a unique, deep bond among those who participated; and often significant accomplishments by both entire groups and individuals.
- In addition, there are four principles of Presencing:
- *Letting Go and Surrendering*, i.e. letting go of the past in order to connect with and learn from emerging future

possibilities;

- *Inversion: Going Through the Eye of the Needle*, i.e. crossing the threshold at the bottom of the U to step into our real power, the power of operating from our highest future Self, with a connection to a deeper state of being that can become present within us and through us, both individually and collectively;

- *The Coming into Being of a Higher (Authentic) Presence and Self*, i.e. connecting our current self with our authentic self; moving toward our real self from the future; entering a deeper state of being where we, as individuals and as communities, experience a fundamental freedom and capacity to create;

- *The Power of Place: Creating a Holding Space of Deep Listening*, i.e. the common factor of presencing journeys taking place within a "container" or "holding space".

And finally, of relevance to this discussion is Scharmer's concept of four levels of listening, i.e., downloading, object-based/factual, empathic, and, in particular, generative listening, or listening from the emerging field of the future – the fourth level of listening, which requires accessing the open heart, an open will, and a capacity to connect to the highest future possibility that wants to emerge.[21] In musical improvisation, this level of listening is of highest interest.

Practitioner Challenges at the Eye of the Needle

According to the work of researchers and scholars in the field, Theory U and Presencing practitioners typically encounter a range of challenges which inhibit the development of their presencing capabilities to a level of mastery. Joseph Jaworski writes, "For me, the explanations of the U-theory in hundreds of pages of books and articles were missing something vital, particularly when they attempted to describe what happens at the "bottom" of the U."[22] A consensus of observations regarding the experiences of practitioners and the obstacles (and objectives) they seek to address might appear as follows[23]:

- the Theory U framework does not seem to have been designed to help practitioners deepen, develop and sustain their overall presencing capacity;
- the phenomenon of reaching a plateau in one's presencing practice has become quite commonplace, if not inevitable;
- in general, practitioners are at a loss regarding how to develop and refine existing and emerging presencing capacities;
- practitioners are perhaps in search of an immersive set of trainings that help build and develop presencing mastery;
- an objective that presencing becomes available as a primary way of engaging our experience, regardless of the situation we are in;
- an assessment of core capacities for engaging presencing which may be deployed as a viable leadership approach for thriving in one's day to day work and life.

Perhaps the above points indicate a general consensus amongst practitioners, that something "more" or "different" is needed to take presencing to the next level,[24] and whichever new approaches or new perspectives are introduced, that they be effective in diverse fractals of society where people, co-workers or citizens will not need to "develop" to a specific action logic but can work with the means at hand.[25]

Musical Improvisation & Theory U

I perceive collective musical improvisation as a non-verbal, interpersonal dialogue unfolding moment by moment in real-time, as the future emerges. The quality of interaction taking place is inherently generative, particularly when engaged in by masterful musicians. As evidenced by the vast body of documented, recorded works available, in the jazz genre especially, the improvisational performances of masterful musicians have been and still seem to be consistently driven by an endeavor to co-create unique, artful outcomes.

The term improvisation itself is rooted in the word "proviso" which means to make a stipulation beforehand, to provide for something in advance, or to do something that is premeditated. By adding the prefix "im" to the word proviso, as when the prefix "im" is added to the word mobile to create immobile, improvise means the opposite of proviso. Thus improvisation deals with the unanticipated, it works without a prior stipulation, it works with the unexpected. Improvisation is about the unforeseen and un-provided-for; it is "the negation of foresight, of planned-for, of doing provided for by knowing, and of the control of the past over the present and future".[26]

Improvisation as an aspect of human behavior can be witnessed in a number of contexts beyond the musical, for example, as a means of adaptation to changing environments, in problem-solving, or in the use of natural language, all of which are unscripted behaviors that capitalize on the generative capacity of the brain.[27] The implication here is that although this discussion seeks to emphasize various facets of masterful or artist-level musical improvisation, the act of improvisation itself, in many other contexts does not require a need to develop to a specific action logic. (Caspari)

Musical improvisation, although a critical identifying component of the jazz genre, occurs in other musical styles as well. Therefore, the reader may encounter that I fluctuate between usage of the phrase "jazz improvisation" and "musical improvisation". In general, the principles of improvisation remain similar regardless of genre; however, usage of the term "jazz" may occur whenever it serves a purpose to further understanding, notably in reference to a distinct range of musical vocabulary which is typically considered as being unique to the music genre of jazz.

Within this discussion, the relevance of musical improvisation in the context of Theory U centers around the following:

- musical improvisation (as well as musical performance, in general) can be viewed as taking place in a *container* or *holding space*, e.g. the stage, the recording studio, or the rehearsal studio;

- ensemble musical improvisation (as well as ensemble musical performance, in general) is a co-creative activity;
- musical improvisation (particularly as observed in the performances of masterful or artist-level musicians) seems to require a deeper quality of attention, consciousness, or awareness, and finally,
- artful outcomes produced via musical improvisation begin to reveal themselves immediately (and thus provide immediate feedback) via action initiated at the threshold of convergence between the present moment and the emerging future.

The implication, expressed utilizing Theory U terminology, is that the inception of masterful, artist-level, ensemble musical improvisation takes place in the generative field as co-presencing at the "eye of the needle", and moves up the right side of the "U". Thus, the "U" movements this writing seeks to describe, begin at the bottom of the "U" with Co-presencing, shifting into Co-creating, and Co-evolving.

By the end of the music performance, the greater We - i.e. musicians, crew, venue personnel and audience – may walk away with the feeling that something inside us has changed, and as a result we are not the same individuals as before. The effect can be momentary, or last a lifetime.[28]

There are indeed plenty of circumstances under which social, conversational and/or co-creative dynamics fail in musical contexts (i.e. "Absencing"), and when they do, the resulting outcomes are not particularly extraordinary. However, when considering various means for intervention within failing or dysfunctional musical scenarios, there exists an abundance of recorded material from which to draw inspiration regarding appropriate action. As such, my perspectives might be viewed as an appreciative inquiry of co-creative, improvisational music performance at mastery level.

"Knowing in Not-knowing" as a Way of Being

As a creative music professional, I have participated in - indeed, it has often been my work to seek out - projects where the objective was to bring together musicians of varying nationalities and cultures[29], and where the ensemble members often lacked a common speaking language. It is possible to assemble a group of masterful musicians in the "holding space" of a rehearsal or on-stage venue, without prior instruction or communication regarding repertoire or musical direction, and expect them to perform artfully, producing co-created works of music on the spot. And create they will, warmly, openly, and generously. Naturally, each individual has engaged in years of deliberate practice beforehand[30], allowing them to confidently and joyfully achieve this objective, and demonstrate a capacity to engage "uncertain and complex circumstances".[31]

As a Presencing experience, the characteristics of masterful, improvised music performance are marked by a level of comfort in evidence, regarding the unforeseen and the unexpected – a "knowing in not-knowing" as a way of being, a negation of the past having control over the present and future, and an intrinsic motivation to co-create from what is. Such is the mindset of the master musical improvisor prior to engaging the social field of presencing: there exists a preparedness for, and perhaps even a savoring of the unknown, accompanied by a confident openness to what might emerge within a fertile holding space rich with undefined possibility - via utilization of the same generative human capacity for improvisation possessed by all of us.

Improvisation is a skill which is mastered by significant numbers of musicians worldwide, meaning, improvisation is a skill which can be acquired and extended until mastery. The connection I would like for the reader to make is that it would seem to follow that such a generative capacity – an ability to creatively engage the unforeseen and unexpected - is something that might be highly useful when engaging an emerging, uncertain future.

Jazz is the music of freedom, with personal autonomy an essential attribute of the improvisational mindset. However, autonomy isn't something that is granted (as is often the case in hierarchical organizations), one has to feel autonomy as something that exists within, nurturing the "desire to be causal agents of one's own life and act in harmony with one's integrated self".[32] Perhaps an increase in facility, competence, or expertise nurtures this sense of agency, which in turn feeds into the daring nature required to improvise, and possibly fail. I find that the vital importance of improvisation as an adaptive skill with which to engage uncertainty is underprioritized in Theory U.

Deep Listening: Discerning the Will of the Spirit of the Group

Masterful music improvisors (and music educators) agree that a deeper attentional quality of listening is a significant driver of the live, musical co-creation which, in the holding space of musical interaction, takes form as the future emerges moment by moment. Equally significant is the ease with which masterful improvising musicians access this deeper source of knowing - or what Scharmer terms as "presencing" - and the dynamics of crystallization, prototyping, and performance output which occur instantaneously in the shared music-improvisational space. I would maintain that, at masterful, peak performance level, the improvising musician's and ensemble's journey toward producing artful outcomes initiates at the bottom of the "U". In other words, for such musicians, the "U" may quite conceivably be a "J". Perhaps one might attribute this deviation from the typical U journey to a primed, mastery mindset - quite possibly the result of a range of acquired skill sets, abilities, and capacities - and a "way of being" which reveals itself even before entering the social field of presencing.

The mix of a musician with a sound that they love, that

they are pursuing and aspiring to is a recipe for a certain kind of intensity. When this intensity gets applied to a spontaneous act such as improvisation, in the right hands, with the right material and the right kindred spirits, the result can be basically the highest level of human achievement manifest, i.e. the Coltrane quartet, the Miles quintet of the 60's ... In this endeavor, the listening part of you is really the leader.[33] - *Jazz Guitarist Pat Metheny*

Deep Listening as a concept appears in the contexts of contemplative education[34], psychotherapy[35], pastoral care[36], and the arts[37]. In Theory U, Scharmer refers to the term "Deep Listening" numerous times, e.g., in the context of dialogue interviews, concerning "Places and cocoons of deep reflection and silence that facilitate deep listening and connection to the source of authentic presence and creativity, both individually and collectively (co-presencing)", and as Open Mind, Open Heart, and Open Will being the three conditions for Deep Listening and Holding.[38] Deep Listening also has a specific context as one of the "Five Mindfulness Trainings" proposed by Zen Buddhist monk Thich Nhat Hanh, where Deep Listening as a practice in this context would be training to respond with calmness and clarity of mind.[39]

I have a personal preference for an understanding of the term Deep Listening which is inspired by the Quaker communal meeting concept of listening in silence to discern "the will of the spirit of the group".[40] The Quaker belief is that conversation may be "Spirit-led", i.e., informed by a dimension of direct, lived experience of transcendence, or deeper knowing and awareness.[41] Deep Listening practice within this context implies a suspended personal agenda, the existence of collective intelligence in the "We", and that this collective intelligence will emerge, through the group allowing it to "let come" – not in due time, but in its own frame of time.

As a musician, this perspective resonates. Part of our maturation process involves learning to "discern the will of the spirit of the group" through attentive listening. Years ago, my Berklee College of Music mentor Herb Pomeroy often instructed us to "interrupt the silence", as a manner of articulating when and how to initiate musical expression as an ensemble, reminding us that when doing so, silence, or the space between the notes, is equally as important as, if not more so, than the notes themselves. In both cases, a focused quality of listening and attunement to one's surroundings is requisite, with an underlying implication that perhaps there may already be an emergence (of music) under-way. Honoring this emergence takes precedence over any ego-centric action to make one's presence known. It's the difference between joining a gathering with respect for the proceedings, or kicking the door open upon entry.

Presencing, Deep Listening, and a concern regarding socio-economic systems operating from a higher quality of attention, consciousness, or awareness in the present moment, are all relat-ed to the psychological process of Mindfulness, a practice which quite possibly is less about merely paying attention to whatever is occurring in the present, and more about carrying forth (co-cre-ative) intention into the present sphere of operation.[42]

Oneness and the Fifth Player

Flamingo The Arusha Jazz Club, Osaka, Japan

I was performing at the top of my game, completely at one with the saxophone - propelling air through the in-strument which had become an extension of my body, si-multaneously channeling impulses of creative expression as if through divine inspiration. The band was on fire; our communication was intuitive, telepathic even. My eyes were closed, but I could see – patterns, shapes, flashes of light. I was in the moment, co-creating with my band-mates each fresh nanosecond of the future as it emerged. I felt a spiritual clarity.

And then suddenly I didn't. We were jamming hard on an open vamp, and I was ready to go to the bridge of the tune. But at center stage facing the audience, my back to the other musicians, I couldn't signal any of my bandmates, both hands being actively in play on the saxophone. The main priority was to sustain the level of energy that had engulfed the jazz club during the improvised passage. As the lead, I felt our collective destinies - the band, the audience, and myself – were in my hands as they worked the saxophone. Such is the urgency of our musical mission. To risk a breakdown in the energy by trying to signal the band or by diluting my focus of attention worrying about how was not an option.

I let go of this extraneous blip of thought, re-focused attention, and continued surging forward with my performance. It's all about trust. We're in this together, and IF we were really in it together, I wouldn't have to signal the band. We'd know by speaking to each other through the music. Jamming on, I began to listen deeply, discerning the will of the group. It didn't matter that I was ready to go to the bridge. The bridge wasn't yet ready to come to us.

This "letting go" meant relinquishing a potentially selfish agenda to manipulate a future outcome, and instead, opening myself to the co-creative field of possibility.

Perhaps such a first-person narrative portrays improvisation as being more of a singular, "ego" pursuit than a collective one. There are, however, additional subtleties taking place in the co-creative, Deep Listening musical "We" space.

Utilizing Kantor's "4-Player Model"[43] (i.e. "mover", "follower", "opposer", "bystander") as an illustration, the first-person perspective above might insinuate my saxophone as the "lead". Therefore, one might assume I'm playing the role of "mover" according to Kantor's model. The actual role, however, needs to be perceived in the context of the music preceding my soloistic offering. A dive into the improvisational waters might possibly constitute an introduction of a completely new idea or direction, support or carry a preceding motif further, provide contrast, e.g., by countering a high-register wail with a low-register moan, or by contributing new perspective via reflection on preceding musical events. I might initiate a phrase with my saxophone which evokes a contrapuntal response from another musician who in turn opens up new territory for all to explore. Who is to say then, that I, the initial "mover", haven't now become the "follower" of the contrapuntal "opposer", whom at present has placed herself into a "bystander" role – all within a single captured moment of continual, fluid role shifts?

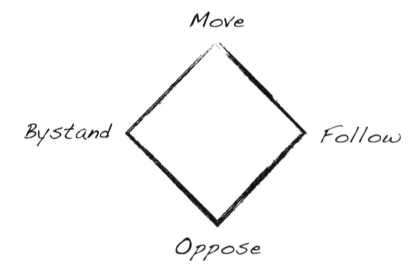

Four-Player Model

Move

Bystand

Follow

Oppose

• Without Movers
there is no Direction

• Without Followers
there is no Completion

• Without Opposers
there is no Correction

• Without Bystanders
there is no Perspective

Adapted from David Kantor ©1995

Figure 1.0 Four Player Model

Note that the shifts I describe are empathic/generative rather than objective/factual, i.e., how Kantor's model might typically apply in Field 2 conversation. It may well be that through it all, my instrument might, from a spectator's auditory perspective, be perceived as the "voice" in the spotlight. But in reality, at peak performance, the "hats" worn may constantly be discreetly and non-algorithmically shifted between all involved. And so, perhaps through this more liberal interpretation of Kantor's "4-Player Model" in action, we can sense a vital fifth-player role emerge: the role of the "whole". A whole which essentially is the emerging musical message, an intricately interwoven co-creation greater than the sum of its parts, that the entire ensemble seeks to "let come" and be carried forth at all times. The above events may register as co-creative dynamics of the move up the right side of the "U". Still, they are all guided by the consistent attentional quality of Deep Listening co-presencing taking place within the group, at the eye of the needle.

We musicians gather with the intention of creating music. Audiences join us as active participants in the musical holding space of co-creation. When the music being performed is improvised, i.e., created from "nothing" in the moment, to becoming "something", the outcome of co-created musical expression will vary, dependent upon the dynamic interactions between the players involved. Additionally, whatever the nature of that which emerges through co-creation, unpredictable as it may be, it will also inform and influence the actions of the players as co-creation continues. Here, the players are indeed operating from the emerging future whole via Deep Listening. This co-created whole, in light of its capacity to inform, influence, and perhaps transformatively affect the proceedings as they occur, certainly warrants fifth-player status in the four-player model. Most musicians would even consider their individual roles as being secondary to that of this fifth-player, the living, co-created whole.

In contrast to levels or types of listening such as downloading, object-based/factual, empathic, active, appreciative listening, or dialogic listening, Deep Listening in musical contexts enables access to a collective, intuitive intelligence. Or, quite possibly, a form of knowledge extending beyond the separateness of a group of individuals who unite and comprise a collective. A "beyond" state which at its best, in my experience, feels more like the "oneness" of a single, living, breathing, intuitive, sometimes prescient metaphysical organism. Perhaps this "beyond state" is the *source*.

Temporal Orientation: It's all in the Groove

While examining personal presencing experiences of Deep Listening in musical contexts, and in the interest of uncovering any novel aspects, I had to ask the question, "In terms of quality of awareness, attention or consciousness from which the participants in a socioeconomic system operate - what might be "different" or unique about the improvisational music ensemble performance experience, in contrast to other "mindful" pursuits?" When I asked myself *how* do I know that I'm "in the moment", or more importantly, how do I know that I'm *not* in the moment - it suddenly struck me: it's all in the "groove". Musical rhythm provides a feedback loop for orientation in the realm of time.

Everything has rhythm – seasons, days, people, flowers, the ocean, and at closer hand, conversations, personal interaction, our movements – everything. Picture a time-lapse video of a city: it breathes, pulsing inward and outward as the city awakens, the sun becomes visible on the horizon, people and traffic appear, the city swarms with activity like a beehive, the sun moves across the sky, as the earth, with its own rhythm, revolves around its axis, the sun disappears behind the horizon, people leave the streets for their homes, lights are turned on, the moon rises, darkness falls – and then it all begins again at the dawn of a new day. And if we were to focus on any one component in that image, we would see a rhythm within the rhythm. Even those of us for whom no day is the same, we have a rhythm as well. A similar microcosm of active potential extends to a single beat of music, teeming with collective co-presencing intelligence which emerges as a phrase, sentence, paragraph, or page in the chapter of a story, eventually converging into an epic musical tale.

The Royal Theatre, Gamle Scene, Copenhagen,

Denmark

The sheet music for first tenor saxophone in Count Basie's "Jumpin' At The Woodside" designated the tempo as being two-hundred eighty beats per minute. "Actually, we're playing at three hundred bpm," the drummer informed me. It wasn't good news. Three hundred beats per minute is about as fast as jazz tempos get, and placed me at the absolute threshold of my abilities as a saxophonist. After a four-measure a cappella break, I was expected to spit out seven choruses of masterful jazz improvisation in front of a full house of thirteen hundred people, while the big band wailed behind me – night after night.

Each note I'd be playing would be spaced roughly sixty-six to one hundred milliseconds apart, over the space of what for me sometimes felt like a life-threatening three or so minutes. I often relied upon a repertoire of four or five different a cappella breaks to get a good jump out of the starting gate; these were often played with variations to keep things interesting for the rest of the band. But once we hit the first beat of the first improvised chorus, the field was open: just drums, piano, upright bass, guitar, and my tenor saxophone in the spotlight. Forty-plus performances, and never once did I have a chance to look up and see the Royal Danish Ballet performing Twyla Tharp's "Come Fly Away" choreography during this segment of the show. I was fully immersed in each nano-moment of music, working the saxophone to keep my notes locked in to the ting-ting-ting-a-ling of the drummer's ride cymbal. It don't mean a thing if it ain't got that swing.

The future can be thought of as something distant, an abstract notion of a few years from now, or perhaps next week, tomorrow, or five minutes from now. At a tempo of three hundred beats per minute – or, five pulses per second, there's a distance of roughly one hundred milliseconds between the beginnings of each eighth note. It's a simple task to picture the threshold of an emerging future located at the tail end of the present note in play, and just before the articulation of the next, as-yet-unplayed future note. In such a situation, the emerging future and all that it holds of possibility for artistic success or bumbling failure, ceases to be an abstract, metaphorical concept from a theoretical framework, and feels intensely, urgently real. Despite being an improvising musician of arguably considerable ability, I found myself nonetheless perched in a balancing act at the cusp of the limits of my ability to - at breakneck speed - execute a skilled, improvisational performance before a paying audience, night after night. At three hundred beats per minute, in keeping with the proposition of Scharmer's Theory U, the quality of musical outcome directly correlates to the quality of awareness, attention or consciousness from which one is able to operate.

Establishing an awareness of time and tempo (i.e., the "pulse" in a piece of music) is an essential step in musical training when learning to perform collectively in an ensemble setting. As student musicians progress in their learning journey, they are exposed to all variants of tempi. The exposure includes terminology and performance techniques utilized for acceleration, deceleration, and the absence of a steady pulse (e.g., *rubato*) during a musical performance.

With practice, musicians begin to develop and maintain intimate familiarity with tempo as a phenomenon. Drummers and percussionists especially are expected to accurately maintain a musical pulse without fluctuation, and therefore devote many practice hours toward "keeping steady time" although an ability to do so is not unique to this group of instrumentalists. As a result of structured practice, developing musicians gradually become individually and collectively adept at intentionally directing consciousness toward a specific point in time when striving to play a particular note, say, for example, on the first beat of a measure, or wherever else specified via the music notation of a compositional work.

A musical piece can be viewed as being comprised of an ordered series of events. In a non-improvisational performance, the ensemble musicians are all well aware of not only what events are approaching, but when they will arrive, and what they will sound like. The music is notated, and each performance is a rehearsed interpretation of the notated. During an improvisational performance, however, the musicians may be able to predict when certain events will happen, but will usually not be able to predict the particular characteristics of these events.[44] In this limited sense, improvising musicians are not separate from the listener in the audience. From both perspectives, expectation accommodates an openness to the mystery of the unknown, an expectation of the unexpected.

In musical contexts, the concept of time as a pulse includes the element of rhythm. Rhythmic patterns occur by emphasizing various subdivisions (or not) within the tempo pulse. Even in silence, awareness of rhythmic sub-divisions exists and leaves room for human interpretation. For example, when seeking to place a note on, say, "one-and" (the eighth note after the first beat/pulse) of a measure, I might intentionally play the note more heavily relative to its theoretical absolute (the mathematical subdivision), if I "feel" doing so will express a particular, desired quality of meaning. The point here is to illustrate that space in between events, even (or perhaps especially) silence, lends itself as a potential contributor to the creation and communication of musical meaning.

The implication is that a beat – which, essentially, consists of a mere moment – can be conceived of as not just a fleeting speck of time, but an organic, living entity to be explored, a universal microcosm within which there is space to operate. The term "universal microcosm" is used here to indicate a space embodying the characteristics of "something much larger" which exists in between successive musical events. If we then consider the idea of "being in the moment", then one "unit" of musical expression relative to the pulse of a beat - in the instant it occurs - represents an event within that very moment. A moment where we musicians find ourselves, present, sensing, and consciously able to make the most of that entity of time and space – musically, creatively, and emotionally, for as long as it lasts, folding co-creative output into the next (presumably) eventful moment, and so on.

Upon its manifestation as musical expression, the masterful improvising musician's ability to direct conscious attention toward any chosen moment in the space of time is audibly evident to the listener. In return, each manifested expression has an audibly detectable influence on the emergent co-creative outcome. As such, masterful musicians, improvisors as well as non-improvisors, are not only able to direct and focus profoundly conscious attention on the present moment, they are simultaneously capable of taking intentional musical action, in any sub-increment of the present moment, with a degree of awareness that their actions will somehow affect the emerging future outcome.

In music, as in life, actions have consequences. Along with an operational fluidity and heightened ability to focus awareness, attention or consciousness in the moment, and for masterful improvisors and their audiences, an openness to the mystery of the unknown, we can add, within the generative, open mind/heart/will container of musical co-creation, a causal awareness which nurtures mutual responsibility, trust, respect, and non-judgment. This is why we musicians listen deeply. Listening guides action, action leads to outcome.

The Theory U framework indicates Presencing as something clearly taking place within the construct of time, e.g., while presencing, we are "present and sensing" *in the moment*, at the threshold of where the *present* meets the emerging *future*, with a desire as practitioners to sustain, or prolong the presencing state. Presencing practitioner focus seems to be directed toward cultivating a richness in the intimate relationship with attention, awareness or consciousness – typically depicted vertically, i.e. as something that moves downward, or "deeper". However, there seems to be little emphasis on the significance of cultivating an intimate relationship with time itself (typically depicted horizontally).

Here, it is relevant to distinguish between Chronos time (i.e., clock time) and time in a musical sense. For example, if musicians ask a drummer to "keep time", they mean for the drummer to communicate a steady musical pulse according to the tempo of the music being performed. In this case, the term "time" is one of convenience, as we're not concerned with the passage of seconds or minutes. Perhaps it is more precise for me to say that we musicians cultivate an intimate relationship with an ordered succession of musical events which, although existing in Chronos time, generally do not occur with any concern for Chronos time. During performance, the focus of our attention is on the events themselves, the spaces in between, and the meaning these hold relative to one another, thereby suspending the social construct of a ticking clock as having any significance.

In hypothesis, the profound quality of awareness that is Deep Listening, from which the participants (musicians) in a socioeconomic system (music ensemble) operate, is perhaps facilitated via an enhanced ability to first direct and sustain consciousness in the present moment, utilizing what I originally dubbed "Time-Rhythm orientation" - although "Temporal Orientation", borrowed from Cognitive Psychology, seems a more practical designation. Philosophers and psychologists do refer to temporal consciousness[45], however, by using the distinction of "orientation", I mean to imply that musicians are able to employ their awareness of temporality as a means of orienting themselves in the psychological present.[46]

This means of orientation allows masterful, musical improvisors to explore a deepening of consciousness within that present microcosmic moment, tapping into the available collective intelligence at hand. Further pursuance into this line of inquiry reveals a study investigating the significance of the human capacity to synchronize, or co-process, time. Researchers have found a connection between the ability to synchronize within a music ensemble setting, and cognitive characteristics - particularly the ability to focus and maintain attention.[47]

Deep Listening is an immersion into the co-created soundscape, resulting in a Flow experience where Chronos time feels suspended, as an ordered succession of musical events unfolds. The future emerges as the present moment, eventually becomes the past, the remnants of which may continue to linger, even with the advent of a new emerging future. This idea of realms of time just "being" touches upon theoretical concepts such as synchronic time perception (versus sequential time perception), or perhaps even more interesting, the theory of eternalism, a.k.a. the "block universe" theory of time, which states that the past, present, and future are all equally in existence, and our consciousness is present at a specific point in time. But just as places do not cease to exist when one leaves them, the past and future are not lost or imaginary simply because we are located in the present.[48]

The theory provides at the very least, a useful metaphor in Theory U context. Consider, for example, these passages via Scharmer:

> When our "self" and our (best/highest) "Self" begin to communicate, we establish a subtle but very real link to our highest future possibility that can then begin to help and guide us in situations in which the past can't offer us useful advice. When these two "selves" talk to each other, you experience the essence of presencing.[49]

Both the concept of Temporal Orientation and the theory of eternalism help bring the idea of a highest future Self closer, as in, "the future exists, right now". For me, this connection leads full circle back to a musical way of knowing. Not only are masterful improvisors able to direct and focus deeply conscious attention on and within the present moment, they are also capable of initiating intentional action in any increment of the present moment while being fully aware of how our actions might affect a future outcome. An image comes to mind, of a skilled juggler with three balls in play, in the "now": past, present, and future.

Sitting here without saxophone in hand, it strikes me as an even more powerful realization when placed in non-musical context: how awareness and intentionality in relationship to a connection between action and causality emerge through Deep Listening.

Deep Listening & Learning

The week before the making of his celebrated "80/81" album, jazz guitarist Pat Metheny brought most of the band he'd hired to record the project - Mike Brecker, Charlie Haden, and Jack DeJohnette, sans saxophonist Dewey Redman - to Ryles Jazz Club in Cambridge, Massachusetts. The group would "rehearse" before a live audience over the course of ten shows. I was on the guest list as a personal guest of Michael Brecker - literally one of the greatest saxophonists to ever walk the face of the earth. Mike was a warm, humble, generous giant, and an inspiring mentor for a number of saxophonists around the world.

I sat front row middle, two shows per night, during all five nights of the engagement, Monday through Friday. The bell of Mike's horn pointed directly at me. Witnessing the process of this music taking shape, powered by these gifted musicians – with particular focus on Mike's improvisational journey from Monday evening's cautious, tentative sight-reading of Metheny's scribbled lead sheets, to Friday night's glorious, virtuous, exuberant, winged flight of soulful tenor saxophone mastery continues to be one of the greatest lessons I've ever had.

This once-in-a-lifetime opportunity for an immersive Deep Listening learning experience at the hands of four of the foremost masters in the history of jazz music, which took place entirely from my perspective and role as an attentive, focused, participatory member of the audience was, mildly put, an epiphany for me. My (at the time) rather basic, theoretic, scale/arpeggio relationship to, understanding of, and approach to jazz improvisation was forever transformed.

The music was complex, and as of Monday's initial show, unrehearsed and clearly unfamiliar to all of the musicians except Pat. Each performance was a display of open mind, open heart, and open will, especially from all of us assembled in the room as the audience. Open mind in the sense of trusting that the musicians would find each other within the sparsely notated framework presented, and lead us somewhere meaningful. Open heart in the sense that all who were present truly wished for the musicians to succeed, and we enthusiastically supported the endeavor from tentative beginning until consummate manifestation. Open will in the sense, for me personally, that this music thing was, at age twenty-one, my chosen vocation, and I desperately wanted to understand what was happening before my ears and eyes, but at first, could fathom very little of it. There was so much searching, probing, and exploration underway on the bandstand, and very little fundament. Jack DeJohnette's drumming teased at an insinuation of steady time, Charlie Haden's acoustic bass reflected his roots performing the free jazz of Ornette Coleman, and was often non-committal in relation to rhythmic or harmonic core. Mike

Brecker had clearly given up on reading what there was of sheet music, and embraced uncertainty, relying upon his ears to guide him.

I came to the realization that Mike wasn't just performing, he was learning – and often failing in the most musical of ways, with Coltranesque sheets of sound laying forth harmonic and melodic possibilities which moved him closer to the truth with each attempt. An iterative cycle of crystallization, prototyping, and actualization; working and re-working passages; reflection-in-action while I sat before him reflecting-on-action.[50] Watching Mike's face, it was clear when he knew he was wrong, but he was never deterred. And through it all, Pat Metheny beamed. He literally smiled like the happiest man on earth, leading the proceedings in a non-judgmental container of trust and openness. As if he knew everything was going to be alright. And so I too refused to give up - after all, as a musician, not as the musician I was, but the best future musician Self I wanted to be - I *had* to understand, I *willed* to know. Something beyond my comprehension was clearly underway, and I refused to remain in the darkness of ignorance. Each night I left the club exhausted, returning early next evening to stand out of the way backstage, where I listened to the group's friendly, often comical banter before securing my usual seat, front row center. The performing musicians never talked about the music, as far as I knew. Backstage, there was no discussion about what had happened, what was about to happen, or what could happen. They simply enjoyed each other's company.

"There is a parallel between music and life, and I also believe that there must be a balance. One should try to get the most out of life, otherwise you won't have much to say through your instrument." [51] - *Saxophonist Michael Brecker*

On Wednesday night during the second show, suddenly it all clicked. What I mean is, it all clicked for me. First, I was reminded of how much practicing I'd have to do, but I already knew that. More importantly, what I began to understand was that in musical improvisation, beyond scale patterns and technical facility, there's a certain energy that exists at the threshold of the present moment and the uncertain, emerging future. It's the energy from a co-creative flame that is fed as a group of musicians come together, with their path of action informed through Deep Listening. It's the same type of energy I would not forsake, many years later, during that evening in Osaka, Japan.

One way of picturing the threshold is as a massive, yet permeable wall of bright light. Before I began to picture it this way, I would often fail at this threshold, by giving up as if I wasn't worthy or didn't have what it takes to pass through. A confrontation took place here, not with the wall of light, but with myself. Walking through required a leap of faith, and I, myself, didn't believe. My Self, however, has always believed– this is why I have practiced deliberately since the age of sixteen – the two just had to be connected. The energy at the threshold is sacred, and it takes commitment to keep the flame burning. This is "the eye of the needle". As an improvising musician, I have to commit to what feels like not a leap of faith - it's more deliberate than that: it's a simple step forward without judgment, without cynicism, without fearing, for example, that I lack whatever it takes to execute that simple step forward. Perhaps the voice of fear whispers more quietly than we think. I have to leave that kind of baggage behind, every time I perform.

What I learned that Wednesday evening of May 29, 1980 is, an authentic Self is not a perfect Self. You bring what you have that is essential and shed everything non-essential. In music, the most essential part is the story all of us have to tell. My particular story may, at times, not be as polished as I'd like it to be, but it is authentic, and when lifted, carried, or born by the combined, authentic stories of my co-creators, it becomes woven into a musical tapestry. Perhaps my bandmates experience a struggle similar to mine at the eye of the needle, but I wouldn't know. As we bare our souls in this generative, musical field of social presencing, I perceive them as the best version of their Selves. Forty years have passed since that defining musical and life lesson at Ryles Jazz Club, yet the insight which emerged during that week in May 1980 continues to inform my evolvement as a musician and as a human being.

Skill Acquisition, Expertise & Mastery

Addressing the earlier Presencing practitioner query regarding what is needed to take presencing to the "next", or mastery level - and perhaps in indirect response to the core question that underlies Theory U and methodology, "What is required in order to learn and act from the future as it emerges?", one might conceivably contemplate the inclusion of a discussion on expertise in the Presencing mastery conversation.

Continual references to mastery-level musical improvisation performance seem to call upon a parallel drawn to the performance dynamic in the social field of presencing, at the "U" movement from co-presencing to co-creation and beyond. According to K. Anders Ericsson, whose work has had a major impact on the trajectory of research regarding expert performance,

> Most people find it inconceivable that the dramatic differences between expert and novice performance can be explained by a series of incremental improvements starting at the novice level. It is common belief that most of the benefits of learning are attained rapidly within weeks or months as is the case for most everyday skills and leisure activities. People are generally surprised to hear that it takes years, even decades, of gradual improvements for even the most 'talented' to reach the highest levels of performance. Even then, the attainment of expert performance requires an extended period of high level deliberate practice, where the duration of practice is limited by the ability to sustain concentration, a capacity that appears to increase as a function of years of practice in the domain. Given that very few individuals sustain commitment to newly acquired skill for more than a few months, much less years, most individuals will never know the upper limit of their performance."

"Research on expertise shows that for everyday performance (e.g. skiing, playing tennis, driving a car, et al.) participants will after some limited period of training and experience, reach an acceptable standard of performance which can be generated without much need for effortful attention. At this point, execution of the everyday activity will attain the characteristics of automated performance. From this point, without conscious effort directed toward maintaining and extending skill, performance levels will taper off and begin to decrease as individuals lose conscious control over intentionally modifying and changing their level of performance. A desire to attain some level of mastery in a domain of expertise is not by itself enough to reach the desired level. Master practitioners across several domains of expertise all describe the critical role played by motivation and willingness to continue work. [52]

Taking these findings into consideration, it should come as no surprise of it being commonplace amongst practitioners that they perceive reaching a plateau fairly early on in their Presencing experience. The time required to attain expertise or mastery level varies across domains, in some cases, anywhere from ten years to several decades.

Notably, Hambrick et al. (2014) dispute the degree to which deliberate practice is as significant a factor in expert performance as argued by Ericsson; Ericsson rejects the arguments presented by Hambrick et al., who offer no alternative theory, but merely wish to debate significance percentages.[53] In my experience as an expert practitioner, deliberate practice is and has always been a significant factor (long before my knowledge of Ericsson's research) in both my emergence as a professional musician and ongoing development as an artist, and is something I would continue to recommend to whoever will listen. Furthermore, much of the discussion between my international colleagues and I, across various social media platforms, or via blogs maintained by respected music professionals, revolves precisely around how deliberately we practice, as well as the content and methodology used in our practice sessions.

The common-sense message here for serious practitioners seems to be, achievement of Presencing mastery requires active effort, commitment, motivation, structured, deliberate practice, and subsequent reflective analysis. If the reader should take anything away from the accounts herein regarding my personal experiences in the music domain, perhaps it might be that an ability to operate from a deeper quality of attention, consciousness, or awareness is not to be taken for granted. The challenges in doing so remain ever present, even after decades of immersive experience, achievement of mastery level, and sustained, deliberate practice.

An additional thought comes to mind: perhaps the shift to a truly distributed, more deeply connected sense of being in the world may take place in a later phase of Presencing mastery, as was the case during my Stage 3 phase of Emergence, where musical improvisation abilities also became more intuitive.[54]

Experienced Presencing practitioners point to meditation and mindfulness as essential foundational practices.[55] If meditation and mindfulness are to be perceived as skills in which expertise or mastery is attainable, then research on expertise may be applicable here as well, indicating a necessity for deliberate practice, in that even prolonged experience within a particular discipline may not lead to expertise or mastery, without considerable effort being invested in conscious control over intentionally modifying and changing the level of performance. Buddhist monks undergo years of training under the guidance of a mentor; in the music domain, we have several hundred years of model musicianship to emulate, an established system of higher education institutions, as well as vast libraries of recordings and published works which enable us to pursue mastery under direct or indirect, even virtual, mentorship.

In the interest of facilitating accessibility to the development and extension of Presencing skill with the means at hand, I propose the idea that practitioners interested in tackling complex societal problems via utilization of the Theory U framework, might, as an exercise in deliberate practice, incorporate conscious exploration of complexity alongside their foundational (and deliberate) practice of meditation and mindfulness. One highly accessible way to explore complexity is through intuitive music listening. Studies published over the past twenty years have suggested that music listening expertise does not need to be taught; in fact, the knowledge gained through formal musical training may be rather tangential to the skills required to be an expert listener. Listening expertise can, for non-performers, instill a sense of co-creation on the music work in progress, whether live or recorded.

> A listener does more than passively experience the music. The listener co-creates the experience along with the performers, making the experience come to life for themselves. Intuitive listening involves experiencing-in-action—that is, perceiving the music as it happens, creating expectations of what may happen, reflecting on what has happened, and interacting affectively with these perceptions. The individual listener is the arbiter of where to pay attention and how much, consciously or unconsciously. This flux of experiencing is constant and inseparable from other aspects of noticing and responding.[56]

The implication here is that many of the skills associated with music performers in this writing, which seem to facilitate their Deep Listening/Presencing ease and mastery, are conceivably scalable to non-musicians, hereunder Presencing practitioners in non-musical contexts.

Deep Listening, From Theory to Practice

"Don't play what's there. Play what's not there." - *Miles Davis*

As a musical director, I began to introduce the above phrase in rehearsals whenever applicable; beyond making me look "cool", there always seemed to be a beneficial outcome in that more "space" was created in the music. Space opens up possibility. I decided to examine the dynamics more deeply: what has to happen for this level of listening to take place?

First, there's the act of acknowledging what is, by perceiving the sounds emanating from the other musicians. Then there's a conscious shift, a "letting go" - although not in the sense of disregarding the musical co-creation in progress. The awareness of 'what is' maintains context as one directs attention toward "what's not there" in the figurative silence of uninhabited musical space, where the possibility of what might be, exists.

Within this realm of possibility, there are many potential emerging futures until, guided by Deep Listening, we musicians co-shift attention toward what gradually begins to unfold as a collectively-chosen path. "Speaking" an intangible whole into existence, initiated by allowing its seedling notes and phrases to be heard and received by others, serves the formation of what is to be. The evolving crystallization of notes and phrases may be new and novel in that we, as individuals or a collective, may never before have produced a performance of that nature.

During moments like these, we may be connecting to and operating from a source of musical knowledge providing collective intelligence in the form of audible clues and fragments of language and history. Patterns absorbed and embodied throughout decades of practice and performance. Our capacity for listening allows us to sense each other's mode of confronting the emerging future. In these intuitive moments of pattern recognition, whether the recognition itself is conscious or subconscious, there exists anticipation, expectation, and predictability. Just as the supposition of a particular consequence often seems to make it more likely to happen simply by directing conscious attention toward the anticipated event, a similar dynamic applies to improvised musical journeys.

During a recent performance, my co-creators and I, present and sensing, found ourselves on a journey of blissful, free improvisation from formlessness to form. Surprisingly, to all of us including the audience, the musical exploration culminated in a quote from "Jean-Pierre" - a Miles Davis composition. The event was remarkable in that it was somewhat out of context; however, our listening had guided us in that direction.

I found it fascinating that a presencing experience could lead to an outcome that, in effect, amounts to downloading - that an emerging future can also present patterns of the past. We connected to a source - in this case, Miles - but it seems we hadn't connected to *the* source. The downloaded performance solution we arrived at - achieved via "sensing from the field/listening from the whole" - was quite effective in eliciting an enthusiastic audience response to the unexpected musical coalescence. In that limited sense, our performance achieved a higher purpose. However, the fact remains that during those few measures of music, we had not created anything profoundly new.

Consequently, it seems that beyond the mastery allowing this somewhat evolved form of downloading to emerge during Presencing, there must exist a tacit agreement between co-creators that we disregard the impulse to re-create, favorable as it may be, rather than create. Additionally, there has to be an awareness of, and capacity for, discernment between various nuances of unrealized potential that inevitably accompany an emerging future. The shift requires a degree of in-the-moment discipline and will, and is perhaps how, as mentioned earlier, an enhanced ability to direct and sustain consciousness in the present moment comes into play, as masterful musicians experience the present moment as a "universal microcosm" within which there is space to operate.

"Operate" seems to be the keyword. When introducing the Presencing journey to unfamiliar ears, a common association accepts the concept as a means of guidance via intuition. As inadequate as such a rudimentary interpretation may be, the usage of the word "intuition" is not entirely off-base. If I've described my musical improvisation experiences at least somewhat accurately, what comes to light is the capability to both invoke cognitive control (evaluation, deliberation, discernment) as well as relinquish this control to an informed intuition, instantaneously. And additionally, a capacity to fluctuate between the cognitive and intuitive at will without interrupting the performance flow. Whereas common "gut" intuition seems to be a momentary state followed by rational, or sometimes irrational mental interpretation, the ability to be guided by informed or "mature" intuition[57] is an operational mode of performance richly grounded in mastery, structures of knowledge, and experience. If such a capacity for high-level performance relies upon a myriad of embodied ways with which to confront and solve various emerging issues, then surely we can learn to let re-creations pass and allow (and have patience for) the novel to arise.

Perhaps this points to an additional dimension or dynamic of Deep Listening and Presencing, toward developing a collective capacity for discerning the profoundly new, a step beyond an acknowledgment of "what's not there" in the silence of uninhabited (musical) space. Toward this end, I've been cultivating a handful of simple practices (however inconclusive they may be at this point) in the interest of discovering methods to facilitate Presencing and Deep Listening in non-musical contexts.

Exploring Complexity

Years ago, on my first music tour to Yaounde, Cameroon, my hosts thought I would appreciate a more immersive cultural experience and checked me into a hotel situated in a local neighborhood. The alternative was a stay inside the walled city of one of the international hotel chains. I agreed.

As we drove up to the hotel on a Saturday shortly after midnight, there were hundreds of people swarming around in the streets out front; there was loud, blaring music, prominent illicit activity, along with street food vendors and party people everywhere. I'm a seasoned solo traveler, and as a musician, I get invited to all kinds of places from the underbelly of the world to the glitzy side. However, this was a cacophony of human activity incomparable to anything I had experienced earlier, even in huge cities. At first impression, it was frightening.

One thing I've learned from extensive international travel: watch and observe. Not in judgment, but to learn. After a while, you can sense the rhythm of the surrounding atmosphere, see patterns in people's movements, figure out who the regulars are and who is just passing through, etc. One also learns to read people's faces and nuances of expression. Initially, what might have sounded like a harsh, aggressive tone of voice can later be understood for what it is: a typical, friendly local greeting. It becomes clear when observing the interaction between two people and the reaction, or lack of, from those in the immediate vicinity.

Gradually I ventured out, further and further away from the hotel. I love sampling local street food and made that my mission. My French language skills are elementary at best, but communicating around food is easy; everybody enjoys sharing their culture through food. Within a couple of days, most of the regulars on the street knew who I was and called out my name whenever they saw me. I talked to everybody: the hotel personnel, shop owners on the street, their kids, police officers, etc. Saturday night, one week later, I was out and about in the same neighborhood that was so frightening when I arrived, but this time laughing, dancing, tasting food, and enjoying the local beer.

I often tell this story as an example of what I understand as "listening to the field". At first glance, from a perspective of not-knowing, it's a way of observing and sensing interactions that appear complex until patterned behaviors begin to emerge more clearly. A means of learning to decipher the "code" of a social field.

Although it's not every day there's an opportunity to explore a foreign culture, I've found other ways of exploring complexity and not-knowing. Through seeking out the unfamiliar, for example, by visiting contemporary art exhibitions, listening to evolved conversations on subjects I don't know much about at lectures and asking questions to learn, or listening to music that I don't understand (practicing intuitive music listening), the unknown becomes less daunting. The exercise itself contributes to my general body of knowledge, and gradually, I've become comfortable in this abstract space. With practice, one begins to sense subtle connections between seemingly disparate crystallizations of human expression within a social field.

Breathing, Listening, and Learning

As a saxophonist and wind instrumentalist, I know that controlling the flow of air is central to proficiency in performance. Without getting into too much technical detail, I am currently exploring a daily instrumental practice centered around the lowest volume threshold where air becomes sound. You might try to imagine a volume so soft it borders on nothingness. In the five decades of practice that have passed since childhood, this is uncharted territory, and I find that the lower extreme challenges my ability to control airflow more than the full-on "blowing" that often takes place during live performance.

The premise for initiating this practice began with the idea that I wanted the sensation of projecting air through my saxophone to feel just as free as a normal human exhalation of breath. I'll spare the reader for the many physical and physiological transactions which take place when playing a wind instrument and suffice to say that the warm-up to this practice routine begins with deep breathing sans saxophone.

The warm-up takes place in silence. In a city-dwelling such as where I live, silence is relative. Here, I combine the discipline of listening for "what's not there" with breathing, acknowledging the bustle of the city, shifting attention past the noise in search of the spaces uninhabited by sound as I inhale and exhale. The hypothesis here being, that to recognize such uninhabited sound space within the chaos of activity, it makes sense to first become comfortable with extended silence and what it "sounds" or "feels" like. An advanced version of the exercise takes place in the tumult of airport departure halls while waiting for flights during layovers: Observe, sense the rhythm of the field, listen for the uninhabited silence, inhale and exhale in controlled cycles, register whatever may emerge, be open for new and unexpected thoughts and ideas. One might also attempt the exercise in nature. This form of directed listening, combined with the mindful, present, "performance" of controlled breathing, seems somehow applicable to enhancing performance capacity on stage, as well as nurturing an engaged, empathic "way of being" in personal life. I wish I'd had the opportunity to test this practice years ago during that week in Yaounde.

A central component of the daily actions mentioned above involves reflection and journaling. Deep Listening plays an instrumental role in my livelihood as a musician, creative leader, educator, and facilitator, and personal relationships as well. It's essential to record and reflect upon not only the triumphs and successes, but also, and in particular, the failures, the lapses, and the missed opportunities for more profound social and relational engagement and the co-creative, beneficial outcomes of these interactions.

Closing Remarks

During this exploration of Theory U and Presencing from the perspective of improvisational music performance, I have sought to illustrate various qualities of the masterful music improvisor's mindset and way of being, which I view as relevant to extending Presencing ability.

I've examined how masterful, improvising musicians may interact in performance scenarios utilizing Deep Listening to inform co-creative action resulting in artful outcomes, and have discussed their ease of access to the social field of presencing, a confident "knowing-in-not-knowing" which they bring to the generative field, and how Deep Listening itself provides an opportunity for profound learning. Furthermore, I have hypothesized regarding Temporal Orientation, implying that a heightened capacity to sustain and direct consciousness in the present allows one to explore a deepening of consciousness within that present moment.

Additionally, I've suggested that achieving mastery in more complex domains requires persistence over the long term, intention, and the cultivation of favorable practices resulting in a consistent level of performance relative to a social field of masterful peers. Toward this end, I propose that by connecting models for achieving expertise, skill in perceiving meaning through various modes of listening and sensing, and a capacity for collaboration, one might develop a scaffolding upon which to extend Presencing ability.

Perhaps most significantly, I point to (and attempt to illustrate) a potential additional dimension or dynamic of Deep Listening and Presencing, revealing itself as a collective capacity for discerning the profoundly new, one step beyond an immediate acknowledgment of the future as it emerges.

Finally, I suggest that enhanced listening-oriented skills exhibited by masterful musicians may be acquired and mastered incrementally by non-musicians and have included practices under development which (with some refinement) may serve to extend Presencing capabilities.

With the intention of bringing Presencing to diverse fractals of society via "the means at hand", I have highlighted an element of inclusiveness, being that improvisation is a generative capacity which all humans possess, music listening expertise is a skill that does not need to be taught, and expertise or mastery in a domain can be achieved in manageable increments over time. Consequently, I maintain that a range of critical skillsets possessed by masterful music improvisors, which facilitate a heightened capacity for Deep Listening and Presencing, are conceivably scalable to non-musicians, hereunder Presencing practitioners in non-musical contexts.

Further steps in my Deep Listening research will include drawing in-depth connections from my current daily practices to various relevant meditative, cognitive, and performance practices. In working toward facilitating Deep Listening journeys for others, future directions for inquiry in the immediate future include:

- How one might enable Presencing practitioners to "feel" the generative capacity of music improvisation (without having to learn an instrument);
- Cultivating my current deliberate practices as described in this chapter, into models for the incremental development of Presencing expertise;
- How one might enable Presencing practitioners to "feel" the human capacity to collectively synchronize, or co-process, time – and "suspend" Chronos time via Temporal Orientation exercises;
- Continued exploration concerning various techniques for engaging "complexity" and developing capacities for "listening to the field"; and finally,
- Continued reflection regarding the habits, practices, and "ways of being" of masterful music improvisors, and how

these may serve to illuminate new inroads to the Presencing experience.

One breath at a time.

References

Barbezat, D. P., & Bush, M. (2014). Contemplative practices in higher education: Powerful methods to transform teaching and learning. San Francisco: Jossey-Bass.

Baylor, A. L. (2001). A U-shaped model for the development of intuition by level of expertise. New Ideas in Psychology. 19, 237–244. doi: 10.1016/S0732-118X(01)00005-8

Bidwell, D. R. (2015). Deep Listening and Virtuous Friendship: Spiritual Care in the Context of Religious Multiplicity. (2015, Vol.35, (p.3-13).) Honolulu: University of Hawaii Press.

Caspari, Anne. (2017, August 30). Presencing and the Scaling Problem. Retrieved November 18, 2018, from https://www.linkedin.com/pulse/presencing-we-space-change-makers-greatest-anne-caspari/

Dainton, B. (2017, June 28). Temporal Consciousness. Stanford University. Retrieved October 31, 2018, from https://plato.stanford.edu/archives/fall2017/entries/consciousness-temporal/.

Deci, E. L., & Vansteenkiste, M. (2004). Self-determination theory and basic need satisfaction: Understanding human development in positive psychology. Ricerche Di Psicologia, 27, 1, 23-40.

Dunn, R. E. (2006). Teaching for Lifelong, Intuitive Listening. Arts Education Policy Review, 107(3), 33-38.

Ericsson, K. A. (2002). Attaining Excellence Through Deliberate Practice: Insights from the Study of Expert Performance. In Teaching and Learning (eds C. Desforges and R. Fox).

Ericsson, K. Anders. (2008) "Deliberate Practice and Acquisition of Expert Performance: A General Overview." Academic Emergency Medicine, vol. 15, no. 11. pp. 988–994.

Fraisse, P. (January 01, 1984). Perception and Estimation of Time. Annual Review of Psychology, 35, 1, 1-37.

Garfias, R., & Kokuritsu Minzokugaku Hakubutsukan. (2004). Music: The cultural context. Osaka: National Museum of Ethnology.

Geller, S. M., & Greenberg, L. S. (2012). Therapeutic presence: A mindful approach to effective therapy. Washington, DC, US: American Psychological Association.

Gunnlaugson, Olen. (2020). Dynamic Presencing: A Journey into Presencing Mastery, Leadership and Flow. Trifoss Business Press, Vancouver.

Gunnlaugson, Olen. (2016 lecture, University of Massachusetts, Boston). Portrait Of The Dialogue Artist.

Hambrick, David Z., et al. (2014) "Accounting for Expert Performance: The Devil Is in the Details." Intelligence, vol. 45, no. 1, Elsevier Inc. pp. 112–114.

Hanh, T. N. (2005). Happiness: Essential mindfulness practices. Parallax Press.

Isaacs, William N. (1999). "Dialogic Leadership." The Systems Thinker, Pegasus Communications, vol. 10, No. 1.

Jaworski, J. (2012, p. 45). Source: The Inner Path of Knowledge Creation. San Francisco: Berrett-Koehler Publishers.

Keller, Peter E. (2013) "Musical Ensemble Performance : A Theoretical Framework and Empirical Findings on Interpersonal Coordination." Proceedings of the International Symposium on Performance Science 2013, pp. 271–285.

Khalil, Alexander. (2010). The Gamelan Project : Teaching , Playing with , and Learning from American Schoolchildren Playing Balinese Gamelan. Freer|Sackler. Retrieved December 5, 2017, from http://archive.asia.si.edu/research/performing-indonesia/article-khalil.php

Kudesia, R. S. (2015). Mindfulness and creativity in the workplace. Mindfulness in Organizations: Foundations, Research, and Applications, 190-212.

Limb, C. J., & Braun, A. R. (2008). Neural substrates of spontaneous musical performance: An fMRI study of jazz improvisation. PLoS one, 3(2), e1679.

Oliveros, P. (2005). Deep listening: A composer's sound practice. New York: Universe.

Peterson, Lloyd. (2006). Interview with Pat Metheny, "Music and the Creative Spirit: Innovators in Jazz, Improvisation, and the Avant Garde". Scarecrow Press.

Pohjannoro, Ulla. (2016) "Capitalising on Intuition and Reflection: Making Sense of a Composer's Creative Process." Musicae Scientiae, vol. 20, no. 2.

Pym, J. (2010). Listening to the light: How to bring Quaker simplicity and integrity into our lives. London: Ebury Digital.

Ricketts, Bobby. (1987). Interview with Michael Brecker, "Jazz Har Det Godt". Musikmagasinet MM Vol. 10.

Ricketts, B. (2017). Deep Listening. Retrieved October 28, 2017, from http://bobbyricketts.com/#deep-listening

Scharmer, C. O. (2009). Theory U: Learning from the future as it emerges. Berrett-Koehler Publishers.

Schön, D. A. (2017). The reflective practitioner: How professionals think in action. London: Routledge.

Skow, B. (2009). Relativity and the moving spotlight. The Journal of Philosophy, 106(12), 666-678.

Sridharan, Devarajan, et al. (2007) Article Neural Dynamics of Event Segmentation in Music: Converging Evidence for Dissociable Ventral and Dorsal Networks. pp. 521–532.

Taylor, Peter J. (2017). Faculty advisor comments to Bobby Ricketts, University of Massachusetts Boston CCT Graduate Program.

Weick, K. E. (1998). Introductory essay—Improvisation as a mindset for organizational analysis. Organization science, 9(5), 543-555.

CHAPTER 9

Arts-based Interventions as a Series of Methods to Access Presencing

Lotte Darsø and Cecilie Meltzer

Introduction

According to Theory U, as a collective, we need focus on moving from an ego-system awareness that cares only about oneself, to an eco-system awareness that cares about the well-being of the whole, including the Self (Scharmer & Kãufer, 2013). Equally, "Pioneering the principles and personal practices that help us perform this shift may well be one of the most important undertakings of our time" (ibid, 2013, p. 2). Here, Scharmer and Kãufer suggest the need for a shift of consciousness; a move from the inner place from where we normally operate, towards a place where we can access the future that wants to emerge. The question is: Which principles and practices can we apply to access the future that wants to emerge? As an overall approach, we suggest working with arts-based interventions.

In this chapter, we will introduce a series of arts-based interventions for the purpose of accessing and transcending the deeper parts of the U-process. In our experience, moving from Seeing to Sensing, Presencing and onwards to Crystallizing, represent the most interesting and challenging parts of Theory U. Our aim in this chapter is to answer the question: How can arts-based interventions prepare and support Presencing, and thereby learning from the future as it emerges?

What can art do? Why art? Briefly put, art is the pathway into our feelings and our humanity (Eisner, 2008). Art can be a gateway through which we can 'escape' the limitations of our mental models and make us aware of new perspectives and new solutions. Art is also a way of accessing our tacit bodily knowledge; that which we do not know that we know (Darsø, 2017). Arts-based interventions offer a range of approaches when examining a given challenge or topic. We see them as unique, as they provide original perspectives, innovative possibilities and added learning from the emerging future (Meltzer, 2016). Here, different artefacts (such as photos, paintings, drawings or sculptures) or expressive art forms (such as singing, movement or drama) may be incorporated as part of the process. This detour via the arts, taking part in creative work, sensing and identifying with a chosen symbol, person, material or artwork, may redirect our attention towards what is meaningful and what makes a difference.

Overall, this chapter will demonstrate and explain how arts-based interventions can assist the Theory U focus and the Presencing process. We will argue that embodiment and identification with an artefact or art form can give people access to deeper layers of knowing of which they were not previously conscious. More specifically, we will introduce arts-based methods that we have found work well for Sensing, Presencing and Crystallizing.

The chapter is organized as follows: After presenting our reflections on Sensing, Presencing and Crystallizing, we will present relevant research findings on thought processes, brainwaves, consciousness and applied quantum theory. Then we will introduce and define a selection of arts-based interventions. We will apply these theoretical frameworks and selected concepts from the field of arts-based research and practice for interpreting our empirical data.

In the following, we have selected four cases derived from different Nordic educational contexts and will argue how they are reciprocal in confirming the empirical applicability of Theory

U. The first two cases were built around Theory U; i.e. moving from theory to practice, whereas the other two cases, meanwhile, were developed and conducted independently of Theory U. When analyzed in a Theory U perspective, the two latter cases implicate Sensing and Presencing; i.e. moving from practice to theory. In the case description, we will present a variety of methods we have developed and explored in practice. We will explain our methods in more detail and exemplify those using empirical data, regarding the participants' experiences and expressed thoughts, feelings and reflections. We *will illustrate how arts-based interventions can offer experiences of relief, illuminate themes, convey deeper understanding and new insights, and provide further awareness of our authentic selves, our patterns of behaviour and our belief systems (Darsø, 2014).* Equally, we will argue and demonstrate how arts-based interventions can provide access to Presencing and one's creative potential. *This process enlightens our will and points us forward from Presencing towards Crystallizing. Before* concluding the chapter, we will outline some critical aspects and considerations regarding the use of arts-based interventions.

Theory U: Sensing

Scharmer illustrates Sensing as a process where perception moves from inside people's heads, looking out across the field, to outside the normal boundaries of the observer. He refers to the field as "the grounding condition, the living soil, from which grows that which only later becomes visible to the eye" (Scharmer, 2007, p. 9). According to him, an indicator of Sensing is when you begin to see yourself as part of the problem, as part of the system (Scharmer, 2007, p. 147). Sensing is related to the Open Heart, i.e. to our feelings. How do we get from Seeing with the Open Mind to Sensing from the Open Heart? This is where art becomes relevant. As Elliot Eisner has stated: "…the arts are largely forms that generate emotion" (Eisner, 2008, p. 3). Through art, we can get in touch with our tacit bodily knowledge. This knowledge can be transformed from being pre-verbal and not conscious into some form or shape that becomes meaningful and begins to make sense. There are several artful ways to enter Sensing, such as music (listening), acting (embodying), focusing and identification.

Presencing

Presencing "means to sense, to tune in, and act from one's highest future potential" (Scharmer, 2007, p. 8). Perception still happens from the field, but now including both the current field as well as the future field, "the beings who surround us" (2007, p. 106). The threshold of Presencing, or the eye of the needle, demands that we shift the inner place from which we operate. It means letting go of our ego and striving to enter a state of openness, willing to be inspired by the future that wants to emerge through our altruistic Self. In a quantum perspective, Presencing means being able to reach an energetic state that leads into the space of potentiality. When Scharmer points out that we can be stopped by the 'Voice of Fear', this can be explained both as fear of losing our ego and fear of the unknown. Dispenza describes this process as going from the conscious to the subconscious, from selfish to unselfish, from the known to the unknown, where we can find answers to shape and create the future (Dispenza, 2014, p. 190).

Crystallizing

According to Scharmer (2007, p. 192), "Crystallizing means clarifying vision and intention from our highest future possibility." He continues by suggesting that this is only possible if we keep connecting to our Source, being our authentic Self, connecting to "the grand will" and beginning to operate from it (ibid, p. 202). The difference between envisioning and crystallizing is the level of attention. Envisioning can be a more superficial process, even created from a Downloading perspective, whereas Crystallizing derives from a more profound process. Crystallization is a defining moment for individuals and groups. In research on innovation, Darsø defined it: "... as the outcome of a process involving collective transformation of accumulated and integrated ideas into a new conceptualization or prototype" (Darsø, 2011, p. 173). Whether for individuals or groups, however, Crystallizing can be quite demanding. Even if people are open towards "letting come" and try to listen to what emerges from within, crystallization does not happen every time. It comes in many, often very subtle, forms, especially when working at a personal level. In our experience, Crystallizing frequently needs a trigger in order to emerge. We will, therefore, outline methods we have successfully worked with in practice after presenting our theoretical considerations.

Theoretical frameworks

How are we to understand "learning from the future that wants to emerge"? And ..." how can we access, activate and enact the deeper layers of the social field?" (Scharmer, 2007, p. 8). What characterizes the mystery of Presencing, and how does this involve thought processes, brain waves, consciousness and quantum theory? In the following, we want to explore consciousness as a central concept for understanding Presencing. According to the International Dictionary of Psychology, consciousness is defined as having perceptions, thoughts, and feelings, and being aware (Chalmers, 1996). Chalmers furthermore characterizes being conscious as an internal subjective quality of an experience (ibid., p. 4).

More than a century ago (1895), Freud introduced the concepts of primary and secondary thought processes, which are complementary. Primary thought processes have a dream-like quality, are associative and nonverbal. Secondary thought processes are analytical, accurate and verbal. Zohar and Marshall added tertiary thought processes, which are unitive, integrative and creative. Corresponding intelligences are Emotional Intelligence (EQ), Intellectual Intelligence (IQ) and Spiritual Intelligence (SQ) (Zohar & Marshall, 2000). To this, we add scientific research about different types of brain waves: Beta waves are our ordinary, everyday consciousness. Alpha waves are slower and give rise to creativity and fantasy. Theta waves can be described as a condition of being half-awake –and half-asleep, which is a meditative state. Delta waves are deep sleep. Finally, gamma waves are linked to a heightened level of consciousness (Dispenza, 2014; Zohar & Marshall, 2000).

Quantum physics, biology, cosmology, brain and consciousness research in the last century indicated that we, as human beings, no longer can see ourselves as separate from the world. Scientists found that "the universe is wholly and enduringly coherent", indicating a connection and communication between all living systems, whether an atom, organism or galaxy (McCraty, Deyhle, & Childre, 2012, p. 66). In quantum physics, which is today as accepted as Newtonian physics, the world is understood as fundamentally inseparable. However, "although quantum fields are mathematically similar to classical fields, they are more difficult to understand because, unlike classical fields, they exist outside the usual boundaries of space-time" (Radin, 1997, p. 158). Everything, both the tangible and the intangible, involves matter (particles) and energy (waves).

However, particles and waves cannot be perceived or studied at the same time, as everything exists as potential in quantum space. What we focus on exists in the moment as particles or waves, but disappears when we stop focusing. According to Dispenza, it is possible to access the space of potentiality in the quantum field if we can create more energy in brain frequency, vibration and wavelength (Dispenza, 2014, p. 226). He demonstrates in several cases that this can be done by changing our consciousness and brain waves through meditation combined with a heightened sensitivity for compassion and gratitude (Dispenza, 2014, 2017). Equally, people may connect to their deeper intelligence and awareness and reach a sense of ease and flow through several types of developmental work, like breathing exercises, heart-focused meditation and listening to uplifting music (McCraty, Deyhle, & Childre, 2012).

Our focus here is, however, the process of *becoming* conscious of something hitherto concealed, the ability to focus our attention, and, in relation to the above, to enact different types of brain waves. In Theory U, Scharmer proposes four levels of attention, which he defines as social fields. Already in 1898, William James proposed that consciousness had a fieldlike quality. Later Rupert Sheldrake suggested that "morphic fields" exist as wholes both within and around an organism. According to Sheldrake, the brain can be understood as a tuning instrument that can access different fields, rather than a container of thoughts, feelings and memories (Sheldrake, 1987). Eventually, Eleanor Rosch emphasized that what designates a field is the integration of intention, body and mind (Scharmer, 2007, p. 149).

Radin connects consciousness to quantum theory: "The idea of field consciousness suggests a continuum of nonlocal intelligence, permeating space and time" (Radin, 1997, p. 159). He suggests that consciousness can "affect the probabilities of events" and that "the strength of consciousness . . . is regulated by the focus of attention" (ibid., p. 160). This is consistent with Scharmer, who, in relation to Presencing, explains that "the I-in-now is the primary spark of intentional and attentive attention", and he continues that "this spark is the key to unlocking the deeper sources of emergence" (Scharmer, 2007, p. 259). We, therefore, want to highlight the importance of the state of consciousness and the focus of attention for accessing the space of potentiality.

What makes artistic work interesting and relevant here is exactly how creative activity and play may move a person into a "potential space", a realm of experience placed between the internal and external reality (Winnocott, 1971). Winnicott saw this potential space as sacred, as it represents a place where individuals express their creativity and experience that life is worth living. Contact with this space may be compared to "heart-based living", where people enter "a global information field that connects all living systems and consciousness", a space supporting positive change and enabling creative solutions (McCraty, Deyhle, & Childre, 2012, p. 64).

Arts-based Interventions

Being creative addresses both the conscious and subconscious mind. Involvement in art-therapy and arts-based learning processes likewise offer creative detours via the arts to discover aspects of the self. In addition, the artwork or outcome assumes a symbolic significance, as it may contain known and foreseen as well as unexpected and surprising elements (Jung, von Franz, Henderson, Jacobi, & Jadde, 1964; Ronnberg & Martin, 2010). Sensing and reflecting upon the initiative to action, the unfolding process and the created product may cause a shift in awareness; moving from an inner programming, seeing challenges as indissoluble or immovable, to the discovery of solutions, not previously seen (Malchiodi, 2007; Meltzer, 2015; Scharmer & Kaeufer, 2010). Preconceived expectations of the future can likewise be altered by adding additional parts to the original artwork, concretizing new and desired outcomes. In this way, artwork may enhance personal development and strengthen the individual's and groups' resources in finding new and more creative ways to tackle challenges encountered in educational or working life (Buswick & Seifter, 2010; Darsø, 2014; Meltzer, 2016; Taylor & Ladkin, 2009).

The research on arts-based interventions has evolved considerably during the last decade (Berthoin Antal & Strauss, 2016; Darsø, 2004, 2016; Karkou, 2010; Mitchell, Weber, & O'Reilly-Scanlon, 2005; Ray & Myers, 1986; Sköldberg et al., 2016). The mentioned research reflects the possibilities in this type of work (Creative Partnerships, 2010; Scharmer & Kaeufer, 2010; Taylor & Ladkin, 2009), as well as providing descriptions of the learning process (Austring & Sørensen, 2006; Malchiodi, 2007; Meltzer, 2015). In the following, we introduce a range of arts-based methods, which are both similar and different. They are similar in the sense that all the methods involve art. The difference is related to purpose, focus and means.

Art-therapy is a therapeutic approach where people with specific emotional and social needs express and examine themes using different art materials. The purpose is to achieve personal development and psychological change. The methods used in arts-based interventions resemble the way one works in art-therapy, as both approaches involve individual participation and self-experience with creative work (Betensky, 1995; Malchiodi, 2007; Taylor & Ladkin, 2009). There are, however, some important differences between participation in art-therapeutic sessions and arts-based interventions.

Arts-based interventions and learning approaches, being used in education and working life, reach out to a far wider audience. Although arts-based learning methods also involve personal development, the intention is not to go deep into an individual's background and life history. Instead, these approaches are educational and learning tools aimed at cultivating personal and/or group development and creativity. Here, the emphasis may be on the creative process, experimentation, developing skills and discovering new perspectives on self, a subject or theme.

The work of Gendlin (2003) and his colleagues provide a valuable contribution when it comes to understanding the value of art-therapy and arts-based methods. To find out what characterized successful therapy, they analysed thousands of recorded therapy sessions. Here, they found that effective therapy was related to people's ability to successfully focus and be receptive to their nonverbal inner experiences, as their unresolved problems and perceived challenges resided in their physical bodies. This corresponds with what the neuroscientist Damasio describes as paying attention to a somatosensory modality characterized by "touch, muscular, temperature, pain, visceral and vestibular" (Damasio, 1999, p. 318). Gendlin developed the method Focusing, suggesting how an individual can discover the felt meaning of an experience by listening inwardly, "sitting with" and witnessing their body/mind sense. According to Gendlin, these bodily felt insights may provide a deeper understanding of the source beneath a challenge or problem and lead to a felt shift; a sense of answers and solutions not yet experienced (Gendlin, 1969, 1986, 2003; Gendlin & Olsen, 1970). Rappaport generated Focusing-oriented art-therapy as a follow up of Gendlin's work, seeking answers to questions or perceived challenges through sensuous and artful approaches (Rappaport, 2009).

Arts-based Inquiry, exemplified in depth below in case 3, is like Focusing and Focusing-oriented art-therapy as it seeks to achieve the bodily feel of an experience (Meltzer, 2018). Arts-based Inquiry was developed and refined by three artists in an ongoing, biannual exploratory workshop (Meltzer, 2015, 2018). They experimented with different arts-based methods to reach a deeper and more authentic understanding of themselves and their artwork. The way this Arts-based Inquiry evolved resembles arts-based action research, as a result here is not considered as an accomplishment, but rather represents "a starting point for further examination, reflection, understanding and change" (Meltzer, 2016, p. 79).

Arts-based Inquiry, however, differs in some ways from Focusing and Focusing-oriented art-therapy, as the chosen symbol or object, for a period, is identified and embodied as part of the self and given a voice of its own. It is an inward-seeking process, combining our common knowledge with the archetypical world of symbols (Meltzer, 2018). Instead of analyzing or evaluating the object using the rational mind, the selected symbol or object is explored and sensed with openness, with no previous projections, judgements or expected answers in mind. With its deep origin in an artefact or symbol, Arts-based Inquiry offers a sense felt route to our tacit bodily knowledge about a perceived challenge, a person or a theme.

To exclude outer visual impressions and support the introspective process, the inquirer keeps his or her eyes closed throughout the inquiry. This part is conducted without interruptions or questions from the co-inquirers (Meltzer, 2018). In this process, the act of being creative, acquiring tacit knowledge through the embodied wisdom in a symbol or artistic expression may provide answers and possibilities not yet known or thought of.

Like Focusing, Arts-based Inquiry can be taught and practised in people's personal lives, at schools and in working life. The method has been adapted and used as part of the training at the non-traditional course Creative Communication at Oslo Metropolitan University (Høgskolen i Oslo og Akershus, 2011). Here, experience with Arts-based Inquiry takes place several times during the course, often in close combination with other exercises. It can, for example, be used when participants examine and become more conscious of their roles in the group, using animal figures as representative of the self; embodying, seeing, sensing and examining themselves from the animals' point of view (Meltzer, 2016).

Artful Inquiry involves creating powerful questions that engage the spiritual dimension and therefore evoke strong passion. These questions are combined with appropriate artistic methods. "Artful Inquiry uses artistic methods to explore the not yet known, i.e. the emerging tacit knowing that can be called forward through these processes. In some instances, the artistic method merges with the reflection process. It becomes the reflection process" (Darsø, 2017, pp. 139-140). At times, this becomes a wordless communion with the material as the material 'speaks back' in awe-inspiring ways. This method involves body, mind, heart and spirit (Darsø, 2017). The context in which this takes place plays an important role, both concerning the physical context, where natural environments are most generative and supportive and to the social and psychological context, where the surrounding community makes a difference; in particular, when trust has previously been developed to form a 'holding space' (Darsø, 2001, 2014).

Empirical cases

In the following, we will describe our experience and learning from many years of practice with arts-based interventions. In cases 1 and 2, we apply Theory U with different participants in an executive Master education in Leadership and Innovation, in case 3, we present an individual story of working with Arts-based inquiry and creative processes; and in case 4, we outline research on a large-scale artistic intervention project. These cases all derive from the educational sectors in the Nordic countries. Our focus is on the processes of Sensing, Presencing and Crystallizing, with particular attention to Presencing.

Case 1: Working with Theory U as a 7-step process

The first case comes from an international executive Master's degree program, Leadership and Innovation in Complex Systems (LAICS). Approximately 20 participants are accepted annually to complete this 2-year part-time education. Alongside they work full time in public and private organizations. At the very first seminar, lasting three and a half days, participants work with theatre rehearsal exercises for most of day three. Towards the end of the day, they work with Image Theatre (Boal, 2000), which involves making human sculptures, in groups of five, in response to the question: What holds you back from creating innovation in your organization? The task is for each participant, quickly, to create a human sculpture to illustrate their situation by positioning their four fellow students and themselves in ways that demonstrate the issues they face. In groups, everyone takes turns in establishing these sculptures. After 10 minutes, we all walk around to look at these human sculptures, which are recreated one at a time. These images are very strong and often quite depressing. We select one or two sculptures to work with to 'solve' them. The main point here, however, is that these sculptures will be recreated at the next seminar to make a shift from Seeing to Sensing.

At this next seminar, the intent is for people to get to know the U-process, both from a theoretical perspective and from direct experience. Moving from Seeing to Sensing begins with the violinist Miha Pogacnik[58] playing a Bach piece. This sets the tone. Music is a very powerful mood changer. Different instruments appeal to our senses in different ways. The violin strings have a unique vibration, and classical music played with intensity can really touch people. The book Artful Creation provides several examples of how music affects people and kindles their soul (Darsø, 2004, pp. 59-66; 93-98).

Afterwards, people are asked to go back to their group and select and embody the human sculpture from the previous seminar that provided the greatest variety of physical posture. Each pose is given a number from 1-5, and then people stand in and sense each position with their eyes closed for about 30 seconds; slowly, they move from one pose to the other, staying 30 seconds in each one and trying to sense what each character feels. This is a very powerful exercise, and people are amazed at how they can feel and somehow understand the different poses by being in them, and thereby sense the complexity of the situation. Two participants wrote the following in their reflection reports; one referring to the human sculptures, the other to an exercise embodying a leader figure:

> The sculptures from the image theatre at seminar 1 are also analogies. We unfolded one of these sculptures in Bled (Slovenia). Circulating between the five characters, we all gained bodily experience of the various positions. It gave rise to an interesting conversation: How did I feel being in a certain position? Did you experience the same, or did you see something different? The bodily sensation allowed us to express how it felt and maybe even see what could be motivating or demotivating for each of the characters. We talked about values. By having multiple perspectives, we could start to discuss solutions. ... The above experience was to me, the first real dive into the U.
>
> Embodying my admired leader behind a mask and trying to act and think as if I was such a leader was a very powerful experience and has changed my relationship with my own superiors and workmates ever since. More specifically, I have become much more aware of people's actions and reactions, and before reacting to their input, I try to evaluate their possible reasoning for their actions (as if looking through their eyes). This practice, together with mentally focusing on those around me who would benefit from my balance, has probably also helped in augmenting empathy and openness in my relationships.

Embodying is an effective approach because it is a way of accessing the body as a seat of knowledge (Pelias, 2008), as most of our knowing is tacit (Polyani, 1966). It is amazing that adopting a bodily position can tell you something about a character's mood and motivation. Standing in another person's shoes is equally powerful and can build understanding and empathy. For more than a decade, we have been using this approach to get people into the Sensing mode when going through the U.

Sensing is an excellent preparation for Presencing, precisely because it affects feelings and body. Through Sensing, we may change brainwaves from beta to alpha oscillations, which are slower and more predisposed to creativity and daydreaming (Capacchione, 2001). This, of course, takes practice.

Practising daily is something that Scharmer strongly recommends. Scharmer talks about Presencing as "connecting to source". Based on the research of Jahn and Dunne, Jaworski describes Source in relation to practice: "There exists an eternally creative Source of infinite potential that lies beyond the orders of time" (Jaworski, 2012, p. 121). "We are capable of establishing dynamic dialogue and resonant channels of communication with the Source – passing information into the Source, as well as extracting information from it. This can be accomplished with practice and discipline, enabling communication between mind and the Source that exceeds conventional expectations... Our channels of reception can be tuned to allow and to amplify the information exchange" (ibid, 2012, p. 118). We will argue that arts-based interventions can open such channels of reception and result in surprising insights and transformational learning. In the following, we present a simple method from our practice applied to achieve Presencing.

The perception of time slowing down is often an indicator of entering the Presencing zone. We use slowing down as a way of opening the space of Presencing when getting to know the U-process at the first level. We start by instructing the participants in how to zen walk. This involves walking very slowly, sensing how one's feet (in shoes) touch the ground while focusing on breathing slowly in and out. When thoughts arrive, simply bid them hello and goodbye. Perhaps something will emerge or stand out during the walk, perhaps not. In the following, we reverse the normal process. Again, a beautiful piece of classical music, played live, helps the participants tune into Presencing. In order to protect the 'magic spell' of the music, we applaud the music before it is played; thereby, when the music stops, people can get up quietly, one by one, and walk back in solitude along a beautiful lake to a designated space. For some people, this is a powerful experience; some get important insights, while others do the zen-walk without gaining any significant new understanding. It is an invitation with no strings attached.

Especially the zen-walk made a big impression on me. I am familiar with meditation, so I just expected it to be a kind of meditation bringing some peace and quiet to my body. But it was so much more than that. I walked for more than two hours, and I felt like some pieces of my puzzle fell in to place. Through the zen-walk, I came to recognize that I use busyness and noise to keep difficult emotions at a distance and the zen-walk helped me instead to stay with the difficult emotions, live them and thereby overcome them without just shutting them down. I try to hang on to this recognition, but I have to admit, it does not always work for me.

In relation to Crystalizing, we have designed a method of drawing and writing with the non-dominant hand (Friis, 2015). The rationale behind it is the doctoral research of Lucia Capacchione, who discovered that the non-dominant hand could reveal tacit knowledge that would not be accessible if only using the rational mind (Capacchione, 2001). Her research is based on findings from brain research on the thinking processes of the two hemispheres of the brain. In most cases, our dominant hand is connected to the left hemisphere, which is related to sequence, analysis, logic, numbers, etc., and our non-dominant hand is connected to the right hemisphere, which is related to images, wholes, colours, daydreaming, fantasy, etc. Capacchione discovered that drawings made with the dominant hand would often be conceptual; that is, governed by our thinking. If trying to draw a table, one would be inclined to draw a flat surface with four legs; that is, the concept of a table. When drawing a table with the non-dominant hand, however, the drawing would turn out very differently, often with many details. It could be a table with a flower vase, a teapot, candles and cups.

Similarly, when writing a question with the dominant hand, the non-dominant hand would come up with surprising answers. In fact, a whole conversation could go on between the hands, as if an invisible force was guiding the process. Capacchione suggests that the body has hidden tacit knowledge, often from childhood, which can become conscious in this way, and that this process can be healing.

For our purpose, this method has worked well for Crystallizing. Coming back after the zen-walk, we ask people to make a drawing with their dominant hand of something that emerged during their walk or attracted their attention. Alternatively, they can draw something that needs their attention. After ten minutes, they are invited to make a similar drawing with their non-dominant hand. For many participants, this has rendered surprising insights. It feels as if the non-dominant hand has a 'life of its own'. Often, the information that is revealed in the second drawing is somewhat idiosyncratic; it feels incredibly important and meaningful to the owner, but may be difficult to explain to others. Several participants have taken this on as a new practice, which they continue in order to get information about issues that would otherwise remain concealed. One participant wrote the following:

> Concluding my experience with Theory U, I did the left-hand/right-hand assignment. ... I did not expect much from it. ...I was tired, and my head was full of all sorts of things, ... Then I switched hands and this drawing appeared (drawing). ...I felt so happy inside, as if I had found an inner source or exposed something that had been concealed for a long time. The message for me was clear: "Theory U is to get down to rock bottom. It is the key to open the door (letting come) and start climbing the stairs of co-creation on the other side."
>
> As I looked through my notes, I noticed the sentence: "I don't like zen- walk, but I like zen- running. It seems to work as a tool I can use for crystallizing."

Case 2: Working with Theory U as Presencing

The following year of the LAICS education, at a seminar on authentic leadership, held at Banff Centre in the Rocky Mountains, the U-process is applied as "principles and practices" with a focus on Presencing (Scharmer, 2007, p. 436). During the first day, people are invited to tell leadership stories with clay. This two-hour session includes individual and group exercises, some of which take place in silence. What makes these exercises particularly interesting is when people find out that their hands can make surprising things with the clay, and in some cases, answer a question they have struggled with for a long time (Darsø 2017). We see this as tacit bodily knowledge that is helped to surface in Artful Inquiry; i.e. asking a powerful question with appropriate artistic material and method.

> We have all got a nice lump of clay. Ed tells us to close our eyes and make our totem animal. We have six minutes. Not much time to think. Just do it. I love working with clay. Have done it a lot when I was a kid. What occurs in my hands is a nice little seal. In a way, it talks to me. Not with a voice of sound, of course. But in my hand some kind of talk is going on. I have sometimes during my life dreamt that I was a seal swimming in the sea in a wonderful, playful, fearless way. Actually, I don't really like deep water and have never been much of a swimmer. But in my seal dreams, I just do it. And now, the seal tells me somehow; I am ready for deeper waters. For a moment, I am the seal going out there. It feels right.
>
> Through his (the facilitator's) skilful guidance, my object of leadership emerged. It came out of nothing, and it has followed me since. The swirl! To me it represents the forces that are there, the energy being created. ... On day four, we glazed and burnt our ceramic object. For me, it continued my thoughts on leadership as energy. ... Facilitation is leadership and leadership of change is to hold the swirl, work with the energy, but from an inner source of intention and authenticity.

Another method offers inspirational experiences with materials from nature, such as branches, grass, twigs, cones, pebbles, berries, etc. A three-hour session from the same seminar starts with an introduction to the artwork of Andy Goldsworthy through a lecture, books and movie clips. Goldsworthy creates temporary installations out of natural materials, such as sticks and stones that he can find in nature. The art-works are ephemeral and vanish quickly or slowly depending on the forces of nature, i.e. the wind, water and sun. Inspired by this, we walk into the forest and people, individually and in groups, begin to collect materials to be used in answering the question: What are the leadership qualities that you want to focus on now? Again, this often results in revelations, even epiphanies, as people seem to communicate with the materials and get messages from nature that touch them deeply. What people get out of this metaphoric work in and with nature is amazing. Nature is a potent teacher and very helpful for Presencing.

> ... the leadership story emerged from both the past and from the future. While sitting there in the grass – looking at the art-creation that my group and I brought to life right there. ... To the sight of this land-art sculpture and still holding on to the co-creational sensation in my body and senses, my leadership story emerged. ... My body and mind were filled up with a sensation, where it became evident that now, I was there.

Later, we take an even deeper dive into the bottom of the U with nature, but this time with an experienced yoga-naturalist guide who is familiar with the U-process. We begin the walk in the forest with breathing and sensing exercises, becoming aware of the sounds and smells of the forest and sensing the space around us, above and below us. We then walk slowly in silence, one by one, with space between us. We are invited to think of the trees as our ancestors and thank them for being there for us. Other exercises involve looking for patterns or focusing on movement in nature. When people are deeply engrossed in sensing, they are given small scrolls with a question to contemplate and asked to find a suitable space for 20-minutes of contemplation. The question is: "What do you offer to the world?" Afterwards, walking back, people share their experiences and insights in pairs. The aim of this session is, among other things, to help people find an everyday practice that works for them.

> Above all, the meditative walking in nature brought me a powerful insight that my current job may be just a bridge to self-understanding and the opening of new horizons through the LAICS journey that would be otherwise unexplored, had I not detoured from my academic career path. This interpretation reinforced my empathy for the concept of synchronicity postulated by Jaworski. The depth of these insightful experiences in Banff reassured (me of) the usefulness and necessity of meditation as a constant and essential practice.

A powerful way to access Presencing is a storytelling ritual. It is important, however, to emphasize that a lot of preparation takes place prior to this ritual. Besides the first experience with Theory U a year earlier, three full days with different arts-based interventions on personal authentic leadership have grounded the participants and helped them to reflect on their leadership and life. They have inquired with their hands, their minds, their bodies, nature, and in dialogue with their trusting community. To prepare for the ritual, people receive five sentence fragments to think about and complete, such as "This is a time when . . . (recalling a time of insight/illumination)".

The ritual takes place in a beautiful space with a mandala, taped on the floor. The mandala has four entrance points. When the process has been introduced, four people step up to the entrance points and begin, one at a time, to state their names and dates of birth. There are seven steps in the ritual, and the process is very moving and potent. Witnessing each other is an important part. The choreography with fixed movement, fixed phrases and vocal announcements, signifies that this is serious; this matters. It is a pledge and thereby becomes an obligation. In Scharmer's vocabulary, this is connecting to Will. Both during and after the ritual, there are tears, vulnerability, love and a high energy field.

Concluding this seminar, everyone tells their leadership story (3-5 minutes), where each person shares a few insights from the sessions.

Accordingly, I believe I have reached the bottom of the U in Banff. Given the challenge of composing a leadership story, I had not written down a single line of my story until about 10 minutes before the stipulated deadline for presenting it. Despite the urgency, I never felt any anxiety or pressure for not having written anything down until so late; as it seemed I knew that my story was already written, except that it was not 'on paper'. As described by Scharmer (and later illustrated by Pogacnik in Bled), the point of inflection at the bottom of the U, when one can deeply listen to the self and sense the highest future possibility (the emerging future), typically happens in a brief instant of insight and immediate action, and that is exactly how I ended up writing my leadership story, i.e. just before reaching the deadline (but ironically, without feeling any urgency or pressure). Now I consider myself to be in an upward process toward crystallizing, proto-typing and performing (the upward process of the U journey), where stating my mission is the first act of this process (crystallizing).

A seminar on authentic personal leadership evidently involves exercises that illuminate "knowing thyself", as Aristotle put it. If crystallizing is about holding on to our highest Self, the altruistic Self, then the premise must be to know that Self. One way to unfold who you are is by drawing self-portraits. This session starts with an introduction showing photos of a range of self-portraits, from ancient times up to today. It is demonstrated how self-portraits often exaggerate certain traits or parts of people, and how they can strive for resemblance or be entirely symbolic. After this introduction, participants have 8 minutes to draw a self-portrait using crayons in A2 format. Afterwards, people make inquiries and interpret this portrait with a trusted friend. Interesting insights often emerge, not least through the other person's observations. Subsequently, the portraits are posted on the wall, where we can look at them all together, and it is astounding how different they are. What have people chosen to focus on? How have they portrayed themselves? Only the face? The whole person? Only the hands? Alone or with others? Is it entirely symbolic? We see this exercise as bridging Presencing with Crystallizing as it can reveal the authentic Self and its purpose.

> On one particular day, we did a meditation walk where the 'small' background question was: "What is your greatest gift to the world?" During the meditation walk, I suddenly saw a picture of myself. I was happy, smiling, and around me was a radiance of positive, yellow energy, and I thought: my greatest gift is that I am spreading happiness and positive energy! Afterwards, I tried to capture this image in a self-portrait.

Case 3: Using Arts-based Inquiry as a way through Presencing towards Crystallization

Although the following process was conducted independently of Theory U, it confirms the applicability of the theory. This case, based solely on a personal account, illustrates how a woman used a character from a dream in an Arts-based Inquiry. By including her experiences in her artwork, she increased her awareness of subconscious and tacit parts of herself. This deep and personal quest, taking her through Sensing and Presencing to Crystallization, caused a lasting change. Her process shows how Arts-based Inquiry can be a starting point where we "can access sensuous and embodied knowledge, foster creativity and reflexivity and uncover deeper and more authentic solutions" to questions arising in the schools and workplaces of tomorrow (Meltzer, 2018, p. 139-140). During the following months, she entered a deep and deliberate process of self-reflection. By surrendering her automatic memory and programming, she transformed her habitual ways of being and acting, resulting in a new and more authentic experience of self.

The woman is an artist. She grew up in a poor family and has only attended primary school. She prefers to stay in her little house, surrounded by fields. Here she feels safe. She knows her neighbours, and they know her. The following process was initiated after spending a week abroad with some friends. It all started with the following dream:

> I am sitting with my grownup son at a table in a small, familiar village square. The atmosphere is calm and friendly. My son is quiet; his lip is a bit deformed. I am talking to a man next to me about the organic goods in the marketplace. When I question him, he replies: "you must find the answer, as you know this better than me."

She is aware that her mentally disabled 'son' in the dream is important, as he, with his unusual appearance, is the odd one out. Her subconscious mind reveals a painful theme that she usually suppresses in her everyday life. As she perceives herself as a slow learner, she, in order not to reveal her ignorance, avoids asking for help. Equally, she often feels like the 'child' in the company of others; being the one that lags behind and lets the 'adults' make the decisions. At the same time, she finds it embarrassing and painful to fill the role of the one who is overlooked and unappreciated, making her feel ashamed and jealous. Nevertheless, and despite her initial resistance towards this part of herself, she chooses to embody her 'son' and let him speak in the following inquiry:

> I am Tom. There is hardly anyone who says my name. I have been sitting at the table next to my mother for a long time. Most of all, I would like to go home, but my mother continues to talk to the man next to her. I sense that the man pretends to not see me. I do not really care, as I am used to it. Maybe it is because my lower lip is so strange. It is as if sitting here together with the people in the square makes me more aware of how alone I am. It feels as if I cannot breathe. I choose to leave my mother and walk into a nearby, familiar field. Here, no one looks at my strange lip. I feel safe. I can sense the wind and listen to the birds. I would like to be with my best friend, Mona. She is a bit younger than I am, but we always have fun

together, exploring the fields, digging holes and finding secret places.

After the inquiry, she shares that it felt good to embody that part of herself. By letting go of her everyday self, she discovers unused resources; the joy of being trivial, spontaneous and easy-going. The following days, however, she can see how diffi-cult it is for her to commit to 'ordinary' people. For her, the free-dom of expression in art means not needing to adapt, be proper or follow the rules. She, therefore, decides to include her experi-ences from the inquiry and her present feeling of sadness by giv-ing voice to her 'son' Tom and his friend Mona in her ongoing artwork.

Half a year earlier she made some peculiar small, burned 'ob-jects' out of old rags. She is still enthusiastic about them, sensing that they represent her core; an authentic part of her, not a copy or imitation of anything. At this point, but without the same en-thusiasm, she starts to create similar objects. Suddenly, it is as if Mona is there with her, taking over the making of her objects, cutting them up and putting them together in new ways. A small figure with a character of its own evolves in front of her. The fol-lowing days, she continues to make several peculiar objects, find-ing joy and excitement in the freedom of finally letting go and doing as she likes.

She continues to share her log notes in the subsequent weeks and months, describing how deeply the inquiry affected her. Now, seeing herself through the eyes of Mona and Tom, she is confronted with numerous painful life experiences, realizing how often she has felt insufficient, stupid and overlooked. She can see how she subconsciously has kept up this pattern in her life, filling the role of the underdog or the little girl. Delving deeply into the feeling of being alone, she also senses the agony within her family and in people she has met, seen and heard about. She can likewise acknowledge that she has always felt com-passion for the oppressed, the poor, the sick, the hungry and the lonely, stating that "Tom has shown me from within what it feels like to be an outcast, a feeling I have done everything to not feel until now ..."

She can, however, also appreciate how her dream and the subsequent inquiry overruled her conscious self. By enabling Tom to speak and be part of her life, she no longer wants to live a life of pretence, escaping her pain. She senses how this shift gradually gives her freedom from previous feelings like jealousy, envy, hatred and anger, continually repeating to herself: "you are not your feelings, but you use your feelings".

One morning, she wakes up and sees an overview of all the situations in her life that activated feelings of inferiority and shame; situations where she had been submissive. This experience makes her understand how her father's abuse during her childhood and her dysfunctional family have had a crucial impact on her way of being. Through this process, she gradually reaches a point of clarification, accepting and integrating the outcast Tom and his qualities as part of herself – a part she needs to consider in her everyday life and not be ashamed of. She shares how she can now meet other 'outcasts' with far greater openness, courtesy, curiosity and compassion:

> Before, I would rather look the other way, wishing they would disappear as they made me feel insecure and stupid. I just wanted them to be normal, like everyone else, or at least stay far away from me. At the same time, I felt attracted to all sorts of outsiders like gipsies, beggars and homeless people.

Being alone had been a core theme in her life. Now she can see that her feelings of secrecy and withdrawal relate to her childhood experiences and the things she could not say to her father. She felt it was crucial not to be alone in this process, as confronting past and well-established patterns of being increased her feeling of vulnerability. It was important to have the ongoing possibility for sharing and contact throughout the following weeks and months. She came to highly value being with others who were sensitive to her needs, as well as to cherish her need to be alone.

This case shows how a person shifted from an ego-system awareness to caring for the well-being of the whole. Her dream made her aware of what she perceived as a challenge. By sharing her dream and the feelings connected to the character Tom, she was able to see herself from a broader perspective (Sensing). Her inquiry, moving towards a state of openness in the now, activated a transference from the known towards an unknown future (Presencing). By letting Mona take over the artmaking and create the outcasts, she produced visual manifestations of the theme she was addressing. Her inner images became 'alive' and present through these objects, supporting and enhancing her process of conscious change.

In this process, she confronted her resistance and fear of the unknown (Voice of Fear). Now, operating from her authentic Self, she cultivated an everyday practice where she relinquished her existing belief systems and usual ways of being (Crystallizing). Repeated encounters with her inner demons, as well as acknowledging the lifelong impact of her childhood experiences, led to a gradual shift. She no longer tried to avoid or suppress her own or other 'outcasts' in her everyday life. To celebrate this inner shift, she sent her objects to an exhibition, symbolizing that she now felt that this part of her was fully integrated and ready to come out into the open.

Case 4: Working with performance methods to foster the poetic self

So far, the described methods and exercises have been sessions lasting 2-4 hours, although in a succession of several days (case 1 and 2) or several months (case 3). The following case is more radical. Sisters Academy is a large-scale experiential artistic intervention and research project that takes place within the Nordic educational sectors. It builds on Sensuous learning and Sensuous Society, concepts coined by Hallberg (Hallberg, 2016). An upper-secondary school is taken over by the performance group Sisters Hope for 2-4 weeks through aesthetic transformation, using light-, sound- and set-design. During this period, the teachers, who have had at least two full days of preparation during the prior six-month period, will teach from a new sensuous perspective, their "Poetic Self". "The poetic self is not a character. It is not a fiction; it is our inner inherent poetic potential that we might not unfold in our everyday lives, but that we discover, give shape and donate our flesh to through performance. By doing so, we experience an expanding spectrum of possibilities, of new spaces in which we can be" (Hallberg & Darsø, 2019, p. 75).

The students also explore their poetic selves during the manifestation. The Poetic-Self exercise can be understood as a deep dive into the U, involving three main steps with time and space for reflection and dialog in between. The first step is total immersion into the sensuous universe of images and memories, guided by inspirational questions (Sensing and Presencing). The second step is creating a tableau by externalizing one's inner landscape with aesthetic materials (Crystallizing). The third step is creating an interactive design, and embodying it together with others (Prototyping). The following quote is from a student who participated in a Sisters Academy intervention:

> Our poetic selves waited for us to find them through broken mirrors. … Facilitated by our amazing teachers, each sense was at constant and heightened attention. One was an ephemeral veil of lace, another a dancing flame. One walked and danced like a queen, yet another offered to paint you with his gaze from the shadows. I found the poetry that had spoken to me my entire life sang in loud, unafraid, shining verses around and around my head, in circles of light and shadow. It was the song of my rebirth, of finding my twin through my poetic self.[59]

Experiences from this case are elaborated in much greater detail in a book chapter (Hallberg & Darsø, 2019). In addition, Hallberg explains this artistic intervention in-depth in her forthcoming doctoral research.

Making sense of the data

With these four cases, we have covered a variety of arts-based interventions and contexts with a focus on both individuals and groups. All four cases illustrate the transformative power of arts-based interventions in relation to Theory U. Cases 1 and 2 portray a progression of experiencing and practising Theory U. Whereas case 1 involves the introduction and initial practice of the U, case 2, which takes place one year later, aims at a deep dive into Presencing in relation to exploring individual authentic leadership. With a few exceptions, the participants are the same and have formed a loving community of trust and respect. Both cases take place in nature. The context of beautiful nature and a loving community strongly support the process, which is both personal and collective (Darsø, 2014). In these cases, the process was guided by the U. Case 3, meanwhile, portrays an individual going through a long-term arts-based intervention, which turns into a deep dive into the U through inquiry and identification. Dealing with difficult subconscious material regarding self, having the courage to feel, stay with and acknowledge the pain, reveals hidden potential and creativity. Finally, case 4 is a radical arts-based intervention taking over an entire school for two to four weeks and transforming it into a sensuous universe. It involves sensuous learning both at an individual and at a collective level.

We begin to summarize our findings by examining the selected excerpts we have presented in the empirical material. In many ways the phases of Sensing, Presencing and Crystallizing overlap. Before concluding the chapter, we explore what prepared and supported people when accessing the deeper layers of the U.

Embodying is evidently a good way of sensitizing people. In the Western world, people are generally focused on their rational minds and on thinking and communicating through Information Technology and social media, whereas their bodies are somewhat estranged. Listening to the body with its abundant tacit knowledge is not the norm. The arts provide ways to appreciate and unfold the wisdom of the body. We see this in our data, as summarized in one of the reflection reports:

LAICS has taught me that including the body in different ways in the processes, such as using analogue tools, body mapping, body metaphors, walk and talks, gives access to new, unexpected insights.

The wisdom of the body is also exposed in the sculpting exercises with clay, where several participants explain how their hands took over and formed items that were surprisingly revealing. These exercises were done with eyes closed, which points back to the research by Gendlin about focusing attention and listening inwardly. It also links to Dispenza's research on the importance of brain waves, such as changing beta waves to alpha or theta waves. Making an artwork or using arts-based methods and materials are ways of slowing down and become inwardly focused, which allows new insights to emerge and become conscious. We see this as a process that goes from Sensing, through Presencing, to Crystallizing.

> In 'Story-finding with clay' I sculpted a tree as my leadership icon, and afterwards, I wrote in my learning journal: "Wow how this session really moved me". My hands formed the clay as if they had started to think by themselves, and in the sculpting process, they lead me to welcoming what I had not really thought of before, which is that my roots and my trunk must support the branches that I reach out to the world.

Passing the threshold of Presencing will often involve painful feelings that have previously been neglected. Scharmer describes this as" bending the beam of attention back onto its source" (Scharmer & Kãufer, 2013, p. 152). Becoming conscious of who you are authentically, for better or worse, and coming to terms with this is essential for accessing one's greater Self and learning from the future as it emerges. There are several examples of this in our data:

> I travel home from Bled as a new person. I think I can say; nothing less ... I closed down for things in Bled I never thought possible. I have had contact with a part of me which had a lot to tell me – and to which, I never listened before. My chronic thirst and the lump in my throat

are gone! It is as if I have got my feelings reorganized inside me. It is as if, there is a new hierarchy inside me ... One of the major changes is that my new path is no longer just a Self-realization project. It has become much larger than myself. On my Zen walk, there was a transformation, where my mission in life was to find small sprouts and get them to unleash their potential. This is my emergent future.

A final example derives from Arts-based Inquiry through identification with an image, in this case, a dream image of a person. It is a deep personal dive into the U, a courageous and frightening venture. However, after an arduous process of sitting with and coming to terms with her hardships and suffering, the person ends up finding her authentic source and creative strength. This is an exemplary story of the Hero's Journey (Campbell, 1993).

Because I now know Tom and Mona from within, I have reached an increased sense of equality. That is a good feeling. I find it difficult to explain, and it might sound strange and banal; I have just noticed that there has been a change: The outsiders can be themselves, not needing to change or adapt. I have found a sense of peace and feel at ease when I meet them.

In the next section, we want to point out some issues that are vital to consider when it comes to the use of arts-based interventions. Until now, we have mostly drawn on positive experiences regarding what worked. However, arts-based methods should be handled with care because the arts involve feelings and may evoke surprises, even crises. The experience and the sensitivity of the teacher, consultant or facilitator is, therefore, an essential ingredient.

Critical aspects and reflections regarding working with Arts-based interventions

There is a wide range of teaching arenas when it comes to creative activity and the use of the arts in schools and workplaces. Whereas some methods work well as tools for learning a specific field of study, other methodologies are used to initiate personal awareness and development (Austring & Sørensen, 2010). Here, the outcome, personal or professional, may differ according to the setting, the theme, the amount of time involved and to what degree a person's feelings and personal experiences are involved in the art-making and the processing of the result. In this context, it is essential to understand, accept and appreciate the ambiguities and uncertainties involved. Changing habitual patterns of living and being takes time, courage, trust in the process and practice (McNiff, 1998). Any developmental work will, therefore, require determination, willingness and self-discipline to return repeatedly to the perceived challenge, despite the resistance and pain it might involve. In this process, it is essential to fully acknowledge the value of having support from a facilitator or teacher, a group or an approving ally, as this may provide a much-needed sense of self-value and of being understood.

Another aspect is that it makes a difference whether the artwork is part of a short-term intervention or is a recurring activity. The program Creative Communication, for instance, provides several repeated arts-based exercises throughout the year (Høgskolen i Oslo og Akershus, 2011). The intention is to create a common thread by offering some repeated practices parallel to the progressing course. One example is drawing a log each morning before the sessions take place; a five-minute spontaneous sketch reflecting the participants' feelings, there and then. Subsequent sharing, seeing and acknowledging each other by presenting their drawings along with a title and a feeling, has shown to build deeper bonds. In another exercise, the participants add new painted 'comments' to their paintings. These painted remarks aim to reflect how their perception of self, their relation to their workplace and their professional sense of identity evolve (Meltzer, 2015). These repeated returns to the same canvas allow them to experience and reflect on the different emotional phases involved in creative processes; phases not unlike those involved in any type of developmental work. In general, these different exercises are performed within a limited timeframe. The reason for this is that it gives people little time to think and analyse the results. It forces them to make quick choices regarding what to include, what to focus on, and which colours to use. Consequently, they tend to use a more intuitive approach, which allows tacit knowledge to emerge.

Regardless of the circumstances, people's response to and involvement in artistic expression may vary considerably depending on how open and familiar they are to this way of working, their sense of security and trust in the facilitator and the group, and whether the given theme in some way or other triggers their personal history or life experiences. All these aspects may influence their instinctive reaction to a given topic, and whether they approach it in an analytical or emotional way. An example of two very different responses happened when two teenagers in the same group were challenged to paint how they perceived anger. One painted fierce sharks in the water, illustrating the danger this feeling represented to her. The other demonstrated how she experienced this feeling; covering the canvas with harsh strokes of red and black paint. These differing responses illustrate the wisdom of the individual psyche, here, revealed as a finely tuned balance between being challenged and maintaining a sense of security, an inner knowing of the degree of involvement they might tolerate at that given time.

A similar variety of responses may be seen when it comes to reviewing and processing a person's creation or final result. According to Moxnes, an authentic exchange is needed to reach deep learning, inner growth and change (Moxnes, 2012). This profound and intense level of sharing, however, balances a fraught line between feelings of security and of anxiety as it involves a possible confrontation with blind, hidden or unknown parts of the self. For the same reason, the place from where a person sees, perceives and understands the artwork may vary considerably. Here, a person, regardless of the instructions, may respond in accordance with his or her conscious or subconscious readiness. Equally, people's understandings of a work of art or creative expression may differ, depending on the degree to which the symbolic result evokes familiar associations or arouses glimpses of a universal and archetypical reality (Jung et al., 1964; Ronnberg & Martin, 2010). A person's focus may likewise alternate between seeing and perceiving the artwork as something entirely or partly separate from the self and as embodied and sensed from within, representing an authority with a voice of its own.

Conclusion

Our primary goal in this chapter has been to explore the question: "How can arts-based interventions prepare and support Presencing and learning from the future as it emerges?" We have demonstrated the empirical applicability of Theory U by describing how different arts-based interventions, whether built around the theory or conducted independently, can implicate Sensing, Presencing and Crystallizing. The cases presented, involving individual and group processes and illustrated through a wide range of arts-based interventions, show the depths and far-reaching effects of these different practises.

Involvement in art and arts-based interventions, like listening to music, sculpting and acting (alpha waves), gives access to tacit knowing and strengthens the communication between the intellect and the body, the conscious and subconscious mind (Sensing). Sensing and letting bodily knowing emerge is a process of supporting subconscious material in becoming conscious. Often people have been struggling with an issue or a question for some time, and by applying an arts-based intervention, the answer emerges 'out of the blue'. People describe how happy they feel when this happens and how grateful they are. In this way, they get important insights about themselves and about the future that wants to emerge through them.

Arts-based Inquiry; embodying, identifying and giving voice to an object, person or artwork (theta waves), support the process of change as it reveals new perspectives and solutions from the emerging future (Presencing). Artmaking (alpha and theta

304

waves), letting go of ego and creating something of real value, can, at this point, support and strengthen individual and group processes. Here, the artwork, containing both the known and the unknown, can come to represent a visible image of a possible future.

According to Scharmer and Kaufer (2013, p. 152), "Stepping into the future starts with attending to the opening of an inner crack.... As human beings, we are on a journey of *becoming who we really are*. The journey to ourselves - to our Selves - is open-ended and full of disruptions, confusion and breakdowns, but also breakthroughs. It is a journey that essentially is about accessing the deep sources of the Self." We have several examples of this in our data. However, getting to know yourself can be both exhilarating and painful.

Nevertheless, it is an important preparation for learning from the future as it emerges. One of the challenges of knowing ourselves is the Voice of Fear (VOF) and coming to terms with difficult emotions that have stayed hidden for a long time. Many of our participants managed to stay with their challenging emotions, whether on a zen-walk in nature or through identification. They came to realize that this can be healing and 'wholing' (making whole). Several participants use the term "finding their inner source".

Essential for accessing Presencing is being able to change brain waves from beta to alpha and theta and to stay focused. This preparation takes practice, whether it be meditation, mindfulness, zen-walk, artistic exploration or simple breathing exercises. We have illustrated how applying arts-based interventions can induce alpha and theta waves and bring about valuable insights that have transformational value for the people involved. However, each individual needs to find his or her way to practice this. What works for one person will not necessarily work for another. Besides, people need to focus on feeling something positive, such as gratitude, love, awe or willingness, as, according to Dispenza's research, this furthers the energy needed for creating the future. A relevant discussion here is how to differentiate between what people want (ego) and what the future wants (Self). We will argue that becoming conscious of who you are, accessing the deep sources of Self through feeling and embodiment, will support a process of altruism. Here, a willingness to stand in the open and be ready to bring the best possible future into being can, in this way, emerge through you.

In this chapter, we have demonstrated how arts-based interventions can support the journey through the U. The arts are related to emotions and can help people access bodily knowledge. Arts-based approaches can catalyse personal development, reveal both hidden energy sources and painful issues, and bring healing, joy and inspiration. These processes facilitate a deep dive into what is truly meaningful for discovering the real purpose, which can energize the Will for creating the future. Based on our experience and empirical data, we conclude that arts-based interventions are well suited for preparing and supporting people in the deepest phases of the U-process.

References

Austring, B. D., & Sørensen, M. (2006). Æstetik og læring. Grundbog om æstetiske læreprocesser: Socialpedagogisk bibliotek. Hans Reitzels Forlag.

Austring, B. D., & Sørensen, M. (2010). Æstetisk virksomhed i pædagogisk regi. Dansk Pædagogisk Tidsskrift, 2, 6-15.

Berthoin Antal, A., & Strauss, A. (2016). Multistakeholder perspectives on searching for evidence of values-added in artistic interventions in organizations. In U. J. Sköldberg, J. Woodilla, & A.

Berthoin Antal (Eds.), Artistic Interventions in Organizations. Research, theory and practice (Vol. 4, pp. 37-59). London and New York: Routledge, Taylor & Francis Group.

Betensky, M. G. (1995). What do you see? Phenomenology of therapeutic art expression. London: Jessica Kingsley.

Boal, A. (2000). Theatre of the Oppressed: Pluto Press.

Buswick, T., & Seifter, H. (2010). Editor's note. Journal of Business Strategy, 31(4), 1-5.

Campbell, J. (1993). The Hero with a Thousand Faces. Hammersmith, London: Fontana Press.

Capacchione, L. (2001). The Power of Your Other Hand, a Course in Channeling the Inner Wisdom of the Right Brain: New Page Books.

Chalmers, D. J. (1996). The Conscious Mind. In Search of a Fundamental

Theory. New York, Oxford: Oxford University Press.

Creative Partnerships. (2010, 08.11.2011). Creative Partnerships Retrieved from http://creative-partnerships.com/

Damasio, A. (1999). The Feeling of what happens. Body and Emotion on the Making of Consciousness. San Diego, New York, London: Harcourt, Inc.

Darsø, L. (2001). Innovation in the Making. Frederiksberg, Denmark: Samfundslitteratur.

Darsø, L. (2004). Artful Creation. Learning-Tales of Arts-in-Business. Frederiksberg, Denmark: Samfundslitteratur.

Darsø, L. (2014). Setting the Context for Transformation towards Authentic Leadership and Co-Creation. In O. Gunnlaugson, C. Baron, & M. Cayer (Eds.), Perspectives on Theory U: Insights from the Field (pp. 97-113). Hershey, PA, USA: IGI Global.

Darsø, L. (2016). Arts-in-Business from 2004 to 2014: from experiments in practice to research and leadership development. In U. J. Sköldberg, J. Woodilla, & A. Berthoin Antal (Eds.), Artistic Interventions in Organizations. Research, theory and practice (Vol. 4, pp. 18-34). London and New York: Routledge, Taylor & Francis Group.

Darsø, L. (2017). Co-creating meaning through Artful Inquiry. In T. K. Chemi, L. (Ed.), Co-creation in Higher Education. Students and Educators Preparing Creatively and Collaboratively to the Challenge of the Future (pp. 131-149). Rotterdam, Boston, Taipei: Sense Publishers.

Dispenza, J. (2014). You are the PLACEBO. Making your mind matter: Hay House Inc.

Dispenza, J. (2017). Becoming Supernatural. How Common People Are Doing the Uncommon. Carlsbad CA, New York City, London, Sydney, Johannesburg, Vancouver, New Delhi: Hay House, Inc.

Eisner, E. (2008). Art and Knowledge. In J. G. Knowles & A. L. Cole (Eds.), Handbook of the Arts in Qualitative Inquiry: Perspectives, Methodologies, Examples and Issues. Thousand Oaks, CA: SAGE Publications.

Friis, S. A. K. (2015). Co-Creation Cards. Copenhagen: U Press.

Gendlin, E. T. (1969). Focusing. Psychotherapy: Theory, Research & Practice, 6(1), 4-15.

Gendlin, E. T. (1986). Let your body interpret your dreams. Wilmette, Illinois: Chiron Publications.

Gendlin, E. T. (2003). Focusing. How to gain direct access to your body's knowledge (3 ed.). London: Rider.

Gendlin, E. T., & Olsen, L. (1970). The use of imagery in experiential focusing. Psychotherapy: Theory, Research & Practice, 7(4), 221-223.

Hallberg, G. W. (2016). Sisters Academy – Radical Live Intervention into the Educational System. In A. Lindelof & M. Reason (Eds.), Experiencing Liveness in Contemporary Performance. Oxon: Routledge.

Hallberg, G. W., & Darsø, L. (2019). Using Performance Methods to Foster Inherent Poetic Potential and Sensuous Learning. In E. Antonacopoulou & S. S. Taylor (Eds.), Sensuous Learning for Practical Judgment in Professional Practice. Volume 2: Arts-based Interventions. (in press) London: Palgrave Macmillan.

Høgskolen i Oslo og Akershus, i. f. y. (2011). Kreativ kommunikasjon. Ledelse av kunstneriske prosesser som bidrag til utvikling på arbeidsplassen. Programplan. Retrieved from http://www.hioa.no/Studier-og-kurs/LU/Evu/Kreativ-kommunikasjon/Programplan-for-Kreativ-kommunikasjon-Ledelse-av-kunstneriske-prosesser-som-bidrag-til-utvikling-paa-arbeidsplassen

Jaworski, J. (2012). Source. The Inner Path of Knowledge Creation. San Francisco, CA: Berrett Koehler Publishers, Inc.

Jung, C. G., von Franz, M. L., Henderson, J. L., Jacobi, J., & Jadde, A. (1964). Man and his symbols. London: Aldus Books Ltd

Karkou, V. (2010). Arts therapies in schools. Research and practice. London: Jessica Kingsley Publishers.

Malchiodi, C. A. (2007). The art therapy sourcebook (2 ed.). New York: The McGraw-Hill companies.

McCraty, R., Deyhle, A., & Childre, D. (2012). The global coherence initiative: Creating a coherent planetary standing wave. Global Advances in Health and Medicine, 1(1), 64-77.

McNiff, S. (1998). Trust the Process. An Artist's Guide to Letting Go. Boston & London: Shambhala.

Meltzer, C. (2015). Understanding the ambiguity and uncertainty in creative processes when using arts-based methods in education and working life. Organizational Aesthetics, 4(1), 46-69. Meltzer, C. (2016). Life in Noah's Ark: Using animal figures as an arts-based projective technique in group work to enhance leadership competence. Organizational Aesthetics, 5(2), 77-95. Meltzer, C. (2018). Using Arts-based Inquiry as a way to communicate creatively in uncovering the future. In E. Antonacopoulou & S. Taylor (Eds.), Sensuous learning for practical judgement in professional practice.

Volume 1: Arts-based methods. (pp 139-166) London: Palgrave Macmillan.

Mitchell, C., Weber, S., & O'Reilly-Scanlon, K. (Eds.). (2005). Just who do we think we are? Methodologies for autobiography and self-study in teaching. Abingdon and New York: Routledge Falmer.

Moxnes, P. (2012). Positiv angst i individ, gruppe og organisasjon: Et organisasjonspsykologisk perspektiv (4 ed.). Oslo: Universitetsforlaget.

Pelias, R. J. (2008). Performative Inquiry. Embodiment and Its Challenges. In J. G. Knowles & A. L. Cole (Eds.), Handbook of the Arts in Qualitative Research (pp. 185-194). Thousand Oaks, Ca, USA: Sage Publications, Inc.

Polyani, M. (1966). The tacit dimension. New Your: Doubleday and Co.

Radin, D. (1997). The Conscious Universe. The Scientific Truth of Psychic Phenomena. San Francisco, CA: HarperEdge.

Rappaport, L. (2009). Focusing-oriented art therapy. Accessing the body's wisdom and creative intelligence. London: Jessica Kingsley Publishers.

Ray, M., & Myers, R. (1986). Creativity in business. New York: Doubleday.

Ronnberg, A., & Martin, K. (Eds.). (2010). The book of symbols. Reflections on archetypal images. Køln: Taschen.

Scharmer, C. O. (2007). Theory U: Leading from the Future as it Emerges. The Social Technology of Presencing. Cambridge, MA: SOL Press.

Scharmer, C. O., & Kaeufer, K. (2010). In front of the blank canvas: Sensing emerging futures. Journal of Business Strategy, 31(4), 21-29.

Scharmer, C. O., & Kāufer, K. (2013). Leading from the Emerging Future. From Ego-System to Eco -System Economies. San Francisco, CA: Berrett-Koehler Publishers, Inc.

Sheldrake, R. (1987). Part I: Mind, memory, and archetype morphic resonance and the collective unconscious. Psychological Perspectives, 18(1), 9-25.

Sköldberg, U. J., Woodilla, J. & Berthoin Antal, A. (Eds.) 2016. Artistic Interventions in Organizations. Research, theory and practice. London and New York: Routledge, Taylor & Francis Group Taylor, S., & Ladkin, D. (2009). Understanding arts-based methods in managerial development. Academy of Management Learning and Education, 8(1), 55-69.

Winnicott, D. W. (1971). Playing and reality. New York: Basic Books.

Zohar, D., & Marshall, I. (2000). Connecting with our Spiritual
   Intelligence. New York and London:
Bloomsbury Publishing.

Chapter 10

Presencing and Negative Capability: Identical Twins or Relatives?

Suneetha Saggurthi and Munish Thakur

I magine a blank canvas. See an artist standing in front of it with a palette. Holding the palette and toying with ideas, the artist gazes at the canvas, allowing different images dance in front of the eyes. What is going to emerge is as much a mystery to the artist as it is to those watching. All that one can feel is the artistic energy that is about to leap onto this blank canvas. Receiving the impulses through the senses and playing with the images that are coming forth are necessary for the painting to come into being. Immersed in the images and becoming one with them, at one point, it all falls into place. The artist knows what has to be presenced. With senses that are alive and pulsating, the painting takes its shape. The painting enters delicately on to the canvas slowly, but instinctually and boldly.

In the act of imagining, playing, becoming one with the image and presencing it are two concepts that are closely related—negative capability (NC) (John Keats) and presencing (Otto Scharmer,) which are the focus of this chapter. As we co-initiated the chapter and began to co-sense these terms, we realized that presencing and NC seem to be connected intuitively with both related to a knowing that takes one to the essence or the inner core or the moment of truth and beauty, and goodness (Bate,

2012; Scharmer, 2009). In this chapter, we intend to presence and crystallize this intuitive connection. We posit that understanding this connection will help ground the U process in a capability that has been lurking behind the process.

The structure of this chapter is as follows. Initially, we discuss the concepts of NC and presencing in detail. We then discuss how they both seem to be related. Subsequently, we present their connection with meaning and leadership.

Negative Capability

The curious phrase (Bate, 1963, p. 237), negative capability (NC) was coined by John Keats, in a letter he wrote to his brother. In the letter, he observed;

> "I had not a dispute but a disquisition with Dilke, on various subjects; several things dovetailed in my mind, & at once it struck me, what quality went to form a Man of Achievement especially in Literature & which Shakespeare possessed so enormously—I mean *Negative Capability*, that is when man is capable of being in uncertainties, Mysteries, doubts, without any irritable reaching after fact & reason—Coleridge, for instance, would let go by a fine isolated verisimilitude caught from the Penetralium of mystery, from being incapable of remaining content with half knowledge. This pursued through Volumes would perhaps take us no further than this, that with a great poet the sense of Beauty overcomes every other consideration, or rather obliterates all consideration" (*KL* I: 193–4 as cited by Ou, 2009, p. 1).

NC seems to be an oxymoron at first sight. It appears that Keats did not have a word to express what he wanted to and therefore perhaps created it using his knowledge of electricity where the negative anode receives impulses passively to combine with the positive cathode to create electricity (Goellnicht, 1976).

Keats developed the concept organically over a period of time while also exemplifying it in his own work (Ou, 2009). He was against one's need to rush to certainty with consecutive reasoning (Bate, 1963, 2012). He lamented the inability to stay in mystery and doubt and opined that running after truth with consecutive reasoning will never get one to the truth. He wanted to convey that rationalism and reasoning are not the only way to understand life's mysteries. In fact, they prevent one from getting to the essence of an issue with focus on the exterior, leading to knowledge that is mediate rather than immediate (Bate, 2012). The obsession with rational analysis, according to him, destroys the imaginative apprehension of the mystery just as a singular focus on describing a rainbow scientifically robs it of its beauty and essence (Goellnicht, 1976).

The phrase traveled from literature to psychology (Bion, 1977), to management (Chia & Holt, 2009; Chia & Morgan, 1996; French, 2001) and even economics (Bronk, 2009). It has been defined as the ability to resist certainty and closure and reach the essence or the core of the matter/mystery by staying passive and receptive, allowing one's imagination to soar and come to an intuitive understanding through sympathetic identification, in a state of diligent indolence (Saggurthi & Thakur, 2016). Diligent indolence, which is a phrase of contraries—diligent and indolent—means to "operate on a sense of idleness" (Bate, 1963, p. 252)-not laziness- without fretting for an answer. This is the state where the body can overpower the mind, and mind can be a "thoroughfare" (Bate, 2012, p. 68) for various thoughts, where they will dovetail with the help of imaginative freedom and sympathetic identification that are integrative. NC can be best expressed in the below lines:

> To look at any thing
> If you would know that thing,
> You must look at it long:
> To look at this green and say
> "I have seen spring in these
> Woods," will not do—you must
> Be the thing you see:

313

You must be the dark snakes of
Stems and ferny plumes of leaves,
You must enter in
To the small silences between
The leaves,
You must take your time
And touch the very place
They issue from
(Poem by Moffit, 1971, as cited by Moustakas, 1990, p. 12)

Presencing

The word presencing was coined by Otto Scharmer (2008, 2009) with an intention, like Keats' negative capability, to express something that was in the field but had no word. When he interviewed innovators and saw how their decisions were informed by a higher future possibility, he was reminded of his own days as an activist, when they acted driven, more by what he called "the felt sense of future possibility" than by the topic itself (Office Hours, October 26, 2017), he looked for a word to describe this but did not find one. He then came across the word "presencing" used by a French translator of Heidegger's work (Scharmer, 2009) and thought "that's a cool word!" (Office Hours, October 26, 2017). He realized that this word succinctly expressed his thoughts.

Presencing, according to Scharmer (2009) is the capacity to connect to the emerging future possibility and to operate in that connection in the now. The word presencing includes all the three meanings that the word can offer which are pre-sense, presence, and be present (Varela & Scharmer, 2000). It has been described as "the blending of sensing and presence, means to "connect with the Source of the highest future possibility and to bring it into the now" (Scharmer, 2009, p. 163). We only know presencing when something presents itself through pre-sensing.

Presencing is seen as an antidote to absencing. The future is absenced. This happens when one is stuck in the past and operates from there. Fettered by the past, one loses the freedom to imagine the future and thus possibilities cannot be seen. Stuck in one truth and in oneself (Scharmer & Kaufer, 2013), it becomes difficult to grasp the inner knowing that is emerging from the field even though it is clear that the past no longer serves either the present or the future (Scharmer, 2009). However, following the past gives one a sense of certainty and control and therefore becomes very difficult to let go of, however desirable a new future might be.

The U journey with both sensing (the current reality) and presencing (the highest future potential) involves participating consciously in a larger social field for change. A social field is a "totality and type of connections through which the participants of a given system relate, converse, think and act" (Scharmer, 2009, p. 4). Acting from this vantage requires answering the questions "who we are and the inner place or source from which we operate, both individually and collectively" (Senge, Scharmer, Joseph, & Flowers, 2005, p. 5). It means focusing on the source of our being with the fundamental question "Who am I? And what am I here to do?" before we begin to act. The "I" here is one's higher self, and the work the purpose of one's existence (Senge et al., 2005, p. 101). One of our colleagues described his presencing experience as follows:

> "When we did the stepping into the field of the future exercise, guided mediation, there I got a clear under-standing of what my future self is telling my current self—and that gave me an idea—it is hard to put into words. Because the presencing moment is like the real embodi-ment of how this feels like ... how does this future-self feel like and what is this energy ... I was getting goose bumps all over and it really felt like ... it's still happening while I am talking about that and then you really connect with this energy and it gives you a spark of the potential that is wanting to arise. I am a very imaginative person. I have pictures of ... I am a very pictureful thinker so ... I have pictures and so I imagine myself in a different environ-ment ... and this gives me really the feeling of sensing or the sensation of what that feels like ..."

NC and Presencing

As we look at our current self and envisage our future self, presencing happens in those moments when the past, the future, and one's authentic self resonate (Scharmer, 2009). We get the essence of the mystery we are seeking in this moment, which we then crystallize. NC, on the other hand, concerns itself about reaching this "penetralium of mystery" (*KL* I: 193–4 as cited by Ou, 2009, p. 1), that is, the sanctum sanctorum or the inner core of the thing that is our object of attention or focus, which in this case is our future self. The sympathetic identification aspect of NC enables us to become this object, that is, assume its identity and enter into the silences in between with its imaginative openness and passive receptivity in a state of diligent indolence and thus reach the essence of the thing we are seeking to know (Bate, 1963, 2012; Goellnicht, 1976; Ou, 2009).

When we juxtapose the two, we can see that the essence of presencing and the essence of intense creativity are the same as they both are about bringing forth or emergence. And NC takes one to the essence. We presence this essence when we act with NC. This essence that comes through NC is the truth which is beautiful (Keats). In other words, NC helps "presence" the moment of truth and beauty.

On delving deeper, we realize that both the concepts have certain common points of deep philosophical considerations/assumptions. Both come from a participatory philosophy (Heron & Reason, 1997). Their ontological assumptions about reality are similar, that is, both stand on the ground that reality is subjective–objective and that they interpenetrate (Heron & Reason, 1997). Epistemologically, this reality can be known through not only a cognitive knowing but also a sensual aesthetic knowing. Both NC and presencing are against the Cartesian split and espouse intimate knowing of the subject (Shotter, 2005) moving toward a Dionysian way of knowing (Heron & Reason, 2013). The foundation of both NC and presencing is awareness and attention—being aware of and paying attention to the sensory impulses that lead to the truth or the heart of the matter. Their focus is on a knowing which is intuitive and immediate (Bate, 2012; Scharmer, 2009).

316

This kind of knowing, as Keats says, is not customary.

Focusing on the subtleties of the concepts leads us to the understanding that both presencing and NC direct our attention to intuitive, instinctive knowing (Bate, 2012; Scharmer, 2009). This knowing can be stifled by the voice of judgment, voice of fear, and voice of cynicism (Scharmer, 2009, p. 245). The social technologies useful to work with these voices (Bate, 2012; Scharmer, 2009) also appear to be related to NC. Open mind, which disarms the voice of judgment and enables seeing, closely approximates the passive receptive aspect of NC. Open heart, which sets aside the voice of cynicism, requires a deeper submission of self (Goellnicht, 1976; Ou, 2009), another aspect of NC, that enhances sensing capacity with sympathetic identification. Once the ego is overcome, one can lose one's self and become "more duck than the duck, more apple than the apple" (Bate, 2012, p. ii), taking one close to the source. Open will, which is to have "no mechanical determinism towards self-love" (Bate, 1963, p. 258), helps set aside fear of loss of identity. This enables presencing because one is in a position to let go, to let come. This is also required for one to be imaginative. With this disinterestedness, one can let one's imagination soar till everything falls in place (Ou, 2009). Thus, we see how the two concepts are entwined with each other. The same is represented in the table below.

Social technology	What it does	Aspect of presencing that it enables	Aspect of negative capability that it is related to
Open mind	Disarms the voice of judgment	Seeing	Passive and receptive awareness
Open heart	Sets aside the voice of cynicism	Sensing	Sympathetic identification
Open will	Sets aside fear of loss of identity	Presencing	Imagination

Having unraveled the common philosophical foundations and the close relationship between the social technology of U and NC, deciphering the differences would help us to understand the complementary relationship between the two concepts. For Keats' NC, the accent is on a "voyage of conception" (Keats as quoted by Goellnicht, 1976, p. 18) with the object of contemplation. "Wander with it, muse upon it and reflect from it and bring home to it, prophesy upon it and dream upon it" where a "doze on a sofa does not hinder it and a nap upon clover engenders ethereal finger pointings" (Keats as quoted by Goellnicht, 1976, p. 18). He says that we do not "go hurrying about," "impatiently from a knowledge of what is to be arrived" but be "passive and receptive," taking "hints from every noble insect that pays us a visit," (Keats as quoted by Goellnicht, 1976, p. 18) where different insights "dovetail," (Keats as quoted by Goellnicht, 1976, p. 40) leading to a deeper awareness of the mystery. This dovetailing is not by means of any rules of logic but an apprehension through imaginative speculations and sympathetic identification.

Presencing, on the other hand, with its fundamental questions and practices, is closely related to the first-person action inquiry (AI) (Torbert & Taylor, 2013) where one acts with intention, making choices with awareness using the practices of autobiographical writing, meditation, art (Reason & Torbert, 2001), and journal writing among other things. We see, sense, presence, and crystallize our choices with the discipline of these practices. When the questions are raised to "What do we collectively wish to create?" it moves to a group level (second-person AI) and collective level (third-person AI). We co-initiate inquiry into issues of mutual concern, co-sense, and co-presence. Along with the personal practices for self, it also includes an interpersonal dialog (Reason & Bradbury, 2013). In other words, it is a journey of conscious and intentional inquiry, "in the midst of the real-time actions of our daily lives" (Torbert, 2006, p. 207).

Whereas the process of presencing can be enabled with specific practices such as journaling, empathy walk, stakeholder interviews, and listening practices (ref. Scharmer, 2009, p.448), NC is developed from life itself. For Keats, the world was a "vale of soul making" (Bate, 2012, p. 35) and "the world a school and the human heart a horn book used in that school" (Bate, 2012, p. 36). The pains and the pleasures of life are to be experienced and accepted to be able to develop NC. This acceptance of life, with all its pleasures and pains and experiencing life's lessons as one lives, "school[s] one's intelligence and make[s] it a soul" (Keats as cited by Bate, 2012, p. 36). This helps in being able to imagine into the other as the self gets liberated from the "egotistical sublime" (Bate, 2012 p. II). Keats, therefore, calls for a life of sensations, meaning thereby to use one's senses—touch, hearing, and sight to experience life and grasp the meaning of the particular experience (Bate, 2012).

The U journey with its practices that leads to presencing becomes a metaphysical or a spiritual journey, whereas NC is more about living life in all its intensity. While the U journey calls for the support of a circle of friends who would hold the space (Scharmer,2009), NC occurs in solitary diligent indolence:

> "I was led into these thoughts, my dear Reynolds, by the beauty of the morning, operating on a sense of Idleness—I have not read any Books, the Morning said I was right—I had no idea but of the morning, and the thrush said I was right" (Keats as quoted by Wigod, 1952, p. 390).

Representing the Resonance

We posit that moments of presencing come about with NC with its imagination as an essential aspect—imagination of possibilities, imagining into the other, imagining into the future, in a state of diligent indolence. And, with heart's affections, all "disagreeables evaporate"(Bate, 2012, p. 48) taking one through the proverbial "gate" or the "eye of the needle" (Senge et al., 2005, p. 93). This emergent future is fraught with mystery. Mystery is also a place of doubt. It is the place where one would prefer "irritable reaching after fact and reason" rather than staying with uncertainty, and doubt. Instead, one would "let go by a fine isolated verisimilitude caught from the penetralium of mystery, from being incapable of remaining content with half knowledge," thus losing the "sense of beauty" that "overcomes every other consideration, or rather obliterates all consideration" (*KL* I: 193–4 as cited by Ou, 2009, p. 1). In other words, it can lead to either repressing the mystery and falling back on the logical analysis or dispersing the energy in anxiety, getting into an activity trap (French, Simpson, & Harvey, 2001).

Between the process of sensing and presencing, there emerges a tiny crack and it is at this opening that NC dovetails all speculations into an insight. In other words, to presence is to open the door to a moment of truth, tune into the truth that NC presents, and act from that truth. Pre-sensing takes us to presencing with NC helping to drop off all that is unimportant and unhelpful. As imagination conceives of different things, sympathetic identification will take one to "the answer," separating all that does not fit in. What then remains is the "holiness of the heart's affections and the truth of imagination." And "what the imagination seizes as beauty must be the truth—whether it existed before or not" (*KL* I: 184-5 cited from Ou, 2009, p. 2). And therefore we propose that "NC is a necessary condition for presencing the emergent future." Strongheart, a participant of the U lab journey shared,

"… my main question for this U lab journey has been: What is my work? And my intention has been around finding meaning and fulfillment in the work that I do. As I stepped through the gate I entered a world of abundance. There were trees and a river and lots of people all around. Everyone was encouraging me and playing about in the beautiful world. I was holding my son's hand and I had the immense feeling that I'm not alone. The world is full of resource and abundance. Joy and play permeated the atmosphere. Golden light shone through the trees and onto my face …. When I entered that world there was complete silence. I had let go of my son's hand and no one from the previous world was there, I was 'alone'. It was dark and at first I could not see or feel anything, I waited. Then what emerged was a profound sense of inner trust, an indestructible faith and trust in my own wisdom. From there, I knew I could help the world simply by showing up in this way. I realized I was teaching and that there were a lot of people waiting to hear what I had to say and to facilitate the discussion. I knew I could do this from a place of deep knowing and co-creation, not from a place of 'I know more than you'. I realized the most important work I have to do in this world is to cultivate, nourish, and deepen this connection of trust in my wisdom (in my Self)" (2017).

When we presence, more often than not, we do so in a symbolic form. The threshold experience at the bottom of U, the point of letting come, has been described as moving through a "sort of inner gate" (Senge et al., 2005, p. 93). This figurative component of the experience of presencing is pre-logical and cannot be grasped by reason. It is a primary knowing (Rosch & Scharmer, 1999) and pre-verbal (Heron & Reason, 2013). These images and symbols are the creative unconscious expressing itself and indicate the spiritual side of human psyche (Neumann, 1973). It is here that NC plays a very important role. What is needed in the moment is to stay with this mystery that the unconscious has thrown up without analyzing it but letting it "permeate" the whole self and be allowed to be "stirred" by it (Neumann, 1973, p. 369). Staying with the sensuous figurative component is important. NC enables one to stay with it without running after the truth with logic and reasoning and allowing the truth to come to them. As we reflect on it, play with the experience, and circle around it, it will speak to our consciousness, our understanding, or the logical self (Neumann, 1973).

NC makes it possible to move into a more intimate and in-depth relatedness with whatever one is beholding or contemplating. With its sustained immersion, receptivity, imagination, and sympathetic identification in a spirit of indolence, we can presence the emergent future as we move beyond our projections and drop down to the soul/spirit. This has creative consequences as doors of perception that were hitherto closed are opened and we can see the heart of reality as it were with the help of our imagination. Once accessed, and insight gained, it is presenced. In the words of Strongheart (2017)

> "Something very concrete and tangible came out of that experience, which is that I'm going to facilitate a workshop on leadership in the next 3 months. The other, tangible and palpable result of the experience was that all day I felt a buzz all around me, an aliveness. I felt incredibly energetic and joyful. It was a field that not only I could feel but others commented on as well. When I described my experience to my counselor later that day, she said she could feel the quality in the room shift."

Crystallizing the Connection: Presencing, Meaning, and NC

The very question "What is at the heart of your work?" or "What is the larger intention that infuses your work and fills it with who you are and your purpose in being alive?" takes it closer to the concept of personal meaning. Meaning is easier to feel than define (Huta, 2016). It gives a sense of purpose, coherence, and significance (Martela & Steger, 2016). It connects a person to the world and vice versa. It is a creative interpretation connecting the inner with the outer world experiences (Dezelic, 2016). It implies the "potential for activity and is thus regulating this activity" (Leontiev, 2012, p. 68); it is "a possibility against the background of reality" (Frankl, 1992, p. 145). Inherent in meaning is a future, and therefore personal meaning can result in a personal project. According to Frankl (1992), one can discover meaning through creating a work, experiencing goodness, truth, and beauty, and adopting an attitude toward inescapable suffering. Meaning is very contextual and can keep changing (Leontiev, 2016). In this context, the focus is on creating something that is meaningful.

Although the psychological definition of experiencing meaning is "feelings of sense, resonance, value, purpose," the metaphysical meaning is "perceiving, building and subjectively participating in a much more deeper and more general phenomena." When this happens, we are closest to life, closest to the source (Huta, 2016, p. 4). Finding meaning is to be "connected to the highest future possibility that can emerge" (Scharmer, 2008, p. 54) and acting from that place. This "experiencing meaning and participating in meaning is what matters most of all; it is the reason we are here" (Huta, 2016, p. 4). However, "It is *how* we are in the unknown that is the context for the kind of meaning that shows up" (Potter, 2017, p. 6). It leads to either discovering the meaning and the emergent future or "inserting meaning" (Potter, 2017, p. 6) into the unknown.

"At first, there is a homogeneous nothingness, which is nevertheless pregnant with potential (e.g., the buzzing vacuum of quantum field theory, the darkness at the beginning of time of many spiritual traditions). Then, somehow (and this is the ultimate mystery), differences arise (e.g., the symmetry breaking of physics, the split between yin and yang of Chinese philosophy). And as soon as you have differences, you have momentum and direction and purpose, things start moving, and by moving they exist (e.g., in modern physics, there is no such thing as space; there is only space-time). And you immediately have relationships between those entities, their roles are defined with respect to one another. Meaning is the fiber of those relationships" (Huta, 2016, p. 4).

The U journey can be perceived as a journey to presence our meaning by connecting to our deepest source, and then prototyping and crystallizing it. It provides a path to know one's meaning by connecting to the "source" that answers the question what is my work? What am I here for? (Scharmer, 2009) And meaning, when presenced, is felt intuitively (Heintzelman & King, 2013). We posit that it is here in presencing one's meaning that NC comes into play. NC helps in staying with the meaning that has been presenced (Potter, 2017). The connection between presencing and NC in the context of presencing one's personal meaning also comes from James Hillman. Meaning in the metaphysical sense can be one's daimon, a Keatsian call that comes from the heart (Hillman, 1996). It is the genius, the highest future possibility that has to be sensed and presenced. To be able to do this, one requires the imaginative perception of NC.

Presencing, Leadership, and NC

The essence of leadership according to Scharmer is presencing as leaders sense and presence the highest future possibility and take actions from the "field of future possibility that wants to emerge" (Scharmer, 2009, p. 186). According to him it is about "acting from the emerging whole" (p.352) and operating from a future space of possibility that wants to appear (Scharmer, 2009).

Twenty-first-century leadership yearns for a "leadership of possibility" (Adler, 2011, p. 208). It has become possible to work backward from imagination and aspiration (Adler, 2011), presence this future and then work toward realizing it, which in the language of the U is the highest future possibility. With the gap between what can be imagined and what can be achieved narrowed considerably (Hamel, 2000, as cited by Adler, 2008), the "defining" question then to be asked (Mau et al., 2004 as cited by Adler, 2008, p. 188) is "Now that we can do anything, what do we want to do?" This is a question about the potentialities and possibilities as much as it is a question about the source which is "What is my work?" It would also involve embracing uncertainty, opening oneself to the unthinkable, sometimes attempting to do the impossible and even willingness to fail. But the fears and risks are balanced by feeling part of something important that is emerging that will make a difference.

NC enables creative leadership (French et al., 2001) that is required to create new emergent future possibilities. According to them, leaders work at the edge of knowing and not knowing and NC helps leaders to be receptive to new possibilities at this edge. With its imaginative openness, it enables leaders to construct a future that is not based on the past but from a future they would like to create. Leaders with their passive receptiveness can view problems from different perspectives in all its complexities , even if discomfiting, and become explorers of new ideas. Not rushing for a closure, they would have the capacity to step back and see the significant connections that arise using all their sensory capacities (Bronk, 2009).

Leading from the emergent future also calls for a capacity to tune into others and be in harmony with the situation or the context. With NC, leaders can "imagine into the other" (Hillman, 2006) and imagine the possibilities. Suspending habitual patterns of thinking, they can stay open to what imagination brings up which provides a "unified" understanding (Depraz, Varela, & Vermersch, 2003, p. 57). Suspension is the place what has been called "[enjoying] our doubts as symptoms in the process of knowledge" (MC Richards, 1964, as cited by Seeley & Reason, 2008, p. 36). It is also a place of empathic attunement to be out there partaking in the existence of the sparrow "that come before window" ... and "pick about the gravel" (*KL* I: 186 as cited by Ou, 2009, p. 39). It suggests "a most gentle, intimate emptiness" (Bamford, 2005, as cited by Seeley & Reason, 2008, p. 36). With the barrier between the self and the subject removed, it would be possible to become one with the field and connect to the source (Rosch & Scharmer, 1999). But giving up self paradoxically needs a strong sense of self (Ou, 2009) and the ability to stay with the existential uncertainty (Von Pfahl, 2011) that emptiness brings. Withstanding this uncertainty, and accepting the situation, with NC, one can gain a deeper understanding of the reality and see the "eachness" of the situation and be affected by this "eachness" (Hillman, 1996, p.124).

A leader has to let go of the past to be able to presence the future. The process of redirecting attention from the past by letting go dissolves the boundaries between the self and the other; the subject and the object. And this is the place where one would move to passive receptivity, receiving impulses like a flower, "budding patiently ... taking hints from every noble insect that favors us with a visit" (Keats as quoted by Goellnicht, 1976, p. 18). These impulses are inspirations and musings, where mind is a "thoroughfare for all thoughts" (Keats as quoted by Goellnicht, 1976, p. 20). According to MC Richards (in Kane, 2003, as cited by Seeley & Reason, 2008, p. 36), "imagination is something that comes to us before it comes out of us." It is an effort of "holding back of our own activity—a form of receptive attentiveness that offers the phenomenon a chance to express its own gesture" (Brook, 1998, as cited by Seeley & Reason, 2008, p. 37). The phenomenon thus comes forth when there is a letting go and surrendering to the process. Surrender of self leads to sympathetic identification and the truth in that moment presents itself and guides the action that would have to be taken.

NC and presencing together bring the sensuous and the sensing body into leadership. Because NC helps grasp the life force that is at work in that concrete situation (Bate, 2012) which is felt through the body. The force is directly experienced through the sense perception which is participating in the experience (Ponty as cited by Abram, 1997). This hidden intensity is "pregnant with potential for something new and creative to happen" (Ladkin, 2008, p. 33). When leadership presences these possibilities with attention and awareness, suspending doubt, cynicism, and fear, they would be engaging with the aesthetics of leadership (Hansen, Ropo, & Sauer, 2007) and its artistic processes with courage, leading beautifully (Adler, 2011). A leader then becomes like the "strings of a lyre, an instrument" "for organizational inquiry, learning, creativity and action" (French et al., 2001; Simpson, French, & Harvey, 2002, p. 1218), without being seduced by the signifiers of the world (Chia & Morgan, 1996).

Conclusion

If presencing is to see from the deepest source and bring it forth through the "U" a journey with its attendant practices, we posit that NC is a capability that would aid this process. With NC, one develops the capacity to slow down and stay with the mystery that comes forth from that inner source and play with imagination till the heart resonates with the image and truth is presenced.

References

Abram, D. (1997). The spell of the sensuous: Perception and language in a more-than-human world. New York, NY: First Vintage Books Edition.

Adler, N. J. (2008). The arts & leadership: Now that we can do anything, what will we do? Learning Landscapes, 1(2), 187–213.

Adler, N. J. (2011). Leading beautifully: The creative economy and beyond. Journal of Management Inquiry, 20(3), 208–221.

Bate, W. J. (1963). Negative capability. In W. J. Bate (Ed.), John Keats (pp. 13–28, 242–263). Cambridge, MA: The Belknap Press of Harvard University Press.

Bate, W. J. (2012). Negative capability. The intuitive approach in Keats. New York, NY: Contra Mundum Press. First edition. (Original work published 1939)

Bion, W. R. (1977). Prelude to or substitute for achievement. In W. R. Bion (Ed.), Seven servants Attention and interpretation (pp. 125–130). New York, NY: Jason Aronson.

Bronk, R. (2009). The romantic economist. Imagination in economics. London, England: Cambridge University Press.

Chia, R., & Holt, R. (2009). Strategy without design. The silent efficacy of indirect action. Cambridge, UK: Cambridge University Press.

Chia, R., & Morgan, S. (1996). Educating the philosopher-manager: De-signing the times. Management Learning, 27(1), 37–64.

Depraz, N., Varela, F. J., & Vermersch, P. (Eds.). (2003). On becoming aware: A pragmatics of experiencing. Amsterdam/Philadelphia, PA: John Benjamins.

Dezelic, M. (2016). Meaning constructs and meaning-oriented techniques: Clinical applications of meaning and existential exploration. Journal of Constructivist Psychology, 537(January), 1–10.

Frankl, V. (1992).Man's search for meaning: An introduction to logotherapy (4th ed.). Part 1 translated by Ilse Lasch. Preface by Gordon w. Allport Beacon Press.

French, R. (2001). "Negative capability": Managing the confusing uncertainties of change. Journal of Organizational Change Management, 14(5), 480–492.

French, R., Simpson, P., & Harvey, C. (2001). Negative capability: The key to creative leadership. In 18th Annual Meeting of the International Society for the Psychoanalytic Study of Organizations, Paris.

Goellnicht, D. C. (1976). Negative capability and wise passiveness. McMaster University. Hamilton, ON, Canada. Open access dissertations and theses. Paper 4675.

Hansen, H., Ropo, A., & Sauer, E. (2007). Aesthetic leadership. The Leadership Quarterly, 18(6), 544–560.

Heintzelman, S. J., & King, L. A. (2013).On knowing more than we can tell: Intuitive processes and the experience of meaning. The Journal of Positive Psychology, 8(6), 471–482.

Heron, J., & Reason, P. (1997). A participatory inquiry paradigm. Qualitative Inquiry, 3(3), 274–294.

Heron, J., & Reason, P. (2013).Extending epistemology within a co-operative inquiry. In P. Reason & H. Bradbury (Eds.), The Sage handbook of action research: Participative inquiry and practice (pp. 366–380). London, England: Sage. Paper back edition

Hillman, J. (1996). The soul's code: In search of character and calling. New York, NY: Random House.

Hillman, J. (2006). War, peace and the American imagination (Vol. 2014). Atlanta, GA: Glenn Memorial Auditorium at Emory University. https://www.mythicjourneys.org/podcast_2feb06.html

Huta, V. (2016). Meaning as a subjective experience. Journal of Constructivist Psychology, 537(March).

Ladkin, D. (2008). Leading beautifully: How mastery, congruence and purpose create the aesthetic of embodied leadership practice. The Leadership Quarterly, 19(1), 31–41.

Leontiev, D. (2012). Personal meaning as a mechanism of motivational process. In D. A. Leontiev (Ed.), Motivation, consciousness and self-regulation (pp. 65–78). Hauppauge, NY: Nova Science.

Leontiev, D. (2016). The divine knot: A relational view of meaning. Journal of Constructivist Psychology, 0(November 2015), 1–7.

Martela, F., & Steger, M. F. (2016). The three meanings of meaning in life: Distinguishing coherence, purpose, and significance. The Journal of Positive Psychology, 9760(February), 1–15.

Moustakas, C. (1990). Heuristic research: Design, methodology and applications. Thousand Oaks, CA: Sage.

Neumann, E. (1973). The origins and history of consciousness. Bollingen series XLII. Princeton university press. Third printing. October 26, 2017. Retrieved from https://courses.edx.org/courses/course-v1:MITx+15.671.1x+3T2017/cb0c2d405df944ce97da1ea01bb9de1f/

Ou, L. (2009). Keats and negative capability. Continuum literary studies series. London, England: Continuum.

Potter, B. (2017). Eudaimonia, faith (Pistis), and truth (Aletheia): Greek roots and the construction of personal meaning. Journal of Constructivist Psychology, 30(1), 57–62

Reason, P., & Bradbury, H (2013). Introduction. Reason, P & Bradbury, H (Eds.), The Sage handbook of action research: Participative inquiry and practice (pp. 1–10). London, England: Sage. Paper back edition

Reason, P., & Torbert, W. R. (2001). The action turn: Toward a transformational social science. Concepts and Transformation, 6(1), 1–37.

Rosch, E., & Scharmer, C. O. (1999). Primary knowing: When perception happens from the whole field. Conversation with Professor Eleanor Rosch, Dept. of Psychology, University of California, Berkeley.

Saggurthi, S., & Thakur, M. (2016). Usefulness of uselessness: A case for negative capability in management. Academy of Management Learning and Education, 15(1), 180–193.

Scharmer, C. O. (2008). Uncovering the blind spot of leadership. Executive Forum, 59(Winter), 52–59.

Scharmer, C. O. (2009). Theory U: Leading from the future as it emerges. San Franscisco, CA: Berret Koehler.

Scharmer, C. O., & Kaufer, K. (2013). Leading from the emerging future: From ego-system to eco-system economies. San Francisco, CA: Berrett-Koehler.

Seeley, C., & Reason, P. (2008). Expressions of energy: An epistemology of presentational knowing. In P. Liamputtong & J. Rumbold (Eds.). Knowing differently: Arts-based and collaborative research methods (pp. 25–46). New York, NY: Nova Science.

Senge, P., Scharmer, C. O., Joseph, J., & Flowers, B. S. (2005). Presence: Exploring profound change in people, organizations and society. London, England: Nicholas Brealey.

Shotter, J. (2005). Goethe and the refiguring of intellectual inquiry: From "aboutness"-thinking to "withness"-thinking in everyday life. Janus Head,8(1), 132–158.

Simpson, P. F., French, R., & Harvey, C. E. (2002). Leadership and negative capability. Human Relations, 55(10), 1209–1226.

Strongheart, Lulu. (2017, October,22nd) Re: Reflections on Live Session #2 Retrieved from https://www.presencing.org/community/discussion/reflections_on_live_session_2

Torbert, W. R. (2006). The practice of action inquiry. In P. Reason & H. Bradbury (Eds.), Handbook of action research (pp. 207–217). London, England: Sage.

Torbert, W. R., & Taylor, S. S. (2013). Action inquiry: Interweaving multiple qualities for attention for timely action. In P. Reason & H. Bradbury (Eds), The SAGE handbook of action research: Participative inquiry and practice (pp. 239–251). London, England: Sage. Paper back edition

Varela, F., & Scharmer, O. C. (2000). Three gestures of becoming aware. Conversation with Fransico Varela. January 12, 2000, Paris.

Von Pfahl, L. (2011). The ethics of negative capability. Nineteenth-Century Contexts, 33(5), 451–466. Wigod, J. D. (1952). Negative capability and wise passiveness. Publications of the Modern Language Association of America, 67(4), 383–390.

CHAPTER 11

Crossing the Threshold of Presencing Using Values and Narrative Coaching

Christine Cavanaugh Simmons
Marcy Strong
Victor Shewchuk

Stepping into the field of the future starts with attending to the opening of an inner crack. Following that crack requires us to let go of the old and 'let grow' something we can sense, but that we cannot fully know before we see it emerge. (Scharmer & Kaufer, 2013)

"There is a crack, a crack in everything. That's how the light gets in" (Cohen, 1992, track 5).

The metaphor of the 'crack' accurately captures the moment when our consciousness is pierced with light and we cross the threshold into the field of the future. This chapter will provide professional leadership coaches with a methodology that consistently guides the leader toward this 'crack', through deep listening to the use of language along the pathway of Theory U. The authors, in working with leaders over time, have observed that the experience of moving through these 'cracks' form generative and agentic identity constituting moments.

The authors will begin with the backdrop of the world's current need for this approach to coaching. The chapter will then lay out the theoretical streams of thought informing our work and then continue with the specific steps for how to use language as meaning making, values awareness and personal narratives as a path into the "Source" out of which a leader can create new realities and new outcomes (Scharmer, 2009). Once the theoretical groundwork is in place, the chapter will delve into the specific tools which include exploration of language as reality and identity constructions, values, values identification questions for gathering recollections of identity constituting narratives, finishing up with levels of listening associated with moving through the 'U'. Finally, we will explore the interior condition of the coach which enables presencing. Examples and direct quotes from coaches will be provided to ground the approach in the experience of practitioners.

Presencing is a state where we connect with our authentic self from the space of generativity and potential in the moment (Scharmer, 2009). It is that moment when one's potential is perceived for the first time and this new potential enables us to decide to enter and 'be' in the future as we interact with the present moment. In the leaders we coach, bringing forth the insights found in the state of presencing is needed more now than ever before. In today's organizations, there is an urgent need for guideposts to help leaders meet the challenges driven by what psychologists refer to as a VUCA (volatile, uncertain, complex and ambiguous) world (Woodruff, 2017). Today's pace of change is unlike anything we have ever seen and VUCA is present in every organizational domain; nonprofit, for profit, and philanthropy. "Today's leaders can no longer rely on best practices, experts or prior learning to face wicked problems or when all hell breaks loose" (Snowden, 2002). Rather, today's leader must be able to inhabit a positive, possible future through a threat lens of VUCA, embrace the threats while focusing on what is emerging with personal values clarity and with the agility to re-author their world (Swart, 2016). These new stories of possibility come through the 'crack' of presencing.

Theoretical Underpinnings of our Approach

The theoretical streams flowing through our approach come from values theory, narrative therapy and social constructionism, which are all decidedly a postmodern take on how we construct our identity and our reality.

Language

There is no better place to begin this review of the philosophy guiding our work than these quotes which convey the power of language to represent our meaning system as well as how language is the portal to a generative future:

"The limits of my language are the limits of my mind. All I know is what I have words for" (Wittgenstein, Hacker, & Schulte, 2009).
"The limits of my language mean the limits of my world" (Wittgenstein, Hacker, & Schulte, 2009).
"All transformation is linguistic" (Block, 2008).
"Such speaking [that alters being] has a direct and lasting impact; in the very act of speaking, it alters the course of events (Erhard, 1984).

These quotes underscore the belief that we create our world through discourse in relationship with each other, which is the world of language and words. The postmodern philosophers have gone so far as to say that we cannot inhabit or build a world for which we do not have the words (Blackmore, 2016). This notion of language is a significant departure from seeing language as simply a mapping device and posits that "meaning is understood as a derivative of language use within relationships" and "because language constitutes what we take to be the world, and rationalizes the form of reality thus created, it also serves as a socially binding force" (Gergen, 2011). Values theorists and creators of values measurement tools have long known that "language is the bridge between inner images and the external world...there is something inherent within written and spoken languages that can alter a person's consciousness...this something is values" (Hall, 1994).

Values

It is with this belief that we create our world through values aware language, that the values and narrative coaching methodology is founded. Values are "the ideals that give significance to our lives that are reflected through the priorities we choose and that we act on consistently and repeatedly" (Hall, 1994). In short, they are energy, they drive our behavior, and they are most often in operation outside of our conscious awareness (Hyatt & De Ciantis, 2014). Values coaching goes beyond the focus on performance or practices in many approaches to executive coaching to guide the leader to their meaning making system and therefore the source of one's life (Lazar & Berquist, 2003). In terms of accessing the state of presencing, values matter because these aspirational ideals, once identified and named, can act as a pulling force from where one is in their values orientation to the emerging future (Hall, 1994). In the process of one on one coaching with a leader, values are detectable in spontaneous speech. Having an understanding that values "are most present in our spontaneous speech, [means that] our values influence our approach to group problem solving, our decision-making, as well as our personal motivation" (Bristol, 2002). Operating from this understanding that values are embedded in the words we use, the coach's ear becomes tuned to listen for the values words and values patterns. This enables the coach to guide the leader to greater awareness of the values that act as stepping stones toward the possible. The coach's ability to support the leader's conscious awareness of their values, is the critical first step (Hall, n.d.).

It is through language and the use of a comprehensive vocabulary of values, mapped to a developmental framework, that allows the coach to guide the leader in the coaching conversation toward presencing in a predictable manner. In the language of Theory U, it is through new values words that carry shared meaning in the coaching dialogue that the emerging future opens.

> It is by languaging that the act of knowing, in the behavioral coordination which is language, brings forth a world. We work out our lives in a mutual linguistic coupling, not because language permits us to reveal ourselves but because we are constituted in language in a continuous becoming that we bring forth with others (Maturana & Varela, 1987).
>
> A new word is like a fresh seed sown on the ground of discussion (Wittgenstein, Hacker, & Schulte, 2009).

With the use of values words, there is a highly intentional use of language, both as the coach listens for values in the words used as well as the coach's introduction of words into the dialogue. Within values coaching, the coach is using a values methodology that is both developmental and goals/means oriented such that the coach can use the model to introduce values words which act as a structure from what is known to what is possible. The importance of having a values-based tool that is constructed with theoretically valid developmental models is critical because it provides values families or tracks. These values tracks provide the necessary pathways that span from the earliest values received from our culture context and family, all the way through to the most integrated and elevated expressions of human actions and endeavors (Hall, n.d.). The authors insist that without a robust tool that names the full range of human values, the practitioner is limited by their own values vocabulary. To use the accessible values from only the coach's personal experience and world view, or to utilize values lists which are limited to 50 or fewer values, is to limit the alternatives toward generating new worlds for the leader. The tools used by the authors to access the inner world of the leader are two methodologies of over 125 discreet values, represented by words with discreet definitions. Without these frameworks, the coach would be subject to their own belief system and priorities guiding the introduction of words to describe a possible future rather than listening and bridging from the leader's own meaning system. This approach is a conscious departure from 'coach as expert' which is often the taken for granted approach in which goals or objectives for change are driven by the coach or negotiated with the leader and/or their organization.

Values provide the seed for an enhanced vocabulary of language describing what has always been felt as personally significant however not yet named. In the coaching process, the coach would only offer a 'scaffolding' vocabulary which is consistent with the client's stated values that link to an idealized, or aspirational self. As the metaphor of scaffolding implies, the offered value word guides the leader from what they are aware of or 'know' into new insights and choices which represent an imagined future self. This process acts as a temporary framework that is put up for support and access to meaning and becomes integrated into spontaneous speech as the client refines their choices among the alternatives along the values path they have been given at the outset of the coaching process.

As a leader begins to talk about their aspirational values, they shift, physically and emotionally. The leader will demonstrate increased excitement, their face will flush, they can become more animated, or alter their cadence of speech as they respond to the values words and definitions. As they continue to talk, new insights arrive, often in the form of "I've never thought about this that way before" or a pause with a "Hunh!".

> A shift in speaking and listening is the essence of transformation. If we have any desire to create an alternative future, it is only going to happen through a shift in our language. If we want a change in culture, for example, the work is to change the conversation–or, more precisely, to have a conversation that we have not had before, one that has the power to create something new in the world. This insight forces us to question the value of our stories, the positions we take, our love of the past, and our way of being in the world. (Block, 2008)

This level of coaching requires that the coach have competency and fluency in the language of values so that they can shift linguistically. This is founded on the understanding that words do not carry meaning, rather that they trigger meaning (Swart, 2016). A values coaching approach means that the coach is orienting to a map of values, listening for what the client wishes to bring into being from a vision or idealized aspiration which then guides the coach to offer values word choices to guide them from a current world view into the desired field of possibility. It is also worth noting that, in one of the values maps used by the authors, there is a value called Word which is placed at the most advanced point on a developmental track (Hall, 1994). This value is defined as:

> the ability to use the power of language to heal and transform the values and world views of the hearers. To communicate universal truths so effectively that the hearers becomes conscious of their limitations, so that life and hope are renewed as the hearer recognizes their place in the larger, universal order. (Hall, 1994)

In values coaching, when the co-creative process of coaching is at its most transformative, the coach is able to guide the leader to see the power of this value, Word, in the exact moment of living into the value. Through the coaching dialogue, it is the sharing of stories which make the values coherent (Bhatkin, 1981). It is only with and through the stories that the coach and the client can inhabit a world of shared meaning.

Narrative

It is the merging of the values mapping tool with autobiographical remembrances that bring the individual's values alive. The theoretical guidance for the use of stories comes from narrative psychology and social constructionism. The use of autobiographical remembrances to give coherence to the values is founded on the belief that stories are how we make sense of our lives and the world and how we communicate with others. Stories also are how we make sense of *ourselves*. It is these expressions of people's experiences of a world that is lived through and all expressions of lived experience engage people in interpretive acts (White, 1997). It's the stories we tell ourselves that we live into and are identity constituting.

> The stories we construct to make sense of our lives are fundamentally about our struggle to reconcile who we imagine we were, are *and might be* ... in the social contexts of family, community, the workplace, ethnicity, religion, gender, social class and culture writ large. Whether aimed at finding meaning in yesterday's conversation around the water cooler or in a 15-year marriage that ended two decades ago, autobiographical reasoning is an exercise in personal integration—putting things together into a narrative pattern that affirms life meaning and purpose. (McAdams, 2008)

Because we know from narrative psychology that we employ narratives to author a sense of self in a unified manner which happens across a lifespan, the inquiry into the values begins with one's life story (McAdams, 1993). How the life story is used in the early stages of reflective inquiry in the coaching dialogue will be explored in depth later in this chapter when sharing the specific steps of the coaching process.

When contracting with the leader to share stories, just the simple use of the metaphor of story or narrative has an impact because the mind immediately perceives story as something outside of ourselves. The minute the mind goes to that place there is an opening to introduce the concept that if we fashion our story of self, we can also re-fashion and evolve that story. The leader begins to understand that our narratives are interpretive acts; self-generated acts of creating self and consequently self's relationship with the world.

It is important to see how "our narrative identities are the stories we live by" (McAdams, 2013). When choice and a sense of agency is coupled with guidance by a coach to include a word or metaphor, that new world of words opens possibility. In many cases, a new possibility can uncover undervalued or previously overlooked stories which become the seed of a new story, or as named in narrative therapy, the preferred or counter narrative (White, 2007). These new narratives are what are found in the light shining through the crack guiding us into presencing.

Through values clarification within a narrative framework, the leader and coach can begin seeking the discontinuity or crack between the two stories of 'Who am I?" and 'What is possible?' This level of self-knowledge and agency to re-story gained from the exploration of old and new stories places the leader in a reflective stance which allows self-observation of their thoughts and actions. Once guided by the coach into a state of self-reflexivity, the leader can think with the coach and co-author a new story, out of the co-created dialogue.

Two of the most important concepts taken from narrative therapy are first, the position of the coach in the coaching relationship and second, how to listen for what is implied (White, 1997). The relationship of the coach to the client has been named decentered and speaks to walking away from the power dynamics in any coaching, consulting or counseling relationship (White, 2007). Though not all coaches interviewed for this chapter used the same nomenclature to describe a decentered stance, each coach spoke of the honoring of each person's resources and uniqueness and stepping away from the expert model for coaching. Decentered coaching is in keeping with the stance of "I in You" and "I in Now" found in the co-creative container constructed by the coach and the leader (Scharmer, 2009). The guiding principles that narrative therapy, with its influences from Foucault, provides an awareness of how a coach carries normative judgements or evaluations and an unconscious authority as the "helper" (White, 2007). A decentered stance by the coach fully embraces the notion that we must decline the invitations to be the expert in people's lives and to fully honor the leader's ideas and resources.

Coaching as decentered but influential means that the relationship is collaborative and respectfully guided by inquiry that influences without imposing the coach's beliefs and values. Instead, it explores the leader's preference for authoring their lives. The coach listens for and is interested in, people's hopes, values, intentions, dreams, beliefs, goals and aspirations (White 1997).

Each coach interviewed indicated how important the very close attention to the linguistic and narrative worlds of the leader is for entering their world of values and aspirations. There was also a shared understanding among the interviewees that before ever hoping to accurately guide the leader toward what they know, which is often 'hidden in the plain sight' of their stories, the coach needs to put the leader's beliefs, preferences, hopes and dreams in the center of the conversation (Morgan, 2002).

This requires the specialized techniques for engaging in listening and framing questions that are unique to narrative therapy. Listening for what is inferred, commonly referred to as double listening, opens the pathway for the coach to listen for what is important by what is implied by the value laden story rather than focusing only on the actual words (White, 1997). The implied important value can be hidden behind a problem story because the leader is blocked from living out a value. Alternatively, if there is an aspirational value that is just beyond the leader's conscious ability to name but can be accessed by a related value in their current values track, bringing it forward enables them to connect into a wider field of meaning for themselves. Both problem and aspirational stories can carry the values that foreshadow an identity shift and a greater sense of congruence and authenticity which flow out of the generative field of presencing (Scharmer, 2009). What the coach is taking in when listening in this way is holistic; nonverbal cues, voice inflection and where the story may fit within a pattern of values. This type of listening bridges both empathetic and generative listening as described by Scharmer (2008). It encompasses empathetic listening in that we are "listening to the story of a living and evolving world" and connecting to the leader from the heart (Scharmer, 2008). Rogers (1980) speaks about how this type of listening and a decentered stance results in

> [the] sensitive ability and willingness to understand the client's thoughts, feelings and struggles from the client's point of view [is] this ability to see completely through the client's eyes, to adopt his frame of reference...". "It means entering the private perceptual world of the other...being sensitive, moment by moment, to the changing felt mean-

ings which flow in this other person... It means sensing meanings of which he or she is scarcely aware.... (Rogers, 1980)

It enables generative listening by diving into meaning for the leader which connects to the emerging future and a deep source of knowing (Scharmer, 2008). Employing rich values frameworks, narrative processes and methods developed in narrative therapy, a coach can be both guide and co-creator with the leader to connect with the state of presencing and the emerging future literally inhabiting the same world of the spoken words together (Scharmer, 2009). Within the context of presencing, values laden narratives provide a means to access deeply held ideals that constitute what meaningfully calls that individual forth into the world, both in terms of action as well as for how they see themselves as part of a larger whole. This enables leaders to craft new solutions as well as step into greater personal capacity to lead.

Values Based Narrative Coaching Alongside Theory U

"Part of becoming a great coach is being able to dance with the emergent" (personal communications). The following step by step process of coaching assumes that best practices established for executive coaching such as ethics, contracting and relationship building etc. have been followed before and during the engagement (coachfederation.org/core-competencies, n.d.).

The image (figure 1) that follows provides a representation of this moment by moment process that most closely resembles our experiences of diving deeply into presencing with our clients.

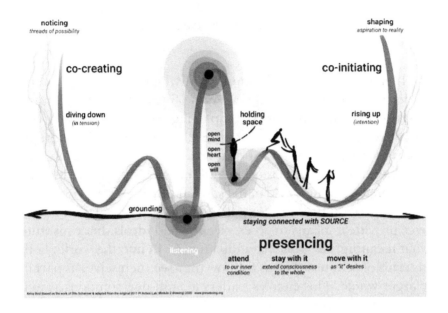

Figure 1. Presencing, Presencing Master Class: Session Two. Adapted from Presencing by K. Bird, 2020. Retrieved from http://www.kelvybird. com/tag/presencing/. Copyright 2011 by Kelvy Bird. Reprinted with permission.

Coaching Process

Each engagement starts with the leader going through a values clarification and prioritization process. As we have emphasized earlier in this chapter, using a tool which is designed with developmental models integrated into the maps, accepted definitions of discreet words that convey specific values, and written reports which provide various looks at the values selected is critical.

Sitting with the reports, the coach and the leader begin to explore priority values, groups of values that form a world view as well as a developmental sequencing of three values groups which are: foundational or deeply integrated early life values, values that are active and consciously lived out in the present and those values which are aspirational and call the leader to the future. Because words, even when they carry a definition, only have meaning that we assign to them, the coach is observant of stories which have energy and aliveness for the leader. This energy and the curiosity about these values laden stories determines a starting point and provides the initial threads of possibility.

"Values are energy words connected by language and it is the energy conveyed in language that makes a dent, a ripple, in working with the leader" (personal communications). Starting with a key value, the coach invites the leader to review a definition of that value and asks about the meaning that it triggers. Listening for the leader's 'first words' is important for the coach as these words from their spontaneous speech are typically highly relevant to how the leader has experienced a given value. The coach's close attention to the patterns and relationships between the values in the stories is mirrored back by pointing out what additional values they have heard in the leader's story.

Initially, while the leader is still gaining an understanding of the values and is warming to the story telling, there is a moving back and forth from Downloading as they orient to the values map and speaking from a point of view as they think about the meaning of the values as lived in their autobiographical memories (Scharmer 2009). It is through the coach's connecting the values selected to values heard in their stories that helps the leader grow in their awareness of their word choice and language, not the coach's, and begin to make the connections to how groups of values, or values clusters, inform their life and their highest purpose (Hall, n.d.). This process connects the leader and the coach to wonder, or "noticing there is a world beyond our patterns of downloading" (Scharmer, 2009). The dialogue enables the coach and leader to see together and this enables the movement down the left side of the U (Scharmer, 2009).

This exploration shifts the coaching conversation from Downloading into Seeing in that the unique value words begin to elicit more specific and meaningful stories and memories (Scharmer, 2009). The coach is listening deeply to the words that the leader is using to understand the meaning it elicits. Then, using questions and bringing forth observations, the coach guides the leader to reflect upon specific metaphors, events, influences and the values that underpin key elements of their meaning system. It is through the focus on values words and their connections to one's meaning system within the autobiographical narrative of "Who am I?" that the leader can begin to see their general attitude toward life which can highlight the basis of what motivates their choices and actions (Cavanaugh-Simmons, 2013).

When bridging into the story telling, it is most effective to begin with the request to look at their life as a story, with chapters and characters. This contracting allows the conversation to proceed with questions that get more directly to the stories that the values elicit. We have found that these questions have a very specific structure which brings the stories out with the greatest ease. Some examples of questions that are most effective are, "Tell me about....", "Describe for me...", "When did (insert value) first show up in your life?", "When were you first aware of something called (insert value)?", "Who in your life has seemed to demonstrate (insert value)?" The method in narrative therapy which allows the leader to think of the value as a character or persona acting outside of the leader is called externalizing (White & Epston, 1990). The process of externalizing is particularly effective if past memories carry a sense of shame or regret (White & Epston, 1990). In these problem stories, externalizing help to separate people's identities from the problems they face and consider their relationships with the problems. "The person is not the problem, the problem is the problem" (White & Epston, 1990). Getting to the details of the specific experiences as well as using their own words is necessary to completely unpack the meaning of the value word to the leader, no matter if the leader views the memory as a crucible, neutral or positive experience.

The following is a typical invitation to share personal stories and guiding the leader gently to focus in on important moments in their life when a particular value was modeled or lived out.

> (Coach) "To make sense of the values words you have selected and bring them to life as we look at them one by one, please share what life events or influences might be associated with that value."

> (Coach) "One of the values that seemed to be of particular importance to you was the value of service."
>
> (Leader) "Yes, I picked that more times than all of the other values. It's been important to me my entire life."
>
> (Coach) "When were you first aware of something called service ?"
>
> (Leader) "I grew up with a Father who was always out in the community. Both my parents were very active in helping people in need and they knew everyone in our small town."
>
> (Coach) "Describe a time that stands out in your mind when you observed your Father and Mother being of service in your small town."

Depending on the scope of the coaching engagement, the coach can begin the process with asking the leader to share their history, even before reviewing the values as just illustrated. The coach can begin by asking the leader to tell the coach about their life, starting with their earliest memories to today. There are well developed processes that the coach can use to conduct a much more in-depth Life Story Interview which can span several sessions (McAdams, 1995).

As the stories are shared, starting with the values that seem to have the most meaning for the leader, the role of the coach is to listen in a way that allows complete openness and the ability to be moved by words and the unique meanings ascribed to them by the leader. "I listen with my whole body. As I am listening I can almost feel a physical sensation of the important words impressing in on me almost like they are leaving a physical impression" (personal communications).

The shift from Seeing to Sensing occurs as the coach and the leader dive deeper into the lived experience of the leader as the stories move forward from earliest memories to current times (Scharmer, 2009). Sensing is the widening of perception to the whole field and being able to see one's experience from a deeper place within the wider system and naturally emerges as the stories connect to the values across the leader's entire life (Scharmer, 2009). "Often, as the storytelling unfolds, the leader will have a moment when they see the through line or the golden thread that is woven into the fabric of their lives, starting from early on to today and how its points to a meaningful future" (personal communication).

Once there is a comfort and flow in the dialogue, the coach is helping the leader to slow down to provide a more detailed understanding of the words and values being discussed within the story that provides its origins and its meaning for the leader. Using the value map's built in path of development, the coach is able to guide the leader, value word by value word, to see the connections in their stories from past to present to future.

(Coach) Can you tell me more about the experience of feeling different from your family?

(Leader) I've always had this sense of a connection to something bigger. When I think of how I was raised, it was very much connected to being Catholic. Although I appreciated the faith, I wrestled with the fear and the guilt that seemed a large part of that experience. This was not my experience of what it felt to be connected to God, a connection to something much bigger than me. On my own, I began to explore why I felt this connection in nature, surrounded by beauty and I found friends that had that same experience. But none of this is what I could share with my family. I tried to share what I felt a couple of times but that was met with concern. I just found it easier to not share.

(Coach) How does that connect with your value of Self-Actualization?

(Leader) I think in those instances, I stopped sharing my whole self so that I would fit in. I didn't want to scare them or make them worry. It was just easier to keep it to myself.

(Coach) How has this shown up in your leadership?

(Leader) In some ways, I still think I am very sensitive to what I share about me. I gauge the room. Sometimes I get told that I am hard to get to know.

(Coach) What I am hearing in your story, is a value

346

that I see you didn't select when you filled this out. Can I bring your attention to Faith/Risk/Vision? Let's look at the definition together. What does this trigger for you?

(Leader) I didn't select it intentionally because that scares me.

(Coach) Can you describe what scares you?

(Leader) That if I told them how I felt about the religion that I would lose my connection to the family.

Even in situations where the leader is telling a story that is steeped in a problem state which they may be interpreting as a situation that is "stuck" or unmoving, the coach is listening closely for the value that is alive just behind the problem. "I am not there to fix their problems, but to offer choices in values to focus on that may help them create a preferred story, often that simple act of choice is creative and therefore transformative" (personal communication).

If a leader is expressing frustration with a situation where there is break down in a process, the value that may be hidden behind the problem is a value for quality and efficiency. The coach, being well versed in the values mapping that is matching to their vocabulary can then inquire about the value that they feel blocked from expressing. Often the leader, upon hearing the value word which is most meaningful for them and which they are feeling blocked from demonstrating, will immediately shift to feeling affirmed in their values and gain new insight for how this value was shaped within them as well as how to move forward through the problem into possibility.

As the coaching session progresses, the leader begins to see the reality they have constructed from these events, their interpretation of these events and, as a result of the self-reflexivity, they begin to see self as constructed or made rather than inherited or static. (Giddens, 1991). The leader then begins to see that there is a multiplicity of possible realities and that they can live a life based on intention, values, purpose and commitments. The coach can facilitate the integration of the past, current and future story of self by asking questions about how their interpretations of these events has changed over time. Inherent to the meaning

making story, the leader will demonstrate that they have extract-
ed lessons and guiding principles from these events. This is a
fundamental insight because it illuminates the agency of choice,
freedom and the construction of a self through interpreting,
learning and re-interpreting important identity constituting
events. Once this insight has been experienced by the leader and
mirrored back by the coach for meaning making, the importance
for life long or permanent self-reflexivity can be reinforced.

A critical next step is to connect the stories so that the leader
can experience how the foundational values shared in their earliest stories are connected to current stories that reflect the values
they are most often focused on demonstrating. When the leader
shares a good memory from the past it will often give them positive images of the future that is now named by the aspirational
values that reflect a vision of a possible future self (Hall, 1994).

The coach can expand the new meaning of this possible future self by introducing words on the same development path or
track as the values explored at the outset of the values review.
This methodology initiates a progression of values fluency within
the leader that enables significant insights of how values evolve
and integrate along with an identification of potential skills to be
integrated towards their vision. If words are worlds as Wittgenstein has said, then the world of the leader becomes expanded to
a wider field. By connecting the foundation, focus and vision values there is a sudden understanding that emerges of what is informing them from the future. "These narratives guide behavior
in every moment and frame not only how we see the past but how
we see ourselves in the future" (McAdams, 2013).

Role of the Coach

The role of the coach as they cross the threshold of presencing is to "hold the leader lightly, truly meet them where they are
at" (personal communications) and to deeply listen to what is
emerging in the formative field by seeing and hearing with the
heart (Scharmer, 2009). It is listening for the meaning beneath
and between the words and making connections which open the

possibility to introduce new values words and thus new worlds for the leader (Brisken, 2009; Lindahl, 2009). This "withnessing" enables reflective dialogue from a decentered stance which generates new forms of experience (Shotter, 2008).

In this state, the coach and the leader are co-creating together as the coach continues to come alongside the meaning being generated by the leader. In this state of "withness" there is a feeling of slowing, both in time and in the conversation as it thickens with meaning, both the coach and the leader are aware of being moved: mind, body and spirit (Shotter, 2008). "There is something I would call silent listening. It happens when I am able to fully merge with the words of the speaker that allows them to speak their true self into it. They can speak more freely and say things they have never said before or even have known about themselves before" (personal communication).

Reflective silence punctuates the questions to delve into the deeper meaning of the values as well as the leader's responses. "When the congruence of the values is clear there is this place that gets created that's a spiritual space. You feel a soul to soul connection with the leader where you both are fully alive" (personal communications). Stillness in this state is where a deep inner wisdom emerges (presencing.com, 2015).

The coach has a feeling of flow with the client, effortlessly following the rhythm of the conversation and sharing authentic and curious questions, or statements that appear in the moment (Csikszentmihalyi, 1997; Corrigan, 2015; Lindahl, 2009). This listening with the whole self also allows images to be perceived and brought into the conversation, often in archetypical images or metaphors.

> "Sometimes the images come along, making a connection to knowing before the words have formed. As I listened (to the leader) I suddenly saw this image of Atlas holding up the world. When I reflected this image to the leader it had deep resonance and I even saw how his body responded to this image. He was able to see something he had not about how he was holding a weight of his world" (personal communications).

It is in that moment of pausing, the shift happens. As coaches we see the shift of energy moving into their body, affect and then connecting to a memory that takes that memory forward into a new understanding. The leader often will say, "I haven't ever said that out loud to anyone!" or "I haven't thought of that before" which can convey the first realization that the state of presencing has been accessed. Presencing opens as we connect deeply with values that inform our source of inner knowing. For the coach, this means fully entering the world of the other's story, with deep witnessing and a heart to heart connection to see the essential self and the core values that are the source of their uniqueness.

> (Leader reflection) I had never thought of the value before. As I sat with the value of Faith/Risk/Vision, I became aware of what it would mean to truly step into the space and honor my own wisdom rather than hiding what I was deeply feeling in order to belong. I sat with my new understanding and I knew that, although it wasn't yet clear, stepping into the space was needed. I felt the weight I'd been carrying lift. I could relax into this new space. I knew I was never going to be the same and that was okay" (personal communications).

Crystalizing occurs when there is a coupling of vision with the leader's desired ends or intent, across the identity they have constructed from their earliest shaping experiences, out to the future (Scharmer, 2009). The leader now can look back at their life from their highest aspirations to see anew how the coherence of their values gives them an expanded sense of self, purpose and possibility. This shared dialogue constructs a universe of meaning aided by self-reflection by the leader, and deep listening on the part of the coach. The leader and coach can work at the level of meaning and emotions. The result is that over several sessions the coach and the leader have a co-created meaning system that is operating from the highest future possibility neither parties would likely have found outside of that container of collective creativity. The process paves the way for significant insights. These insights become vivid, enduring memories of the coaching encounter that continue to act as catalysts for a personal values shift.

After the initial values coaching sessions, the leader takes the insights into action which realizes the prototyping and performing stages of Theory U. The values clarification work enhances their leadership identity, resulting in seeing their life within a narrative structure. With the ability to articulate what their priority values are and where they came from in a narrative structure, the leader can craft a "Who am I?" story that they can share as a way to connect, inspire and guide others (Shewchuk, Cavanaugh-Simmons, & Strong, 2017).

For the coach to fully come alongside the leader requires both an open mind, open heart and open will that flows into the exploration (Scharmer, 2009). It is the holding of the relationship and the feeling of heartfelt connection with the leader so that the coach is moved with the depths of their stories, memories and experience. The co-creation of understanding between coach and leader is also adaptive, often pointing the way to the next 'right' action for the leader. The mental images and/or a knowing in the body for how to act come alive and are important to document because they often foreshadow the enacting and embodying of the leader's new behaviors and what they will look like.

The Interior Condition of the Coach

"When coaching, you prepare and then you let go of the outcome" (personal communications). To hold the space for presencing in this coaching process requires significant personal preparation for the coach. Though this process starts with technical preparation by understanding values reports to chart the mapping of the coaching path and questions, it is important that this preparation does not cloud the coach's ability to see what is emergent. To coach with an open mind in this capacity requires significant personal preparation and awareness - that awareness consists of self-awareness of one's own triggers, values world view and judgements that could block deep listening and connection with another (Corrigan, 2015; Scharmer, 2009). "You have to prepare but all the while you are aware that when you look at the values the leader has chosen you don't condescend or elevate based on your own values" (personal communications). This is especially important because the review of values reports through the developmental lens can cause inferences and projections based on the values of the coach. Being able to see and separate these biases enables the coach to take a stance that is decentered. Without consciously stepping away from old assumptions based in power which are unconsciously assumed by the profession and having knowledge, the coach could unconsciously impair their ability to maintain an open mind and a willingness to listen for what is conveyed by the leader's own words, narrative and meaning making. "When I really see a leader for all their gifts and how only they can be the expert in their life story I feel a sense of connection and sheer privilege in being able to step into their interior world" (personal communications). "After you have enough practice with the technique and the values maps are well ingrained in your head, it makes it much easier to just trust the process. Just let them tell their stories. It's not work at all. You just listen for the patterns and help them see the connections" (personal communication).

Sitting in a values coaching experience with another requires, and brings to the forefront, a coach's own expression of the value of "Presence" or "the ability to be with another person that comes from inner self-knowledge that is so contagious that another person is able to ponder the depths of who he or she is with awareness and clarity" (Hall, 1994). This requires that the coach approach the session with an open heart extending empathy and love to both the client into themselves (Scharmer, 2009). "Just before the session starts, I connect with myself and affirm that I want to show up in the way that is best for the client. I let go of any doubt and I focus on deep caring and welcoming possibility" (personal communications). By connecting with our highest self, we create the safe space that enables both the coach and the client to show up without fear (Bird, 2016).

To live into this value of presence, many of the coaches we interviewed described the practice of centering and slowing down both in breathing and activity prior to the session to enable them to be in the moment and in deep connection with another. "Before the start of a session, I seek out time to be still. I focus on going inside and slowing down. I focus on my breath by taking three slow, full and deep inhales and exhales until my mind quiets. Sometime more are required. I know I am ready when my mind is quiet. I feel receptive, more aware of physical and emotional sensations. I am ready to be moved" (personal communication). "I just seek silence. I might sit under a tree and do deep breathing, whatever I might have the time and space for to just get as silent inside as I can" (personal communications).

As the session starts, it is through the coach's ability to be completely present, open in mind, heart and will, that the coach is able to "inhabit the sacred space" the coaching connection creates (personal communication). This sacred space or "dialogic container" holds the coach and leader in a place of emergent meaning making (Corrigan, 2016). As these containers can collapse without a deep connection, it is essential to hold the space well (Corrigan, 2016). Through the course of the session with the leader, the coach continues to hold this container with attention tuned into the nuances of the leader's language and their physical and emotional changes. This stance of "withness" requires a continued awareness of the coach's inner state and an ongoing maintenance of openness (Shotter, 2008). "I slow down. I slow down my breathing and I am listening with my whole body" (personal communications).

The coaches interviewed all spoke about the somatic level of knowing and sensing which included; slowing down of cognitive and physiological functions, having a feeling of flow with the client, effortlessly following the rhythm of the conversation, having a sense of time out of time and of knowing that is felt through the body, personal awareness of the physical feeling of being moved or impressed when taking in the stories shared by the leader, a noticing of the hypersensitivity of sight and hearing, and a physical sense of diving down into the dialogue to come up and experience the light of expanded awareness. "I can literally feel when there is this diving down. The quality of light in the room can change, it's quite a strong visual cue to me and I have learned to sink into my body even more" (personal communications).

Through this connection and "withness", the coach can fully enter world of their words with reverence and respect as they progress through the Theory U stages (Drake, 2015; Scharmer, 2009; Swart, 2013, Shotter, 2008). *"In this place we meet a "knowing" beyond literal understanding of words, concepts, and impressions.* An intuitive muscle comes online, and it's an absorbent place" (Bird, 2016).

Conclusion

As the world continues to grow more complex, the ability of leaders to access their highest self through presencing is critical and essential. Values and narrative based coaching is one means to access the deep wisdom of this state. Helping make implicit values systems explicit through this coaching process enables the leader to reflect and construct an enhanced view of themselves in their own unique context. Beyond having technical competence in these methods, the coach plays a special role of holding the container for presencing to occur and for wisdom to move through. "I have come to trust that this liminal state will emerge if the leader is ready. The opening to walk across that threshold of the known into the unknown is there in every moment" (personal communications).

The authors would like to thank the coaches they interviewed for generously sharing their stories and experiences for this chapter.

References

Bakhtin, M. M. (1981), The dialogic imagination: Four essays. Austin, TX: University of Texas Press.

Bird, K. (2011, October 29). Presencing master class 2010-12 [Blog post]. Retrieved from http://www.kelvybird.com/tag/presencing/

Bird, K. (2016, April 19.) Steady, to scale [Blog post]. Retrieved from http://www.kelvybird.com/tag/otto-scharmer/page/2/

Blackmore, L. (2016). The Quotable Wittgenstein. Jovian Press.

Block, P. (2008). Community: The structure of belonging. San Francisco, CA: Berrett-Koehler.

Briskin, A., Erickson, S., Ott, J., & Callanan, T. (2009). The power of collective wisdom and the trap of collective folly. San Francisco, CA: Berrett-Koehler.

Bristol, S. (2002). Why values matter. Retrieved from https://www.lj-map.com/Values@Hand/Why_Values_Matter.htm

Cavanaugh-Simmons, C. (2013). Three stories leaders tell: The what and way of using stories to lead. Gold River, CA: Authority.

Cohen, L. (1992). Anthem. On The future [CD] New York, NY: Columbia Records.

Corrigan, C. (2015). Hosting and holding containers. In B. Bushe, & R. Marshak (Eds.), Dialogic organization development: The theory and practice of transformational change (pp. 291-304). Oakland, CA: Berrett-Koehler.

Corrigan, C. (2016). Hosting dialogic containers: A key to working with complexity. OD Practitioner: Journal of the Organization Development Network, 48(2), 21-29.

Csikszentmihalyi, M. (1997). Finding flow: The psychology of engagement in everyday life. New York, NY: Basic Books.

Drake, D. (2015). Narrative coaching: Bringing our new stories to life. Petaluma, CA: CNC Press.

Erhard, W. (1984). A way to transformation. Retrieved from http://www.wernererhard.com/heart.html

Gergen, K. (2011). The Self as Social Construction. Psychological Studies, 56(1), 108–116. doi:10.1007/s12646-011-0066-1

Giddens, A. (1991). Modernity and self-identity. Self and society in the late modern age. Cambridge, UK: Polity Press.

International Coach Federation. (n.d.). Core competencies. Retrieved from https://coachfederation.org/core-competencies/

Hall, B. (n.d.). The omega factor: A values based approach for developing organizations and leadership. Retrieved from http://www.valuestech.com/gui/OmegaFactor4.pdf

Hall, B. (1994). Values shift: A guide for personal and organizational transformation. Rockport, MA: Twin Lights.

Hyatt, K. & De Ciantis, C. (2014). What's important: Understanding and working with values perspectives. Tucson, AZ: Integral Publishers.

Lazar, J., & Berquist, W. (2003). Alignment coaching: The missing element of business coaching. International Journal of Coaching in Organizations, 1(1), 14-27.

Lindahl, K. (2009). Practicing the sacred art of listening: A guide to enrich your relationships and rekindle your spiritual life. Woodstock,

VT: Skylight Paths Publishing.

Maturana, H., & Varela, F. (1987). The tree of knowledge. The biological roots of understanding. Berkeley, CA: Shambala Press.

McAdams, D. (1993). The stories we live by: Personal myths and the making of the self. New York, NY: William Morrow.

McAdams, D. P. (1995). The life story interview. Retrieved from https://www.sesp.northwestern.edu/foley/instruments/interview/

McAdams D. P. (2008). Personal narratives and the life story. In O. John, R. Robins, & L. Pervin (Eds.), Handbook of personality: Theory and research (pp. 242-264). New York, NY: Guilford Press.

McAdams, D. (2013) The redemptive self. Oxford, UK: Oxford University Press.

McAdams, D. (2013). Narrative identity. Current Directions in Psychological Science. 22 (3), 233–238. doi:10.1177/0963721413475622.

Morgan, A. (2002). International Journal of Narrative Therapy and Community Work. Adelaide, AU: Dulwich Centre Publications

Presencing Institute. (2015). Principles and glossary of presencing. Retrieved from https://www.presencing.com/principles

Rogers, C. (1980). A way of being. Boston, MA: Houghton-Mifflin.

Scharmer, O. (2008). Uncovering the blind spot of leadership. Leader to Leader, 47, 52-59. Retrieved from https://www.presencing.com/resources/uncovering-blind-spot-leadership

Scharmer, O. (2009). Theory U: Leading from the future as it emerges. San Francisco, CA: Berrett-Koehler.

Scharmer, O., & Kaufer, K. (2013). Leading from the emerging future: From ego-system to eco-system economies. San Francisco, CA: Berrett-Koehler.

Shewchuk, V., Cavanaugh-Simmons, C., & Strong, M. (2017). Words for Worlds: Developing Leaders through Values and Narrative Processes at the University of Alberta. In R. Koonce, P. Robinson, & B. Vogel (Eds.), Developing Leaders for Positive Organizing: A 21st century repertoire for leading in extraordinary times (pp.389 – 401). Bingley, UK: Emerald Publishing.

Shotter, J. (2008). Conversational realities revisited: Life, language, body and world. Chagrin Falls, OH: Taos Institute Publication.

Snowden, D. (2002). Complex acts of knowing: paradox and descriptive self-awareness. Journal of Knowledge Management, 6(2), 100-111. doi.org/10.1108/13673270210424639

Swart, C. (2016). Re-authoring leadership narratives with and within organizations. OD Practitioner: Journal of the Organization

Development Network, 48(2), 21-29.

White, M. (1997). Narratives of therapists' lives. Adelaide, AU: Dulwich Centre Publications

White, M. (2007). Maps of narrative practice. New York, NY: W. W. Norton and Company.

White, M. & Epston, D. (1990). Narrative means to therapeutic ends. New York, NY: W.W. Norton & Company.

Wittgenstein, L., Hacker, P.M.S., & Schulte, J. (2009). Philosophical investigations. West Sussex, UK: Wiley-Blackwell Publishing.

Woodruff, M. (2017). How to Thrive in a VUCA World: The psychology of navigating volatile, uncertain, complex and ambiguous times. Retrieved from

https://www.psychologytoday.com/blog/spotting-opportunity/201707/how-thrive-in-vuca-world

CHAPTER 12

Perspectives on Voices of Resistance with Experience-based Coaching

Katherine J. Train

"Our deepest fear is not that we are inadequate. Our deepest fear is that we are powerful beyond measure. It is our light, not our darkness, that frightens us most." – Marianne Williamson, *A Return to Love*

Introduction

These words aptly describe the deep seated and insidious human fear of rising to greatness. They are often inadvertently attributed to Nelson Mandela, one of the truly great leaders of our time recognized as a pivotal role-player in dismantling apartheid in South Africa. They speak to widespread human aspiration and challenge evident in the number of times they are quoted in the context of Mandela. To presence the emergence of a better future requires facing some of the most deep rooted of fears.

Fear is but one of the three voices of resistance addressed in Theory U. "The capacity to operate from the deeper levels of the U can only be developed to the degree that a system deals with the forces and challenges of resistance" (Scharmer, 2009, p. 247). The voices of judgment, cynicism and fear act as powerful forces of resistance in opposition to open mind, heart and will necessary for presencing at the bottom of the U. A tendency to resistance manifests in the relationship between past self and future Self. At this meeting point of past into future, interior restraints and conditioning influences surface to challenge greatness. They require explicit attention to ensure a person can invoke a state of presence at will, rather than relying on elusive and transient peak states.

Scharmer (2009) describes the voices of resistance as enemies that block the entrance to the deeper territories of the interior world and the potential for courageous, creative and human-relevant innovation that resides there. Enemies because they show up to hijack the best intentions towards presencing. We might consider them as counter-forces to emergent change, serving to maintain the status quo and resist progress and development towards a more human-centered world.

Significant change requires facing complex systemic uncertainty, usually together with multiple stakeholders and complex inter-personal and power dynamics. Favorable circumstances, and a fortunate configuration of stakeholders may determine that a leader, or critical mass of stakeholders, attain a peak experience of presence. Wicked problems, however, surface with, and indeed trigger, less than ideal circumstances.

As coaches working with clients in the Theory U framework we probably observe the downfall of significant change processes due to an inability in leaders initiating or facilitating change to maintain a state of presence. So how do we facilitate them to attain and maintain a state of presence, as a reliable discipline, beyond its appearance as an occasional peak experience?

As pointed out by Scharmer, this journey is often the road less travelled since it demands a deep interrogation with less than comfortable parts of our interior world.

In her recent book Forged in Crisis: The Power of Courageous Leadership, Nancy Koehn (2017) describes the journeys of five courageous and history-altering leaders. In each case they were, as leaders, not born into leadership, but forged during their lifetime. It is of significance that, when plotting their biographies, Koehn identifies in each one of them, a journey in which, through life crises, they transformed themselves from the inside out. She describes how each of them used life setbacks as material to grow their skills and emotional strength, and to minimize personal weakness. They consciously worked on past self, with a vision of future Self, to make a lasting impact on history.

I suggest the voices of resistance are enemies while we deny them and push them away. As shadow representations, however, their denial serves to strengthen them, encouraging them to resurface when our guard is down. We may also choose to communicate with them as a key to release past limiting patterns acting as trigger conditions to the voices. As trusted allies they provide a portal through which we encounter the limitations of the past self. Thereby accessing the needs required to engage the future Self.

Understanding the process and mechanisms by which a leader switches between presencing and absencing lays the foundation for a disciplined practice to invoke a state of presence at will. The voices of resistance as judgment, fear and cynicism, show up in many guises, sometimes managing to dress themselves to masquerade as presence. It is important to recognize their early stages and signs, to understand their genesis and to facilitate leaders to clear them before they trigger absencing. Since many of the indicators are covert rather than overt, working with presence leading to significant change requires that we, as coach, notice covert cues and facilitate a sensemaking process in the client of dynamics operating below the surface.

In this chapter I present a framework as a basis for skills for coaches to facilitate the recognition and clearing of the voices of resistance in a client. It lays out a mechanism of action and methods to help coaches identify the limiting voices before they trigger absencing. The chapter aims to contribute to an understanding of the interior constraints expressed through the voices that come about partly through inherent human characteristics and partly through biographical conditioning influences.

The framework, firstly, proposes a mechanism to aid in the recognition and understanding of the appearance of the voices of resistance. It follows with coaching methods drawing on psycho-phonetics (Tagar, 2006), and a descriptive phenomenological (Merleau-Ponty, 2002) and enactive (Thompson, 2007) approach to disarm and transform inherent and conditioned influences. Methods are described in the context of the voices of resistance and intending toward their transformation to open mind, heart and will. The mechanisms and methods are illustrated with examples from leadership coaching case studies in organizational scenarios where open mind, heart and will are compromised by judgment, cynicism or fear. Examples aim to illustrate the often subtle, insidious and covert nature of these voices.

Recognizing the Voices of Resistance

The voices of resistance find expression as a dynamic interplay in the space between presencing and absencing. At the meeting point of the future Self with the past self, trigger conditions may be activated to initiate a reactive, defensive switch from a state of presence to a state of absence. Recognizing the early signs and stages of the voices, understanding the typical types of trigger conditions and knowing how the conditions have developed in the individual's biography, lays a foundation to disarm and transform them into the ground for presence.

Switching from Presencing to Absencing via the VOR

Presencing is a harmonious expression of the individual self, identified with and expressed through the collective field. It requires the ability of a person to initiate fluid and flexible shifts in focus between their own center and the space of the field and is characterized by an ability to engage with multiple, potentially ambiguous, truths (Herdman Barker & Torbert, 2011). It is also expressed in an ability to share in and understand the experience of others from their perspective (Cook-Greuter, 2000). Absencing, on the other hand, pre-empted by blinding and desensing, results in rigid adherence to one's own truth, becoming locked within one's own boundaries. It is expressed as absorption in self and an inability to relate empathically with others and the collective field (Scharmer, 2009).

Presence may occur as a spontaneous and automatic peak state in response to optimal conditions between and amongst people within an enabling environment (Wilbur, 2006). However, if the state is automatically and unintentionally achieved, it may just as easily dissipate. As the future Self encounters the past self, trigger conditions (Merleau-Ponty, 2002; Preston, 2007; Preston & de Waal, 2002)"title" : "Phenomenology of perception", "type" : "book" }, "uris" : ["http://www.mendeley.com/documents/?uuid=ab0ced09-4095-40e6-bdd1-e7c727cf1887"] }, { "id" : "ITEM-2", "itemData" : { "ISBN" : "0140-525X, 0140-525X", "ISSN" : "0140-525X", "PMID" : "12625087", "abstract" : "There is disagreement in the literature about the exact nature of the phenomenon of empathy. There are emotional, cognitive, and conditioning views, applying in varying degrees across species. An adequate description of the ultimate and proximate mechanism can integrate these views. Proximately, the perception of an object's state activates the subject's corresponding representations, which in turn activate somatic and autonomic responses. This mechanism supports basic behaviors (e.g., alarm, social facilitation, vicariousness of emotions, mother-infant responsiveness, and the modeling of competitors and predators, in the form of reactions, provoke resistance, and like the flick of a switch the light of broad-focused presence may be replaced with the inward-focused darkness of absence.

The alternative to relying on fortuitous states of presence is to go the long road of understanding the triggers that flick the switch, taking steps to address the interior restraints and conditioning influences at the base of the triggers (Preston, 2007)first detailed in Preston and de Waal (2002b and invoking presence as a conscious and chosen state.

Trigger Conditions for Activation of VOR

Triggers leading to the activation of voices of resistance may come in various forms. When coaching individuals and groups I observe two primary areas of focus, the first as natural protective influences and the second as biographical conditioned influences. Both entail a trigger in the environment touching on an area of sensitivity, causing a reaction, with a concurrent response into an attacking, protective or defensive attitude.

Environmental stimuli may present a real risk requiring a protective fight or flight response. Alternatively, they may present a perceived risk by reminding a person of conditioned protective, defensive responses learnt earlier in life, where there is no current biological or psychological risk.

In the former, a common influence triggering a natural protective response is observed where conditions challenge the endurance of leaders beyond what is biologically reasonable or even safe. Working long hours, compromising sleep patterns, limited relaxation or down time, excessive screen time and cross-time-zone travel are all conditions that provoke physiological stress responses that mimic a fear response. Providing ongoing empathic attention and care to others, without necessary self-care in place may result in physical, emotional and spiritual exhaustion and a need to withdraw, regroup and recharge, often perceived as cynicism (Maslach, 2003; Maslach, Jackson, & Leiter, 1997). Attention to such conditions ensures adequate self-care necessary for presencing.

In the latter, areas of sensitivity in self, not adequately addressed, or cared for, by self, may act as red alert buttons, and when pushed, activate previously learnt protective and defensive behaviors. Causing us to close off and contract into self. A discussion of the mechanism for the activation of biographical conditioned influences will be presented in the section *Genesis of trigger conditions for voices of resistance* below.

It is important, here, to distinguish between maintaining open heart, mind and will with a vulnerability that is well contained and cared for by self, and openness that exposes vulnerability that is raw and needy of attention from others. When vulnerability is well wrapped, we can open it to others in safety. When we have denied, or abandoned our own vulnerability, its exposure is risky. Particularly when there is a wish for acknowledgement or validation of vulnerability from others, which may be observed in, for example, an excessive need for feedback and affirmation.

Early identification of both natural protective and biographical conditioned influences provides the ground for adequate self-care necessary for presencing. The identification and acknowledgement of conditioned influences also serves as the first step in engaging a process of exploration of the interior world. This enables an encounter with the interior restraints that reside there.

Early Stages and Signs of the Voices of Resistance

Explicit expressions of fear, cynicism and judgment, and the clusters of behaviors they represent are hard to miss. When the heart is racing and we feel paralyzed to move forward, we are aware of fear. When a person is rude and hateful, we recognize the voice of cynicism. However, not all stages and signs are clearly discernable. Knowledge of the stages of manifestation and early signs enable us to recognize them in time and to put habits in place to ensure their transformation.

Voices of resistance may be identified as belonging to three emergent stages. They are, as recorded in Table 1, external direct, internal suppressed and external indirect.

Table 1

Stages and Signs of the Voices of Resistance

Stage	Stage 1 External direct	Stage 2 Internal suppressed	Stage 3 External indirect
Characteristics	Occasional, expressed outward, directed towards the target	Frequent, expressed primarily inward, directed towards the self	Frequent, expressed outward and inward, directed towards others in the environment
Signs of fear	Inactivity, over-activity, delaying tactics	Anxiety, nervousness	Procrastination, passive aggression

Signs of cynicism	Avoidance and denial of feelings of others	Avoidance of people, suppression of own feelings	Depersonalisation, gossip, slander, spreading rumour
Signs of judgment	Over-thinking, over-researching, flawed logic, circular arguments	Self-doubt, clouded thinking	Rationalising of feelings, destructive criticizing

Stage 1 External direct. Stage 1 is characterized by occasional expressions of resistance directed outward from the focal actor towards a target, be it another person, group of people, task or project. They are openly expressed and without a hidden agenda. Stage 1 manifestations of the voices of fear include the use of delaying tactics and may be observed in expressions of inactivity or over-activity or an experience of fatigue without a physical cause. The voices of cynicism may express themselves, during the early stages, as avoidance or denial of feelings of others, or by intellectualizing feelings. Resistance in the form of judgment presents itself in the initial stage as over-thinking or over-researching, or an inability to recognize when enough-is-enough. It may also be observed in flawed logic and circular arguments.

Stage 2 Internal suppressed. Expressions of a direct, external nature continuously affronted and frustrated, may progress to stage 2, where the external manifestation is suppressed and directed inward in the focal actor. Stage 2 expressions may progress from stage 1 in current time. Alternatively, they may have developed as biographical conditioning influences earlier in life and manifest directly as stage 2 or 3 expressions in current time. During stage 2 one recognizes habitual patterns of resistance, in the will, of excessive caution as a result of anxiety or nervousness. Voices of cynicism directed towards the self may manifest as suppression of feelings in self, as avoidance of others who come across as needy, or indeed, in severe cases as avoidance of people in general. Cynicism is also, frequently, expressed as dislike of aspects of self, or the self as a whole and may be observed in a compromise to self-care. During this stage, voices of judgment appear as self-doubt, showing up in many guises. For example, seeking out ever greater qualifications, or needing to gain more and more experience before venturing out to express one's creativity.

Stage 3 External indirect. A further thwarting or misunder-standing of efforts leads resistance into stage three where it becomes insidious, endemic and directed anywhere and everywhere. As unsavory as this may sound, voices of cynicism in the form of corridor gossip, backstabbing and rumormongering are a common and widespread frustration in organizations. Rationalization and procrastination are frequently observed as covert mechanisms founded upon a base of fear. Cynicism, or depersonalization, is a strategy with widespread expression in service organizations, used to protect the self from prolonged exposure to perceived difficult feelings of others.

The subtle stages and signs of the voices find expression in dances of resistance amongst and between focal actors. Tom, a senior manager working on a water sustainability program, had fresh and innovative ideas. He was coordinating a team for an international launch. He, however, had difficulty communicating with his immediate superior. She questioned his launch program. He found himself second-guessing the program in communications to her. He explained away his hesitancy as a need to be strategic and collaborative, finding reason to initiate more research and revise his methods. Upon examining his caution in greater depth, however, he noticed that he perceived his senior colleague's questions as being critical and judgmental. He recognized his caution as fear. Further examination revealed a deep-seated and frequent fear of rejection in the face of a perceived critic.

Depersonalization, a voice of resistance often observed in people working in service industries, is identified as a component of burnout along with exhaustion and reduced sense of accomplishment (Maslach, Schaufeli, & Leiter, 2001). Burnout was described in the 1970s by the psychiatrist Herbert Freudenberger as a scourge of our times. It commonly occurs in the caring professions where the work requires ongoing and sustained empathy towards others. A component of empathy is a shared affect experience between an agent and the person being served, in that the agent experiences the experiences of the other. If ongoing and unmanaged, it may result in the need to shut off to protect self from the repeated difficult experiences of stress or suffering of others. The mechanism of shutting off is expressed with cynicism or depersonalization.

Discerning the subtler expressions of the voices of resistance requires familiarizing oneself with their stages and signs alongside an understanding of how they come about in the biographical conditioning of the individual. Early recognition enables greater success in bringing about their deactivation.

Genesis of Trigger Conditions for VOR

Voices of judgment, cynicism and fear frequently emerge as expressions of protective and defensive behavior in response to real or perceived threats in the environment. In the event of a real threat, the resistance hopefully serves as a useful messenger to moderate choices. Perceived threats, unsubstantiated by a real threat, however, are stimulated as a result of biographical conditioned influences accrued during previous life experiences, particularly early childhood. They habitually inhibit the potential of the leader to consistently maintain a state of presence.

The genesis of biographical conditioned influences may be understood by the following mechanism.

Memories as sense-feel-sound mental images. Memories of life experiences are organized as clusters of associated thought, feeling and embodied experience and stored as mental images, also known as representations, including associated sensations and meanings made of them (Steiner & Sardello, 1999). Ongoing associated life experiences serve to expand the mental images but are built upon the foundation of previous meanings made of and attached to these mental images. They also include associated emotional affect and bodily responses such as breathing and heart rate patterns, and facial and postural expressions (Damasio, 1996; Steiner & Sardello, 1999; Tagar & Steele, 2008) accrued as the prevailing state of being at the time of the initial experience. The mental images may be thought of as sense-feel-sound-images.

For instance, a mental image associated with a response of disapproval at being late accrued during childhood may be accompanied by a prevailing state of anxiety and guilt experienced whilst growing up and being reprimanded for being late. It may include the postural memory of a tight stomach and shallow breathing.

Mental image as sensation, emotion response and meaning conclusion. Mental images evolve in the interiority throughout life, but particularly so in the first years of childhood. As we journey through life, clusters of sense impressions emerge as sensation within the interior world. A response of either sympathy or antipathy occurs to everything that enters the interior experience. For instance, an experience of being late for a harsh disciplinarian teacher at school may be associated with fear and an accompanying pounding heart and shortness of breath. The sense impressions include any noteworthy facial and bodily expressions of the teacher as she communicated her disapproval. A feeling of dislike for the teacher may have ensued. The experience is also met with reasoning, working on the experience and coming to a meaning. To make meaning of the response and the teacher's behavior one might have concluded that the teacher was unfair and a bully. Meaning conclusions, together with associated sensations and sympathy/antipathy response are stored as mental images (Steiner & Sardello, 1999). The interior world is made up of an intricate and complex web of these mental image complexes.

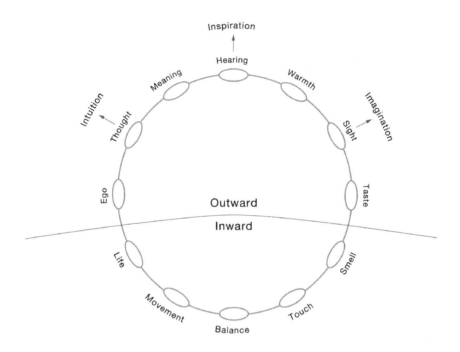

Figure 1. The genesis of mental images in the interior world.

Mental images remain stored with the original associated meaning unless new reasoning is applied to them in order to change the meaning. Significantly, the original meanings are usually gleaned from a young and immature reasoning capacity. In an open, nurturing and supported environment, mental images will be upgraded with the continuously evolving and maturing reasoning capacity. However, in many cases, the biographical upbringing is distorted in varying degrees and clusters of mental images forego a reasoning upgrade and continue to be reinforced by distorted perceptions (Preston & de Waal, 2002)cognitive, and conditioning views, applying in varying degrees across species. An adequate description of the ultimate and proximate mechanism can integrate these views. Proximately, the perception of an object's state activates the subject's corresponding representations, which in turn activate somatic and autonomic responses. This mechanism supports basic behaviors (e.g., alarm, social facilitation, vicariousness of emotions, mother-infant responsiveness, and the modeling of competitors and predators. Thus, determining that the past self is populated by mental images representing limiting patterns of meaning conclusions. The 'lateness' mental image may endure into adulthood with a pervasive experience of anxiety in anticipation of being late and an experience of being bullied into time adherence.

Automatic action primed by mental images. According to the Perception-action hypothesis (Preston & de Waal, 2002)cognitive, and conditioning views, applying in varying degrees across species. An adequate description of the ultimate and proximate mechanism can integrate these views. Proximately, the perception of an object's state activates the subject's corresponding representations, which in turn activate somatic and autonomic responses. This mechanism supports basic behaviors (e.g., alarm, social facilitation, vicariousness of emotions, mother-infant responsiveness, and the modeling of competitors and predators when we perceive the world of people and things again, perceived characteristics of those people or things will automatically activate associated mental images. The threat or even the thought of being late for an appointment would be experienced with feelings of fear or anxiety and the accompanying bodily sensations. This includes the behavior of another person, which automatically activates our own mental image of similar or associated behavior. It then automatically proceeds to a primed response, unless actively inhibited (Preston, 2007)first detailed in Preston and de Waal (2002b. If we empathize with a person who is going to be late for an appointment, our own associated mental images, with sensations and behaviours, will be activated, unless actively inhibited or transformed.

Similarly, if we perceive another person's state or situation it automatically activates our own mental image of that state or situation, and the activation of the mental image automatically primes associated bodily responses and action, unless inhibited.

In this way, perception of another person or situation, either directly observed, imagined or even suggested is automatically processed according to the context of our own past experiences, leading to an automatic response. The thoughts, affect and embodied experience of the past experience is in this way triggered, and re-experienced, when we imagine, observe or infer the similar situation of others.

What is noteworthy here, is that the mental image and all associated experience may well remain in a pre-reflective space, meaning that we are not consciously aware of it, but that it is accompanied by subtle bodily sensations and emotions none-the-less. It likely remains a part of the general background noise of daily life. Also significant is that even though we are not aware of it, it has an undermining effect on wellbeing (Preston & de Waal, 2002)cognitive, and conditioning views, applying in varying degrees across species. An adequate description of the ultimate and proximate mechanism can integrate these views. Proximately, the perception of an object's state activates the subject's corresponding representations, which in turn activate somatic and autonomic responses. This mechanism supports basic behaviors (e.g., alarm, social facilitation, vicariousness of emotions, mother-infant responsiveness, and the modeling of competitors and predators. One might find that at the end of a day in which there are a sequence of time pressures and risks of being late, one feels drained or exhausted, but not sure why.

Decision and action pre-empted by bodily sensation. As a continuation of the perception/action mechanism, decision-making processes are determined by bodily marker signals that arise in and through bio-regulatory processes expressed as bodily sensations, again, usually not in conscious awareness (Bechara & Damasio, 2005; Bechara, Damasio, Tranel, & Damasio, 1997). They are coupled with corresponding emotions. In this way decisions are guided by biases associated with culturally and historically determined mental images. Patterns of behavior are repeated, and decisions are based upon previous experiences in cultural or historical life.

In the case of an empathic interaction with a stressed person, the observation or imagination of that person's experience acts as a trigger to a conditioned event in the agent's own life, together with the associated bodily sensations. The experience stimulated in the empathizing person is biased according to their cultural or historical experiences.

__Limiting and painful mental images.__ When past experiences, and the associated meaning conclusions, are limiting or even painful, the mental image, when triggered by reminders in the environment, surfaces with the limiting or painful experience. It creates congestion, or an area of no-go in the interiority so as to avoid re-experiencing the associated pain. The congested areas resist the invocation of the Source of future potential. It is the emotion response and corresponding bodily sensations that define the no-go zones.

The activated mental image in turn, automatically primes or generates previously learnt responses. Responses learnt through primary stressful events (Bechara & Damasio, 2005), accumulated during the lifespan, are activated in response to similar events in current personal or work life. Accordingly voices of resistance may be activated as a result of biographical conditioned influences. These as learnt defensive behavior primed in response to perceived stressors, and because of earlier learned defensive habits.

The mechanism described above may be viewed in the context of voices of cynicism frequently observed in people working in human services. People who have had previous similar experiences of adversity in their own lives to those with whom they empathize, are more likely to experience a compromise to their own wellbeing in an ongoing attempt to empathize (Baird & Kracen, 2006; Jenkins & Baird, 2002)..

Sharon is managing a center providing trauma services to people experiencing family abuse, bullying or xenophobia. Whilst working with a young female client on a legal case of abuse she becomes identified with the client to the extent that she becomes physically ill, needing to withdraw from the case for weeks at a time. As the case progresses it transpires that the facts of the case, at the acknowledgement of the child, have been embroidered in an attempt to 'get back' at the stepfather. At this point Sharon becomes so enraged with the client that she has to be restrained because she 'could have murdered her'. The accumulated effect of a number of similarly disappointing cases has led to her being mistrustful of extreme stories of clients. In reflecting on her responses some time after the case has passed Sharon recognizes the extent to which her work reminds her of her own experiences of childhood abuse with an alcoholic father. Her volatile engagement with clients swings between wanting to protect them and being angry with them for getting into such situations.

Opening one's heart and feelings to others requires feeling with them. When the experience of others with whom one is working is reminiscent of challenging experiences in one's own life, this provokes memories, resurfacing challenging thoughts and feelings. Unless a leader has developed capacities of regulation relevant to the previously conditioned challenge, it surfaces an experience of past difficulty. The result is to retract into self-preservation mode. In this context judgment, cynicism and fear are used to keep others, and their difficult experiences, at bay (Maslach, 2003).

How do we let go of the old self and the stuff that needs to die with it? A large proportion of perception and action occurs below the surface of conscious awareness. We notice cues in the world and act upon them in an automatic manner. This means that we are not consciously aware of them. If we stop and think, we may, even then, not be aware of them, but are left with a vague bodily and affective experience associated with them. It is into this pre-reflective space that the voices of resistance find their expression.

The section on methods to follow aims to illustrate that awareness of these influences, and information about their genesis, is available to a client through embodied experiential markers, which, in turn become increasingly available to awareness with the skillful facilitation of embodied experiential techniques by a coach. These methods present a roadmap to aid exploration at the meeting point between the future Self and the past self and provide a basis for which to face the force of resistance that the voices represent.

Methods to Disarm the Voices of Resistance

The journey down the U, of suspending, redirecting and letting go may be marred by the voices of resistance. Trigger conditions as a result of natural protective and biographical conditioned influences may activate their appearance, compromising presence. Biographical conditioned influences, as mental image clusters of sensation, associated emotion response and meaning conclusion, act as triggers to their activation. While mostly in a pre-reflective state and not in conscious awareness, they none-the-less are accompanied by subtle bodily sensations and emotions. As a result decisions and actions are preempted by measurable bodily markers (Bechara, Damasio, Tranel, & Damasio, 2005).

Being present to experience brings to awareness the subtle sensations associated with bodily markers. Thus, the mastery of *staying with experience* is paramount to presencing.

Experience provides both a portal to explore, understand and disarm the natural and conditioned influences that trigger the voices of resistance and at the same time results in the invocation of presence. It, however, struggles for a verbal vocabulary. To recognize the internal shift from open heart or compassion, to, say, cynicism and depersonalization requires awareness and a language. Equally, the reverse shift from absencing to presencing, from being caught in the singular, closed walls of the self to an empathic engagement with the collective field, requires a method and a language to surface and disarm the voices of resistance, and to invoke presence.

This next section sets the scene for experience as fundamental to dealing with the voices of resistance, to presencing, and to learning from the emerging future. The section provides a description of experience, and methods for bringing awareness to experience through the body, to surface the interior world and to enable an encounter with the interior restraints.

The aim of this approach is to introduce skills for coaches to guide a client to be aware of experience and to interrogate the interior world of conditioned influences as triggers to the voices of resistance.

Presence and Experience

Experience and presence are mutually sustaining states of being. Staying with experience ensures presence and when one maintains a state of presence one is more present to experience. In this paragraph I present a way of being whereby a *focus on experience* is a thing to do.

This begs the questions: "What is experience?" and "How do we bring awareness to experience?" For the purpose of this discussion, experience is described as an expression of the world as it is perceived inwardly. It is an account of the interior processes that contribute to reality as perceived in the interior world by first-person perception. This is distinct from an abstract and conceptual interpretation of the world as assumed from a third-person account of reality. Focusing on experience involves paying attention to the inward perception of the world and requires developing an enhanced awareness of the interior processes residing there.

Frequently in coaching we default to an interpretive mode of interaction with clients: making meaning of a client situation or scenario with an interpretation or conclusion of what we hear or observe. What is described here is refraining from any such interpretations and staying with the experience of the client as it presents itself. Furthermore, encouraging the client to stay with their experience too. And, again, encouraging them to refrain from interpreting or drawing conclusions. The methods presented in this chapter set the stage for a further sensemaking of the interior restraints by the client themselves. The sensemaking process does not form a part of this chapter.

The following discussion of ways of 'being in the world' and 'seeing the world' and of the interior and exterior world aims to enhance the understanding of experience and lay a foundation for the methods to follow.

Ways of 'being-in-the world' and 'seeing the world'. It is through the internal perception of the external world that reality of the world is created. There is no direct cause-and-effect link, however, between the nature of stimuli in the outer world, the nature of the impressions they make on inner awareness and how they might be experienced. Between stimulus and experience lie the biographical conditioned influences acting as a filter through which the world is make sense of. In this regard, we identify two distinct ways of 'seeing the world', each having a subtle impact on 'being-in-the-world'.

The naïve attitude. In the first instance, we may take a naïve attitude, commonly assumed in everyday life, that the exterior world is an independent world 'out there'. In this attitude experiences are taken for granted to be outwardly just as they are experienced inwardly. Objects, including other beings, are considered from the perspective of how they are experienced, regardless of whether they are that way or not. In this attitude, a person will account for their interior condition to be a result of exterior conditions.

Anne, a marketing manager, is in charge of making decisions for large corporate campaigns. She has been working for the company for over twenty years and has gathered a vast experience in the field. She is, however, withdrawn from active engagement with the management team, sitting distractedly in meetings and fiddling with papers while others are talking. She speaks cynically of the entire organization. When encouraged to open up, she expresses anger and frustration, which she ascribes to the fact that a colleague of hers persistently avoids asking for recommendations and overriding her decisions. In this attitude, Anne draws a direct link between her anger and frustration and the colleague's behavior.

The reflective attitude. Alternatively, we may take a reflective attitude, with an understanding that interior experiences are perceived through filters as mental images constructed according to current and historical culture and context. In this reflective attitude we break with the habitual naïve attitude of a content-directed interior world and direct attention to focus on awareness. We regard the world of things, self and others from the perspective of this interior awareness.

Upon instruction, Anne suspends the habit to direct her attention towards the colleague and redirects her attention to her own interior world. When asked to direct her attention to her body, she experiences a sensation in her arms and legs, which she names as disempowerment. She recognizes that under the anger and frustration is an experience of disempowerment. In this state, Anne has redirected her attention in a reflective attitude to her awareness and the stimuli that meet her awareness from her own interior world.

The processes of suspending and redirecting correspond to the first two of the three gestures of the opening process depicted in the Theory U: Leading from the future as it emerges figure, The Opening Process of the U (Sharmer (2007, p.37). In this case directed by an individual towards their inner world, rather than to the group process as is the case in the U process.

From the reflective perspective, the interior of the individual is subjective, is accessible by first-person account, and is susceptible to interpreting processes within the individual. And interpreting processes are led by mental images as biographical conditioned influences. By assuming this reflective attitude to experience, we are able to shine a light into the interior world and to begin to discern the layers that reside there, one of them being the mental images of biographical conditioning influences acting as triggers to the activation of the voices of resistance. Awareness of the residing layers enables a leader to discern what is required for the reverse shift back to presencing.

By training a leader to habitually engage a process of assuming a reflective attitude, thereby noticing and making meaning of the interior conditions, they become increasingly aware of the early stages and signs of the voices of resistance.

The interior and exterior world. In Theory U Scharmer highlights the importance of the *interior condition* of an intervener or leader in determining the success, or lack thereof, of an intervention. The interior condition reflects the qualities of the interior world and is the source from which actions emerge. The interior condition may be represented by the future Self, as a manifestation of the highest future potential. But equally, it may be represented by the past self with its limiting biographical conditioned influences and operating from the habitual cognitive space of downloading. Actions are, consequently, representative of either the future potential self or the limited self.

The interior space, known as the blind spot, is invisible to the social field, contrary to the visibility of actions and behavior that emerge from it. As the following discussion aims to show, a significant portion of the interior space, and the motivations that arise from there to drive action, is habitually invisible to self-awareness too. It may, however, with *experience awareness*, become increasingly visible, so that past limiting patterns associated with biographical conditioned influences may be revealed and potentially released.

The layered interior world. The interior world is distinct from the exterior world or the environment in which it is embedded and represents an imprint thereof. The interior world is, however, made up of elements with increasing proximity and intimacy with the core self or "I" from which the Source emanates during presencing. A characteristic of experience is this "I', capable of awareness, and also the originator of awareness. Experience may be regarded as the imprint of all stimuli perceived by awareness that originates from outside of that awareness (Tagar, 1994). In this context, the interior world is made up of the impressions of all stimuli perceived by this awareness.

Inputs in the form of impressions reach awareness from stimuli originating from the outer world of other beings and things, but also from aspects of the self.

Inputs from the world of other beings and things are directly perceived through the senses, imagined or inferred by objects or events reminiscent of them.

Inputs from the self originate as psychological and bodily content: psychological such as thoughts, feelings, memories, images and associations, drives and motivations; and bodily in the form of sensations of touch, warmth, movement, balance, pleasure or pain. Inputs originating from bodily sensations are sensed as life processes and sense of wellbeing through the interoceptive senses. Inputs as gesture, posture, facial expressions and voice prosody are sensed as balance and motion through the proprioceptive senses. This will be discussed in more detail later on.

Thus, a layer of the interior world is interior in that thoughts, feelings and bodily sensations are a part of the blind spot, but exterior to core awareness. This is important since it is by recognizing this layer of interiority, capable of being sensed by awareness that enables us to interrogate the limiting patterns of past self. It is essential to distinguish between these layers of interiority since it is into this outer layer of the interior, of emotional and bodily content, that the core "I" awareness works on the past limiting patterns that reside as biographical conditioned images.

Passive and active sensing of the outer and inner world. The extent to which we encounter the impressions of experience with "I" awareness is variable. Sensing, leading to experience of sensation, is a dual process: the world comes to meet me, and I make sense of it (Merleau-Ponty, 2002; Tagar, 2006). The meeting point between "I" and the world of objects and other beings, and also the interior world of bodily sensations and emotions may be passive or active. In passive sensing the world invades the interiority and overwhelms the "I". The flooded "I" is reflected in limited awareness of experience of the world, self and others. In active sensing, the "I" comes to meet the world at the meeting point between world and self, consciously making sense of it, and results in heightened awareness of experience.

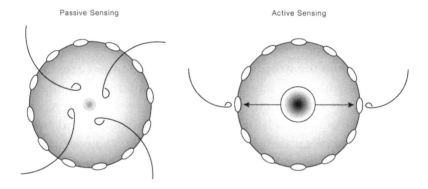

Figure 2. A comparison of passive and active sensing.

The outer circles, in both diagrams of figure 2, represent the interiority of the self, with the core circles representing the "I" awareness. In the left-hand diagram, in passive sensing, the interiority is invaded by sense impressions but the "I" has little awareness of them. Even though there is limited awareness in current time, however, a residue of the sense impression remains undigested and imprinted in the body (Legrand, 2006). Active sensing, represented in the right-hand diagram occurs with presencing when the "I" is consciously aware of a larger proportion of sense impressions.

To go back to the discussion of the genesis for the activation of the voices of resistance, a mechanism is described to account for biographical conditioned influences as triggers to their activation. It describes how through the "I", sensation, met with an experience of sympathy and antipathy is processed and integrated with reasoning into meaning conclusions. The interior blind spot, when invisible to "I" awareness is susceptible to harboring trigger conditions for the voices of resistance. Stimuli in the environment sensed passively bypasses "I" awareness and, in accordance with biographically conditioned mental images, primes automatic action. However, active sensing of experience brings awareness to the blind spot and enables the biographical conditioned images to be brought to awareness in order that new meaning may be made of them with a vision of future Self. In this way the interior world of past self may be transformed from the inside out.

On becoming aware. In active sensing we encounter the foundation for presence, with the dual function of engaging the future Self, transforming the past self with new meaning and engaging presence.

I bring this discussion into context with a continuation of Anne's story. On becoming aware of the exterior world and the layers of the interior world with a reflective attitude she shone a light into a previously opaque and unaware area of the interior world. The exterior world is represented by the perceived behaviors of the colleague. Anne's habitual focus of awareness is on the colleague, blaming the colleague for her discomfort. The outer layer of the interior world is clothed in a layer of cynicism and withdrawal. On first examination and following an instruction of active sensing of bodily sensations, an inner layer of anger is revealed. A further internal interrogation, guided by a coach, identifies two further layers of emotional and bodily content that are named as frustration and disempowerment. At this point, Anne recognizes that disempowerment is, and has been, a common theme throughout her life.

Thus, the habitual interpretation of the perceived exterior world occurs through the filter of the biographical conditioned influence of disempowerment. On further interrogation, she identifies the experiences of disempowerment as stemming from interactions in her childhood. Many years later it still acts as a trigger to her cynical and withdrawn demeanor in management meetings via the interior conditions of disempowerment, frustration and anger.

The two sections to follow will present two methods that facilitate an opening to the interior world for a client in order that they may become increasingly aware of the early stages and signs of the voices of resistance as limiting influences, and also of the mental images as biographical conditioned influences.

This will be presented as methods for experience surfacing and embodied experience by guiding a client to a reflective attitude and awareness of experience and guiding a client to active sensing of their experience.

Experience Surfacing: Guiding a Client to a Reflective Attitude and Experience Awareness

While we experience all of the time, the inner world of experience is usually not the focus of awareness. The inner processes that form and mold the interior perception of reality remain hidden. This blind spot is the source of action in the world, including expressions of the voices of resistance. Correspondingly, motivation driving action is frequently automatic and unconscious, hidden to awareness of the actor him or herself. Content of the internal world, including biographically conditioned mental images, is also hidden from view. In the naïve attitude, as we interact with and respond to the world, this interior world of experience is commonly also not in the conscious awareness of the actor. This naïve attitude tends to be the default attitude and so, as we respond to stimuli, we tend to respond with a primed default response.

Although the blind spot is generally invisible to the social field, interesting research reveals that aspects of the inner world are reflected externally through subtle bodily signals (Ekman & Friesen, 2003; Gallagher, 2005), and through mirroring mechanisms (Gallagher, 2012; Gallese, 2017), readable by others. A close and intimate connection between the inner world and the body presents an opportunity for coaches to gain indirect access to the experiential inner world of the client.

Fascinating research conducted by Paul Ekman, and colleagues, reveals the extent to which emotional experiences are reflected as micro-expressions that flash across the face, even when the emotion is suppressed or repressed. These expressions are shown to be universal, common to all people of all cultures. They are also available for interpretation by a trained coach or practitioner. Similarly posture and gestural expression as well as the tone of voice and prosody, reflect aspects of the interior world.

Recent neuro-scientific research on empathy also reveals the extent to which people automatically and unconsciously mimic and mirror the micro-expressions of each other resulting in emotional contagion (Hatfield, Cacioppo, & Rapson, 1994). Also, with progressive skill, enabling a coach to glean aspects of the interior condition of a client.

An understanding of these two factors provides a basis for an embodied experiential approach to coaching whereby aspects of the interior of another person can become more visible to the experience and awareness of a trained coach. Correspondingly, responding to the tone of the interior world in a productive manner facilitates the client to more awareness of their experience.

The relationship we assume to experience. A person may assume one of a number of positions in relation to their experience, identified and categorized by Yehuda Tagar (1994, 2006) as being reacting, sensing, feeling, beholding and speaking. A trained coach is able, by observing micro-expressions of the face and body, to identify the position in which a client is oriented towards their experience. By responding to the client in a manner appropriate to the specific position, the coach can encourage the client to engage more deeply with their experience.

Psychophonetics methodology of experience awareness. As an embodied experiential method psychophonetics methodology of experience awareness (PMEA) (Tagar, 1994) enables a coach or practitioner to observe and notice the relationship a person assumes to their experience. It enables a practitioner to identify the position a person assumes to their experience as reacting, sensing, feeling, beholding or speaking.

Reacting. In reacting a person responds with an instinctive, automatic and unconscious coping behaviour to triggers in the environment. It serves the purpose of defending against a perceived threat in the environment that reminds the person of a specific event. In this position a person is automatically responding to biographical conditioned influences with a primed response. It is in this category of relationship to experience that the stages and signs of the voices of resistance find their expression.

Sensing. In this position a person is encountering their experience. It is the way in which the experiencer becomes more aware of themselves and their experience through the body. The senses form the connection between the person and their environment. Sensing, as active sensing in the PMEA methodology, occurs when an outer and an inner phenomenon reaches awareness and becomes an inner experience.

Feeling. This may be seen as the most inward relationship that a person has to their experience and comes about with a welling up and radiating of *feeling* within, described as, for example, sadness or joy.

Beholding. When beholding a person inwardly observes their own experience, manifesting as the capacity to be aware of awareness. It consists of the activity of drawing one's attention to the internal dynamics of a previous experience currently under examination and is expressed in the reflective attitude.

Speaking. In speaking the person is expressing something about the experience. Speaking may not necessarily be verbal but could also be in writing, drawing, painting, or with a gesture as in acting. Speaking is significantly a consciously chosen act in contrast to reacting, as an unconscious, automatic act. In PMEA speaking comprises three interrelated activities of intending, emoting and urging.

Intending. The internal act of thinking leading into the act of expression, examples being an expression of cultural understanding, acknowledging judgment, identifying contradictions and evaluating anticipated actions.

Emoting. This is the emotional prelude of leading feelings into speaking, examples being acknowledged and expressed openness, shyness, disappointment, patience and inner strength.

Urging. This is the expression of consciously chosen motivation and determination, as in, for example, listening, mimicking gesture, purposeful use of silence, commitment and follow through.

Thus, by applying the observational techniques of PMEA, a coach can determine the position a client assumes in relation to their experience. By responding appropriately in accordance with the particular position the client is in, the coach enables the client to bring their "I" awareness into greater intimacy with the structures of experience. This creates a foundation on which to be aware of the conditioned influences as a basis for further sensemaking thereof.

In the previous discussions we refer to emotional and bodily content guiding an interrogation of the interior world. The following section serves to elaborate on the relationship between experience, mind and body and how an awareness of embodied experience facilitates the interrogation process.

Embodied Experience: Guiding a Client to Active Sensing of Their Experience

Experience occurs as a result of an active mind in a living body. Recent interpretations of how we understand the world focus on the embodied role of cognition (Thompson, 2007; Varela, Thompson, & Rosch, 1991). No longer is cognition understood to be a function purely of processing symbols in a disembodied brain, but rather the mind present in and through the body. Correspondingly, experience is a function of the mind in and through the body and serves as a point of connection between the mind and the body. With this as a foundation, a skilled coach is able to guide a client to their experience through the body, and more specifically though active sensing through the body.

The sources of experience, one from the body and one from the mind, find their meeting point and are integrated in awareness by the "I". Sensing and perception come about through the body. Reasoning and conceptualizing occur as a result of the mind.

The embodied nature of experience. The mind and body are united in experience. Perception and action abilities are dependent upon the body and its sensing capacities. An embodied perspective contributes significantly to an understanding of how we experience the world. Prior to the 1970s, it was considered that information processing not in conscious awareness occurred as the manipulation of symbols or pattern recognition in the brain. A more recent understanding, however, takes the view that these unconscious processes are made up of bodily and emotional processes not yet accessible to conscious awareness, but that have covert or overt bodily experience (Thompson, 2007; Varela et al., 1991).

Research conducted by Antonio Damasio and his colleagues determine that decisions are pre-empted and determined by subtle, usually covert but measurable bodily markers. The earlier discussion in *Genesis of trigger conditions for VOR* describes a mechanism according to which trigger conditions for the voices of resistance are determined by biographical conditioned influences, made up of mental images formed during the lifespan. Figure 1 illustrates the process by which mental images are formations of sensation, emotion response and meaning. Experience, as sensation, enters the interior world via sense impressions of the body. Clusters of sensations are processed with an emotion response as sympathy or antipathy and elicit a further experience of like or dislike. Reasoning works on experience and makes meaning of it. Meaning conclusions, including the like/dislike response and corresponding bodily sensations become embedded as mental images and form the interior condition of the past self. The like/dislike responses and bodily sensations correspond to the bodily and emotion processes as unconscious processes that preempt and determine decisions and actions.

The interior world consists of inputs as sense impressions

from the outside world of objects and other beings but also sense impressions from an aspect of the interior world itself in the form of emotional and bodily content. The "I" encounters the impressions of experience with varying awareness. We may passively sense impressions where the impression is met with limited, or no, perception by the "I". In this case the "I" does not become involved and sensation remains below conscious awareness. We may actively sense by bringing awareness to encounter sense impressions, becoming aware of sensations and activating perception.

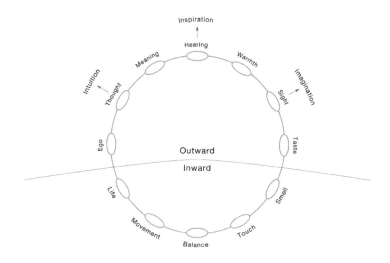

Figure 3. Twelve primary sense foci. Adapted from "Man's Twelve Senses in Relation to Imagination, Inspiration, Intuition" by R. Steiner, 1981, *Anthroposophical Review, 3,* p. 12. Copyright for the works of Rudolf Steiner have expired following the 70-year term of copyright protection.

Sensing is not only passive or active, but also involves a breadth of perceiving options not usually brought to daily awareness. By bringing active awareness to the full extent of sensing activity, we engage a reservoir of nuanced experience. The diagram below reflects twelve primary foci of sense impression (Steiner, 1981). The top eight are directed primarily outwards to the world of objects and other beings. The lower four are directed inwards to the interior world of self. The outwardly directed sense foci are further divided into those directed towards the material world and those directed towards the immaterial world of other beings.

The outwardly directed sense foci directed towards the immaterial world are:

Ego. With this focus we experience the being of another.

Thought or concept. With this focus we experience the grasping and understanding of a concept or meaning. It is expressed in the meaning conclusions associated with mental images.

Meaning or speech. With this focus we experience a tone associated with speech and the meaning attached to the tone. This meaning and tone sense is distinct from pure vibrational quality of sound. It is represented in voice intonation and prosody. It is recognized in the meaning attached to language.

Hearing. With the sense of hearing we experience the vibrational quality of sound.

The outwardly directed sense foci directed towards the material world are:

Warmth. With the sense of warmth we experience the temperature of a substance. A sense of warmth is also associated with feeling as may be expressed in enthusiasm or interest towards an object or person.

Sight. Sight reveals an experience of how an object responds to light, either allowing it to pass through or not.

Taste. The sense of taste requires contact of our saliva with the chemical nature of substance.

Smell. The sense of smell reveals an experience of the gaseous emissions of an object.

Sense foci directed inwardly towards one's own body are:

Life. With the focus of life, one gains an experience of the wellbeing of our own body and interior world. It may represent an experience of thirst, hunger, fatigue or pain. This focus is experienced through the mediation of the interoceptive senses and the autonomic nervous system and may be represented in heart rate and pressure, breathing depth and rate.

Movement. With this focus we gain an experience of our own internal and external movement. There is a connection between this focus and our emotional content, as evident in the phrase "I was moved to tears". The experience is mediated by muscle and tendon spindles of the proprioceptive sensory system.

Balance. This focus provides us with an experience of our own sense of balance and equilibrium and is representative of our own internal organization. It is experienced through the mediation of the semicircular canals in the ears.

Touch. With the sense of touch, we experience our boundaries and the point at which we end.

Through these twelve primary foci the exterior world of things and other beings and the mid-interior world of bodily self are available as stimuli to awareness. By encouraging active sensing by a client in all areas of sense focus, so the world of experience may be brought to light as the ground for interrogation of the past limiting influences. The sense foci directed inwardly towards one's own body reveal the bodily and emotion processes as points of entry to the mental images of biographical conditioned influences. The sense foci directed outwardly towards the immaterial world are points of entry to the inter-personal dynamics that act as triggers to biographical conditioned influences.

The relationship that a client assumes to their experience, observable through embodied experiential techniques as they recount the presenting issue in a coaching session, presents the roadmap for the coach to guide active sensing as an exploration of experience for the client.

In conclusion, this chapter describes two primary limiting influences acting as triggers to the voices of resistance. These influences are natural influences and biographical conditioned influences. The chapter presents a description of a biographical conditioned mechanism to account for the limiting interior influences of past self, acting as triggers to the voices. The mechanism is placed in the context of early signs of the voices of fear, cynicism and judgment that, when not dealt with adequately, become entrenched and difficult to shift. It describes three stages through which these forces of resistance progress from an external, direct expression, through an internal, suppressed expression towards an entrenched external and indirect expression.

A focus on experience, through the keyhole of embodied experience, is presented as a method through which to gain access to the limiting influences, both natural and biographical conditioned. This is in order that they may be interrogated with a view to transformation by the future Self.

The chapter presents two techniques that form part of psychophonetics methodology applied to coaching. They enable a trained coach to facilitate a client to access their experience in order that the limitations of the past self may be acknowledged, explored, and potentially transformed with a vision of future Self, thereby disarming the limiting voices of resistance.

References

Baird, K., & Kracen, A. C. (2006). Vicarious traumatization and secondary traumatic stress: A research synthesis. *Counselling Psychology Quarterly*, *19*(2), 181–188.

Bechara, A, Damasio, H., Tranel, D., & Damasio, A.R. (2005). The Iowa Gambling Task and the somatic marker hypothesis: some questions and answers. *Trends in Cognitive Sciences*, *9*(4), 159-62; discussion 162-4. https://doi.org/10.1016/j.tics.2005.02.002

Bechara, A., & Damasio, A. (2005). The somatic marker hypothesis: A neural theory of economic decision. *Games and Economic Behavior*, *52*(2), 336–372.

Bechara, A., Damasio, H., Tranel, D., & Damasio, A. (1997). Deciding advantageously before knowing the advantageous strategy. *Science*, *275*(5304), 1293–1294.

Cook-Greuter, S. R. (2000). Ego development: Nine levels of increasing embrace. *Journal of Adult Development*, *7*(4), 227–240.

Damasio, A. (1996). The somatic marker hypothesis and the possible functions of the prefrontal cortex. *Philosophical Transactions of the Royal Society of London*, *351*, 1413–1420.

Ekman, P., & Friesen, W. (2003). *Unmasking the face: A guide to recognizing emotions from facial clues*.

Gallagher, S. (2005). *How the body shapes the mind*. Oxford: Clarendon Press.

Gallagher, S. (2012). Empathy, simulation, and narrative. *Science in Context*, *25*(03), 355–381.

Gallese, V. (2017). *Mirroring , a liberated embodied simulation and aesthetic experience* .

Hatfield, E., Cacioppo, J., & Rapson, R. (1994). *Emotional contagion*. Paris: Cambridge University Press.

Herdman Barker, E., & Torbert, W. R. (2011). Generating and measuring practical differences in leadership performance at postconventional action-logics. In A. H. Pfaffenberger, P. W. Marko, & A. Combs (Eds.), *The Postconventional Personality: Assessing, Researching and Theorizing Higher Development*. SUNY Press.

Jenkins, S. R., & Baird, S. (2002). Secondary traumatic stress and vicarious trauma: A validational study. *Journal of Traumatic Stress, 15*(5), 423–432.

Legrand, D. (2006). The bodily self: The sensori-motor roots of pre-reflective self-consciousness. *Phenomenology and the Cognitive Sciences, 5*(1), 89–118.

Maslach, C. (2003). Job burnout: New directions in research and intervention. *Current Directions in Psychological Science, 12*(5), 189–192.

Maslach, C., Jackson, S. E., & Leiter, M. P. (1997). *The Maslach Burnout Inventory Manual*.

Maslach, C., Schaufeli, W. B., & Leiter, M. P. (2001). Job burnout. *Annual Review of Psychology, 52*(1), 397–422.

Merleau-Ponty, M. (2002). *Phenomenology of perception*. London: Routledge.

Preston, S. D. (2007). *A perception-action model for empathy*. (T. F. D. Farrow & P. W. R. Woodruff, Eds.), *Empathy in Mental Illness*. Cambridge: Cambridge University Press. https://doi.org/10.1017/CBO9780511543753.024

Preston, S. D., & de Waal, F. B. M. (2002). Empathy: Its ultimate and proximate bases. *The Behavioral and Brain Sciences, 25*(1), 1-20; discussion 20-71.

Scharmer, C. O. (2009). *Theory U: Leading from the future as it emerges*. San Francisco: Berrett-Koehler Publishers, Inc.

Steiner, R. (1981). Man's twelve senses in their relation to imagination, inspiration and intuition. *Anthroposophical Review, 3*(2).

Steiner, R., & Sardello, R. (1999). *A Psychology of Body, Soul and Spirit*. New York: Anthroposic Press.

Tagar, Y. (1994). *The methodology of experience-awareness (Unpublished Resource)*. Melbourne.

Tagar, Y. (2006). *Fundamentals of psychophonetic: The literacy of experience - the basic modes of non-verbal communication and their applications (Unpublished resource)*. Cape Town.

Tagar, Y., & Steele, R. (2008). *Psychophonetics counselling and psychotherapy*.

Part 1: conversational counselling (Unpublished resource). Melbourne.

Thompson, E. (2007). *Mind in life: Biology, phenomenology, and the sciences of mind*. Cambridge: Harvard University Press.

Varela, F., Thompson, E., & Rosch, E. (1991). *The embodied mind: Cognitive science and human experience*. Massachusetts: MIT Press.

Wilber, K. (2006). *Integral Spirituality*. Boston: Integral Books.

CHAPTER 13

Criticality and Creativity in Presencing

Hayo Reinders and Jay Hays

Introduction

This chapter introduces readers to a new topic: Critical Presencing. Whilst some aspects will be known and accepted by scholars and practitioners familiar with notions of presence and presencing (Kaiser et al, 2014; Reams et al, 2014; Scharmer & Yukelson, 2015), others may seem, at first, contrary or incompatible with conventional understandings. Such is the nature of paradox , and in this chapter the authors raise and attempt to resolve a number of contradictions, ambiguities, and indefinite propositions about presencing and its relationship to creativity and criticality. It may be that paradox, irrelevance, flights of fancy, and intuitive musings are precisely what is needed to springboard constructive creativity and innovation. They probably occur to and for us all, but often virtually unconsciously or quickly dismissed (Croskerry, 2015). Drawing on Potter (2017), an individual who is critically present (or presencing) would be aware of these springboards and their potential value, as well as how he or she is attending to and dealing with them.

One premise emphasised here is that the more conscious

thinkers are of these thoughts and when and how they come the more productive they will be. Greater critical awareness, along with discipline in applying certain learning habits and skills, can lead to faster and more repeatable innovations and successful responses (Cloud, 2017; Klein, 2017). This chapter, indeed Critical Presencing, is largely about attaining and sustaining that critical awareness so essential for learning, resilience, and innovation. We discuss what Critical Presencing is, why it's important, and how to develop it.

In brief, Critical Presencing is a synergistic merging of two, till now, distinct concepts and disciplines: presencing and Critical Learnership. This fusion permits us to obtain the greatest possible value from presence and presencing, criticality, and continuous and purposeful learning. Each of the concepts and disciplines are explained fully in the body of this chapter, and their individual components and their interrelationships identified and illustrated.

The crux of our unfolding discussion hinges on the following understandings and propositions.

As used here, presencing implies two main purposes and states: (1) intentional action to be present, as in mindful awareness of one's purposeful engagement in and interaction with the world (task, situation, other persons); and (2) intentional action to bring into presence desirable ends—to make material the immaterial, the intuitive, the possibilities sensed though not yet manifest.

Critical Learnership (Hays & Reinders, 2017), a new way of thinking about and structuring how we approach learning, might be thought of as a critical-analytical thought process and set of strategies for continually upsetting mental models (Helfat & Martin, 2015; Hurni & Grösser, 2017; Lozano, 2014) and the levels of comfort that surround them. It is intentional, proactive, disruptive, and anticipative learning for the future

We will sometimes use the abbreviation CL for Critical Learnership.

Critical Presencing (CP) represents what we see as a logical and valuable convergence of Critical Learnership and presencing. There is much to be gained from such a union, if CL and CP operate as we theorise. Embedding presencing in a matrix of criticality may imbue the result with greater credibility and legitimacy than might otherwise be the case. The critical frame for presencing may also lead to [*the bringing into being of*] more practical and sustainable products, services, or ideas. This aspect explains, in part, our assertion that criticality and creativity may be complementary processes rather than oppositional.

Most importantly, merging Critical Learnership with presencing may permit a mastering of the presencing function leading to its continuous acceleration, extension, and replicability. In return, CP may enhance the learning process and outcomes. These interrelated elements may all operate as a virtuous cycle (Kornel, 2018).

Critical Presencing, then, represents a system whose main elements are presence, learning, and criticality. When optimal, these elements (or subsystems) operate synergetically to mutually enhance one another and produce the best possible system outcomes. How and why this all happens is the focus of the various subsequent sections of the chapter.

The main thesis of "Criticality and Creativity in Presencing" is embodied in the following suppositions:

1. Presencing is essential for preparing to contend with problems and exploit opportunities before they become manifest; that is, before it is too late to effectively stave them off or bring them to fruition while they may still be capitalised upon. This is the "seeing over the horizon" feature of presencing (see, for example, Peschl & Fundneider, 2017).

2. The presencing function can be learned and enhanced (but learning is not necessarily an automatic part of the presencing process). While presencing is increasingly a focus of attention in the literature, little has been said about how one masters the discipline.

3. Not all products, services, solutions, or ideas resulting from the presencing process are necessary or worthwhile from a "greater good" perspective; some may even be counterproductive.

4. Critical Learnership is essential for resilience and sustainable innovation and development. This holds true at individual, team, organisation, community, and society levels.
5. Given the state of the planet and 21st Century business and social challenges and demands, sustainable innovation and development are crucial (Holden, et al, 2017).
6. Presence is a key feature of Critical Learnership (Hays & Reinders, 2017); without it, engagement in the world of problems and opportunities might easily be superficial and short-sighted (thus unsustainable or counterproductive), and the learning therefrom squandered.
7. Bringing criticality to presencing (through Critical Learnership) increases the probability that (a) what is presenced contributes to the greater good (or at the minimum does more good than harm to the planet), (b) the presencing process is as effective as possible, and (c) we learn through and from the presencing process.

This chapter explains each of these postulates and positions them, where best supported, within the relevant extant literature on sustainability, learning, complexity and emergence, and presencing, paying particular heed to relationships amongst systemic elements, whist attempting to broaden and extend the existing set of theory, principles, concepts, and applications.

In terms of chapter structure, following this brief introduction and overview, we cover, in turn, short sections on presence and presencing, Critical Learnership, and Critical Presencing, the conjunction of presencing and Critical Learnership. We, then, provide a mini-case portraying a moment in the life of a busy executive faced with a seemingly insurmountable dilemma. We use the case to practically ground Critical Presencing, illustrating its principles and the thinking and discipline that go along with it.

Concluding points of the chapter include a critical discussion of presence, presencing, and learning, and how they can and should be thought of as complementary parts of a better whole. While calls for new learning agendas are common and approaches to learning continually evolve, for example, the role of presence in learning has been largely overlooked.

In the model of Critical Learnership put forward here, presence plays a central role. Reflective action and *learning-in-the-moment* (Hays, 2017), for instance, so necessary to responsive and responsible behaviour, are simply impossible without presence.

Critical Background: Presencing

For present purposes, presencing (Scharmer, 2009) implies two main purposes and states: (1) intentional action to be present, as in mindful awareness of one's purposeful engagement in and interaction with the world (task, situation, other persons); and (2) intentional action to bring into presence desirable ends—to make material the immaterial, the intuitive, the possibilities sensed though not yet manifest.

With respect to the first point, presence is a quality of being and engagement: being fully, mindfully, critically, and authentically involved in affairs of the moment, while at the same time aiming to see self and situation in their larger context, balancing immediate concerns with longer-term implications (Lombard & Jones, 2015). Presence, then, is an attribute of the wise and improving one's ability to attain and sustain it a noble aspiration.

In addition to presence as a quality, as understood in this context, it is also a capability and a disposition: presence is a deliberate and skillful endeavour.

Deci, et al, (2017) inform us that such engaged presence confers a mindful, purposeful, and focused attentiveness and inquisitiveness to individuals' experiences with the intent of understanding their meaning and significance. They argue that this state of awareness supports "autonomous regulation", and that "people who are more aware in these ways are also more likely to orient toward intrinsic aspirations such as personal growth, intimate relationships, and contributing to community than toward the extrinsic goals of gaining wealth, fame, and a favorable image" (p. 112), attributes of the wise (Hays 2016; Hays, 2017). They add that mindfulness is increasingly important in the busyness of the current age characterised by distractions, competitions for time, and other tensions that leave little space for people to be present for their moment-to-moment lived experiences. Their ideas on "interest taking" and self-regulation are particularly germane to the notions of criticality and creativity in presencing.

Presencing, Point 2, relies on these same skills and dispositions but allows the individual to range further, virtually, in time and space—not bound to the moment but able to return to the moment with the substance of his or her travels. (It is not so much a concrete thing with which the "traveler" returns, but an approximation—a rich description with sufficient contextual character that it can be presenced by others—a believable possibility may be comprehended, the picture of which is compelling.

Critical Presencing is a synergistic merging of two, till now, distinct concepts and disciplines: presencing (Scharmer, 2009) and Critical Learnership (Hays & Reinders, 2017). This fusion permits us to obtain the greatest possible value from presence and presencing, criticality, and continuous and purposeful learning. The more objectively conscious thinkers are of their thoughts and whence and how they come the more productive they will be. Greater critical awareness, along with discipline in applying certain learning habits and skills, can lead to faster and more repeatable innovations and successful responses (Cloud, 2017; Klein, 2017). These habits and skills are presented in a series of publications by Scharmer, Senge, and others.

They are basically to "wake us up" and keep us awake, to critically reflect on our behaviour and what is going on around us and in the world; to develop our sensitivity to circumstances and attune us to possibilities; and to direct us toward purpose. This discipline helps us see and contend with our "blind spots" (Fotaki & Hyde (2015), and is, in part, our notion of criticality. Being aware of possibilities and what is holding us back from realising them leads to emergence—our notion of creativity—and, thus, individual, team, organisational, or community transformation. Critical Presencing is largely about attaining and sustaining that critical awareness so essential for learning, resilience, and innovation.

Critical Learnership

Critical Learnership (Hays & Reinders, 2017) is a way of thinking about and restructuring how we approach learning. It enables continual learning, unlearning (Downs et al, 2015; Voelpel et al, 2004) and reinvention through building certain skills and favourable dispositions and introducing strategies founded on paradoxical principles of sustainability and discontinuity (Hays, 2015). As the authors have stated,

> Critical Learnership provides the motivation and mechanisms to undo impediments, see new possibilities, and reinvent self and practice. It acknowledges that we are always perfectly incomplete: works in progress striving continually toward a better future of our own making (Hays & Reinders, 2017).

This quote provides the basic premise on which the conjunction of Critical Learnership and Critical Presencing rests: envisaging and bringing into being a desired future.

Convergence of Critical Learnership and Presencing

The notion of "Critical Presencing" is new or has been alluded to using different terminology. It represents less a departure from than a subtle refinement to the way presencing is typically described. The point to emphasise is that presencing—profound capability that it is—is not necessarily objective, ethical, or wise. Embedding presencing in a matrix of criticality may imbue the result—the bringing into being of compelling visions of the ideal future state—with greater credibility and legitimacy than might otherwise be the case. The critical frame for presencing may lead to more practical and sustainable products, services, or ideas. Most importantly, merging Critical Learnership with presencing may permit a mastering of the presencing function leading to its continuous acceleration, extension, and replicability. This comes about through the critical reflective process, arguably a strong, if not essential contributor to learning and transformation (Jones & Charteris, 2017). The convergence is basically an integration of criticality, presence, and learning towards self-mastery (King & Haar, 2017), organisational effectiveness, innovation, and sustainability.

To illustrate and explain Critical Presencing, the vignette below, developed from actual organisational casework, portrays the complex and competing challenges with which modern leaders must contend. More to the point, the thoughts shared and actions taken by Frankie, a public service executive, are characteristic of Critical Presencing at work.

From Problems to Possibilities	
The walk from the boss's office to hers was a somber one. Confirmation that the department would be announcing redundancies for 1000 employees nationwide was bad enough. Frankie would personally have to break the news to her direct reports, most of whom she knew well and respected. This would be emotionally wrenching, as Frankie knew from previous dismissals. And it couldn't come at a worse time. Frankie had no idea how her small team could meet the mandate to bring operations into the 21st Century whilst reducing the budget by an additional 100,000,000 within three years. It seems we are being asked the impossible—again—she thought to herself and sighed.	1 2 3

As she sat at her desk and gazed out the window at the busy street below, Frankie allowed herself to indulge in a few moments of private self-pity. She was quite conscious of the moments slipping away and the thoughts flitting through her mind, many already shaping toward solutions. After a few minutes, Frankie determined to just "be" for a short time. She knew that great ideas often come to her when she "unfocuses" and does not judge or dismiss ideas as they flow into and through her mind. She rang her executive assistant, Laurie, and asked to not be disturbed for a quarter of an hour.	4 5 6
Frankie reminded herself to ignore the specific challenges facing her and to set aside the tentative solutions that first came to mind; she needed only to create a space for possibilities and stay attentive to thoughts and images that would appear. Frankie sat quietly for ten minutes or so then realised that her strategy was not working this time—no immediate brilliant ideas or clear strategies to approach the problems facing her and her department. But several thoughts had come to mind that she realised were important.	7 8

First, Frankie acknowledged her lifelong tendency to attack problems head-on by herself, practically, boldly, and often successfully (explaining her quick rise through the ranks in public service). At the same time, she was quite aware that this won her only grudging respect amongst peers, at best, and guaranteed no buy-in from stakeholders. Even with the best ideas, Frankie knew that she could not solve her organisation's problems on her own.	9
Second, Frankie realised that even if their current challenges could be successfully dealt with, that new and perhaps bigger problems would inevitably arise. More significantly, it began to become clear that moving the organisation into the 21st Century with fewer resources than ever was virtually impossible until and unless the existing concept of the organisation could be re-imagined. The bottom line for Frankie, arrived at from this line of thinking, was that (a) she shouldn't spend too much time trying to solve any related problem on her own and (b) that the department should not waste resources thinking about solving current problems, but rather envision future circumstances, say five years from now, and design the organisation for that world.	10 11

Frankie started to become excited thinking what that world might be like—its probable challenges and unfolding opportunities—and what kind of organisation might best serve its public and other stakeholders in those circumstances. She knew intuitively that they'd have to throw out the current blueprint and draft an inspired institution and roadmap to creating it built on new or reinterpreted principles, values, and possibilities. Frankie believed she could show leadership in imagining a viable future state and undoing the traps of the present, but realised that she could not do it on her own. She buzzed her EA on the intercom: "Laurie, get hold of the other directors. We are going to schedule an off-site to reinvent ourselves." "Sure thing, Boss", Laurie replied. "That sounds... um, ...interesting."	12

Critical Presencing Virtually Realised

The vignette immediately above not only depicts a situation that many managers and leaders have to face, but also reveals, at least partially, Critical Presencing at work. The brief analysis that follows explicates aspects of the case that bear on or demonstrate principles, behaviours, and thinking associated with CP. The dozen annotations in the column alongside the narrative are keyed to the points below that we would like to emphasise.

1. Laying-off individuals is never easy. Frankie likely feels some measure of disappointment, sadness, or stress associated with the task. This does not set a constructive stage for the more technical and managerial tasks that she will have to deal with at the same time. An individual critically present will know what he or she is feeling, his or her responses to it, objectively think through the implications,

403

and, what, if anything, should be done about them.

2. One of those tasks is reengineering her organisation for the 21st Century, no small challenge for anyone. The critically present individual will strive to disentangle affective and physical issues and find healthy and effective ways to partition and deal with them. A particular challenge that must be overcome in envisaging possible futures and architecting strategies to proceed is "stepping outside" the assumptions and beliefs that govern the way we understand the world and how things work. We have to know what they are and their limitations. This arises from Critical Learnership and feeds Critical Presencing.

3. Frankie's reengineering task is made the more difficult due to impending budget cuts, on the order of 30M reductions per year. This means, bluntly, doing more with less.[60] It is likely the case that these forced reductions along with the mandate to reinvent the organisation may actually force a dramatic change, for only that will be viable. Here, it is key to envisage possibilities rather than impediments. This is where creativity, energised by tensions in present circumstances, comes into play.[61]

4. Critically present, Frankie is attentive to thoughts, emotions, and feelings; she is consciously processing—watching her thinking, so to speak, rather than just thinking. It could be profoundly significant to know when, how, and from where ideas and intuitions come from. These associations can provide the springboards to forward learning (Hays, 2015).

5. Frankie realises that she—like many others—tends to jump to problem-solving (if not solutions), which shortcuts the process of thinking through issues more fully. Realising this tendency, she consciously commits to distance herself from problems and or slow down in directly trying to solve them.

6. Having learned from reflecting on past experiences, Frankie knows the value for her in "spacing"—that is, allowing time and space to allow insights and intuitions to visit. When not directly and actively involved in trying to

solve a problem or make a decision, the thinker has more time to just observe insights and intuitions and let them wander comfortably.[62]

7. The critically present individual recognises the importance of non-judgemental, open-mindedness, accepting as possibilities, or springboards to the possible, the ideas, insights, and intuitions that arise, even (and especially) when they might be dismissed as absurd, irrelevant, unrealistic, improbable, and likewise.[63]

8. To be critically present means that one is critically aware of thoughts and objectively conscious of the thinking process, including whether or not it is productive, and when it is time to change course. Here, Frankie realises she is "on to something", while not having found an immediate and practicable solution.

9. Long critically reflective[64], Frankie knows her strengths and shortcomings, her tendencies and their implications. Here, she acknowledges her inclination to do things herself, to solve problems and make decisions on her own. She is critically aware of the up- and downsides of this tendency, and, in this case, is likely to opt for a more collaborative approach to dealing with the challenges her organisation faces.

10. Having had a short contemplative period, Frankie has been "visited" by some pretty important insights and intuitions. Her realisations concerning the dramatic changes required, under sparse circumstances, can lead to creative foresight.[65] She knows that modest, incremental change will not produce radical transformation and that entirely new possibilities must be entertained.[66]

11. Frankie has come to see that (a) she can't do much on her own and (b) that she and her organisation have to leave the past (and present) behind to envisage a possible future that is dramatically and fundamentally different than the current one. Without knowing what, she is beginning to see how: through collective creativity and co-construction of the future (Boon et al, 2016).

12. Fortunately, Frankie is positive and optimistic about pro-

ceeding, and keen to get others involved. She'll need the energy to keep going and to mobilise others over the long haul ahead. She is cognizant of the fact that her organisation of the future cannot physically resemble its current form and that even its personality (corporate culture) might have to change. Frankie needs to learn to be a new person (collaborative, for example, and prepared for the challenges and opportunities five years hence, which are, at present, barely discernible.[67] Collectively, they need to learn to be a new organisation, underpinned by new or revised principles and values bearing on structure and operations. The great challenge will be learning forward, unlearning the habits and beliefs of the present, and continually evolving on the way to a future state largely imagined at the outset, and adapting and correcting on the go as the environment and context become more tangible.[68]

Frankie's story and the authors' interpretations of it cannot account for all aspects of Critical Presencing, but it is hoped that readers get a sense for what it means, how it might be applied, and how valuable it might be to individuals, teams, and organisations. The vignette brings into focus several elements of CP, including the importance of:

1. Knowing oneself through critical reflection	Frankie ensures she takes time out from the busy and stressful flow of work to interrogate and critique her thoughts, feelings, and behaviour, knowing her strengths and weaknesses, and then determining the most productive courses of action.

2. Mindful attention to one's thoughts, feelings, and internal states	Frankie permits her musings and flights of fancy but has trained herself to attend to her thoughts and feelings, and to interrupt this mindless wandering and either focus practically on matters at hand or purposefully and carefully track and mine her flow of thoughts.
3. Knowing just how present one is in the midst of activity	The hardest time to be mindful is when caught up in busyness and drama. Frankie continually assesses her behaviour within the context of the present. What is happening? How am I responding to it? Is this effective? Am I on "auto-pilot" or am I in control?
4. Non-judgemental acceptance (or at the least observation) of ideas and images that arise in or flow through the mind	Frankie trains her openness and is always on the lookout for censoring and dismissal of ideas. She allows them space and time to evolve and mature before passing judgement.
5. Intentional "spacing" (through meditation, daydreaming, rhythmic swimming or running, quiet walks)	Busyness and tension undermine creativity and consideration of possibility. Effective manages like Frankie create opportunities to "get away" mentally and / or physically. The best solutions often come when we are not thinking about the problem.

6. Critical awareness and objective assessment of thoughts and thinking, and their productivity and effectiveness	Mindfulness. Meta-cognition—thinking about thinking. Constructive and objective critique. In-the-moment reflection. These are the hallmarks of Critical Presence, and Frankie appears to practice them religiously.
7. Imagining and envisaging possible future states	This may be the crux of creativity and divergent thinking. The key skill is the ability to recognise limitations of current models, paradigms, and "taken as givens", instead seeing what is not established or obvious... admitting the potential of possibilities that others might fail to see or discard. Frankie attempts to do this while accepting that she cannot (or should not) do it on her own.
8. Generating multiple possibilities	The more the ideas the better (and sometimes the more absurd, outrageous, impractical, novel, risky, unpopular, and so on) the more likely to be genuinely radical and transformative.
9. Considering a range of implications for any number of possibilities	Frankie recognises that enlisting her fellow directors will be crucial in coming up with inventive new ways of organising and structuring the organisation's work, and that working through a process of design and critique will reveal better ways forward as well as gaining requisite ownership.

10. Speculating on skills and knowledge needed in potential future states, and how they may be acquired and developed	This is a necessary, practical step in preparing for and bringing forth an emerging future. The dramatic and required organisation change Frankie and her colleagues will be undergoing will succeed to the degree that they understand and overcome their current limitations vis-à-vis the envisaged future state. Their effective Critical Learnership will be essential.
11. Identifying and limiting, if not discarding, the assumptions, beliefs, and perspectives that impede performance or progress	This is a key feature and skill in Critical Learnership. Frankie seems to be competent and attentive in this regard. She knows they will have to surface their beliefs and biases and work hard to replace them with new ways of thinking and acting in keeping with their emerging new organisation.
12. Developing strategies to bring into being or get closer to ideals and future possibilities	Frankie knows she needs to reinvent herself, just as the organisation must undergo its own transformation. She sees they have a chance to adopt new values and operating principles. She apparently has a plan to collectively envisage the future ideal organisation and reverse engineer the ways of being and capacities needed to realise the desired future state. She will need to be a role model for purposeful self-transformation.

Linked to the vignette with Frankie, the table above presents a dozen skills and dispositions indicative of Critical Presencing. The list is no doubt incomplete and often intangible, but, even so, highly instructive of capabilities that we can build toward more effective, creative, and constructive thinking and acting. [69]

Conclusions

Presencing (Scharmer, 2009) offers great potential to organisational innovation and societal progress. However, that potential may not always be realised and may, in worst cases, be counterproductive, the result of well-intentioned organisations and communities bringing perceived possibilities into being that do not serve the greater good. *Critical Presencing*, a merger of Critical Learnership (Hays & Reinders, 2017) and presencing, represents a clear step forward in the scope and practical application of presencing. It serves to make presencing more deliberate, repeatable, and fulfilling; and, if our logic holds true, Critical Learnership can make presencing more constructively creative. It is served by subjecting perceived possibilities through critical, objective scrutiny and enhancing the learning and learning process associated with presencing.

As has been asserted, Critical Learnership is vital to sustainable development and innovation (Hays & Reinders, 2017), and can play an important role in presencing. Through interplay among presence, Critical Learnership, and sustainable development, *Critical Presencing* can lead to individual, team, and organisational outcomes that contribute to the greater good and long-term sustainability. It does this by increasing individuals' conscious engagement in the world while imposing a critical stance to what is known, what needs to be learned, and what must be unlearned, then reconstructed (Hays, 2016). Being always present and critically mindful, individuals are more likely to see objectively the merits and disadvantages of the way things are, why they may be so, and what needs to be done differently.

Critical Learnership seeks to reduce the tendencies (and drivers) to shortcut, compromise, or postpone scrupulous solutions and decisions in favour of the preferred (preferred often being perceived as faster, cheaper, less risky, politically popular, more predictable, and the like). Presence puts us in the picture, yet allows us to stand outside it. It thus permits the perspective necessary to see these tendencies critically [whilst surfacing our blindspots (Fotaki & Hyde, 2015; Shaw, 2016)] and enables us to make better decisions and solve problems more effectively (Epstein, 2017). This is enabled through the mindful critical reflection and ethical scrutiny operating throughout the presencing process. Trained to be more attentive and effective learners, individuals and teams simply know what they are doing, how, and why, continually interrogating purpose, process, and outcomes for merit and ways to improve.

Presencing offers the promise of bringing to fruition products, services, and ideas. Critical Learnership increases the likelihood that these products, services, and ideas add value to the world without costing unduly, that we learn from the process, and that the presencing function may be enhanced and widely distributed. Combined, presence, presencing, and Critical Learnership serve to amplify our strengths and to overcome our shortcomings.

To some, presencing may seem abstract and impractical. The seven steps of Theory U (Scharmer, 2009), for example, involve and depend on a very sophisticated set of capabilities and dispositions. The language may seem foreign to would-be practitioners and the process too involved and time-consuming. And the behaviours associated with presencing may be subtle and almost imperceptible. Unless, for example, an individual puts the images, thoughts, and feelings into words as he or she envisions a future possibility or critically reflects on an experience, no one would know this busy process is going on. Even if attempted, verbalising an intuition taking form might be next to impossible; and, unfortunately, few of us countenance the "half-baked" ideas and musings of others (and have learned to keep our own to ourselves). We say "unfortunately" because rejections, criticisms, and self-censure kill ideas before they have a chance to become creative solutions and innovations (Watts et al, 2017; Zabelina & Robinson, 2010).

These same people who might too readily dismiss presencing

for its speculative and immaterial nature are probably also those who tend to be less creative, innovative, adaptable, and embracing of risk. The world needs people who can see beyond conventional boundaries and are willing and able to go there (Hays, 2015). Presencing provides at least part of that capability. Scharmer and his adherents have given us extraordinary insight and instruction with respect to sensing and envisaging possibilities—to lead from an emerging future. Irrespective of the efficacy of the process, it does need to be made more accessible, better understood, and applicable to people so that organisations and societies may reap its benefits.

In the first sentence of this concluding section, we noted that presencing has profound potential to make a difference. We believe this potential applies to individuals, teams, organisations, and communities. Having considered this at length, we also believe that the value of presencing can be improved, extended, and made more predictable. It consists of skills and process that can be honed, individually and collectively. Critical Learnership increases the chances that presencing skills can be improved and the process made more repeatable. Moving toward Critical Presencing increases that potential. It has us deliberately, consciously, and critically engage our skills and dispositions towards viable and desirable futures, learning and improving as we go. With sustained effort, we may over time develop mastery. With mastery, our sustainability is virtually assured.[70]

The title of this chapter, "Criticality and Creativity in Presencing" infers that presencing involves both criticality and creativity. It does; or at least it could. Most individuals familiar with presencing would probably agree that the *bringing into be* of presencing is a creative, constructive act. But, not every creative act is necessarily constructive in the positive sense, as many innovations have proven costly in the long run. Criticality brought to bear on the *bringing into be* increases the likelihood that what is envisaged as possible and how realised will be better for the planet: more sustainable, more widely beneficial. This is constructive creativity and innovation. At the same time, bringing criticality to bear on presencing through Critical Learnership increases the probability that what we create and how we create it becomes sustainable.

412

The big implication, here, is that the skills and processes of creativity can be learned and improved in and through presencing.[71] More empirical evidence, of course, to make that claim conclusively is needed. It is probably also the case that as creative capability increases that presencing will become more productive as well.

In the vignette presented earlier, we saw that Frankie was evincing skills of Critical Presencing, including creativity. She demonstrated critical reflection and awareness, engaged presence, and purposeful and prospective learning. While she did not envisage the future operating model for her organisation, Frankie had a sense of how she and her fellow directors could proceed in co-designing it. As a part of this emerging *coming into being*, Frankie was deliberately undergoing a process of personal transformation she believed necessary to lead organisational re-invention. As a critical learner, one would predict Frankie's survival through what might be a long and tumultuous organisational change. Her resilience will be shown as she learns, adapts, and becomes.

As a subtle and sophisticated set of capabilities and dispositions, Critical Presencing may not come automatically to everyone (or anyone, for that matter). Developing CP mastery may be a life's work, as with other qualities of wisdom.[72] We do not have a comprehensive curriculum, yet, for building Critical Presencing, so can prescribe no guaranteed set of instructions. However, we have identified the twelve CP attributes listed below the vignette about Frankie. We encourage practitioners and scholars to take up these Critical Presencing skills and dispositions as competencies to be further defined and explored. Specific ways of instructing, coaching, and assessing to be tested-out will be a valuable next step. As we learn more about Critical Presencing, how it works, the difference it makes, and how it is enhanced and diffused, we get that much closer to realising our vision of more creative, constructive, and sustainable organisations and society.

References

Adams, R., Jeanrenaud, S., Bessant, J., Denyer, D., & Overy, P. (2016). Sustainability-oriented innovation: a systematic review. *International Journal of Management Reviews*, Vol. 18, No. 2, pp. 180-205.

Aguilera, M., & Bedia, M. (2018). Adaptation to criticality through organizational invariance in embodied agents. *Scientific Reports*, Vol. 8, No. 1, pp. 1-11

Ahmadi, S., Henning, J., & Goli, F. (2017). Awakening teachers to their presence: an experiential course in body wisdom. *The Practitioner Scholar: Journal of Counseling & Professional Psychology*, Vol. 6, No. 1, pp. 92-107.

Alvis, J. (2018). Making sense of Heidegger's 'phenomenology of the inconspicuous' or inapparent (Phänomenologie des Unscheinbaren). *Continental Philosophy Review*, Vol. 51, No. 2, pp. 211-238.

Banson, K., Nguyen, N., Bosch, O., & Nguyen, T. (2015). A systems thinking approach to address the complexity of agribusiness for sustainable development in Africa: a case study in Ghana. *Systems Research and Behavioral Science*, Vol. 32, No. 6, pp. 672-688.

Bernato, R. (2017). *Futures Based Change Leadership: A Formula for Sustained Change Capacity*. Rowman & Littlefield.

Bohle, D. (2016). From knowledge intensive to wisdom based services. *Integral Leadership Review*, pp. 132-144.

Bonnett, M. (2015). Sustainability, the metaphysics of mastery and transcendent nature. In *Sustainability* (pp. 25-39). Routledge.

Boon, A., Vangrieken, K., & Dochy, F. (2016). Team creativity versus team learning: transcending conceptual boundaries to inspire future framework building. *Human Resource Development International*, Vol. 19, No. 1, pp. 67-90.

Brewer, G. D. (2007). Inventing the future: scenarios, imagination, mastery and control. *Sustainability Science*, Vol. 2, No. 2, pp. 159-177.

Chlopczik, A. (2014). Magic moments–Otto Scharmer's Theory U and its implications for personal and organizational development. *Gestalt Theory*, Vol. 36, No. 3, pp. 267-278.

Cloud, J. P. (2017). Education for Sustainability Benchmarks Focus on "Thinking about the Thinking". The Cloud Institute for Sustainability Education. Downloaded at: https://greenschoolsnationalnetwork.org/ education-sustainability-benchmarks-focus-thinking-thinking/.

Croskerry, P. (2015). Clinical decision making. In *Pediatric and Congenital Cardiac Care* (pp. 397-409). London: Springer.

Deci, E., Ryan, R., Schultz, P., & Niemiec, C. (2015). Being aware and functioning fully. *Handbook of Mindfulness: Theory, Research, and Practice*, p. 112.

De Smeta, A., & Janssensb, N. (2016). Probing the future by anticipative design acts. In *Proceedings of DRS 2016: Future Focused Thinking* (Vol. 6, pp. 2795-2808).

Dhiman, S. (2018). Mindfulness in the workplace: meaning, role, and applications. *The Palgrave Handbook of Workplace Spirituality and Fulfillment*, pp. 177-210.

Downes, M., Grummell, B., Murphy, C., & Ryan, A. (2015). A case study in learning to unlearn. *The Adult Learner*, pp. 104-111.

Epstein, R. (2017). Mindful practitioners, mindful teams, and mindful organizations: attending to the core tasks of medicine. In *Distracted Doctoring* (pp. 229-243). Springer.

Ergas, O. (2017). *Reconstructing 'Education' through Mindful Attention: Positioning the Mind at the Center of Curriculum and Pedagogy*. Springer.

Forsyth, B., & Maranga, K. (2015). Global leadership competencies and training. *Journal of Leadership, Accountability and Ethics*, Vol. 12, No. 5, pp. 76.

Fotaki, M., & Hyde, P. (2015). Organizational blind spots: splitting, blame and idealization in the National Health Service. *Human Relations*, Vol. 8, No. 3, pp. 441-462.

Grossman, P. (2015). Mindfulness: awareness informed by an embodied ethic. *Mindfulness*, Vol. 6, No. 1, pp. 17-22.

Grisold, T., & Kaiser, A. (2017). Leaving behind what we are not: applying a systems thinking perspective to present unlearning as an enabler for finding the best version of the self. *Journal of Organisational Transformation & Social Change*, Vol. 14, No. 1, pp. 39-55.

Gunnlaugson, O. (2011). A complexity perspective on presencing. *Complicity: An International Journal of Complexity and Education*, Vol. 8, No. 21, pp. 1-18.

Gunnlaugson, O., & Walker, W. (2014). Deep presencing leadership coaching: Building capacity for sensing, enacting, and embodying emerging selves and futures in the face of organizational crisis. In *Perspectives on Theory U: Insights from the field* (pp. 128-137). IGI Global.

Hays, J. (2014). Theory U and team performance: PRESENCE, PARTICIPATION, AND PRODUCTIVITY (CH. 10; PP. 138-160). IN GUNNLAUGSON, O., BARON, C., & M. CAYER (EDS.), *PERSPECTIVES ON THEORY U: INSIGHTS FROM THE FIELD*. HERSHEY: IGI GLOBAL.

Hays, J. (2015). *Chaos to Capability: Educating Professionals for the 21st*

Century. Monograph Series, No. 1. Auckland: Unitec.

Hays, J. (2016). Transformation and transcendence for wisdom: the emergence and sustainment of wise leaders and organisations (Ch. 7; pp. 133-154). In Küpers, W. & D. Pauleen (Eds.), *Handbook of Practical Wisdom: Leadership, Organization and Integral Business Practice*. Gower.

Hays, J. (2017). A wise course: educating for wisdom in the twenty-first century (Ch. 8; pp. 185-210). In Küpers, W., & Gunnlaugson, O. (Eds.), *Wisdom Learning: Perspectives of 'Wising Up' Management Education*. Farnham: Gower.

Hays, J., & Reinders, H. (2017). Critical Learnership: a new perspective on learning. *International Journal of Learning, Teaching and Educational Research*, publication details pending.

Heinonen, S., & Hiltunen, E. (2012). Creative foresight space and the futures window: using visual weak signals to enhance anticipation and innovation. *Futures*, Vol. 44, No. 3, pp. 248-256.

Helfat, C., & Martin, J. (2015). Dynamic managerial capabilities: a perspective on the relationship between managers, creativity, and innovation. In, *The Oxford Handbook of Creativity, Innovation, and Entrepreneurship*, 421.

Henriksen, D., Mishra, P., & Fisser, P. (2016). Infusing creativity and technology in 21st century education: a systemic view for change. *Journal of Educational Technology & Society*, Vol. *19*, No. 3, pp. 27-37.

Holden, E., Linnerud, K., Banister, D., Schwanitz, V. J., & Wierling, A. (2017). *The Imperatives of Sustainable Development: Needs, Justice, Limits*. Routledge.

Hurni, D., & Grösser, S. N. (2017). Innovation management with an emphasis on co-creation. In *Dynamics of Long-Life Assets* (pp. 45-68). Springer International Publishing.

Iñigo, E., & Albareda, L. (2016). Understanding sustainable innovation as a complex adaptive system: a systemic approach to the firm. *Journal of Cleaner Production*, Vol. 126, pp. 1-20.

Intezari, A., Pauleen, D. J., & Rooney, D. (2014). Is knowledge enough? The case for research that leads to a better world. In *28th ANZAM Conference, "Reshaping Management for Impact*.

Jahn, D., & Kenner, A. (2018). Critical Thinking in Higher Education: How to foster it using Digital Media. In *The Digital Turn in Higher Education* (pp. 81-109). Wiesbaden: Springer.

Jones, M., & Charteris, J. (2017). Transformative professional learning: an ecological approach to agency through critical reflection.

Reflective Practice, Vol. 18, No. 4, pp. 1-18.

Kabongo, J., & Boiral, O. (2017). Doing more with less: building dynamic capabilities for eco-efficiency. *Business Strategy and the Environment*. No page numbers; accessed on-line. DOI: 10.1002/bse.1958.

Kaiser, A., Kragulj, F., & Gächter, S. (2014, September). Recent developments and approaches to knowledge creation and learning in systems. A proposal for further innovation. In *European Conference on Knowledge Management* (Vol. 2, p. 524). Academic Conferences International Limited.

Kerr, F. (2014). *Creating and leading adaptive organisations: the nature and practice of emergent logic* (Doctoral dissertation). University of Adelaide.

King, E., & Haar, J. (2017). Mindfulness and job performance: a study of Australian leaders. *Asia Pacific Journal of Human Resources*, Vol. 55, No. 3, pp. 298–319.

Klein, J. T. (2017). Creativity, design, and transdisciplinarity. In *Creativity, Design Thinking and Interdisciplinarity* (pp. 53-68). Singapore: Springer.

Kornel, A. (2018). Blending art and science. In *Spinning into Control* (pp. 133-152). New York: Palgrave Macmillan.

Koskela, V., & Schuyler, K. G. (2016). Experiences of presence as a key factor toward sustainability leadership. *Journal of Leadership Studies*, Vol. 9, No. 4, pp. 54-59.

Küpers, W. (2014). To be physical is to inter-be-come–beyond empiricism and idealism towards embodied leadership that matters. In *The Physicality of Leadership: Gesture, Entanglement, Taboo, Possibilities* (pp. 83-107). Emerald Group Publishing.

Kyrö, P., Mylläri, J., & Seikkula-Leino, J. (2011). Meta processes of entrepreneurial and enterprising learning–the dialogue between cognitive, conative and affective constructs. *Entrepreneurship Research in Europe: Evolving Concepts and Processes*. Cheltenham: Edward Elgar Publishing, pp. 56-84.

Léautier, F. (2014). Risk management approaches. In *Leadership in a Globalized World* (pp. 177-207). Palgrave Macmillan UK.

Lombard, M., & Jones, M. T. (2015). Defining presence. In *Immersed in Media* (pp. 13-34). Springer International Publishing.

Lozano, R. (2014). Creativity and organizational learning as means to foster sustainability. *Sustainable Development*, Vol. 22, No. 3, pp. 205-216.

Lundgren, H., & Poell, R. (2016). On critical reflection: a review of

Mezirow's theory and its operationalization. *Human Resource Development Review*, Vol. 15, No. 1, pp. 3-28.

Miron-Spektor, E., and Erez, M. (2017). Looking at creativity through a paradox lens: Deeper understanding and new insights. In Lewis, M., Smith, W.K., Jarzabkowski, P. & Langley, A. (Eds.), *Handbook of Organizational Paradox: Approaches to Plurality, Tensions and Contradictions*. Oxford University Press.

Odero, E. A. (2017). Lean thinking, value-creation processes, leadership, organizational culture and performance of universities: a conceptual analysis. *Imperial Journal of Interdisciplinary Research*, Vol. v3, No. 4), pp. 353-368.

Olson, G., Worsham, L., & Giroux, H. (2015). *Politics of Possibility: Encountering the Radical Imagination*. Routledge.

Osberg, D. (2018). Education and the future. In *Handbook of Anticipation* (pp. 1-20). Springer International Publishing.

Pelling, M., O'Brien, K., & Matyas, D. (2015). Adaptation and transformation. *Climatic Change*, Vol. 133, No. 1, pp. 113-127.

Peschl, M., & Fundneider, T. (2017). Uncertainty and opportunity as drivers for re-thinking management: future-oriented organizations by going beyond a mechanistic culture in organizations. In *ReThinking Management* (pp. 79-96). Springer.

Potter, P. (2017). *Becoming a coach: Transformative Learning and Hierarchical Complexity of Coaching Students*. Doctoral dissertation, Fielding Graduate University.

Proctor, T. (2014). *Creative Problem Solving for Managers: Developing Skills for Decision Making and Innovation* (4th Ed.). New York: Routledge.

Purser, R., & Milillo, J. (2015). Mindfulness revisited: a Buddhist-based conceptualization. *Journal of Management Inquiry*, Vol. 24, No. 1, pp. 3-24.

Raimond, P. (1996). Two styles of foresight: are we predicting the future or inventing it? *Long Range Planning* Vol. 29, No. 2, pp. 208-214.

Reams, J., Gunnlaugson, O., & Reams, J. (2014). Cultivating leadership through deep presencing and awareness based practices. *Leading with Spirit, Presence, and Authenticity*, pp. 39-58.

Reinders, S. (2017). The sensuous kinship of body and earth. *Ecopsychology*, Vol. 9, No. 1, pp. 15-18.

Rubenstein, L., Ridgley, L., Callan, G., Karami, S., & Ehlinger, J. (2018). How teachers perceive factors that influence creativity development: applying a social cognitive theory perspective. *Teaching and Teacher Education*, Vol. 70, pp. 100-110.

Sadler-Smith, E., & Shefy, E. (2007). Developing intuitive awareness in management education. *Academy of Management Learning &* *Education*, Vol. 6, No. 2, pp. 186-205.

Serrat, O. (2017). On resilient organizations. In *Knowledge Solutions* (pp. 245-250). Singapore: Springer.

Scharmer, C. (2009). *Theory U: Leading from the Future as it Emerges (The Social Technology of Presencing)*. San Francisco: Berrett-Koehler.

Scharmer, O., & Yukelson, A. (2015). Theory U: from ego-system to eco-system economies. *The Journal of Corporate Citizenship*, Vol. 58, pp. 35-40.

Senge, P. M. (1998). Personal mastery. *Leading Organizations: Perspectives for a New Era*, pp. 411-423.

Senge, P., Scharmer, C., Jaworski, J., & Flowers, B. (2007). *Presence: Exploring Profound Change in People, Organizations and Society*. London: Nicholas Brealey.

Shaw, R. (2016). The logic and limits of leadership blindspots. *Leader to Leader*, Vol. 80, pp. 12-17.

Sinclair, A. (2015). Possibilities, purpose and pitfalls: Insights from introducing mindfulness to leaders. *Journal of Spirituality, Leadership and Management*, Vol. 8, No. 1, pp. 3-11.

Steyn, J., & Buys, A. (2011). Creativity and 'eureka' in science and engineering. *South African Journal of Industrial Engineering*, Vol. 22, No. 2, pp. 1-17.

Varsos, D., & Assimakopoulos, N. (2016). A systems approach to alternative paradigms for organisation and organisational change. *International Journal of Applied Systemic Studies*, Vol. 6, No. 4, pp. 302-326.

Voelpel, S., Leibold, M., & Tekie, E. (2004). The wheel of business model reinvention: how to reshape your business model to leapfrog competitors. *Journal of Change Management*, Vol. 4, No. 3, pp. 259-276.

Wang, Z., Chen, L., & Anderson, T. (2014). A framework for interaction and cognitive engagement in connectivist learning contexts. *The International Review of Research in Open and Distributed Learning*, Vol. 15, No. 2, pp. 121-141.

Warburton, K. (2003). Deep learning and education for sustainability. *International Journal of Sustainability in Higher Education*, Vol. 4, No. 1, pp. 44-56.

Watts, L., Mulhearn, T., Todd, E., & Mumford, M. (2017). Leader idea evaluation and follower creativity: Challenges, constraints, and capabilities. *Handbook of Research on Leadership and Creativity*, pp. 82-99.

Wuolle, V. R. (2017). *Conscious Evolution as Catalyst for Emerging Community* (Doctoral dissertation, Marian University).

Zabelina, D., & Robinson, M. (2010). Don't be so hard on yourself: self-compassion facilitates creative originality among self-judgmental individuals. *Creativity Research Journal*, Vol. 22, No. 3, pp. 288-293.

Zhang, Y., Waldman, D., Han, Y., & Li, X. (2015). Paradoxical leader behaviors in people management: Antecedents and consequences. *Academy of Management Journal*, Vol. 58, No. 2, pp. 538-566.

CHAPTER 14

Sensory Templates and Presencing

Claus Springborg

Introduction

In this chapter, I will introduce the concept of Sensory Templates (Springborg, 2015, 2018) developed on the basis of recent research in the field of embodied cognitive metaphors (Barsalou, 2010; Barsalou & Wiemer-Hastings, 2005; Bergen, 2012; Johnson, 2007; Lakoff, 2012; Lakoff & Johnson, 1980; Svensson, Lindblom, & Ziemke, 2007; Svensson & Ziemke, 2005; Wilson, 2002). The theory of Sensory Templates identifies the neurological mechanism whereby humans ground concepts in somatic states as the deepest assumptions upon which actions, thoughts, and emotions are based.

Understanding the theory of Sensory Templates is important in relation to Theory U because it can be used both as a pedagogical tool for facilitating the movement through the U and as a theoretical tool for generating deeper understanding of the nature and importance of presencing in the U process. I developed the concept of Sensory Templates during my PhD at Cranfield School of Management. The main finding of my research was that managers unconsciously use somatic states as templates upon which they build their comprehension of managerial issues and envision their own possibilities for action in relation to these issues (Springborg, 2015, 2018).

In brief, a sensory template is a somatic state that the individual uses to represent phenomena, such as commitment, freedom, self, manager, employee, leadership, power, vision, value, mission, ethics, control, motivation, collaboration, competition, negotiation, communication, innovation, and inclusion. Every time the individual thinks, speaks about, or interacts with a given phenomenon, they activate the corresponding somatic state. Sensory templates serve the function of enabling and supporting actions in relation to the phenomenon it is used to represent. One may, for example, comprehend the concept of "freedom" as analogue to the somatic state of unrestricted physical movement – even when discussing forms of freedom that are not necessarily connected to physical movement, such as economic freedom. Using this somatic state to represent "freedom" enables the individual to conceive of freedom as something that can be achieved by removing anything that limits the individual's possibility to act. As we shall see below, using different somatic states to comprehend a phenomenon enables the individual to envision and carry out different courses of action relating to this phenomenon – some of which are highly efficient and some of which are not.

I begin the chapter with a summary of the U process, followed by an introduction to the metaphorical and embodied view of cognition upon which I have based the concept of Sensory Templates. I then present the concept of Sensory Templates illustrated by two cases from my research on sensory templates (Springborg, 2015, 2018). In both cases, changes in sensory templates led to changes in the managers' comprehension of an important organisational issue, the courses of action they were able to envision, and their ability to deal efficiently with the organisational issue. Afterwards, I look closer at the three main movements of the U (sensing, presencing, and realising) and show that knowledge of how sensory templates operate can deepen our understanding of these movements, and significantly add to our ability to facilitate them. I argue that cultivating awareness of inner felt sense through the use of a sensorimotor vocabulary can help facilitate to facilitate both "sensing" and "presencing"; and that grounding our concepts in aspects of the somatic states we find at the bottom of the U can help facilitate "realising". For example, instead of grounding our concept of "commitment" in somatic states, such as, pushing through barriers or using tensions to control movement, one may ground the concept of "commitment" in the somatic state of surrender that one feels at the bottom of the U. Similarly, instead of grounding the concept of "freedom" in somatic states of unrestricted physical movement, one may ground it in the somatic state of inner emptiness found at the bottom of the U. Redefining what somatic states we use to represent our concepts in this way will ground our perception, thinking, and, consequently, our action in the state found at the bottom of the U and allow individuals to move into action from that inner place. In short, grounding more and more of our concepts in aspects of the state we feel at the bottom of the U facilitates "realising".

Thus, the theory of Sensory Templates is important to facilitators working with Theory U because it makes it easier to translate theory into concrete, pragmatic methods, such as the cultivation of felt sense, the use of sensorimotor vocabulary to speak about this felt sense, the grounding of concepts in the somatic states felt at the bottom of the U – and other such practices, which I elsewhere have called Somatic-Linguistic Practices (Springborg 2018, Chapter 7). In short, Theory U tells us *what* to do. The theory of Sensory Templates tells us *how* to do it.

The U

The U theory describes a learning process that consists of a three-fold movement of sensing, presencing, and realising. The purpose of engaging in this learning process is to formulate courses of actions that support the whole system of which the individual is a part. The U process can be both an individual and a collective process. Sensing mainly consists of seeing your own automatic participation in the creation of your moment-to-moment experience. When you see how you are constantly and automatically co-creating your present experience, you are to some extent no longer in the grips of this automatic process – you have suspended it. It may still be continuing in a sense, but your awareness is no longer limited by it. Thus, each time you see some aspect of how you participate in the creation of your own experience, your awareness of the whole expands (sensing). When you are no longer in the grips of this automatic process, you feel inner stillness and calmness. From this place of stillness, you can perceive your situation with increased clarity and fresh eyes (presencing). Finally, when you act from this place and from what becomes clear to you in this place, your actions will be supportive of the whole, and your actions will have the power to move people because they articulate and embody latent movements that are already present in the whole (realising). What is primarily added in the U process compared to other learning processes, such as Kolb's learning cycle (Kolb, 1984) or Argyris and Schön's double-loop learning (Argyris, 1976, 1982; Schön, 1975), is the emphasis on the state of presencing. Understanding both how to arrive at presencing through the sensing phase and how presencing impacts action in the realisation phase is key to the U process.

The word "presencing" is coined from the words "presence" and "sensing". It is the core practice in Theory U of being present with the whole of what one is sensing, without using past experience to filter it. This practice opens one to a receptive mode in which one can perceive what Otto Scharmer calls "the future as it emerges" (Scharmer, 2009). This emergent future is normally hidden because we use fixed ideas and concepts formed from past experience to filter our sensory perception. One can say that we, in our normal state of consciousness, filter out the emergent future, because it has no relevance when experienced from the viewpoint of the past. This is analogue to the way we filter out car noise and bird song when we are listening to a friend speak at an outdoor café. We do so because we categorise our friend's speech as relevant, and the other sounds as irrelevant (or in the language of Gestalt Psychology as foreground and background respectively). Thus, the emergent future is found in the sensations we habitually filter out as irrelevant. Presencing is the practice of including experience we would normally dismiss, and in this way make ourselves open to perceive the emerging future.

According to Theory U, the road to presencing passes through various stages of becoming aware of the process through which we come to perceive the world in a particular, habitual, and limited way. By becoming aware of this process, we can sidestep it, and this opens us to new insights and ways of acting. For example, noticing and sidestepping the habitual assumption that encyclopaedias have to be edited by a central editing unit paved the way for the conception of Wikipedia. Similarly, noticing and sidestepping the habitual assumption that manufacturing companies have to have a stock of spare parts paved the way for Toyota's famous just-in-time production system. Noticing and sidestepping the habitual assumption that music had to be sold as collections on physical CD's paved the way for iTunes where songs could be purchased individually as mp3s. Noticing and sidestepping the habitual assumption that financial information systems should be marketed to corporate purchasers (i.e. IT-managers) enabled Bloomberg's success when they in the 80s designed *their* systems based on the needs of the users (i.e. analysts and traders). Such ideas may seem obvious in hindsight. However, noticing and sidestepping habitual assumptions is no easy task. We are often thoroughly unaware of how we use the past to filter and shape the present. What appears to us as our naked present experience is, in fact, already filtered and shaped by our past. We may, for example, have a feeling that we see the entire system of which we are a part, but that we are helpless to change it. This very feeling of helplessness may seem like a naked fact. However, it is a conclusion that we have drawn about the system. It is an interpretation of the system. It is part of how we construct our experience of the system. Becoming aware of the interpretation process through which we create our moment-to-moment experience, is a practice of continuously discovering that more and more of what we felt were facts, really are our own creation. Therefore, a central challenge for practitioners and facilitators of Theory U is how to bring about this continuous discovery process. In other words, how to become present with one's experience, without unknowingly shaping it by using past experiences. In this chapter, I propose that a shift from analytical thinking to felt sense as a mode of engaging with our experience, and a shift from abstract to sensorimotor vocabulary as a mode of speaking about our experience is key to meeting this challenge.

The road onwards from presencing passes through various stages of creation and brings into existence what was perceived during presencing. According to Theory U, presencing leads us to perceive what is occurring with such clarity, that no decision-making concerning the future course of action is needed. What we need to do simply becomes obvious to us. Thus, the creative action in the realising phase follows spontaneously from the perspective we have gained during the presencing. When moving into action, there is a risk that we return to a way of viewing ourselves as separate from the system (rather than as participating in its continuous creation). This is because we often think about change in terms of "rolling out change programs" and "dealing with resistance to change". These ways of thinking about change imply that the change agent is separate from the system that needs to change. Peter Senge sums this up by saying that: "Just as moving down the U requires refraining from imposing preestablished frameworks, moving up from the bottom of the U involves not imposing our will" (Senge, Scharmer, Jaworski, & Flowers, 2005, p. 91). Thus, another central challenge for the practitioners and facilitators of the U process is how to refrain from imposing their will as they move into action. In this chapter, I propose that grounding our concepts in the somatic states found in the experience of presencing is key to meeting this challenge. For example, instead of grounding the concept of "change" in the somatic experiences of rolling something out or pushing through resistance, it is possible to ground it in the somatic experience of open space, which allows any change without any resistance.

The metaphorical and embodied view of cognition

The concept of Sensory Templates is based on newer developments in cognitive science. It is based on the emerging view of cognition as metaphorical and embodied. Before presenting the concept of Sensory Templates, it is useful to describe these developments in some detail.

Cognitive Metaphor Theory (Grady, 1997; Lakoff & Johnson, 1980, 1999) claims that humans develop understanding of new/abstract domains of experience by drawing on understanding of well-known/concrete domains of experience. For example, we can understand negotiations in terms of warfare, life in terms of a physical journey, organisations in terms of machines, commitment in terms of self-imposed restrictions, and change in terms of physical manipulation.

The metaphorical view of cognition emerged from the observation that the so-called dead metaphors used when speaking a language idiomatically can be grouped according to the underlying metaphor. In Cognitive Metaphor Theory, it is proposed that these groups of commonly used metaphorical expressions are evidence of a deeper metaphorical structure of our understanding (Lakoff & Johnson, 1980). In English, for example, we find a range of metaphorical expressions commonly used when referring to negotiations, such as, "he was defending his position well", "she shot down his arguments", "we need to keep our powder dry", "we've been fighting over this for weeks", "his attack was right on target", or "she won/lost the negotiation." Common to all these expressions is that they describe negotiations by using words related to warfare, such as defending, shooting down, keeping powder dry, fighting, attack, on target, and winning/losing. This can be taken as evidence that humans commonly understand negotiation in terms of warfare. Lakoff and Johnson (1980) identified many clusters of common expressions where one domain was being described by using terminology from another domain. Based on this linguistic evidence, they argued that such expressions show that we organise our understanding of one domain of experience (the target domain) by seeing it in terms of another domain of experience (the source domain). The reason we have so many common expressions about negotiation, which contain words from the domain of war, is that we get to grips with the more abstract phenomenon of "negotiation" by seeing it as analogue to the more concrete phenomenon of "warfare" or "physical combat". Examples of other cognitive metaphors include: Life is a journey ("he had come to a crossroad in his life", "her life was going uphill", "he was at a standstill in his life"), affection is warmth ("she gave him a warm welcome", "it took a while for him to warm up to her", "she gave him the cold shoulder"); and anger is heat ("he boiled over", "she exploded", "he flared up").

Two interrelated consequences of the metaphorical nature of cognition are important for the exploration of the Theory U movement. First, this view shows that using different cognitive metaphors will make different courses of action appear obvious or natural. Second, cognitive metaphors support the individual in acting by highlighting certain (relevant) aspects of experience and hiding other (irrelevant) aspects. Thus, using cognitive metaphors is an important part of how we participate in the creation of our own experience. And because cognitive metaphors 'curate' our experience by highlighting certain aspects of experience while hiding others, the resulting experience will reinforce our use of these cognitive metaphors.

To understand this, we may think of the cognitive metaphors that organisational theorists have used to understand organisations. Gareth Morgan (Morgan, 1980) used the Cognitive Metaphor Theory to group organisational theories according to the cognitive metaphor they are based on. For example, in scientific management theory organisations are seen as machines, in contingency theory organisations are seen as living organisms in an ecosystem, in theories of learning organisations, organisations are seen as brains, in organisational culture theory organisations are seen as cultures. Because these theories are based on different cognitive metaphors, they each offer very different perspectives on organisations and supports very different ways of acting in relations to organisations – including different ways of *managing* organisations.

Understanding organisations as analogue to machines enables and supports managers to manage organisations by planning efficient workflows, defining clear objectives, and controlling performance through measurements. However, this cognitive metaphor hides the value of humans beyond their ability to perform clearly defined tasks and the importance of employees questioning the predefined workflows in ways that may lead to innovations and adaption of the organisation to changes in the environment. By hiding these aspects of experience, it reinforces the view that organisations are analogue to machines. In contrast, understanding organisations as organisms enables and supports managers to manage organisations by seeking to find a good fit between the organisation and the organisation's environment. This includes finding a good fit between the needs of the organisation and the needs of the employees, beyond the need for earning a living. This leads to the creation of more democratic organisations, where employees have more autonomy, responsibility and influence on the decision process. Thus, the actions that seem natural when operating from one cognitive metaphor can be very different from, and even contrary to, the actions that seem natural when operating from another cognitive metaphor.

Since the use of cognitive metaphors are an important part of how we participate in the creation of our own experience and makes us act in ways that create systems that reinforce those cognitive metaphors, seeing the cognitive metaphors from which we operate is a very useful way to practice the sensing phase in the U process. I will return to this below.

Cognitive metaphor theory has developed considerably since it was launched in the 80s, primarily through the discovery of primary metaphors (Grady, 1997) and by adopting certain research findings from the field of embodied cognition (Barsalou, 1999, 2010; Johnson, 2007; Johnson & Rohrer, 2007; Lakoff, 2012; Wilson, 2002)

Whereas the cognitive metaphors found in Gareth Morgan's work on organisational theory varies between individuals; Joseph Grady (1997) found that certain cognitive metaphors seem to be universal since expressions based on these cognitive metaphors are found in practically all languages. For example, in all languages one can find expressions where "friendliness/hostility" is understood in terms of "warmth/cold", where "knowing" is understood in terms of "seeing", "understanding" in terms of "grasping", "more/less" in terms of "up/down", "happy/sad" in terms of "up/down", "purpose" in terms of "movement towards a destination", "difficulties" in terms of "weight", "causation" in terms of "physical forces", etc. The universality of primary cognitive metaphors seems to indicate that they are more fundamental than other cognitive metaphors – such as the cognitive metaphors identified by Gareth Morgan.

Primary metaphors draw on somatic states – sensory, bodily experience – such as grasping, seeing, temperature, the up/down or front/back dimensions of the body, and various forms of movement, tension, and relaxation. This seems to indicate that our cognition is grounded in sensory, bodily experiences and that abstract concepts are understood through analogues to concrete somatic states. This argument is already present in the early work of Lakoff and Johnson (1980) but is more fully developed with the finding of primary cognitive metaphors.

That abstract concepts are grounded in analogues to somatic experiences finds support in research findings from the field of embodied cognition (Barsalou, 1999, 2010; Johnson, 2007; Johnson & Rohrer, 2007; Lakoff, 2012; Wilson, 2002). Embodied cognition refers to a wide variety of theories, but one of the most important propositions put forward by scholars in the field of embodied cognition is that all our concepts are grounded in reactivations in the sensorimotor systems in the brain. For example, the concept of "affection" is literally represented by slight activations in the neurons, which are also used to register warmth. Similarly, whenever we use the concept of "understanding", we activate the same neurons, which were originally developed to coordinate the movements through which we grasp physical objects. The same is the case with the rest of the primary cognitive metaphors mentioned above.

There is mounting empirical support for the hypothesis that all concepts, including abstract concepts, are grounded in activations in the sensorimotor systems, that is, in somatic states. Cacioppo, Priester, and Berntson (1993) found that activating arm-flexion/extension, which are actions related to pulling things closer or pushing them away, made test subjects judge Chinese ideograms more or less favourably. Tom, Pettersen, Lau, Burton, and Cook (1991) found that asking people to shake or nod their heads (as in disagreement or agreement) under the pretence of testing whether the headphones would stay on the head during head movement, made the participants less/more likely to accept a pen that had been lying on the table during the experiment as a gift after the test. Both results support the hypothesis that affective states are represented through somatic states and that activating the somatic states in non-obvious ways brings about the affective states. Pulvermüller, Härle, and Hummel (2001) found that participants activated motor cortices relating to moving head, hand and leg respectively during the task of recognising words related to these body parts – even when only minimal actual movement (of pressing a button) was required to communicate the completion of the task. This result indicates that "words are cortically represented by cell assemblies whose topographies reflect the words' lexical meanings" (Pulvermüller et al., 2001, p. 163). This finding was later confirmed and strengthened by Tettamanti and his team in a similar experiment where no physical movement was required (Tettamanti et al., 2005). Joshua M. Ackerman, Christopher C. Nocera, and John A. Bargh (2010) tested the link between somatic states and abstract concepts suggested by the theory of primary metaphors in a series of experiments. For example, linguistic evidence points to concepts such as "seriousness" and "importance" being represented through somatic states of sensing weight. Ackerman and his team asked 54 random people to read resumes on either light or heavy clipboards. Those who read a resume on a heavy clipboard judged the job applicant as more competent and more seriously interested in the job than those who read the same resume on a light clipboard. Those who read the resume on a heavy clipboard also assessed their own judgment as more precise and their participation in the research as more important than those who read the resume on the lighter clipboard. Similar connections were found between somatic states of rough texture and the concepts of "harshness" and "difficulty" and between physical hardness and the concepts of "stability", "rigidity" and "strictness".

The metaphorical and embodied view of cognition provides insight into the depth of our participation in our moment-to-moment experience. Furthermore, it suggests that awareness of somatic states is key to understanding this participation. In the following section, I present the concept of Sensory Templates, which emerged from a study of how managers unconsciously use somatic states as templates upon which they build their comprehension of managerial issues and their own possibilities for action in relation to these issues.

Sensory templates

If we understand all abstract phenomena metaphorically as analogue to concrete somatic states, as suggested in embodied cognition (Barsalou, 2008, 2010; Wiemer-Hastings & Xu, 2005), then managers must build their understanding of various aspects of their work, including the issues they face within their organisation, by seeing them as analogue to various somatic states. Somatic states used in this way are what I call sensory templates. Thus, sensory templates are some of the most fundamental assumptions from which we operate.

Since sensory templates are cognitive metaphors, they will, like any cognitive metaphor, enable and support certain courses of action and not others. If we see motivation as analogue to pushing or pulling physical objects in a specific direction, then all our actions of motivating (self or others) will be abstract forms of pushing or pulling. If we, on the other hand, see motivation as analogue to the stream found in a river, then all our acts of motivating will be abstract forms of unblocking and guiding the flow of the flow of the river. As we shall see in the sections regarding the realising phase, the sensory templates based on the somatic experience of being at the bottom of the U are more conducive to generativity than other sensory templates.

In my PhD research, carried out at Cranfield School of Management, I found that the use of one sensory template can make a managerial issue appear to be an unsolvable problem, whereas the use of another can make the same issue appear to be a relatively simple matter to deal with. I worked with 60 managers from both public and private sector organisations and all levels of management. All participants had at least three years' experience as managers with employee responsibilities. At the beginning of the research, I asked all managers to relate an important issue they were currently facing in their work life that they had tried to solve for years and which seemed unsolvable to them. Next, I asked the managers to create pictures, drawings and poems that described the inner felt sense they experienced when they thought about and discussed the problem. Through the pictures, drawings, and poems and by listening closely to the metaphorical expressions the managers used when describing their problem, I obtained information about which somatic states they used to represent the problematic situation and various key aspects of it. Next, I guided the managers to find alternative somatic states they could use to represent the issue. Afterwards, I sent them back to their organisations with the encouragement to remember these new somatic states when dealing with the problem. After a month, I once again interviewed the managers about their issues. When the managers changed the sensory template through which they represented the problematic situation, this situation often changed (to the astonishment and relief of the managers themselves) from appearing to be an unsolvable problem to appearing as a relatively simple matter. This indicates that a manager often perceives a situation as unsolvable, not because it *is* unsolvable in any objective sense, but rather because *none of the actions afforded by the sensory template the manager uses to represent the problematic situation are useful in dealing efficiently with this situation.* To illustrate this, I present a summary of two cases. The names used are not the managers' real names.

One manager, Anna, was part of a management team. At the beginning of the research, Anna stated that her challenge was how to ensure commitment to the decisions made within the management team. She experienced that she would meet with her fellow managers and make decisions about what to do, and then she would see each manager return to their departments and do something different. When Anna explored what somatic states she used to represent this situation, she discovered that she saw "commitment to decisions" as analogue to "moving towards the same physical destination". Inversely, she saw the current "lack of commitment" as analogue to "moving in different directions". Using *this* Sensory Template made it natural for Anna to deal with the situation by trying to change the managers' trajec-

tories and ushering them towards the same destination. However-
er, she had so far been unsuccessful. First, because it was very
difficult to convince her fellow managers that they should operate in the way she thought best and second because she did not
believe that it was a viable solution to impose her will on her colleagues. Thus, the problem seemed unsolvable. However, working with the photographs, Anna discovered an alternative somatic state, she could use to represent the situation. The revelation
came when she took a picture of a scarf left on a bench. She initially did not understand why she had taken this picture. However, speaking about the picture she said: It kind of feels lonely. It is
just left there and not in touch with anything. Immediately upon
mentioning the lack of physical touch, Anna exclaimed: That's it.
The issue is not lack of common commitment; the issue is that we
have no relationship to each other. She then remembered that
whenever she got a new group of employees, the first thing she
did was to ensure that they built relationships because, as she
said: without relationships, nothing works. She already had a
toolbox to facilitate relationship building. She had just never
thought about using this in relation to the management team.
When she began doing this, the collaboration in the management
team finally began to work. Thus, the moment Anna changed the
sensory template through which she understood the situation,
from seeing it as analogue to the somatic experience of ushering
things towards the same physical destination to seeing it as analogue to the somatic experience of bringing separate things into
physical contact, she was able to imagine new courses of action,
which enabled her to deal efficiently with the issue.

Another manager, Becky, had a customer service department
in which the employees felt unappreciated. This led them to
speak harshly to each other – and to the customers. Becky had for
years tried to raise the employees' sense of being appreciated.
She had, among other initiatives, organised an event, where all
employees from the other departments visited the customer service department to allow the customer service employees to show
what they did and how their work benefitted the organisation as
a whole. Such initiatives would usually have a positive but very
time-limited effect. The general feeling in the department would

quickly revert to the sense of not being appreciated. Becky felt this to be a Sisyphus work. Time and again, she would put in an effort raise the employees' morale, and as soon as she turned to other matters, the morale would plummet back down. This was the sensory template Becky used to understand the situation – and which had not afforded any efficient course of action. As Becky explored what alternative sensorimotor states that could represent the situation, she at some point took a picture of a bicycle wheel and said that the situation reminded her of riding one's bicycle with the breaks on. Using *this* sensory template enabled a different course of action, namely searching for the friction and removing it. Searching for the friction, Becky became aware that the manager of the customer service department demanded that all decisions should be approved by him. This included decisions the employees were fully competent to make themselves. Becky was immensely relieved at realising this. She said: I don't know how to raise the morale of a whole department, but I *do* know how to tell a manager that he has to change his leadership style: making sure that his employees are competent and then allowing them to get on with their work. As long as Becky saw the issue as analogue to rolling a boulder up a mountain, she would engage in actions aimed at raising the morale and ensuring it stayed there. The issue seemed unsolvable because the type of actions afforded by this sensory template were inefficient. When she changed the sensory template and understood the issue as analogue to physical friction, she began to explore how she could identify and remove the friction. This sensory template *did* afford actions that were efficient in dealing with the issue, and thus, Becky no longer perceived the issue as unsolvable.

These examples show how it is possible to become aware of the sensory templates managers use to represent managerial issues, and that representing such issues through different sensory templates can mean the difference between experiencing an issue as either unsolvable or as a relatively simple matter because different sensory templates enable managers to imagine different courses of action.

In the following, I will explore how knowledge of sensory templates can enrich our understanding of the three movements of the U and of how to facilitate them.

Sensing – transformation of perception

"Learning to see begins when we stop projecting our habitual assumptions and start to see reality freshly. It continues when we can see our connection to that reality more clearly" (Senge et al., 2005, p. 41)

The first part of the U movement is sensing. This movement consists first of *suspending* our assumptions and mental models as we observe a given system so that we may see this system afresh, and second of *redirecting* our awareness so that we can perceive our own participation in the creation of this system. *Suspending* allows us to see the whole system instead of being limited to the part of the system that seems relevant given our assumptions. However, seeing the whole system can make one feel like a victim within this system, without any possibility to influence it. *Redirecting* is realising one's own participation in creating and reproducing the system and the mode in which the system operates. This can be an empowering experience. If one participates in creating the system one is also able to influence the system. One can say that redirecting is a continuation of suspending; in that one suspends the assumption that the system is separate from one's self. Thus, the main challenge of sensing is to see our own participation in our experience: First, by seeing our participation in our perception (suspending) and second seeing our participation in the systems of which we are a part (redirecting).

Knowledge of how sensory templates operate can help us meet this challenge. We can become aware of our own participation in our experience by using inner felt sense to examine which somatic states we use to represent various abstract phenomena and to examine how this influences our engagement with the system of which we are a part in ways that make us reproduce the system in its current form. When we see how perception, action, and the larger system of which we are a part unfold from the sensory templates we use, we see that we are at the mercy of *our own creation*. Seeing this dispels the sense of being a victim of this creation.

When we engage with organisational issues, we use words, such as, "commitment", "freedom", "self", "manager", "employee", "leadership", "power", "vision", "value", "mission", "ethics", "control", "motivation", "collaboration", "competition", "negotiation", "communication", "innovation", and "inclusion." Each of us represents these phenomena through particular sensory templates. Depending on which sensory template we use, different courses of action (including emotional responses) in relation to the phenomenon will seem natural and obvious to us. When we follow the kind of actions that seem natural and obvious to us given the sensory template we use, we participate in the reproduction of the particular mode in which the whole system operates.

For example, one manager in the research mentioned above, Catharine, was part of a central unit who analysed data from many teams across the world, and based on these analyses formulated action plans and determined which projects to proceed with and which to abandon. Her issue was that one of the teams she worked with proceeded in secrecy with projects that according to the analysis would never produce a return on investment. This made her angry, and she blamed the team for being both stupid and egotistic. At the same time, the organisation had decided to make "collaboration" an explicit value and part of all managers performance assessment. Therefore, she feared that involving others in the fight with the team would be seen as a lack of ability to collaborate and reflect negatively on her personal performance assessment. During the research, Catharine changed the sensory template through which she represented "people". She realised that people are not like water that one may easily pour from one glass to another. Instead, she came to see people as a large sticky mass that was not easily moved. As long as she saw people like water, she felt that giving them the result of the analysis ought to be sufficient to make them change their behaviour – that is, to immediately abandon the projects that would not bring a return on investment. When she began to see people as a large sticky mass, she first realised that the 'rouge' team had noble qualities including a desire to do something good for the local population and an entrepreneurial spirit seeking to create something great. She also realised that she admired these qualities much more than the qualities of control that her own work represented. Second, this change of sensory template gave her a sense of calm and relaxed patience, because if people are like a sticky mass, it is obvious that they will not move quickly. Third, she began to involve others to put pressure on the mass from more than one side. Again, this is the only obvious thing to do with a large sticky mass. And since she did this with sincere patience instead of blame, it was not taken as a sign of poor collaboration skills. The team eventually abandoned the problematic project and focused their energy on the more promising projects in their portfolio. When Catharine changed the sensory template through which she represented the people in the team, she changed her perception of them, from seeing them as primarily stupid, to seeing them as people who desired to do great and noble things and naturally fought for what they believed in. In consequence, the actions that seemed obvious changed from blaming and fighting directly with the team to patiently presenting the results of her analysis to the relevant people throughout the organisation and thus applying pressure on the team from multiple sides. And finally, this changed the system of which she was a part, from one where she was fighting a battle on two fronts against the team and against the performance assessment process of the organisation, to one in which she was supported by the structure of the organisation. This was summed up in the change from feeling despair about being part of an organisation she felt didn't work to noticing that it *did* in fact work – provided that she knew how to act within it. In this example, we see how a change of sensory templates involved both suspension and redirection.

Facilitating sensing – cultivating felt sense through the use of sensorimotor vocabulary

When we think about a phenomenon, the somatic states that

we use to represent this phenomenon, the sensory template, is activated. Therefore, it is possible to detect which sensory templates we use to represent a phenomenon simply by paying attention to and describing the subtle changes in our felt sense that occurs when we think about this phenomenon. It is key to understand that the felt sense we experience when thinking about a phenomenon is not *produced* by the phenomenon, but rather is the very *tool we use to comprehend* the phenomenon, i.e. the felt sense is produced by one self as a means of representing the phenomenon in a way that enables action.

For example, when thinking about "happiness" or telling stories about times when we felt happy, most people are able to detect a certain inner lightness or possibly a sense of bubbles floating upwards in the body. This is because the sensation of lightness and bubbles is the somatic state most people use to represent the concept of happiness. Similarly, thinking and speaking about "commitment" or "patience" will produce particular inner somatic states. Many people will feel "commitment" as a sense of self-imposed control of one's impulses to move away from the trajectory to which one is committed, while "patience" for many people will feel like an inner sense of holding back one's impulses to act, a sort of self-induced paralysis. For others, engaging with these concepts will involve different somatic states. The somatic states the individual feels when engaging with a particular concept are likely to be the sensory templates the individual use to ground these concepts. Sometimes one concept can be tightly associated with another, and in those cases, one may primarily sense the somatic state in which the other concept is grounded. If, for example, the concept of "power" for one individual is related to "fear", then speaking about power may lead the individual to primarily feel the somatic state in which the concept of "fear" is grounded rather than that in which the concept of "power" is grounded. However, it is beyond the scope of this chapter to deal with such intricacies in detail (see Springborg, 2018, p. chapter 7).

Thus, some of our deepest assumptions, our sensory templates, can be detected through a well-developed awareness of one's inner felt sense. The ability to notice subtle changes in our inner felt sense is one that needs to be cultivated. A simple way to cultivate felt sense is by describing one's experience purely through sensorimotor vocabulary. If, for example, we are aware that we feel happy, we may ask ourselves: What is the actual sensory experience that I call happy? If we are aware that engaging with a particular concept feels tedious, or thrilling, or boring, or scary, we may ask ourselves: What is the actual somatic experience that we call tedious, thrilling, boring, or scary?

If it is true that our concepts are grounded in reactivations in our sensorimotor systems, as claimed by the embodied view of cognition, such questions are both valid and important. We are not adding something artificial to the experience by describing it in terms of sensorimotor words, but on the contrary, we are describing how we are already grounding these concepts in somatic states. Of course, one can justifiably object and point out that we may not have sensorimotor words that adequately describe the somatic state in which we ground a particular concept and that by forcing ourselves to describe it through the sensorimotor vocabulary we *do* have at our disposal, we distort this experience. This is true; however, our sensorimotor vocabulary is likely to distort our experience less than more abstract vocabulary. Thus, practising describing our felt sense through sensorimotor vocabulary is a way to practice the more general skill of moving our attention to the felt sense – without interpreting this felt sense in any habitual way.

Noticing what somatic states we use to ground a concept is noticing some of our most fundamental assumptions, and in doing so, we both suspend these assumptions and see a very fundamental level of our own participation in the creation of our experience. Thus, describing our experience through sensorimotor vocabulary can be used as an important practice for developing our capacity for sensing – the first movement in the U process.

Presencing – transformation of self and will

"In my experience, the part that people struggle most to understand," said Betty Sue, "is the bottom of the U –

presencing." "That is really the heart of the heart," said Peter. "It's the essence of the whole theory, and perhaps what we really may be discovering about shifting the whole" (Senge et al., 2005, p. 219)

At the bottom of the U something happens, which can be difficult to describe beyond the effects of it. The effects include increased receptivity, awareness of one's participation in the process that generates one's experience and the systems of which one is a part; a direct rather than analytical form of knowing, an increasingly fluid and decentralised sense of self, a commitment that is a surrendering rather than an act of will power, and compassionate and spontaneous action that springs from a perception of the whole and simultaneously supports this whole.

The presencing that brings about such effects can be conceptualised in different ways. In the following, I will propose that our knowledge of how sensory templates operate can illuminate the mystery at the bottom of the U in ways that are helpful when facilitating the movement through the U. As mentioned above, sensory templates serve the function of enabling and supporting action. Therefore, when we, in our acts of comprehension, activate sensory templates, we will feel a pull towards the actions implied by this sensory template. If we comprehend our colleagues as analogue to separate physical entities that scatter in several different directions and which we must gather, this act of comprehension literally activates the neurological circuits and muscles we use for the physical action of gathering scattered objects together. If we comprehend the morale in a department as analogue to a heavy boulder, that we need to roll up a mountain, this act of comprehension literally activates the neurological circuits and muscles we would use for such a physical task. Such activation is only a slight priming in the nerves and muscles, but we feel it as a pull towards the specific type of action.

Thus, when we suspend our assumptions, we relinquish our attempts at doing something with the phenomenon we are looking at. We look at it without trying to draw conclusions, problem solve it, change it, modify it, influence it, or even comprehend it. All assumptions and actions are enabled and supported by the activation of sensory templates. Thus, the more assumptions and related impulses for action we suspend, the fewer sensory templates we activate.

This absence of (or at least a lessening of) the inner priming of our neurological and muscular systems is felt as inner stillness because fewer active sensory templates mean less activity in our sensorimotor systems. Thus, the experience of stillness at the bottom of the U can be explained as the neurological phenomenon of fewer active sensory templates. But the experience of fewer active sensory templates has several other aspects apart from stillness. First, from embodied cognition, we know that we use the same neurological circuits for both cognitive tasks and perception. When we use our sensory circuits less for generating sensory templates, we can use them more to receive sensory perceptions. This can explain why, at the bottom of the U, we feel more perceptive, receptive, and awake. Second, many of the sensory templates we use are various forms of muscular tension. Rolling a boulder up a mountain involves muscular tension. Gathering scattering entities involves muscular tension. If we represent seizing an opportunity as analogue to grasping a physical object, this involves muscular tension. If we represent avoiding a threat as analogue to pushing something away, it involves muscular tension. If the sensory templates we relinquish when we suspend are states of muscular tension, the state at the bottom of the U will feel comparatively relaxed, open and free. Third, many of the sensory templates we use are static and/or predictable. Even though rolling a boulder up a mountain, gathering scattering entities, grasping physical objects, or pushing away physical objects, all contain a certain degree of movement; this movement is static in the way that it is repetitive and predictable. If the sensory templates we relinquish when we suspend are static or repetitive, the state at the bottom of the U will feel comparatively alive, spontaneous, and contain a pronounced element of surprise and unpredictability. Fourth, sensory templates pull us into action, the state at the bottom of the U where these sensory templates are suspended can be experienced as a profound and effortless sense of grounding or a relaxed form of patience where one is not pulled into any particular action or a relaxed form of commitment that springs from an absence of anything pulling one away from one's path rather than from a personal effort to stay on the path in spite of the forces pulling one away.

Thus, seeing the state at the bottom of the U as the state of fewer active sensory templates can explain why this state feels simultaneously receptive, awake, relaxed, open, free, alive, spontaneous, unpredictable, grounded, patient, and committed. Which of these aspects are most prevalent depends upon which sensory templates we have relinquished and what aspects of the experience of the activity of sensory templates we focused on before moving our awareness to the bottom of the U.

It is because we use relational words to describe the state at the bottom of the U that it can appear to be paradoxical. Because the bottom of the U is an emptiness, an absence of assumptions, when we let our awareness rest there, we feel simultaneously more still and more alive. The sense of stillness comes from comparing the empty state with the noise of our habitual mind, and the sense of aliveness comes from comparing the empty state with the deadness in the routines of our habitual mind. Similarly, at the bottom of the U, we feel simultaneously free and committed. This is because the sense of freedom derives from comparing the emptiness with the bondage of following the habits of our mind, and the sense of commitment derives from comparing the emptiness with the defocused mode of operating when we follow the many opposing pulls of our fragmented mind. Thus, the state at the bottom of the U is no more paradoxical than the fact that the number "two" is simultaneously *greater* than "one" *and lesser* than "three". The state at the bottom of the U deserves reverence, not because it is paradoxical, but because it holds everything we ever search for, and being aware of it gives us the capacities mentioned at the beginning of this section.

Thus, our knowledge of sensory templates can help us understand why the bottom of the U feels like it does – including why it initially can give us a sense of being a paradoxical state.

Facilitating presencing – making sensory templates explicit

To facilitate presencing it is useful to describe the experience of it. However, when we use abstract concepts to describe this experience, we can encounter difficulties since we do not know in advance what sensory templates other people use to ground these abstract concepts. Other people may well ground the abstract concepts we use to describe the experience at the bottom of the U in somatic states that are very different from the somatic states we encounter there. The solution to this would be to qualify one's descriptions of the experience of presencing by being explicit about the inner felt sense in which one grounds one's abstract conceptions. This point can be well illustrated by looking at a conversation between Otto Scharmer, Joseph Jaworski, and Betty Sue regarding the nature of presencing (Senge et al., 2005, pp. 220–223).

Otto Scharmer states that for him "presencing is about 'pre-sensing' and bringing into presence – and into the present – your highest future potential. It is not just 'the future' in some abstract sense but my own highest future possibility as a human being", and he continues: "The key is that your highest future possibility is related to your own highest purpose or intention. It's more an intention you build for yourself, for your life, perhaps even before you are born" (Senge et al., 2005, p. 220).

Joseph Jaworski agrees with the notion of presencing as sensing a future that wants to emerge. However, he sees the intention as coming from life or God rather than from a higher self. He says: "For me, it's being an instrument for life itself, to accomplish, in a sense, what life or God, or however you want to put it, wishes for me to accomplish... For me, 'Bring it to reality as it desires' means using ourselves as an instrument for something better to emerge, being open to our larger purpose. I believe that everyone is born with a destiny or a purpose, and the journey is to find it" (Senge et al., 2005, p. 221). For Jaworski, presencing is heeding the "call to service that most of us deny throughout our whole life" (Senge et al., 2005, p. 223).

Betty Sue recognises what Jaworski is speaking of, but astutely adds that: "what troubles some people about the phrase 'instrument for something better to emerge' is that it sounds as if you're an unthinking tool or slave" (Senge et al., 2005, p. 222).

If we look at this small piece of conversation, it is possible to see how inattention to the somatic states in which abstract concepts are grounded can lead to confusion and the illusion of disagreement. No doubt that Scharmer grounds the concept of 'one's highest future potential' and 'highest future self' in somatic experiences he has had during presencing. However, his emphasis on self seems to Jaworski to lack the somatic experience of 'physically letting go of something'. Jaworski captures this somatic experience in the phrase being 'an instrument for something better to emerge'. However, it is fully possible that the felt sense in which Scharmer grounds the concept of 'highest future self' *does*, in fact, include this somatic experience of letting go of something. It seems plausible to me that Scharmer would capture the sense a letting go in the letting go of his everyday self (as opposed to his higher self). Furthermore, Sue points out that some people may ground the phrase being an 'instrument for something better to emerge' in the experience of being a slave, by which she may well refer to the somatic experience of being coerced by external forces. This all shows that it is important to qualify how one is using abstract concepts by being explicit about what somatic states one uses to ground these concepts. Had Scharmer been explicit about the felt sense in which he grounded the concept of 'highest future self', and this had included the somatic experience of letting go of the tension related to 'ego will', Jaworski may not have had any disagreement with him. And for Jaworski not to be misunderstood in the way Sue points out that many people may misunderstand him, he would do well to be explicit about the somatic states in which he grounds the concept of being 'an instrument for something better to emerge'. In particular, by explicitly stating that this is a state in which one feels free, rather than coerced by external forces.

Thus, our understanding of how sensory templates operate lead us to see the importance of facilitating presencing, not merely by describing abstract conceptions of this state, but by explicitly describing the somatic states these conceptions are grounded in.

Becoming intimately familiar with the felt sense experience at the bottom of the U can help us tune in to this state directly. Instead of detecting and suspending our assumptions one by one, we can move our awareness to the felt state that is simultaneously completely still and completely alive, completely free and completely committed, and let then this state suspend our assumptions and pacify our minds for us.

Realising – transformation of action

"Such knowing is open rather than determinate, and a sense of unconditional value, rather than conditional usefulness, is an inherent part of the act of knowing itself," said Rosch. Acting from such awareness is "spontaneous, rather than the result of decision making," and it is "compassionate... since it is based on wholes larger than the self." (Senge et al., 2005, p. 99)

Realising is the part of the U process where we act from the inner state and the understanding, we have found at the bottom of the U. The main characteristic of such action is that when we sense the state at the bottom of the U, we spontaneously act in ways that are both in support of the whole and very efficient. The main challenge of realising is to move into action without forgetting or disconnecting from the state we got in touch with at the bottom of the U. If we have intense, collective, and repeated experiences of the state at the bottom of the U, this will help us move into action without forgetting this state. However, our knowledge of how sensory templates operate can further help us meet the challenge of moving into action in ways that are informed by the states we encounter at the bottom of the U.

First, because our actions are enabled and supported by sensory templates, when we move into action, we forget the states at the bottom of the U if these sensory templates are not aligned with this state. If we ground our understanding of negotiations in somatic states such as those felt during a tug-of-war or during physical combat, then merely uttering the word: "negotiation" or thinking about this concept will activate in us these somatic states – and this can take our awareness away from the states at the bottom of the U.

We can prevent this from happening by grounding more and more of our concepts in the states we experience at the bottom of the U. In other words, we can begin to use the states found at the bottom of the U as sensory templates for more and more of our concepts. We could, for example, use the state of profound aliveness and vitality found at the bottom of the U as sensory template to represent our understanding of negotiation. This will profoundly alter both how we feel about negotiations and how we negotiate.

That people who go through the U process, in fact, *do* begin to change the somatic states in which they ground important concepts is evident in how the authors of Presence (Senge et al., 2005) speak about how their engagement with the U process (and similar practices from various spiritual traditions) over time has changed how they experience concepts such as "commitment", "freedom", and "self".

Many people represent the phenomenon of "commitment" as a self-imposed control, i.e. using muscular tension to block one's impulses to move away from the trajectory to which one is committed. By contrast, Joseph Jaworski speaks about "commitment" as a form of surrendering, i.e. a form of relaxation. When Jaworski refers to "surrendering into commitment" he grounds the concept of commitment in the somatic state found at the bottom of the U, rather than in the somatic state of self-imposed control and tension.

Peter Senge reflects on a similar change relating to the concept of "freedom" when he writes that "there are two types of freedom: outer freedom and inner freedom... Outer freedom is what we usually mean when we talk of freedom: whether or not forces outside me are limiting my actions. Inner freedom is more subtle. It concerns the extent to which our actions are governed by our habits. We can appear free in the sense of no one is controlling us, yet our actions are completely predetermined by our habitual ways of thinking and acting in reaction to our circumstances" (Senge et al., 2005, p. 223). What Senge is calling outer freedom and sees as the most common way to conceive of freedom, is grounded in the sensorimotor experience of nothing restricting our physical movements. By contrast, the inner freedom is grounded in an aspect of the state found at the bottom of the U, namely the openness we feel when we have suspended our habits of mind.

Similarly, the authors describe of how engagement with the U process can change the concept of "self" from being seen as analogue to our sensorimotor experiences of being a physically separate entity to being seen as analogue to the state of ever-changing creative emergence, found at the bottom of the U: "Just as the theory of electromagnetic fields, and, later, of quantum fields transformed the Newtonian worldview of isolated particles, this emerging science potentially transforms the particular nature of the isolated self" (Senge et al., 2005, p. 188).

Thus, our knowledge of how sensory templates operate reveals that an important part of the realisation phase of the U movement is that the somatic states in which our concepts are grounded change, and that this allows us to move into action, while preserving the felt sense connection to the state at the bottom of the U.

Facilitating realising – using the bottom of the U as the sensory templates for action

Since the actions that seem obvious to us spring from the sensory templates we use, changing the sensory templates we use is key to the realising phase of the U movement. We could tell a manager to carry out specific actions that will support the whole. However, if this manager did not operate from the sensory templates that make these actions seem natural, then the actions carried out by this manager would be little more than empty imitations. Unless the actions in the realisation phase flow from the somatic states found at the bottom of the U, they will not hold the power they could hold. Thus, grounding the concepts, we use for acting in various aspects of the state found at the bottom of the U is an important part of the facilitation of realising.

The idea that it is important to relate all our concepts to the whole is also found in the philosophy of Baruch Spinoza. Spinoza saw "God or nature" as the whole of which *everything* is a part. Bertrand Russell describes this part of Spinoza's philosophy in the following way: "Love towards God... must hold the chief place in the mind... Every increase in the understanding of what happens to us consists in referring events to the idea of God, since, in truth, everything is part of God. This understanding of everything as part of God is love of God. When all objects are referred to God, the idea of God will fully occupy the mind. Thus the statement that "love of God must hold the chief place in the mind" is not a primarily moral exhortation, but an account of what must inevitably happen as we acquire understanding" (Russell, 1945, pp. 575–76).

Spinoza's God or nature is very similar to the Taoist notion of Source. And speaking about the Taoist Source, Elenor Rosch in her interview with Joseph Jaworski and Otto Scharmer said: "There's this awareness, this little spark, which is completely independent of all the things that we think are so important – achievement or nonachievement, even being alive or dead, or awake or asleep. This supposed world actually radiates from that. This is the way things happen, and in the light of that, action becomes action that supports the whole, action that includes everything and does everything that's needed." Action that originates from this connection with Source appears "without conscious control – even without the sense of 'me' doing it – a spontaneous product of the whole." And such action, said Rosch, "can be shockingly effective" (Senge et al., 2005, p. 104).

As we saw in the above-mentioned cases from the research on sensory templates, once the managers had changed their sensory templates, the new courses of action that followed this change were not something the managers decided upon, they simply did what seemed obvious and natural to them when they built their understanding of the situation upon the new sensory template. If the issue is like riding the bicycle with the breaks on, the natural thing to do is to identify and remove the cause of friction. One does not have to decide this. It is given by the nature of the problem. In the same way, when we use the various aspects of the state found at the bottom of the U as sensory templates for our various concepts, then our actions automatically change. We can begin to feel "commitment" as analogue to the state of surrendering, "freedom" as analogue to the emptiness of the state, "self" as analogue to the ever-changing creative manifestation of the state, "peace" and "power" as analogue to the stillness of the state, "inspiration" and "curiosity" as analogue to the lightness of the state, "motivation", "enthusiasm", "strength", "courage" and "engagement" as analogue to the aliveness and energy of the state, "commitment", "support", "confidence" and "patience" as analogue to the settledness of the state, etc. If we do not ground our concepts in aspects of the somatic state at the bottom of the U, we are likely to lose the connection to this state as soon as we move into action in the realisation phase of the U process. On the other hand, the more our concepts are grounded in aspects of the somatic state at the bottom of the U, the more we will be able to move into action during realisation in ways that are supportive of the whole and "shockingly effective".

Conclusion

According to Theory U, "the challenges we face require us to become aware and change the inner place from which we operate... our invisible realm, in which our source of attention and intention originate" (Scharmer, 2009, p. 10). According to the theory of Sensory Templates, the inner place from which we operate, which gives rise to our use of attention and our intention, is the somatic states in which we ground our concepts. From this point of view, the U process is a process of becoming aware of the sensory templates in which we habitually ground our concepts and shifting these sensory templates, so we ground more and more of our concepts in the presencing state, the state found at the bottom of the U. The theory of Sensory Templates is important to facilitators working with Theory U, because it makes it easier to translate theory into concrete, pragmatic methods, such as the cultivation of felt sense, the use of sensorimotor vocabulary to speak about this felt sense, the grounding of concepts in the somatic states felt at the bottom of the U, and other Somatic-Linguistic Practices (Springborg, 2018, p. chapter 7). In short, Theory U tells us *what* to do. The theory of Sensory Templates tells us *how* to do it.

References

Ackerman, J. M., Nocera, C. C., & Bargh, J. A. (2010). Incidental haptic sensations influence social judgments and decisions. *Science*, *328*(5987), 1712–1715.

Argyris, C. (1976). *Increasing Leadership Effectiveness. Contemporary Sociology* (Vol. 7). John Wiley and Sons, Inc.

Argyris, C. (1982). The Executive Mind and Double-Loop Learning. *Organizational Dynamics*, *11*(2), 5–22.

Barsalou, L. W. (1999). Perceptual symbol systems. *The Behavioral and Brain Sciences*, *22*(4), 577–660.

Barsalou, L. W. (2008). Grounded cognition. *Annual Review of Psychology*, *59*, 617–45.

Barsalou, L. W. (2010). Grounded Cognition: Past, Present, and Future. *Topics in Cognitive Science*, *2*(4), 716–724.

Barsalou, L. W., & Wiemer-Hastings, K. (2005). Situating abstract concepts. In D. Pecher & R. Zwaan (Eds.), *Grounding cognition: The role of perception and action in mamory, language, and thought* (pp. 129–163). New York: Cambridge University Press.

Bergen, B. K. (2012). *Louder than words: The new science of how the mind makes meaning*. New York: Basic Books.

Cacioppo, J. T., Priester, J. R., & Bernston, G. G. (1993). Rudimentary determination of attitudes: II. Arm flexion and extension have differential effects on attitudes. *Journal of Personality and Social Psychology*, *65*(1), 5–17.

Grady, J. E. (1997). *Foundations of meaning: primary metaphors and primary scenes*. University of California, Berkeley.

Johnson, M. (2007). *The meaning of the body: Aesthetics of human understanding*. Chicago: The University of Chicago Press.

Johnson, M., & Rohrer, T. (2007). We are live creatures: Embodiment, American Pragmatism, and the cognitive organism. In T. Ziemke, J. Zlatev, & R. M. Frank (Eds.), *Body, Language and Mind Volume 1: Embodiment* (pp. 17–54). Berlin, New York: Mouton de Gruyter.

Kolb, D. A. (1984). *Experiential learning: Experience as the source of learning and development.* Englewood Cliffs, NJ: Prentice-Hall, Inc.

Lakoff, G. (2012). Explaining embodied cognition results. *Topics in Cognitive Science, 4*(4), 773–85.

Lakoff, G., & Johnson, M. (1980). *Metaphors We Live By.* Chicago: University of Chicago Press.

Lakoff, G., & Johnson, M. (1999). *Philosophy in the Flesh: The Embodied Mind and its Challenge to Western Thought.* New York: Basic Books.

Morgan, G. (1980). Paradigms, metaphors, and puzzle solving in organization theory. *Administrative Science Quarterly, 25*(4), 605–622.

Pulvermüller, F., Härle, M., & Hummel, F. (2001). Walking or talking? Behavioral and neurophysiological correlates of action verb processing. *Brain and Language, 78*(2), 143–68.

Russell, B. (1945). *The history of Western philosophy.* New York: Simon and Schuster.

Scharmer, C. O. (2009). *Theory U: Leading from the future as it emerges, second edition.* Oakland, CA: Berrett-Koehler Publishers Inc.

Schön, D. A. (1975). Deutero-learning in organizations: learning for increased effectiveness. *Organizational Dynamics, 4*(1), 2–16.

Senge, P., Scharmer, C. O., Jaworski, J., & Flowers, B. S. (2005). *Presence: An exploration of profound change in people, organizations, and society.* New York: Doubleday.

Springborg, C. (2015). *Art-based methdos in management education.* Cranfield University.

Springborg, C. (2018). *Sensory Templates and Manager Cognition: Art, Cognitive Science and Spiritual Practices in Management Education.* London: Palgrave Macmillan.

Svensson, H., Lindblom, J., & Ziemke, T. (2007). Making sense of embodied cognition: Simulation theories of shared neural machanisms for sensorimotor and cognitive processes. In T. Ziemke, J. Zlatev, & R. M. Frank (Eds.), *Body, Language and Mind Volume 1: Embodiment* (pp. 241–270). Berlin, New York: Mouton de Gruyter.

Svensson, H., & Ziemke, T. (2005). Embodied Representation : What are the Issues ? In N. J. Hillsdale (Ed.), *Proceedings of the 27th Annual Conference of the Cognitive Science Society* (pp. 2116–2121). Lawrence Erlbaum Associates.

Tettamanti, M., Buccino, G., Saccuman, M. C., Gallese, V., Danna, M., Scifo, P., … Perani, D. (2005). Listening to Action-related Sentences Activates Fronto-parietal Motor Circuits. *Journal of Cognitive Neuroscience, 17*(2), 273–281.

Tom, G., Pettersen, P., Lau, T., Burton, T., & Cook, J. (1991). The role of overt head movement in the formation of affect. *Basic and Applied*

Social Psychology, 12(3), 281–289.

Wiemer-Hastings, K., & Xu, X. (2005). Content differences for abstract and concrete concepts. *Cognitive Science, 29*(5), 719–36.

Wilson, M. (2002). Six views of embodied cognition. *Psychonomic Bulletin & Review, 9*(4), 625–636.

Endnotes

[1] This metaphor was inspired by a talk of Bernat Corominas-Murtra: "Open-Ended Evolution: Characterization, Consequences and Paradoxes" at the Konrad Lorenz Institute, Klosterneuburg, AT (March 2, 2017).

[2] Without going into details, by making use of an argument from quantum physics, Kauffman (2014; 2016, p 33f) shows that in the domain of Actuals the law of the excluded middle (i.e., either A exists, or A does not exist) applies, while Possibles do not necessarily obey this law. Possibles ontologically can exist and can not exist at the same time (until they get realized; i.e., they become Actuals).

[3] Apart from giving the example of a sculptor shaping matter and being shaped in an almost "intimate" relationship with matter (Scharmer 2007, p 170).

[4] Dynamic Presencing has developed more recently from research and practice with my MBA students internationally, several communities of practice as well as my longer term research in presencing (Gunnlaugson et al., 2013; Gunnlaugson & Scharmer, 2013; Gunnlaugson 2007; 2006); complexity and contemplative approaches to presencing (Gunnlaugson, 2011a, 2011b); conversational leadership (Gunnlaugson, 2012; Gunnlaugson, 2015); intersubjectivity (Gunnlaugson, 2011a; 2009); generative dialogue (Gunnlaugson and Moore, 2009; Gunnlaugson 2007; 2006), Bohmian dialogue (Gunnlaugson, 2014); integral theory & consciousness development (Gunnlaugson, 2014; Boiral et. al, 2013; Gunnlaugson, 2005, 2004) and consciousness-based forms of transformative learning (Gunnlaugson, 2008; 2007).

[5] In this first journey of Dynamic Presencing, each lifeworld invites us into an immersion with an essential dimension of our presencing nature that with sufficient practice and mastery, becomes potentially accessible to us at any moment and situation.

[6] 1 Among the very few places, that I'm aware of, that are working with such an integration are Integral without Borders and Pacific Integral.

[7] The ideas presented at the end of this chapter are being implemented in the 9-month program, Into the Dark (www.intothedark.dk) and were initially developed during the three-year education programme Sustainable Co-Creation with Michael Stubberup, Steen Hildebrandt and Arawana Hayashi. The programme ran from 2013-2016 and was a joint venture between Presencing Institute and Leadership with Heart (http://www.synergaia.vision/sustainablecocreation/).

[8] I believe there is at least one more way in which we use the U process, namely, as a process tool, for structuring a process that may run for hours, days, month or years.

[9] The same is implied in Lev Vygotsky's widely used concept of the zone of proximal development (ZPD).

[10] It is perhaps worth noting, that the name of Torbert's theory, Action Inquiry, may be seen as a deliberate attempt to connect the reflective mode of inquiry, which Kierkegaard referred to as "facing backwards", with an action oriented "forward" mode (Torbert, 2004).

[11] The late 4th pp. quality of vertical inclusion is a central aspect of this chapter. In that connection it might be important be aware of the tendency of early 4th pp. to collapse the vertical spectrum of levels into what Wilber (in Laloux, 2014, p. xi) describes as "two columns", one being right and the other wrong. Reducing problems to an Ego-column versus an Eco-column potentially constitutes a Theory U version of this 4.0 reduction of a spectrum to a polarity.

[12] Since much of the research on later levels of development is done with groups of people who are interested in development it is hard to say what percentage of the general population are at levels beyond 4th pp. Cook-Greuters large reserch from USA in 1999, which involved a diverse sample of 4510 people showed that only 2 % were at 5.0, Construct-Aware or higher (Cook-Greuter, 2019, p. 19).

[13] In the following I will follow O'Fallon and Wilber's understanding that concrete, subtle and causal, correspond to Open mind, Open heart and Open Will, respectively (Fitch & O'Fallon, 2014. P. 119. Wilber, 2017, p. 617).

[14] Process Oriented Phycology, or Process Work was developed by Arnold Mindell around 1980 and revolves around three process levels that are extremely similar to the basic levels of the U. In his book from 2017, Conflict Phases, Forums and Solutions for our dreams and body, organizations, Governments, and planet, Mindell introduced four "Phases of deep democracy" that conflicts move through. The first two phases occur in Consensus Reality (The mind level). First phase is 'Just being' or "Lets, enjoy", where we are not inclined to deal with any tension, or problems. In phase two, 'Tension or conflict', we can't avoid it. The polarity that was avoided or hidden comes up and we identify strongly with one pole. The third phase, 'open to the other', or 'roll switching' occurs at the level of Dreamland (Open Heart) and here we are softening up and more open to our own nonverbal communication and to the other side. Finally, at the Essence Level (Open Will) is phase four, Detachment, we sense how the universe moves us. Here we relax and get a detached overview, and an openness to the flow of all the phases.

[15] In the Inner Compass of Stewardship, the MetAware tier (5th and 6th pp.) is represented by the outer circle (fullness) and the dot in the center (emptiness) and regarded as the larger space of awareness of awareness, in which the integration of concrete and subtle can deepen.

[16] The triangles in figure 3 are partly inspired by the Leadership-from-the-heart triangle (Hildebrandt & Stubberup, 2015, p. 170). The words "Obligation" and "Synergy" at each side of the triangles are suggested points to contemplate in relation the individual and collective drivers of development, adapted

from the Leadership-from-the-heart system.

[17] In this endeavor, the micro-phenomenological method of "explicitation interview" (Petitmengin, 2017) might be helpful since this approach is particularly suited to heighten awareness of the complex relationship between the words we use and the various experiences behind them.

[18] Ericsson, K. A. (2002). Attaining Excellence Through Deliberate Practice: Insights from the Study of Expert Performance. In Teaching and Learning (eds C. Desforges and R. Fox).

[19] Ericsson, K. A. (2002). Attaining Excellence Through Deliberate Practice: Insights from the Study of Expert Performance. In Teaching and Learning (eds C. Desforges and R. Fox).

[20] Keller, Peter E. (2013). "Musical Ensemble Performance : A Theoretical Framework and Empirical Findings on Interpersonal Coordination." Proceedings of the International Symposium on Performance Science 2013. pp. 271–285.

[21] Scharmer, C. O. (2009). Theory U: Learning from the future as it emerges. Berrett-Koehler Publishers.

[22] Jaworski, J. (2012, p. 45). Source: The Inner Path of Knowledge Creation. San Francisco: Berrett-Koehler Publishers.

[23] Gunnlaugson, Olen. (2019). Dynamic Presencing: A Journey into Presencing Mastery, Leadership and Flow. Trifoss Business Press, Vancouver.

[24] Gunnlaugson, Olen. (2019). Dynamic Presencing: A Journey into Presencing Mastery, Leadership and Flow. Trifoss Business Press, Vancouver.

[25] Caspari, Anne. (2017, August 30). Presencing and the Scaling Problem. Retrieved November 18, 2018, from https://www.linkedin.com/pulse/presencing-we-space-change-makers-greatest-anne-caspari/

[26] Weick, K. E. (1998). Introductory essay—Improvisation as a mindset for organizational analysis. Organization science, 9(5), 543-555.

[27] Limb, C. J., & Braun, A. R. (2008). Neural substrates of spontaneous musical performance: An fMRI study of jazz improvisation. PLoS one, 3(2), e1679.

[28] Ricketts, B. (2017). Deep Listening. Retrieved October 28, 2017, from http://bobbyricketts.com/#deep-listening

[29] E.g., the "One Song" Project (1996-1998) Københavns Amts Musikudvalg, Copenhagen Denmark.

[30] Ericsson, K. Anders. (2008). "Deliberate Practice and Acquisition of Expert Performance: A General Overview." Academic Emergency Medicine, vol. 15, no. 11. pp. 988–994.

[31] Pohjannoro, Ulla. (2016). "Capitalising on Intuition and Reflection: Making Sense of a Composer's Creative Process." Musicae Scientiae, vol. 20, no. 2.

[32] Deci, E. L., & Vansteenkiste, M. (2004). Self-determination theory and basic need satisfaction: Understanding human development in positive psychology. Ricerche Di Psicologia, 27, 1, 23-40.

[33] Peterson, Lloyd. (2006). Interview with Pat Metheny, "Music and the Creative Spirit: Innovators in Jazz, Improvisation, and the Avant Garde". Scarecrow Press.

[34] Barbezat, D. P., & Bush, M. (2014). Contemplative practices in higher educa-

tion: Powerful methods to transform teaching and learning. San Francisco, Calif: Jossey-Bass.

[35] Geller, S. M., & Greenberg, L. S. (2012). Therapeutic presence: A mindful approach to effective therapy. Washington, DC, US: American Psychological Association.

[36] Bidwell, D. R. (2015). Deep Listening and Virtuous Friendship: Spiritual Care in the Context of Religious Multiplicity. (2015, Vol.35, (p.3-13).) Honolulu: University of Hawaii Press.

[37] Oliveros, P. (2005). Deep listening: A composer's sound practice. New York: Universe.

[38] Scharmer, C. O. (2009). Theory U: Learning from the future as it emerges. Berrett-Koehler Publishers. p. 44.

[39] Hanh, T. N. (2005). Happiness: Essential mindfulness practices. Parallax Press.

[40] Pym, J. (2010). Listening to the light: How to bring Quaker simplicity and integrity into our lives. London: Ebury Digital.

[41] Gunnlaugson, Olen. (2016 lecture, University of Massachusetts, Boston). Portrait Of The Dialogue Artist.

[42] Kudesia, R. S. (2015). Mindfulness and creativity in the workplace. Mindfulness in Organizations: Foundations, Research, and Applications, 190-212.

[43] Isaacs, William N. (1999). "Dialogic Leadership." The Systems Thinker, Pegasus Communications, vol. 10, No. 1.

[44] Sridharan, Devarajan, et al. (2007). Article Neural Dynamics of Event Segmentation in Music : Converging Evidence for Dissociable Ventral and Dorsal Networks. pp. 521–532.

[45] Dainton, B. (2017, June 28). Temporal Consciousness. Retrieved October 31, 2018, from https://plato.stanford.edu/archives/fall2017/entries/consciousness-temporal/.

[46] The psychological perception of the present moment(s) within the context of ever-present change on a temporal scale. Fraisse, P. (January 01, 1984). Perception and Estimation of Time. Annual Review of Psychology, 35, 1, 1-37.

[47] Khalil, Alexander. (2010). The Gamelan Project : Teaching , Playing with , and Learning from American Schoolchildren Playing Balinese Gamelan. Freer|Sackler. Retrieved December 5, 2017, from http://archive.asia.si.edu/research/performing-indonesia/article-khalil.php

[48] Skow, B. (2009). Relativity and the moving spotlight. The Journal of Philosophy, 106(12), 666-678.

[49] Scharmer, C. O. (2009). Theory U: Learning from the future as it emerges. Berrett-Koehler Publishers. p. 41.

[50] Schön, D. A. (2017). The reflective practitioner: How professionals think in action. London: Routledge.

[51] Ricketts, Bobby. (1987). Interview with Michael Brecker, "Jazz Har Det Godt". Musikmagasinet MM Vol. 10.

[52] Ericsson, K. A. (2002). Attaining Excellence Through Deliberate Practice: Insights from the Study of Expert Performance. In Teaching and Learning (eds C.

Desforges and R. Fox).

[53] Hambrick, David Z., et al. (2014). "Accounting for Expert Performance: The Devil Is in the Details." Intelligence, vol. 45, no. 1, Elsevier Inc. pp. 112–114.

[54] Taylor, Peter J. (2017). Faculty advisor comments to Bobby Ricketts, University of Massachusetts Boston CCT Graduate Program.

[55] Gunnlaugson, Olen. (2019). Dynamic Presencing: A Journey into Presencing Mastery, Leadership and Flow. Trifoss Business Press, Vancouver.

[56] Dunn, R. E. (2006). Teaching for Lifelong, Intuitive Listening. Arts Education Policy Review, 107(3), 33-38.

[57] Baylor, A. L. (2001). A U-shaped model for the development of intuition by level of expertise. New Ideas in Psychology. 19, 237–244.

[58] www.mihavision.com

[59] Posted on 20 September 2015 by Student, Sisters Academy #3, The Boarding School, Inkonst, Malmö, Sweden

[60] The authors agree that the "doing more with less" oxymoron-paradox can serve as a guiding principle for sustainable action rather than just the complaint often heard. It seems others agree; see Odero (2017) and Kabongo and Boiral (2017) as examples.

[61] See Hays's (2015) work on converting chaos to capability.

[62] See Dhiman (2018) for supporting ideas.

[63] These ideas come from our work with Synectics Creative Problem Solving process. See Proctor (2014) as one of many useful references on Synectics CPS method.

[64] There are countless references on critical reflection. Two we have found useful in recent years are: Jahn and Kenner (2018) and Lundgren and Poell (2016).

[65] See Heinonen and Hiltunen (2012) and Raimond (1996) for more on creative foresight.

[66] Pelling et al, (2015) and Varsos and Assimakopoulos (2016) are amongst references distinguishing between incremental and radical transformation.

[67] Here, the notions of "over the horizon" thinking and sensing emergent possibilities before fully manifest apply. Refer to Bernato (2017), Hays (2014), and Hays (2016) for background.

[68] Grisold and Kaiser (2017) and Hays (2015) take up these ideas and applications.

[69] Items, here, have been distilled from multiple sources and gathered over a decade of research, including Forsyth and Maranga (2015), Hays (2015), Kerr (2014), and Kyrö et al, (2011). Complementing the more mainstream sources, the authors have also been influenced by Buddhist psychology and philosophy and Zen principles and practices (see Epstein, 1995; Goldstein, 2002; or Suzuki, 2002), or as crossover examples Ahmadi et al, (2017), Purser and Milillo (2015), and Sadler-Smith and Shefy (2007).

[70] The concept of mastery appears to have been popularised by Senge (see, for example, his source cited herein as 1998). We have been following mastery literature for some time, and relevant additional sources include Warburton (2003), Brewer (2007), and Bonnett (2015).

[71] There is increasing support for this assertion in general. See Henriksen et al, (2016) or Rubenstein et al, (2018) as examples. Creativity in presencing and the influence of criticality will need further investigation.

[72] See Hays (2016) or Intezari, Pauleen, & Rooney (2014) for more on wisdom and mastery.

Made in the USA
Middletown, DE
13 January 2021

31429893R00255